a-z of careers & jobs

THE TIMES

a-z of careers & jobs

13th edition

Edited by:
Susan Hodgson

KOGAN PAGE

Publisher's note

Every possible effort has been made to ensure that the information contained in this book is accurate at the time of going to press. Neither Kogan Page nor the editor can accept responsibility for any errors or omissions, however caused. No responsibility for loss or damage occasioned to any person acting, or refraining from action, as a result of the material in this publication can be accepted by the editor, the publisher or any of the authors.

First published in Great Britain in 1984 by Kogan Page Limited
Thirteenth edition 2006

Kogan Page Limited
120 Pentonville Road
London N1 9JNA
www.kogan-page.co.uk

The views expressed in this book are those of the author, and are not necessarily the same as those of Times Newspapers Ltd.

British Library Cataloguing in Publication Data

A CIP record for this book is available from the British Library.

ISBN 0 7494 4627 7

Typeset by Saxon Graphics Ltd, Derby
Printed and bound in Great Britain by Bell & Bain, Glasgow

Preface

There is plenty of good news in today's job market. High levels of employment, wide access to higher education courses and an extensive array of other training options are all in your favour, whether you are looking for your first job or considering career moves and changes of direction at any stage in your working life. With so much to consider, being able to access all the right information can really help you make career decisions in the most well-informed way.

The internet is a marvellous resource, and most organisations advertising vacancies, describing education and training opportunities or providing careers guidance offer good current information on their websites and those websites are listed at the end of each career profile in this book. You still need to know where to begin though, and a guide like this offers an ideal starting point, giving you enough information to plan your next step and clear details on where to find out more. It also allows you to make quick comparisons between one occupation and another, whether this is in terms of salary, entry qualifications or the range of skills you need to enable you to fit in and get on.

If you know there is a job that interests you, this book gives details of where to get further information. If you are at the 'I'm not really sure what I want to do' stage, then brief but comprehensive information on many different occupations can clarify your thinking.

Ideas about work are changing. Few of us expect to have one career that lasts throughout our working lives – we may change direction through choice or because labour market requirements oblige us to do so. We want our work to be rewarding and satisfying, especially since it takes up so much of our time, energy and commitment. For these reasons, being well informed about any career decisions that we make is important, and this book will help that process.

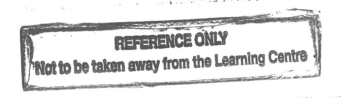

Susan Hodgson
Careers Adviser

Abbreviations

A level	Advanced level
AS level	Advanced Special level
AVCE	Vocational A level
CAM	Communication, Advertising and Marketing Foundation
Edexcel	Edexcel Foundation
Edexcel (BTEC)	Comprises ULEAC (University of London Examination and Assessment Council) and BTEC (Business and Technology Education Council)
GCE	General Certificate of Education
GCSE	General Certificate of Secondary Education
GNVQ	General National Vocational Qualification
GSVQ	General Scottish Vocational Qualification
H grade	Higher grade (SCE)
HNC/HND	Higher National Certificate/Higher National Diploma
HTC	Higher Technical Certificate
LSC	Learning Skills Council
NC/ND	National Certificate/National Diploma
NVQ	National Vocational Qualification
QCA	Qualifications and Curriculum Authority
SCE	Scottish Certificate of Education (equivalent to GCSE)
SNC/SND	Scottish National Certificate/Scottish National Diploma
SQA	Scottish Qualifications Authority
SVQ	Scottish Vocational Qualification
SWAS	Social Work Admissions System
TEC	Training and Enterprise Council
UCAS	Universities and Colleges Admissions System

Qualifications

Scottish readers should be aware that in order to simplify the text the editor has referred to qualifications required in terms of GCSEs, A levels and NVQs or equivalent. NVQs are directly equivalent to SVQs but Scottish National and Higher Qualifications are not equivalent to GCSEs and A levels. A new qualification, the Advanced Higher, does equate to A level but most universities still express their entry requirements in terms of the Higher. Full details of all Scottish qualifications can be found on the SQA website. The easiest way to compare the points awarded for A levels and Highers is using the Universities and Colleges Admissions Service (UCAS) tariff calculator. Relevant Scottish sources of further information have been included where appropriate.

Financing your future

If you've been thinking long and hard about your career, you've probably discovered that further training could enhance your job prospects. After all, a further period of academic study or vocational training can really make a job applicant stand out from the crowd. Yet, whilst finding a suitable course may not be a problem, finding the money to pay for it could be.

That's where a Career Development Loan (CDL) can help. Available from three major banks, CDLs are the result of a government initiative to help make sure a lack of money doesn't get in the way of vocational training. The Learning and Skills Council will pay the interest on the loan while you are studying and for up to one month afterwards. You can then spread the repayments over 1 to 5 years afterwards. Over the last 17 years, Career Development Loan have helped tens of thousands of people to give their careers a lift.

No interest while you study

You can apply for a Career Development Loan from The Co-operative Bank for any amount between £300 and £8,000, knowing that you will not have to repay a penny whilst you study – or for up to one month after you have completed your course. The rate of interest is fixed as soon as your loan is agreed.

For example, say you are applying for a 12 month course which starts on 1 March 2006. You don't pay anything for

Useful points of contact

www.ucas.com
Details of, and current entry requirements for most higher education courses in the UK. The tariff calculator that can be found in the News section removes the need to grapple with the new points system (www.ucas.com/higher/tariff/calc/index.html).

www.statistics.gov.uk
This site includes various surveys about the labour market, including the New Earnings surveys, which are published annually. These are retrospective, but they still provide helpful information on relative salaries in different fields of employment.

www.ssda.org.uk
Information about the 25 existing sector skills councils and any aspirant sector skills likely to be licensed in the near future.

www.qca.org.uk
The Qualifications and Curriculum Authority accredit and monitor qualifications in schools, colleges and at work in England, Wales and Northern Ireland. Details of the national qualifications framework showing the equivalence between all qualifications are available here.

www.sqa.org.uk
The Scottish Qualifications Authority is responsible for the development, accreditation, assessment and certification of qualifications other than degrees in Scotland. Information on these and their equivalence to qualifications in the rest of the UK can be found on this site.

The right path for you?

What is purchasing & supply?

People have been purchasing or 'procuring' things for thousands of years, striking agreements or arrangements between two parties for the provision of a desired object or service and in receipt of that object or service there is a form of payment made by the receiver. It sounds very simple and obviously in today's global economy this is an integral business function that, if done well can help bring considerable success to an organisation. Essentially purchasing and supply management involves buying the goods and services that enable an organisation to operate.

A purchaser may be responsible for sourcing raw materials from suppliers worldwide, bringing them into the organisation, to enable production of goods for customers. Additionally this could involve the purchasing of marketing, advertising or IT related services. Purchasing and supply management is the link in that chain which manages the interface between the supply market and the organisation. Its importance lies in the fact that a company can spend more than two thirds of its revenue buying its goods and services, so even a modest reduction in purchasing costs have a significant effect on profit.

What personal skills do I need?

To succeed in purchasing you will need to demonstrate a wide variety of skills such as good business sense, financial management, good communication skills as wells as creativity and innovation.

The right skill set is obviously reflected by the salary offered by an organisation. Average salary entry levels for individuals with no purchasing experience can be up to about £17k. However salaries are rising rapidly and a good graduate moving into purchasing and supply management could expect a quick promotion. Many purchasing directors especially in a large organisation can command salaries well in excess of £100k.

Where could I work?

One of the most beneficial things about a career in purchasing is that a well-qualified purchasing professional can walk into a wide range of environments

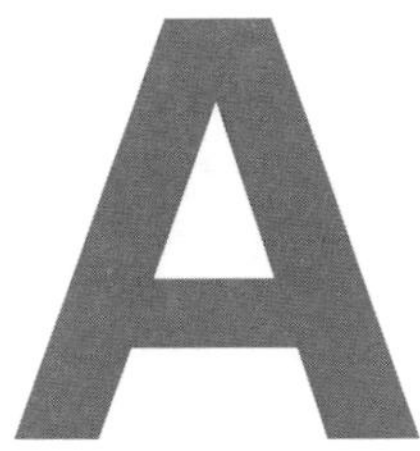

ACCOUNTANCY

(*see also* Taxation)

Members of the accountancy profession are involved in the financial transactions of businesses, including the preparation and verification of accounts, auditing and analysis.

Accountants

Accountants deal with such matters as auditing, analysing, verifying and interpreting clients' accounts, advising on taxation, executorship and trusteeship, and liquidations. An accountant provides and maintains the financial records and helps companies to make business decisions based on this information. Daily procedures such as keeping records of payments, salaries, VAT and National Insurance contributions are also part of an accountant's job. The accountant is also required to provide annual records as an account of the year's trading, which are certified by an outside accountant known as an auditor. However, an accountant will also be expected to help companies plan for the future by providing analysis on market trends, costs and business risk.

Accountants employed in industry and commerce or by local authorities are more concerned with financial planning and the allocation of funds. After qualifying, some accountants specialise in areas such as taxation, auditing or management consultancy. They may also specialise in clients from a particular field, for example music or the theatre. In the public sector, the range of career opportunities covers everything from central and local government to health and further/higher education. Accountants work in companies ranging from small partnerships to huge multinational offices. For those with ambition, job prospects are good. One in three professionally qualified chairs and chief executives of the top 100 UK companies trained as accountants, and 40 per cent of their directors are also trained accountants.

There are several professional bodies that oversee training, accreditation, professional development and standards in accountancy. These different bodies are each responsible for a specific type of accountancy, eg, chartered, certified, management or public sector. Once you have decided which types of accountancy appeal to you, any employer who appoints you will know which training route and professional body is the one you should qualify with.

Qualifications and Training

Accountants must obtain membership of one of the many professional bodies. Minimum educational requirements are GCSEs plus at least two A levels or equivalent. Ninety per cent of those training to be chartered accountants in England and Wales are graduates. Most graduates also need at least three grade Bs at A level.

For those with at least two A levels or equivalent there is the Association of Accounting Technicians (AAT) to Associate Chartered Accountant (ACA) fast-track route. Students can enter the AAT at intermediate level and qualify as an ACA in four years.

For the Institute of Chartered Accountants of Scotland, all entrants must hold a degree. It is generally compulsory for students to undertake a period of practical training – of three to four years' duration – in addition to taking professional examinations before being admitted as a professional member of an institute.

Personal Qualities and Skills

A surprising amount of your time is spent dealing with and explaining things to people, so good communication skills are essential. You also have to possess discretion and integrity, and an ability to interpret financial data. A good grasp of business trends and the ability to work under pressure are all important.

info

Institute of Chartered Accountants in England and Wales, PO Box 433, Chartered Accountants' Hall, Moorgate Place, London EC2P 2BJ; 020 7920 8100; www.icaew.co.uk; e-mail: careers@icaew.co.uk

Financial Training Company (FTC), 7–13 Melior Street, London SE1 3QP; 020 7407 5000; www.financial-training.com

Chartered Institute of Public Finance and Accountancy, 3 Robert Street, London WC2N 6RL; 020 7543 5600; www.cipfa.org.uk; e-mail: choices@cipfa.org

Institute of Chartered Accountants of Scotland, CA House, 21 Haymarket Yards, Edinburgh EH12 5BH; 0131 347 0100; fax: 0131 347 0108; www.icas.org.uk; e-mail: caeducation@ icas.org.uk

Association of Chartered Certified Accountants (ACCA), Student Recruitment and Training, 29 Lincoln's Inn Fields, London WC2A 3EE; 020 7396 5800; www.accaglobal.com; e-mail: info@accaglobal.com

Chartered Institute of Management Accountants, 26 Chapter Street, London SW1P 4NP; 020 7663 5441; www.cimaglobal.com; e-mail: cima.services@cimaglobal.com

Institute of Internal Auditors – UK and Ireland, 13 Abbeville Mews, 88 Clapham Park Road, London SW4 7BX; 020 7498 0101; fax: 020 7978 2492; www.iia.org.uk; e-mail: info@iia.org.uk

Careers in Accountancy (Kogan Page)

Accounting for every profession

There are lots of myths and misunderstandings about what it means to be an accountant. Is it boring, just counting other people's money all day? Do you have to wear a suit and sit in a lonely office?

The answer is no.

Accountancy and finance have always been at the heart of every business, but now the profession holds more challenges and opportunities than ever before. There are a wide variety of exciting career options throughout the corporate, public and practice sectors, often leading to senior management positions.

Almost any company you name will employ accountants in a variety of roles, and often they are the people who make the big decisions about how a company is run.

Modern accountants don't just count figures and write reports, most of the business leaders who control Britain's companies or act as advisers to them are qualified accountants. They are also skilled in communication, problem-solving and people management.

The advantage of having a recognised professional accountancy qualification is that throughout your career any company you want to work for will know that you have the skills and knowledge to do your job to the highest standards. There is a lot of work involved in passing your exams but once you've done them your future success is assured.

ACCA has always been associated with flexibility and freedom of choice and this has never been more true. Entry to the accountancy profession can begin at 16, by registering on the CAT accounting technician scheme straight after leaving school.

The role of an accounting technician is to support the work of qualified accountants. They can work in any sector, and often assist in such tasks as audit, taxation, and maintenance of financial records and statements. The level of responsibility and the range of work can vary with the size of the organisation, and as a CAT graduate you are ideally placed to move on to the ACCA Professional Scheme.

Alternatively, registration on the ACCA Professional Scheme can take place after A Levels. You can take advantage of the opportunity to study for a BSc in Applied Accounting, with the Oxford Brookes University. You would be eligible for this additional award as a result of this innovative partnership without having to attend university full-time.

Many people begin their ACCA studies after completing a relevant degree in accounting, finance or business, or indeed any other discipline, often while embarking on a training scheme with an employer at the same time. We have students with degrees ranging from archaeology to zoology building successful, demanding and rewarding careers.

Once you're with ACCA you could choose to work for a car manufacturer, in a multinational bank, for a football club, a charity or for the government. Whether you go for one of these or for one of the countless other types of businesses that exist today, an accountancy qualification will mark you out as the sort of person who should be making the decisions.

Each year, thousands of students join ACCA, from over 170 countries, knowing that they are embarking on a future that is diverse, challenging and constantly surprising. ACCA qualifications enable you to work in the widest variety of roles for the most diverse range of employers. They are also recognised all over the world, so there really are no limits to where they can take you.

For more information on the huge range of opportunities ACCA can offer, visit **uk.accaglobal.com/uk**, contact us on **0141 582 2000** or email **students@accaglobal.com**

Starting Salary

Starting salaries for graduates range from £18,000 to £27,000, depending on the size and type of organisation you work for – the highest salaries are paid in London by the large accountancy firms and management consultants. At senior levels salaries range from £40,000 to £70,000 +.

Accounting technician

Accounting technicians work in a variety of roles, often alongside professionally qualified Chartered Accountants. They are involved in the day-to-day practical work of accountancy and finance, including the preparation of information and accounts and the interpretation of computer information, such as audit tax and payroll. Accounting technicians are widely employed in public finance, industry and commerce, and private practice. Their roles range from accounts clerks to finance managers. A growing number of accounting technicians provide a range of services direct to the public and manage their own practice. Many go on to qualify with the senior chartered accountancy bodies.

Qualifications and Training

The Association of Accounting Technicians' (AAT) Education and Training Scheme offers open access, although candidates must demonstrate numeracy and literacy. The scheme, which usually takes three years part-time, is competence-based and accredited at NVQ levels 2 to 4. Central assessments are combined with relevant work-based assessments during the training period. The three stages of the scheme are Foundation (NVQ level 2 in accounting), Intermediate (NVQ level 3 in accounting) and Technician (NVQ level 4 in accounting). The AAT also offers the following specialist qualifications: NVQ in audit (internal), available at levels 3 and 4; NVQ in payroll administration available at levels 2 and 3; AAT Diploma in Government Finance; AAT Bookkeeping Certificate.

Personal Qualities and Skills

You have to be thorough and methodical and to enjoy working with figures. Good ICT skills are becoming increasingly important, and you need to be happy working as part of a team but also managing your own workload.

Starting Salary

Starting salaries range from £9,000 outside London to £14,000 in London. With experience you can earn more than £20,000 but £13,000, to £15,000 is more usual elsewhere.

info

Association of Accounting Technicians, 154 Clerkenwell Road, London ECIR 5AD; 020 7837 8600; www.aat.co.uk; e-mail: aat@aat.org.uk

'Student guide to the AAT accounting qualification' (Association of Accounting Technicians): available to download on www.aat.co.uk/docs/students/guide.pdf

ACTOR

see Performing Arts

ACTUARY

Actuaries play a key role in businesses that require an understanding of financial risk management. They are able to analyse past events, assess current risks and predict future financial trends. The majority are employed by insurance companies and consultancies. Others work in areas such as investment, banking and healthcare. The work offers management opportunities, often at the highest level, with actuaries having a commercial as well as a technical role. It is a small but influential profession with good opportunities for career progression. This profession is likely to grow. Because the financial world is so complex, the entry requirements are high, but if you do have the right qualifications the profession offers excellent prospects.

Qualifications and Training

Nearly 95 per cent of entrants to the profession are graduates, though the actual minimum entry qualification is A level mathematics grade C. Preferred degrees are mathematics, economics, statistics and engineering. You can also take degrees and postgraduate courses in actuarial science; some employers insist on these. These courses normally include some exemptions from professional actuarial examinations. Training is on the job with an insurance company or a firm of management consultants. Unless you have exemptions, training and qualifying takes five to six years.

Personal Qualities and Skills

Actuaries need to be highly numerate and able to translate numerical data into clear language that can be understood by the less mathematically minded.

info

Actuarial Education Company (ActEd), 31 Bath Street, Abingdon, Oxfordshire OX14 3FF; 01235 550005; www.acted.co.uk

The Association of Consulting Actuaries, Warnford Court, 29 Throgmorton Street, London EC2N 2AT; 020 7382 4954; www.aca.org.uk

Faculty of Actuaries, Maclaurin House, 18 Dublin Street, Edinburgh EH1 3PP; 0131 240 1300; www.actuaries.org.uk

Financial Services Skills Council, 51 Gresham Street, London EC2V 7HQ; 020 7216 7366; www.fsnto.org.uk

Government Actuary's Department (GAD), Finlaison House, 15–17 Furnival Street, London EC4A 1AB; 020 7211 2601; www.gad.gov.uk

Faculty and Institute of Actuaries, Napier House, 4 Worcester Street, Oxford OX1 2AW; 01865 268200; www.actuaries.org.uk/files/pdf/careers/employers.pdf

Starting Salary

Graduates joining the profession start at between £23,000 and £26,000. With qualifications and experience you can command an extremely high salary, ranging from £40,000 to more than £100,000.

ADVERTISING

(*see also* Marketing, Market Researcher *and* Public Relations Officer)

Communication is the heart of this complex industry, providing a wide range of openings, many with agencies that plan, organise and run advertising campaigns. Working on behalf of clients, advertising agencies study the product or service to be advertised and its market. They then plan how it should be sold and distributed, and how the media might be used to the best advantage in this process.

Account executive

Account executives are responsible within the agency for a particular client or group of clients. They interpret the client's wishes; coordinate and supervise the work of others within the agency, such as creatives, account planners, copywriters and scriptwriters; seek advice from other experts such as media executives; and then present the ideas most likely to meet with the client's approval.

Account planner

Account planners consider the client's brief and work to identify the ideal audience and optimum method of getting the client's message across. They analyse market research and other data and provide the creative team with the information that will help them develop the most effective campaign. They may also work on forward planning for the agency, identifying likely future clients based on market data they have researched.

Art editor/executive director

This position involves coordinating the work of the creative department, which converts the client's original intentions into a visual form for approval. Others, including copywriters, may elaborate upon this.

Artist

(*see also* Art and Design)

Agency artists prepare initial visual layouts of adverts, posters and displays, and produce final artwork for printing. They need to be competent in using design software.

Copywriter and scriptwriter

The writers in the agency produce headings, text, jingles and copy for articles in journals, and scripts for films and commercials. Copywriters often work closely with the Art Editor and visualisers.

Media executive

Media executives provide expert advice on the advertising medium – for example, television, cinema, posters, newspapers, journals – that will best suit a particular campaign, and negotiate the most economical rates.

Qualifications and Training

Degrees and diplomas in advertising, business studies, English, marketing, or media studies provide a good background but are not an essential entry qualification or a guarantee of success. Degrees in design are an advantage if you want to work on the creative side. It is a very competitive sector and any work experience you can offer is as important as your qualifications. The Institute of Practitioners in Advertising (IPA) organises some structured work placements, but any relevant experience you can get is worthwhile. The Communications and Marketing Education Foundation (CAM) is phasing out its certificate and diploma courses. Most training is on the job, and in larger agencies this may include some structured courses.

Personal Qualities and Skills

As you may be dealing with anyone, from clients to members of the creative team, excellent communication skills are a must. For most jobs in advertising you have to be persuasive, enthusiastic, confident, very well organised and able to work under pressure. For creative positions you must be imaginative and quick to come up with new ideas, not put off by criticism, and good at teamwork.

Starting Salary

Most new entrants to the sector earn between £10,000 and £20,000. The larger agencies based in London pay the highest salaries. For copywriters, the range is from £12,000 to £18,000.

info

The Advertising Association, 7th Floor, Artillery House, Artillery Row, London SW1P 1RT; 020 7340 1100

CAM Foundation Ltd (Communications and Marketing Education Foundation Ltd), Moor Hall, Cookham, Maidenhead, Berkshire SL6 9QH; 01628 427120; www.camfoundation.com; e-mail: info@camfoundation.com

Institute of Practitioners in Advertising, 44 Belgrave Square, London SWIX 8QS; 020 7235 7020; www.ipa.co.uk

Creative and Cultural Skills, 11 Southwark Street, London SE1 1RQ; 020 7089 5866; www.ccskills.org.uk

AERIAL ERECTOR

Aerial erectors fix aerials to roof structures along with the necessary cabling to feed televisions, VCRs and radio receivers. Many installers also offer cable and satellite dish installation, and a number of businesses specialise in these areas as well as offering standard communication aerial installation.

Qualifications and Training

Formal qualifications are not necessary as training is often given on the job by experienced colleagues. Formal training is given in all aspects of aerial and satellite installation through the Confederation of Aerial Industries Ltd (CAI). The ability to drive is an advantage.

Personal Qualities and Skills

Good colour vision and a head for heights are essential. Being reasonably fit is useful when climbing up ladders and getting in and out of lofts or onto roofs. You have a lot of customer contact and work in people's private homes, so you need to be polite, friendly, helpful and trustworthy.

Starting Salary

Starting salaries range from £13,000 to £16,000 and can rise to £19,000. There are a lot of short-term contracts in this work.

info

Confederation of Aerial Industries (CAI), Fulton House, Fulton Road, Wembley, Middlesex HA9 0TF; 020 8902 8998; www.cai.org.uk; e-mail: office@cai.org.uk

Local Job Centre Plus and Careers/Connexions Centres

AGRICULTURE

(*see also* Farming)

The work in agriculture involves cultivating crops and raising livestock for food, energy and raw materials.

Agricultural contractor

Agricultural contractors employ experienced workers and managers to provide specific help to farmers at certain times of the year. About 60 per cent of farms use contractors from time to time.

Qualifications and Training

While qualifications are not essential, NVQs are available in relevant subjects. These, together with certificates at national or advanced national level in agriculture or agricultural contracting, from a college of agriculture, improve chances of finding employment.

Personal Qualities and Skills

Agricultural contractors must have an appreciation of farmers' needs, combined with efficiency, reliability and a good business sense.

Starting Salary

Variable, depending on whether or not the contractor is an employee or running his or her own concern, and the size of the operation, but in the region of £10,000 to £25,000.

Lantra is the Sector Skills Council for the environmental and land-based sector. For further information on training, education and careers within the environmental and land-based sector contact: Lantra Connect, Lantra House, Stoneleigh, Kenilworth, Warwickshire CV8 2LG; 0845 707 8007; www.lantra.co.uk; e-mail: connect@lantra.co.uk

Agricultural engineering

see Engineering

Agricultural surveying

see Surveying

AMBULANCE SERVICE

Most of the work in the ambulance service is directly with patients, providing pre-hospital care and transportation in response to emergency and urgent calls, or providing transport for those unable, for medical reasons, to make their own way to hospital. There are two distinct areas of front-line work: Accident and Emergency and Patient Transport Services.

Ambulance care assistants

Ambulance care assistants are mainly concerned with transporting elderly, infirm or handicapped people to hospital. They work within Patient Transport Services (PTS) and are mainly involved in routine transportation work. Such work does not involve emergency duties but staff are trained in Basic Life Support Skills, First Aid and Patient Care. Staff may also work in hospital units.

Ambulance control and communication

Staff requirements vary among ambulance services, although most require a good general standard of education. Control staff can move to ambulance duties providing they meet the entry requirements and successfully complete the selection process.

Ambulance paramedics

Paramedics are trained to use advanced life support techniques and administer a range of drugs for the emergency treatment of a number of conditions. In order for paramedics to maintain their qualification, they must update their skills regularly and prove their competence through examination, and are only allowed to practise if they are state registered. They must comply with Council for Professions Supplementary to Medicine (CPSM) regulations. There has to be a paramedic on each emergency ambulance.

Ambulance technicians

Ambulance technicians work alongside paramedics responding to 999 and urgent calls. They make decisions on the treatment and transportation of ill and injured patients. Their work involves a wide range of skills, including resuscitation, oxygen and some drug therapy, fracture splintage, wound dressing and pain relief. The type of work undertaken by both technicians and paramedics is varied and demanding. Both paramedics and technicians are trained in advanced driving skills and may work in ambulance motor vehicles, air ambulances or on motorcycles.

Emergency medical dispatcher

Emergency medical dispatchers work in central control rooms answering calls from GPs and the public, and ensuring that resources are deployed effectively and efficiently. Some ambulance services run a despatch prioritising system for emergency calls, which are analysed and placed in order of priority. When a caller gives information about a life-threatening situation, staff give advice over the phone while the ambulance travels to the scene.

Qualifications and Training

Ambulance care assistants need to be over 18 years of age and to have had a full current UK driving licence for at least one year and often two. Some ambulance services simply require a good standard of education, while others specify GCSEs or equivalent, including English and maths. Selection includes a medical assessment to ascertain that applicants are physically fit with good eyesight. Training takes up to three weeks, covering moving and handling techniques, first aid, basic patient care skills and safe driving techniques.

Technicians must meet the minimum ambulance care assistant requirements, although frequently services will require higher academic qualifications. Some services allow for direct entry technicians and others recruit internally from the ambulance care assistant grade. Technicians spend up to three weeks on an intensive driving course followed by six to nine weeks training in pre-hospital emergency care. This includes regular examinations and assessments. They then work under supervision for up to a year gaining experience completing competency assessments.

Paramedics must have at least one year of experience as a technician and then pass written and practical examinations. Intensive training lasts 10 to 12 weeks. Technicians and paramedics are required to attend regular training and reassessment. Paramedics re-qualify every three years.

Control and Communication staff requirements vary among services; most require a good general standard of education. Control staff can move to ambulance duties providing they meet the entry requirements and successfully complete the selection process.

Personal Qualities and Skills

Ambulance personnel must be honest, show initiative, have good people skills, a caring personality and be prepared to work with all types of people. They have to be well organised and work well as part of a team, though able to make their own decisions when necessary. They must stay calm under pressure and be good communicators. Physical fitness is essential as staff regularly lift patients and equipment.

Control and Communication staff need strong powers of concentration because calls involve assimilating a lot of information quickly and making decisions rapidly. They must be able to take clear notes and operate high technology equipment.

Technicians and paramedics require a high level of technical knowledge, a cool head in emergencies and the manual dexterity to carry out treatment in awkward conditions. Paramedics need to cope with advanced theoretical studies and be able to apply clinical judgement in emergencies.

Starting Salary

A trainee ambulance care assistant starts on just over £9,000. A fully qualified assistant earns just under £14,500. A qualified technician earns £19,000 and a paramedic (leading ambulance person) earns £21,400. There are some additional responsibility payments available, and annual pay rises usually apply from April each year.

info

Recruitment is through individual ambulance services; they advertise locally and are listed in telephone directories. Details of these services and private ambulance providers are available from the Ambulance Service Association.

Ambulance Service Association, Friars House, 157–168 Blackfriars Road, London SE1 8EZ; 020 7928 9620; www.asancep.org.uk

Ambulance Service Institute, 23 Clifton St, Bury, Lancs BL9 5DY; www.asi-international.com/

British Paramedic Association (BPA), 28 Wilfred Street, Derby DE23 8GF; 01332 746356; www.britishparamedic.org

Health Professionals Council, 184 Kennington Park Road, London SE11 4BU; 020 7582 0866; www.hpc.uk.com

NHS Careers provides leaflets and a telephone helpline: 0845 60 60 655; www.nhscareers.com

Skills for Health, 1st Floor, Goldsmiths House, Broad Plain, Bristol BS2 0JP; 0117 922 1155; www.skillsforhealth.org.uk

ANIMALS

(*see also* Veterinary Science *and* Zoology)

There is a wide range of occupations that involve working with animals. An obvious prerequisite for anyone wanting to work in this field is to have a love of animals and concern for their welfare.

Animal groomer

Animal grooming is a growing industry, with more dog and cat owners using the services provided by grooming salons of which there are 2,000 in the UK. Most are small private businesses, and some are part of other establishments, including pet shops, garden centres, boarding and breeding kennels. Some mobile groomers visit animals in their own home.

Each breed has different requirements and there are many types of coat, which all require specialist skills and techniques. The work involves bathing, shampooing, drying, clipping, trimming and brushing a variety of long- and short-coated animals. Specialist procedures include nail clipping, teeth cleaning, ear care and treatments for parasites.

Qualifications and Training

There are two main routes into training: a fee-paying course at a private grooming training centre or learning on the job. Candidates with practical animal-grooming experience may enrol for the City and Guilds Dog Grooming Certificate 775. This two-part exam, with a written paper and a practical element, tests candidates' skills on three different types of animal. This qualification shows employers that the groomer has had correct training and gives customers confidence that the groomer is competent.

The Advanced Grooming Diploma tests the expertise and skill required of the experienced groomer working in a commercial environment. A good working knowledge of the Kennel Club Breed Standards, styles and trimming techniques is required in order to pass all components. The exam consists of a written paper and seven practical modules, which can be taken over a period of time until all seven are complete, working at a timescale to suit the individual.

Starting Salary

This varies from area to area, and hours and rates of pay are negotiable. A general range is £8,000 to £12,000, but more if you run your own business.

British Dog Groomers Association, Bedford Business Centre, 170 Mile Road, Bedford MK42 9TW; 01234 273933; fax: 01234 273550; www.petcare.org.uk; e-mail: info@petcare.org.uk

Lantra Connect, Lantra House, Stoneleigh, Kenilworth, Warwickshire CV8 2LG; 0845 707 8007 (Lantra Connect – Helpline); www.lantra.co.uk; e-mail: connect@lantra.co.uk

Local Job Centre Plus and Careers/Connexions Centres

Animal technician

Animal technicians are a specialised and distinct group of professionals who are responsible for the care and welfare of animals used in biomedical research. Governments around the world require that new medicines have been extensively tested on animals before allowing human clinical trials. Testing is also undertaken on veterinary medicines and other products which may have an effect on human health. Animal technicians are responsible for caring for the animals, undertaking observations, sampling for the scientific studies, and ensuring that the strict laws controlling their use are followed at all times. Applicants should have a genuine desire to work with animals and must demonstrate concern and respect for their wellbeing.

Qualifications and Training

The minimum entry qualifications are five GCSEs at grade C or above, but some entrants have A levels or a degree. The Institute of Animal Technology offers five levels of qualification, from a basic one-year certificate to a postgraduate MSc. You can get exemption from certain modules of these courses if you can offer sciences at A or degree level. These qualifications can be taken as distance learning modules or at local colleges through day release courses.

Personal Qualities and Skills

You have to be comfortable handling animals and you must be kind, caring and calm when doing so. You also have to accept that you will have to do things that are stressful for animals, so you need to be prepared for this. You must be practical, thorough and meticulous, since you have to record scientific information accurately.

Starting Salary

Salaries for trainees range from £10,000 to £12,000 and from £12,000 to £15,000 for qualified technicians, but there is no national agreed rate for this work. A senior laboratory manager can earn up to £35,000.

Institute of Animal Technology, 5 South Parade, Summertown, Oxford OX2 7JL; www.iat.org.uk

Association of the British Pharmaceutical Industry, 12 Whitehall, London SW1A 2DY; 020 7930 3477; www.abpi.org.uk

Universities Federation for Animal Welfare (UFAW), The Old School, Brewhouse Hill, Wheathampstead, Hertfordshire AL4 8AN; 01582 831818; www.ufaw.org.uk

Dog trainer

(*see also* Kennel Work)

Dog trainers work with dogs in a wide variety of occupations, some as self-employed trainers of domestic pets and others in specific occupations such as the Police, the Armed Services and HM Customs & Excise. Dog trainers are also used by the Guide Dogs for the Blind Association and the Hearing Dogs for Deaf People, and by other groups of people with disabilities.

Depending on the context of the work, trainers will teach dogs to obey commands, learn rules of behaviour, seek out illegal substances, or restrain suspected criminals. In the case of guide dogs, they are trained to ensure that their owners are guided safely around obstacles and through gaps. Guide dog mobility instructors work with guide dogs to complete their training and introduce the dogs to their new owners and train them together. Trainers working with domestic animals often deal with dogs with behavioural problems as well as general obedience training.

Qualifications and Training

No specific qualifications are required for self-employed dog trainers. For those who work in organisations, in-house training is usually given. The Guide Dogs for the Blind Association requires a minimum of three GCSEs (including English language). Training is in-house and will lead to an NVQ or City & Guilds qualification. There are three-year apprenticeships for guide dog mobility trainers.

Personal Qualities and Skills

Dog trainers need a great deal of patience and good communication skills with both dogs and their owners and other people. Much of the work is outdoors, so prospective trainers need to be prepared to work in all types of weather.

Starting Salary

Salaries range from £8,000 to £11,000 as a trainee. Some training posts also provide living accommodation. Salaries are rarely high in this field, since many of the employers are charitable or voluntary organisations. Part-time work is sometimes available.

info

BBCi: www.bbc.co.uk/cbbc/wild/working/dogtrainer.shtml

Guide Dogs for the Blind Association, Burghfield Common, Reading RG7 3YG; 0870 600 2323; www.gdba.org.uk; e-mail: guidedogs@guidedogs.org.uk

Hearing Dogs for Deaf People, The Grange, Wycombe Road, Saunderton, Princes Risborough, Buckinghamshire, HP27 9NS; 01844 348100; www.hearing-dogs.co.uk; e-mail: info@hearing-dogs.co.uk

Dogs for the Disabled, The Frances Hay Centre, Blacklocks Hill, Banbury, Oxon OX17 2BS; 01295 252600; fax: 01295 252668; www.dogsforthedisabled.org

British Institute of Professional Dog Trainers, Bowstone Gate, Nr Disley, Cheshire SK12 2AW; www.bipdt.net/

Groom

Grooms look after all aspects of the horse's welfare. Their duties include grooming and strapping, mucking out, feeding, cleaning tack, saddling up, exercising and leading both mounted and dismounted, elementary veterinary care and sick nursing, preparation for and travelling with horses by road, sea and air and care of the horse when at grass. Grooms work in racing stables, hunting establishments, private stables, studs and breeding concerns, riding schools, occasionally (seasonally) with polo ponies and at trekking centres.

Qualifications and Training

No formal qualifications are necessary but it is recommended that grooms take the British Horse Society examinations stages 1, 2 and 3 in Horse Knowledge and Care, which comprise the Grooms Certificate. Alternative options are NVQs in Horse Care, levels 1, 2 and 3.

Training is usually on the job and should be sufficient to prepare students for exams. There are also courses of varying lengths to prepare students for particular exams; however, the fees are often high. Funding may be available for the achievement of British Horse Society qualifications providing that the person is not eligible for any other type of funding.

Personal Qualities and Skills

A love of horses is essential, plus patience and the willingness to work long hours and perform many routine tasks. A heavy goods vehicle driving licence may be an advantage.

Starting Salary

Stable staff generally earn the national minimum wage. In some cases food and accommodation may be free, in others they may be deducted from the wage. The hours may be long. The BHS issues guidelines on salaries for those with BHS qualifications; details are on their website.

info

British Horse Society, Stoneleigh Deer Park, Kenilworth, Warwickshire CV8 2XZ; 08701 202244; fax: 01926 707800; www.bhs.org.uk; e-mail: enquiry@bhs.org.uk

The BHS Guide to Careers with Horses £3.50 plus 50p p&p. Available from the BHS Bookshop (address as above); Order line: 08701 201918; Online bookshop: www.britishhorse.com

Lantra Connect, Lantra House, Stoneleigh, Kenilworth, Warwickshire CV8 2LG; 0845 707 8007 (Lantra Connect – Helpline); www.lantra.co.uk; e-mail: connect@lantra.co.uk

Kennel work

Kennel staff ensure that the animals in their care have clean accommodation, are fed a regular and nutritious diet, kept clean and well groomed and given sufficient exercise. Where animals are sick or recovering from an operation, the kennel staff must also be able to provide adequate nursing care.

There are a number of different types of kennel – greyhound kennels train dogs for racing, hunt kennels for hunting – and they involve a lot of outdoor work, exercising the dogs and perhaps travelling to meetings. There are quarantine kennels licensed by the Department for the Environment, Food and Rural Affairs (DEFRA) and breeding kennels where duties also include weaning and training puppies, preparing dogs for shows and possibly handling them. Boarding kennels look after animals while their owners are away. Some of the racing and quarantine kennels are large operations situated near racing stadia, airports and ports but others may be smaller, family-run concerns.

Qualifications and Training

No formal qualifications are needed to work in kennels and most employers prefer school leavers to train on the job. The NVQ level 2 in Animal Care and the National Small Animal Care Certificate are nationally recognised by the industry and provide a good base for further study. Many training organisations and agricultural colleges throughout the country offer this qualification. Entry requirements vary depending on the institution.

Personal Qualities and Skills

Good health, general fitness and stamina are required for this manual, physically demanding, outdoor work. Kennel staff must be unsentimental about animals but at the same time have a genuine concern for their wellbeing; they require patience and a placid but firm nature. A willingness to work long days, weekends and public holidays is also required.

Starting Salary

£150–200+ a week.

info

Lantra Connect, Lantra House, Stoneleigh, Kenilworth, Warwickshire CV8 2LG; 0845 707 8007 (Lantra Connect – helpline); www.lantra.co.uk; e-mail: connect@lantra.co.uk

Animal Care College, Ascot House, High Street, Ascot, Berkshire SL5 7JG; 01344 628269; www.animalcarecollege.co.uk; admin@rtc-associates.freeserve.co.uk

Our Dogs, 5 Oxford Road, Station Approach, Manchester M60 1SX; 0161 228 1984 (weekly magazine featuring job offers and advertisements from kennels. Also publishes *Cats*)

Local Job Centre Plus and Careers/Connexions Centres

Running Your Own Boarding Kennels (Kogan Page)

Jockey

Jockeys are employed by trainers of flat racing and National Hunt (jump) racehorses to ride horses at race meetings. They may ride for one trainer or for several. To become a jockey it is necessary first to work in a racing stable as an apprentice jockey or stablehand.

Only those showing most talent – about 1 in 10 – are chosen to ride in a race. The others remain as stablehands, and may be promoted to Head Lad (this title applies to boys and girls).

Stable lad

Stable lads (who may be boys or girls) do a lot of labouring work, mucking out, fetching straw, filling haynets and sweeping. They must also learn to groom and exercise the horses, and usually become responsible for a certain number of their 'own'. On race days, a stable lad will accompany a horse, groom him, walk him round before the race and lead him into the winner's enclosure if he wins.

Qualifications and Training

No specific educational qualifications are needed to become a jockey. Some experience of riding is useful but serious training is given by the stable. The racing industry has introduced NVQs, levels 1, 2 and 3 in racehorse care and management, and Foundation and Advanced Modern Apprenticeships. Flat-racing apprenticeships start at 16 and last until the age of 24. National Hunt apprenticeships start at 17–18 and last until the age of 25.

There is a nine-week training course available at the British Racing School in Newmarket, funded by racing, and open to school leavers who wish to work in a racing yard. Pupils are taught to ride, look after horses and carry out elementary stable management. The Northern Racing School at Doncaster runs a 10-week residential course for school leavers who wish to work in a racing yard and for those already in the industry who wish to further their training as stable staff. Training is compulsory for all 16- to 19-year-olds employed by the industry.

Personal Qualities and Skills

Apprentice jockeys must be prepared to work long hours in all weather conditions. At 16, flat-racing apprentices should weigh 7–8 stone (44–51 kg), girls 8–9 stone (51–57 kg); National Hunt jockeys may be heavier. Jockeys need strong hands and arms, and must be able to deal with nervous horses in a calm, confident and unemotional way. Jockeys must also be able to work within the strict, rather conservative traditions of the racing world.

Starting Salary

Apprentice jockeys and stablehands over 19 with a year's experience earn about £140 a week. Apprentice and conditional jockeys receive their normal wage plus half the riding fee when racing. Racing jockeys' salaries vary according to their success; there is a rate per ride plus a percentage of the prize money.

info

British Racing School, Snailwell Road, Newmarket, Suffolk CB8 7NU; 01638 665103; www.brs.org.uk; e-mail: careers@brs.org.uk

British Horseracing Board (BHB), 42 Portman Square, London W1H 6EN; 020 7396 0011; www. bhb.co.uk; e-mail: info@bhb.co.uk; 'Careers in the horseracing industry' can be downloaded from the website

Northern Racing College, The Stables, Rossington Hall, Great North Road, Doncaster DN11 0HN; 01302 861000; www.northernracingcollege.co.uk; info@nrcdonc.demon.co.uk

Riding instructor

Riding instructors teach people, individuals or groups, how to ride horses. They may also accompany riders who hire horses by the hour, and be required to help train horses and look after them, cleaning tack and stables. The work includes teaching in riding schools and clubs and in summer camps, training competition riders and occasionally sitting as a judge or examiner.

Qualifications and Training

To take the British Horse Society's Assistant Instructor certificate, candidates must be members of the society and, if under 18, have four GCSEs, one of which should be English. On completion of Stages 1, 2 and 3, the Preliminary Teaching Test, an approved first aid certificate and 500 hours of teaching experience, they are awarded the Assistant Instructor's certificate.

There are several methods of training: at a riding school, paying fees for instruction, board and lodging – the courses can be as short as three months or as long as a year, depending on the type of course; or as a BHS Apprentice at a BHS approved riding centre, doing stable work while receiving instruction. This takes approximately one year. Pupils pay for their keep. For more information on the BHS apprenticeship scheme, contact the BHS Approvals Office. After being awarded the Assistant Instructor's certificate, candidates may take the Intermediate Instructor's exams after reaching the age of 20. At 22, Intermediate Instructors may go on to take the British Horse Society Instructor's certificate. The Fellowship may be taken from 25 years of age.

Personal Qualities and Skills

Patience and authority, but above all a love of horses, are essential for this work. A riding instructor must enjoy being out of doors and get on well with people, especially children.

Starting Salary

£8,000–10,000 for an Assistant Instructor as a rough guide; salaries vary depending on whether instruction is being provided, accommodation and stabling for the instructor's own horse and the instructor's age and experience.

British Horse Society, Stoneleigh Deer Park, Kenilworth, Warwickshire CV8 2XZ; 0870 120 2244; www.bhs.org.uk

RSPCA inspector

Inspectors for the Royal Society for the Prevention of Cruelty to Animals (RSPCA) deal with complaints from the general public about the alleged ill-treatment of animals and also perform more routine tasks. Inspectors have no power to take an animal from its owner unless the owner legally signs it over.

They may caution people and, in some circumstances, the organisation will ensure that cases go before the courts. Inspectors also visit boarding kennels, pet shops and riding schools. They can be involved in physical rescues, often working unsociable hours and driving considerable distances.

Qualifications and Training

Applicants require GCSEs or equivalent in English language and a science, a valid driving licence and the ability to swim 50 metres fully clothed. Experience of working with animals is desirable.

About 20 inspectors are recruited each year from over 2,000 applicants. Training lasts six months and covers animal welfare legislation, basic veterinary training, mountain and boat rescue techniques, investigation skills, interview techniques, court work, animal-handling techniques, media training and public speaking. After written examinations, students serve six months' probation before becoming fully qualified. Minimum age for entry is 22.

Personal Qualities and Skills

Inspectors have to be very good at handling animals of all kinds. They must be calm, kind and authoritative. They need excellent interpersonal skills, be able to be assertive, to deal with both sensitive and potentially confrontational situations. They must be able to speak in public, whether it is in court or in a classroom.

Starting Salary

Salaries start at around £14,500 and senior inspectors earn £20,000 plus. Inspectors also receive travel and accommodation allowances.

RSPCA Chief Superintendent (Training), RSPCA, Wilberforce Way, Southwater, Horsham, West Sussex RH13 9RS; www.rspca.org

Zoo keeper

Keepers look after animals in zoos, mucking out their living quarters, preparing their food, feeding them and engaging in all other aspects of animal husbandry. There is increasing emphasis on education, public relations and research. Keepers work long hours – from 8 am to as late as 7 pm – much of the time outdoors and the work is often physically demanding.

Qualifications and Training

No specific qualifications are needed although an interest in biology or natural sciences is advantageous. On-the-job training is by a correspondence course followed by a City and Guilds qualification. However, many applicants for posts in zoos have done courses in Animal Care or Welfare. These are available at First, National and Higher National Diploma level and there are also related degree courses. Graduates are more likely to enter posts in education and research. Applications for such jobs far exceed the number of places available, and zoos prefer people to enquire only when a vacancy is advertised.

Personal Qualities and Skills

Affection and respect for animals, combined with an unsentimental approach, are essential. Keepers must have practical common sense, an interest in education and conservation and the ability to communicate effectively with the public.

Starting Salary

Salaries range from about £8,000+ to £13,000+.

Association of British Wild Animal Keepers; www.abwak.co.uk (Contact details for members of the Association can be found on the website)

Careers Working with Animals (Kogan Page)

ANTHROPOLOGIST

Anthropologists study the development of human societies, making comparisons between different communities and cultures. This academic discipline is linked with the other social sciences and with evolutionary biology. Much of the work still concerns non-industrial, 'primitive' or rural cultures, but changes brought about by contact with more sophisticated outside influences and pressures from 'modern' societies are an important aspect of study and many anthropologists now undertake research in urban or industrial societies. The career involves a combination of research, teaching and finding out more about the people being studied by going to live with them over a period of time.

Increasingly, anthropologists are finding employment as consultants, for instance in the development, health and humanitarian fields and in such professions as journalism, human resource management, planning, tourism and heritage, museum curatorship and medicine.

Qualifications and Training

A good degree in anthropology. Postgraduate study is usually required.

Personal Qualities and Skills

Those wishing to embark on this career must normally be committed to an academic way of life, although there is growing demand outside universities. Field researchers must be prepared to spend long spells abroad, often in basic conditions. Physical and mental stamina is required, as well as independence and resourcefulness. Anthropologists must be prepared to work on their own. However, as anthropology has diversified, so the ways of working life adopted by anthropologists have become more varied too and they now work in every imaginable setting, from offices and day-care centres to out in the field. Linguistic ability is useful.

Starting Salary

Salaries vary; around £12,000–14,000 is a rough guide. Salaries may be very different when working on overseas projects.

Royal Anthropological Institute, 50 Fitzroy Street, London W1T 5BT; 020 7387 0455; fax: 020 7383 4235; www.therai.org.uk; e-mail: admin@therai.org.uk

ANTIQUE DEALER

The buying and selling of antiques for profit entails expert knowledge of the field, combined with sound managerial and business sense. Comparatively few people make a living at this trade, and many businesses are family concerns. Dealers frequently specialise in particular types of antiques, and trade among themselves as well as with private buyers and sellers. Dealers may sell from shops, antiques markets, antiques fairs and from home. An increasing number trade on the internet using auction sites such as eBay as well as their own websites.

Qualifications and Training

No specific qualifications are required, although a broad artistic background may be useful. The accepted route into the business is via a job with an established antique dealer, which provides an opportunity to learn the trade.

Personal Qualities and Skills

Above all, you must be genuinely interested in the antiques you are dealing with. You need a keen eye for detail, and the ability to investigate thoroughly. A sound financial head and the ability to get on well with people are also extremely important.

Starting Salary

Most antique dealers are self-employed, so income varies enormously. Some antique dealers employ assistants who earn around £10,000 to £12,000. A dealer running his or her own successful business at the upper end of the market, or with highly specialised expertise, can earn £50,000, but this is unusual.

British Antique Dealers' Association, 20 Rutland Gate, London SW7 1BD; 020 7589 4128; www.bada.org; e-mail: enquiry@ bada.demon.co.uk

ARCHAEOLOGY

Archaeology is the examination of the human past through the study of buried remains and artefacts.

Archaeologist

Archaeology – building up a picture of the past – is both an art and a science. Archaeologists use highly technical and scientific methods of discovery, analysis and identification to reconstruct and study men and women from the past using their material remains. The evidence is collected through fieldwork, including excavations, where clues are sought in objects, their surroundings, the ground itself and the remains of living things. The evidence is then analysed, subjected to experiment, assessed, identified, catalogued, conserved and possibly exhibited. Archaeologists usually specialise in a particular period, technique or geographical area. Opportunities for full-time, permanent positions are limited; consequently competition is fierce for the few jobs available. These are to be found in central and local government, museums and universities, independent units and trusts, as well as a variety of positions in commercial operations. Job availability is closely related to building and development work. Some work includes the opportunity to spend time abroad.

Qualifications and Training

There are several degree courses in archaeology and most people who work as archaeologists will also have a postgraduate qualification and some work experience of volunteering on archaeological digs. There are also postgraduate courses in archaeological conservation.

Personal Qualities and Skills

Archaeologists need to be practical, thorough and very careful and observant. They should be able to work well as part of a team, or as a team leader. They need to have a real passion for and commitment to their work.

Starting Salary

Salaries are relatively low in this work. Many people start as volunteers and salaries of £9,000 to £11,000 are usual. A fieldwork supervisor earns around £14,000 to £15,000 a year.

Archaeological surveying

see Surveying

ARCHITECTURE

Architecture is a profession requiring the practical combination of imaginative design with scientific and technological principles, to produce designs for new buildings and for the extension, or renovation, of those already existing.

Architect

Architects are professional experts in the field of building design and construction. They advise individuals, developers, local authorities and commercial organisations on the design and construction of new buildings and the area around them. Architects are also involved in the restoration and conservation of historic and existing buildings. In its wider definition the professional association for architects, RIBA, says, 'Society looks to architects to define new ways of living and working, to develop innovative ways of using existing buildings and creating new ones.'

Architects create designs based on information supplied by the client on the function of the building, the proposed budget and the site. An architect needs to have an understanding of structure, finance, planning law and design, and in many building projects acts as the coordinator in a team of specialist consultants such as engineers, builders and interior designers.

The architect works to the client's requirements and produces working drawings for the builder. These show dimensions, materials and how everything will be put together. An architect will also negotiate with local authorities and submit the designs to planning officers for approval. On large jobs there will be a team of architects working with engineers and other specialists, and it may take months to prepare all the drawings and schedules. Alternatively, very small jobs take only a few weeks. After the contract documents have been prepared and a builder selected, work begins on the site. The architect visits frequently as the building goes up. This can involve tramping around in boots and a hard hat, climbing up and down ladders as well as taking the chair at site meetings.

Opportunities exist for employment in private practice, with local authorities, in research, teaching, central government and some industrial organisations. Increasingly, interior design and companies working in associated fields employ architects as part of their team. Specialist areas can include domestic, public building and retail architecture. The use of computer-aided design packages plays a significant part in the work of architects.

Qualifications and Training

Candidates should have passes in at least two subjects at A level, or one A level and two AS levels, together with passes in at least five other subjects at GCSE level. Subjects should be drawn from academic fields of study and include maths, English language and a separate science (physics or chemistry), or a double certification in science. Training takes a minimum of seven years, but only five of those are spent at a school of architecture. After a three-year degree course, students spend a year in an architect's office. Students often work abroad during this year or work in other parts of the building industry. Another two years' further study to obtain a diploma or higher degree are followed by a further year of working in an office, ending with a professional practice exam to become registered as an architect with the Architects' Registration Board and a corporate member of the RIBA. This allows the use of the title Architect in business. Part-time training is an alternative offered by a few schools for students already working in an architect's office on a day-release basis. Membership of the Royal Institute of British Architects (RIBA) and Royal Incorporation of Architects, Scotland (RIAS) is open to students while studying and also to those who are fully qualified.

Personal Qualities and Skills

Architects must have artistic ability and be imaginative, but at the same time need to be able to understand and apply technical information. They must adopt a practical approach to their work and be able to communicate their ideas and instructions to a variety of people. Business acumen, a professional approach, discretion and willingness to conform to a strict code of conduct are very important.

Starting Salary

While completing their two years' practical training, architectural students may expect to earn between £12,000 and £16,000; when fully registered this will increase to about £21,000, and thereafter be dependent upon position, experience and employer. £32,000 is the average.

info

Royal Institute of British Architects (RIBA), Public Information Line, 66 Portland Place, London W1B 1AD; 020 7580 5533; fax 020 7255 1541; www.architecture.com; e-mail: info@inst.riba.org (There is a comprehensive careers section on this website.)

Architects' Registration Board (ARB), 8 Weymouth Street, London W1N 3FB; 020 7580 5861; www.arb.org.uk; e-mail: information@arb.org.uk

Royal Incorporation of Architects in Scotland (RIAS), 15 Rutland Square, Edinburgh EH1 2BE; 0131 229 7545; www.rias.org.uk; e-mail:information@rias.org.uk

Architectural technologist

Architectural technologists work alongside architects and other professionals as part of the building design and construction team. Technologists can negotiate the construction project from inception to completion. Specific, specialist skills could include surveying land and buildings, preparing and undertaking feasibility studies, presenting design solutions, analysing and detailing drawings, and managing and applying computer-aided design (CAD) techniques.

Qualifications and Training

A degree in architectural technology, an HNC/HND in Building Studies (with specific additional units) or an NVQ level 4 in Architectural Technology lead to Associate Membership of British Institute of Architectural Technologists (BIAT) and the designation ABIAT.

Personal Qualities and Skills

Architectural technologists should be able to work both as part of a team and on their own initiative. Attention to detail is necessary, as is the ability to take account of other professionals' needs. Effective communication skills are necessary when working as part of the team, liaising with clients or tendering for contracts and they should feel comfortable with new technology and innovative concepts.

Starting Salary

Junior technologists, £11,000–13,000; qualified technologists with three years' experience, £12,500–14,000; senior technologists with appropriate educational qualifications and 10 years' experience, up to £25,000.

Chartered Institute of Architectural Technologists (CIAT), 397 City Road, London EC1V 1NH; 020 7278 2206; Freephone (UK only) 0800 731 5471; www.biat.org.uk; e-mail: careers@biat.org.uk

Modelmaker

see Modelmaker

ARCHIVIST

In the course of business many organisations and people create or collect archives. These include government agencies, local authorities, universities, hospitals, businesses, charities, professional organisations and families and individuals. Archives may be books or papers, maps or plans, photographs or prints, films or videos, or computer-generated records. Archives are intended to be kept permanently, to preserve the past and allow others to discover it.

It is the job of the archivist to preserve and exploit this archival heritage and the information contained within it. This includes assisting visitors or users, promotional work including exhibitions, presentations or media liaison, as well as the curatorial skills of selecting archives for preservation and interpreting them for archive users.

Qualifications and Training

This is a small profession, requiring a strong academic background. Entrants should have a good degree and an interest in heritage and information management, and good customer service skills. The recognised qualification is a postgraduate Diploma/ MA, usually taken as a one-year full-time course at one of five universities in the UK and Ireland.

The Society of Archivists also offers an in-service diploma to graduates who are currently employed in archives or records management. Competition for places on these courses is fierce, and substantial practical paid or voluntary experience is required for applications to be successful. Lists of graduate placements are kept by the Society of Archivists' Training Officer and in addition, many local archives are also prepared to accommodate occasional volunteers interested in a career in archives.

Personal Qualities and Skills

Archivists must be good communicators, able to relate to and encourage a wide variety of people. They must also be ready to accept and exploit the technological advances that will continue to have a profound effect on demands for and use of information. A logical mind is essential for identifying and sorting archives before they can be interpreted or used effectively, and although archivists are not researchers, an understanding of research skills is helpful in all aspects of their work, particularly advising users. Archivists need to be prepared to continue their development after qualification, acquiring management, budgetary and other relevant skills.

Starting Salary

Salaries for new entrants range from £18,000 to £23,000. Business organisations, central government and universities usually offer higher pay than local authorities.

info

The British Library, 96 Euston Road, London NW1 2DB; 020 7412 7332; www.bl.uk

Business Archives Council, c/o Ms F Maccoll, Rio Tinto plc, 6 St James Square, London SW1Y 4LD; 020 7753 2123; www.businessarchivescouncil.com

Museum, Libraries and Archives Council, 16 Queen Anne's Gate, London SW19 9AA; 020 7272 1444; www.mla.gov.uk

The National Archives, Kew, Richmond, Surrey TW9 4DU; 020 8876 3444; www.nationalarchives.gov.uk

Society of Archivists, Prioryfield House, 20 Canon Street, Taunton TA1 1SW; 01823 327030; www.archives.org.uk

ARMY

The Army is the largest of the three armed services and offers a wide range of career opportunities at basic and officer entry level. As a solider you start as an infantryman, a gunner or a tank operator, and officer training is offered by all the Army's regiments. Army careers include nursing, medicine, dentistry, engineering, information technology, catering, finance and human resources. There are also opportunities for civilians in many of these fields. Visit the Army's online Careers Service for details on the full range of career options. The Army also offers special gap year opportunities, if you want to try the Army life between school and university.

Qualifications and Training

Officers

Officer recruits are normally aged 18–29 and of graduate calibre. The Army recruits graduates from all disciplines to all areas of the Army. All officers are awarded an initial three-year Short Service Commission (SSC) on commissioning from Sandhurst, and this is the minimum length of commitment. An SSC can be extended up to a maximum of eight years. After two years' SSC service, officers can apply to convert to an Intermediate Regular Commission (IRC), which provides up to 16 years' service. After two years' IRC service, officers can apply to convert to a Regular Commission, which provides service up to the age of 55.

Sponsorship

Cadetships and bursaries are available for those studying for a recognised first degree. All successful applicants complete 11 months' officer training at the Royal Military Academy, Sandhurst.

Soldiers and Servicewomen

Eligibility is determined by the results achieved on the Army Entrance Test (known as BARB). This assesses an applicant's ability for training by using computer touch-screen question and answer techniques. Entry is from age 16 to 30. Recruits usually enlist on an open engagement by which they agree to serve for 22 years, although it is possible to leave after a minimum of four years' service provided a year's notice is given.

Personal Qualities and Skills

Applicants must be British or Commonwealth citizens, born of British or Commonwealth parents and have been resident in the UK for the past five years. All candidates must be medically fit, intelligent, have the ability to work in a team and show dedication, courage, patriotism and a sense of responsibility.

Starting Salary

Soldiers: £11,152; Graduate officer cadet: £20,173. Army personnel receive other benefits such as accommodation, food and travel allowances.

Army Recruiting Group, FREEPOST 4335, Bristol BS1 3YX; 08457 300 111; www.army.mod.uk

Local Army Career Information Offices

ART AND DESIGN

There are many different careers in art and design and artists work with many different mediums. Popular areas include fashion and textiles, jewellery, furniture, interior design, graphic design, industrial design and photography. Less commercial applications include painting and sculpture.

Artist

Only a very few artists are able to earn a living solely by the sale to clients of original work. Many more work as designers in advertising, industry and publishing, the latter also offering opportunities for illustrators, particularly for covers and jackets of children's books, or teach art in a school or college.

There are limited opportunities for work as a community artist, community arts officer (encouraging art in the community) and artist-in-residence.

Qualifications and Training

For the majority of artists, academic qualifications are necessary. These range from two-year diploma courses for 16-year-olds with some GCSEs or equivalents, to degrees. Many degree courses require the completion of a one-year Foundation course. A portfolio of work is normally required alongside academic qualifications for entry to art-related courses. Art teachers require appropriate teaching qualifications; *see also* Teaching.

Personal Qualities and Skills

The qualities required vary according to the work undertaken. Creativity, talent and imagination are all important, as well as enthusiasm and, in some cases, the ability to work as part of a team and to meet deadlines.

Starting Salary

Teachers' salaries start at over £18,000. Salaries are very unpredictable. Many artists take on casual jobs to support their creative careers.

info

Arts Council, 14 Great Peter Street, London SW1P 3NQ, 020 7333 0100; www.artscouncil.org.uk

Design Council, 34 Bow Street, London WC2E 7DL; 020 7420 5200; www.designcouncil.org.uk and www.yourcreativefuture.org.uk; e-mail: info@designcouncil.org.uk

Creative and Cultural Skills, 11 Southwark Street, London SE1 1RQ; 020 7089 5866; www.ccskills.org.uk

Graphic designer

A number of different disciplines come under the umbrella heading of graphic design. These can include design studies, film and animation work, typography and lettering, illustration, printing processes, display and exhibition work, technical graphics for engineering, calligraphy, packaging and design for advertising, corporate identity and multimedia. Graphic design incorporates drawing and presentation skills and requires an understanding of colour, lettering and patterns. Many graphic designers work in three dimensions using specialist computer software. A high level of technical skills is therefore expected along with design ability. A rapidly growing area in graphic design is the field of new media, with new opportunities in multimedia, digital imagery and computer-aided design/manufacture.

Qualifications and Training

There are a wide number of degree and HND graphic design courses available. Many offer specialist modules such as graphic design with print media, interactive media, publishing, typography, illustration, plus many more. Graphic design can also be studied within a more general Art and Design qualification. Entry requirements to degree level Art and Design qualifications might also require a Diploma in Foundation Studies in Art and Design.

Personal Qualities and Skills

Design skills and good computer literacy skills are essential. You should be able to work in a team and to client requirements. Presentation skills are also useful.

Starting Salary

£12,000–16,000.

Design Council, 34 Bow Street, London WC2E 7DL; 020 7420 5200; www.designcouncil.org.uk and www.yourcreativefuture.org.uk; e-mail: info@designcouncil.org.uk

Chartered Society of Designers, 1 Cedar Court, Royal Oak Yard, Bermondsey Street, London SE1 3GA; 020 7357 8088 www.csd.org.uk

Illustrator

Illustrators create illustrations for a range of clients using painting and drawing skills. The main area of work is within print media although technical and medical illustrators are also employed in industry and medicine respectively (*see also* Medical Illustration). Illustrators work to a client's brief and produce ideas incorporating design and creative ideas. Increasingly, computer-generated illustrations are also expected in this sector. Many illustrators work in a freelance capacity, and will often require representation through an agent to find work.

Qualification and Training

It may not be necessary to have a qualification to find work as an illustrator, as employment can be found by presenting a good portfolio of work. However, a diploma or MA in Graphic Design or Illustration might provide a good basis for entry into the profession.

Personal Qualities and Skills

Design and artistic skills. Ability to develop good client relationships and to interpret client briefs. Ability to work in a variety of styles. Self-motivation and marketing skills.

Starting Salary

Illustrators tend to be self-employed and are paid per illustration.

Association of Illustrators, 81 Leonard Street, London EC2A 4QS; 020 7613 4328; www.theAOI.com

Design Council, 34 Bow Street, London WC2E 7DL; 020 7420 5200; www.designcouncil.org.uk and www.yourcreativefuture.org.uk; e-mail: info@designcouncil.org.uk

Industrial product designer

Trained designers work within industry with engineers who have created products. These range from household goods and furniture to specialised equipment for science, industry and commerce. Designers are concerned with creating products that both look attractive and are efficient and convenient in use. The competition for the sale of new goods, from suitcases or spectacles to cassette players or cars, has resulted in an increased demand for the services of industrial designers.

Qualifications and Training

Employers recruit from those with an HND or degree in a design-related subject; some courses offer specialist modules in industrial design. Entry to such courses is normally via a National Diploma course after GCSEs or a Foundation course at an art college after A levels. Applicants for art and design courses are expected to have a portfolio of their artwork when interviewed.

Personal Qualities and Skills

As well as artistic ability, an understanding of mass-production processes is necessary; the industrial designer should also be able to work as part of a team, to schedule and recognise the needs of the consumer.

Starting Salary

Starting salaries range from £15,000 to £20,000, and experienced designers working for large companies can earn as much as £40,000.

info

Design Business Association (DBA), 32–38 Saffron Hill, London EC1N 8FH; 020 7831 9777; www.dba.org.uk

The Design Council, 34 Bow Street, London WC2E 7DL; 020 7420 5200; www.design-council.org.uk

Institution of Engineering Designers, Courtleigh, Westbury Leigh, Wiltshire BA13 3TA; 01373 822801; www.ied.org.uk

Local Job Centre Plus and Connexions/Careers Centres

Interactive media design

(*see also* Information and Communication Technology)

Interactive media design is a new and highly popular area within art and design. There are now over 500 multimedia courses in the UK. Multimedia design draws on both technical and design skills, and is used in designs for interactive media products such as websites, CD ROMs, interactive TV and computer games. Career opportunities exist in a wide variety of organisations, from corporations with websites to specialist producers of computer games.

Qualifications and Training

Technical and design skills are essential. Many general courses in Art and Design also have a multimedia option, although there are now specialist multimedia and interactive design courses available. The majority of employers expect an HND or degree.

Personal Qualities and Skills

Strong design and IT abilities are essential, as are the ability to work within a team and to understand the requirements of the organisation if employed on a company website. The development of new multimedia products such as computer games and CD ROMs would also require an understanding of business and marketing principles.

Starting Salary

Starting salary approximately £18,000 although experienced designers can achieve £40,000+.

British Computer Society, 1 Sanford Street, Swindon, Wiltshire SN1 1HJ; 01793 417417; www.bcs.org.uk

British Interactive Multimedia Association, 5–6 Clipstone Street, London W1P 7EB; 020 7436 8250; www.bima.co.uk

British Web Design and Marketing Association, PO Box 3227, London NW9 9LX; 020 8204 2474; www.bwdma.com

UK Web Design Association, Fareham Enterprise Centre, Hackett Way, Fareham, Hampshire PO14 1TH; www.ukwda.org

Skillset, Prospect House, 80–120 New Oxford Street, London WG1A 1HB; 020 7520 5757; www.skillset.org

Careers and Jobs in IT (Kogan Page)

Interior designer

(*see also* Interior Decorator)

Interior designers work for commercial organisations as well as undertaking private commissions. They are responsible for the interiors of buildings (whereas an architect is responsible for its shell). Interior design can cover materials for floors and ceilings, fitments and fittings, and colour schemes, along with electrical and spatial planning. The commercial organisations may be offices, hotels, pubs, stores or banks. Interior designers may work with architects, have their own consultancies, or work in design units within large organisations.

Qualifications and Training

Entry to art school and college via a Foundation course is the same as for an industrial product designer (see page 37). Once at art college, the student may specialise in interior design.

Personal Qualities and Skills

A natural aptitude for art, the ability to work as part of a design team, and to present work to customers are necessary.

Starting Salary

£13,000–20,000 according to experience and ability.

Design Council, 34 Bow Street, London WC2E 7DL; 020 7420 5200; www.designcouncil.org.uk and www.yourcreativefuture.org.uk; e-mail: info@designcouncil.org.uk

Signwriter

Signwriters design and paint company names and logos on to shop fronts and the sides of vans and lorries; they may also paint estate agents' signboards and a wide variety of other temporary signs and notices. Signwriters increasingly use a range of materials and techniques, including computer technology, to create signs. The letters are often formed from plastics, metal or wood and stuck on to the background.

Some signwriters are in business on their own; others work for commercial signwriting companies.

Qualifications and Training

There are no formal academic entry requirements for this type of work, but artistic talent combined with an interest in lettering is important. Some graphic design courses include typography and signwriting and provide wider training. Some commercial signwriting firms take on trainees and NVQs in Assembly, Fabrication and Manufacturing Processes and Signmaking are available at level 2.

Starting Salary

Many signwriters are self-employed and earnings vary greatly.

Local Job Centre Plus and Careers/Connexions Centres

Art therapist

see Therapy

Arts administration

This is the administration and management of theatres, orchestras, opera houses, ballet companies and arts centres. The Arts Council, responsible for the promotion of art throughout the country, has its own administrative staff. The British Council, responsible for displaying British arts abroad, also employs a small number of staff.

Qualifications and Training

Experience is often more important than formal qualifications, although a good general education is expected; many entrants are graduates. Commercial awareness plus a knowledge of and interest in the arts is essential. Postgraduate courses such as an MA in Arts Administration can be studied part- or full-time.

Personal Qualities and Skills

You have to be good at dealing with the public and also with artists, so a full range of interpersonal skills is important. You must be well organised, a very good administrator and have good ideas about marketing, publicity and fund raising. Basic accounting skills are useful.

Starting Salary

Salaries start at around £11,000 to £12,000 and are often linked to local authority pay scales. £18,000 is a typical salary once you have some experience.

info

Arts Council, 14 Great Peter Street, London SW1P 3NQ; 0845 300 6200; www.artscouncil.org.uk; e-mail: enquiries@artcouncil.org.uk

Scottish Arts Council, 12 Manor Place, Edinburgh EH3 7DD; 0131 226 6051; www.sac.org.uk; e-mail: help.desk@scottisharts.org.uk

Arts Marketing Association, 7a Clifton Court, Clifton Road, Cambridge CB1 7BN; 01223 578078; fax: 01223 245862; www.a-m-a.co.uk; e-mail: info@a-m-a.co.uk

ASTRONOMER

Astronomers study the sun, planets, stars, galaxies and other objects in the sky, analysing the radio, infrared, optical, ultraviolet, X and gamma radiations they emit, to find out how they work. Some of these radiations do not penetrate the earth's atmosphere, so observations by satellite are necessary as well as from the ground. Modern astronomical detectors are usually based on electronic methods and give results which can be analysed by computer.

Qualifications and Training

To become a research astronomer, a good degree in physics or maths is necessary and it is possible to do degrees in astronomy or astrophysics. This is normally followed by postgraduate study and research. Various grants are available to support students undertaking such courses.

Astronomy-related careers at an engineering or technical level are also open to those with skills in applied physics, electronics, computer hardware and software, optics and mechanical engineering.

Personal Qualities and Skills

Astronomers need curiosity and imagination; they must be able to make logical deductions from the available observations. Working long and unusual hours and travelling to remote observatories may also be involved.

Starting Salary

Post-doctoral salaries start at around £18,000; technical salaries after training are around £15,500–22,000, depending on qualifications.

The Library, Royal Astronomical Society, Burlington House, Piccadilly, London W1V 0NL; 020 7734 3307; www.ras.org.uk; e-mail: info@ras.org.uk

Public Information Officer, Royal Observatory Greenwich, National Maritime Museum, London SE10 9NF; 020 8858 4422; www.rog.nmm.ac.uk

AUCTIONEER

(*see also* Land and Property)

The auctioneer's work involves the sale by auction of property of all kinds, including buildings (houses, farms and estates), livestock, and goods such as furniture, antiques, paintings, glass, toys, carpets and china. The work also entails valuations for various purposes, including investment and insurance.

Qualifications and Training

An auctioneer's work involves the valuation of land and property, so surveying or valuation qualifications are necessary. There are two components to qualifying as a Chartered Surveyor or Valuer. First is successful completion of a Royal Institution of Chartered Surveyors (RICS) accredited degree or diploma, followed by enrolment onto the Assessment of Professional Competence (APC). This is two years' practical training while in employment, finishing with an RICS professional assessment interview. One-year full-time and two-year part-time postgraduate conversion courses are also available.

Personal Qualities and Skills

Attention to detail is important for this job, together with a practical attitude and an aptitude for figures. In fine art auctioneering, a certain flair and the ability to distinguish a fake from the genuine article are essential.

Starting Salary

Trainees starting at 18, £8,000–9,000; graduates with relevant degrees, £11,000–13,800 rising to £19,000+ or higher in London.

Royal Institution of Chartered Surveyors, 12 Great George Street, London SW1P 3AD; 020 7222 7000; www.rics.org.uk/afa

AUDIOLOGY TECHNICIAN

Audiology technicians carry out tests to assess the presence, nature and extent of a hearing loss, using complex and advanced techniques. They take aural impressions for individual moulded ear inserts, fit and instruct the patients on how to use hearing aids, and review their progress.

Qualifications and Training

Four GCSEs at C grade or equivalent, in English, maths, physics and another science and two A levels, one of which must be a science. Training involves two years of combined theory and practice while in employment, leading to an Edexcel (BTEC) qualification in medical physics and physiological measurement, or NVQ equivalent.

Personal Qualities and Skills

Candidates must be patient, have a clear speaking voice and the ability to get on with people.

Starting Salary

Trainee £8,000+. Once qualified, depending on grade, £15,000–30,000+.

British Society of Audiology, 80 Brighton Road, Reading RG6 1PS; 0118 966 0622; fax: 0118 935 1915; www.thebsa.org.uk

British Society of Hearing Aid Audiologists, Bridle Croft, Burgh Heath Road, Epsom KT17 4LF; 01372 725348; www.bshaa.co.uk; e-mail: information@bshaa.com

BANKING AND FINANCE

Banking

Banks provide a delivery point for financial services. The most obvious side of banking is the high street branches but other work includes international banking (financing foreign trade and providing an overseas banking service for UK customers); corporate finance (dealing with the requirements of large companies); human resources, recruitment, training and staff development; insurance; computer services; marketing; training; and trust work (when a bank is appointed as executor or joint executor of a will).

The recent reduction in the number of bank branches and the growth in internet and telephone banking is a trend that is expected to continue, with some opportunities being offered in bank call centres, although some are now located abroad.

Commercial

Commercial banks provide financial services to individuals, small businesses and large organisations. They usually have high street branches and provide such services as bank accounts, cash transactions, cheque clearing; credit and debit cards, loans (including mortgages), foreign currency; and advice on insurance, pensions and savings products. Most commercial banks also offer telephone and online banking facilities for their customers. Junior posts involve routine office work and dealing with customers by telephone and in person. With experience the work will involve building links with business, solving complex customer queries and making business decisions. There are also specialist opportunities in IT, human resource management and marketing.

The Bank of England

This is the banker to the government. It is concerned with the financial structure of Great Britain, with other banks in the country and with operating accounts for overseas central banks. The Bank of England is responsible for the printing, issue and withdrawal of British banknotes and it also controls interest rates and raises short-term government finance. The monitoring of economic developments at home and abroad provides information for the Bank, the Treasury and other government departments. It does not offer banking facilities to the general public. Specialists such as economists, statisticians and librarians are recruited in addition to other banking staff.

Investment Banks

These are generally financial houses, which started from trading as merchants and have expanded their role to financing the trading and commercial activities of others, especially in the international marketplace. An investment banking group nowadays includes the following services for its clients: corporate finance and advisory work, banking for governments, institutions and companies, investment management and securities trading.

Qualifications and Training

Each bank has different entry points, recruiting school leavers after GCSEs and A levels as well as graduates. Structured training programmes often provide access to qualifications of the Institute of Financial Services in England and Wales or Chartered Institute of Bankers in Scotland (CIOBS). As well as covering traditional areas of banking there are a range of new qualifications such as certificates in Commercial Banking in the Networked World, Capital Markets, and the New Economy and E-Finance.

The Chartered Institute of Bankers in Scotland first-level qualification (the Certificate in Financial Services) requires no previous qualifications for entry. Students completing the certificate can progress to the Associateship and Membership examinations. NVQs level 2–4 in providing financial services are available.

Most banks welcome applications from graduates who have qualified from a range of disciplines such as law, accountancy or business. There are also vacancies for individuals seeking a career in information technology.

Personal Qualities and Skills

Accuracy, integrity, good powers of concentration, attention to detail and a clear mind are essential for success in a banking career. It is important to be able to get on with people and to work as a member of a team.

info

British Bankers Association (BBA), Pinners Hall, 105–108 Old Broad Street, London EC2N 1EX; 020 7216 8800; www.bba.org.uk

Chartered Institute of Bankers in Scotland (CIBS), Drumsheugh House, 38b Drumsheugh Gardens, Edinburgh EH3 7SW; 0131 473 7777; www.ciobs.org.uk/

The Financial Services Authority (FSA), 25 The North Colonnade, Canary Wharf, London E14 5HS; 020 7066 1000; www.fsa.gov.uk

Financial Services Skills Council, 51 Gresham Street, London EC2V 7HQ; 020 7216 7366; www.fssc.org.uk

Institute of Financial Services (IFS), IFS House, 4–9 Burgate Lane, Canterbury CT1 2XJ; 01227 762 600; www.ifslearning.com

Starting Salary

Starting salaries in most commercial banks are around £12,000 to £13,000, or £15,000 to £21,000 for graduates. Salaries tend to be higher in investment banking and commence at around £25,000 to £30,000.

Building societies

The traditional function of building societies is to attract savings and investments from the public, and then use these funds to make loans for home ownership. However, more recently most building societies have moved into offering a range of financial services, such as banking, insurance, credit cards, investment, estate agency and unsecured lending, but the savings and loan activities remain the most important. The number of building societies has decreased since deregulation as many have converted to banks and there are now 65 in the UK.

Building society assistants deal with customers' enquiries and are expected to sell some of the society's financial services, as well as being responsible for routine and administrative tasks. With the increase in telephone and internet banking the number of jobs in building society branches has decreased, but some call centre work is available.

Building society managers work with customers on mortgage and loan applications, financial planning queries and with customers facing repayment difficulties. They may be in charge of a single large branch or a number of small branches, where they have responsibility for managing staff and ensuring targets are met.

Qualifications and Training

Assistants need four GCSEs or equivalent including English and maths. Competency-based on-the-job training is common and can include the opportunity to take Chartered Institute of Bankers (CIB) or Chartered Institute of Bankers in Scotland (CIOBS) modules or examinations. Those with CIB/CIOBS Associateship qualifications can move into management. Graduates are also recruited into management training posts; entry can be from any degree discipline and further professional training is available through CIB/CIOBS.

Personal Qualities and Skills

Honesty and discretion are essential as well as good communication, mathematical and IT skills. The ability to market financial products is becoming increasingly important. Managers need negotiating, decision-making and problem-solving skills, in addition to good people management skills.

Starting Salary

Assistants earn from £9,000 to £15,000 depending on qualifications and experience. Graduate trainees start on £16,000–18,000+.

info

Building Societies Association, 3 Savile Row, London W1S 3PB; 020 7437 0655; www.bsa.org.uk

Institute of Financial Services, 4–9 Burgate Lane, Canterbury, Kent, CT1 2XJ; 01227 818609; www.ifslearning.com

Chartered Institute of Bankers in Scotland, Drumsheugh House, 38b Drumsheugh Gardens, Edinburgh EH3 7SW; 0131 473 7777; www.ciobs.org.uk

Careers in Banking and Finance (Kogan Page)

Economist

see Economist

Financial adviser

Financial advisers provide advice on all aspects of financial planning to a wide range of clients. They work with individuals and corporate clients and other groups of people such as societies or charities. They can offer advice on such diverse matters as loans, mortgages, pensions, investments and other financial products and services.

Their work involves meeting clients and explaining financial products and services to them clearly and carefully. They have to assess people's different financial circumstances in order to advise on the most suitable products. They conduct in-depth research into different products and liaise closely with banks, building societies, insurance companies, etc – the financial product suppliers. They are often self-employed, so they also have to be good at marketing and promoting themselves and seeking out new clients.

There are approximately 75,000 financial services advisers working in the UK, and almost half class themselves as independent rather than tied advisers. Being independent, however, does not necessarily mean being self-employed. Both tied and independent financial services advisers may work for an organisation or may be self-employed. Many independent advisers work for firms which themselves are known as independent financial advisers.

Tied advisers work for financial services companies, insurance companies, investment firms, banks and building societies. Some are employed by estate agencies, law firms and by retailers that have developed financial services as a part of their business.

Qualifications and Training

You don't have to be a graduate, though degrees in business studies, accountancy or financial services can give you an advantage. Many employers are happy to take people from a wide range of working backgrounds and do not require academic qualifications. You nearly always need a driving licence, and some employers set lower age limits of 21 or older for trainers.

All entrants to the professions have to pass the Financial Planning Certificate examinations parts 1, 2 and 3 or the Certificate for Financial Advisers in order to be licensed by the Financial Services Authority. A lot of the training is provided on-the-job and when you start you often learn by shadowing a more experienced adviser.

Personal Qualities and Skills

You need excellent communication skills: able to talk convincingly to corporate clients and sensitively to private individuals. You must be smart, well organised and highly motivated – this is a competitive sector. You need good numeracy and IT skills and the ability to deal with highly complex information.

Starting Salary

Most advisers earn a basic salary, plus commission from the products they sell. Starting salaries for tied advisers are between £10,000 and £15,000; successful advisers earn in excess of £70,000.

An experienced independent financial adviser can expect to earn between £30,000 and £40,000 – based on performance a successful adviser can earn in excess of £100,000.

info

Society of Financial Advisers (SOFA), 20 Aldermanbury, London EC2V 7HY; 020 8989 8464; www.sofa.org; e-mail: info@sofa.org

Chartered Insurance Institute, 42–48 High Road, South Woodford, London E18 2JP; 020 8989 8464; www.cii.co.uk; e-mail: customer.serv@cii.co.uk

Institute of Financial Planning, Whitefriars Centre, Lewins Mead, Bristol BS1 2NT; 0117 945 2470; www.financialplanning.org.uk

Association of Independent Financial Advisers (AIFA), Austin Friars House, 2–6 Austin Friars, London EC2N 2HD; 020 7628 1287; www.aifa.net

Institute of Financial Services (IFS), IFS House, 4–9 Burgate Lane, Canterbury, Kent CT1 2XJ; 01227 818609; www.ifslearning.com; e-mail: customerservices@ifslearning.com

Investment work

Investment Analysts

Investment analysts analyse the financial markets to advise on the best investments for clients. Investment managers rely on their information. There are two main types of investment analyst. First are those who work for stockbrokers and undertake their own analysis to provide information for fund manager clients. The aim is to generate 'buy and sell' orders for the stockbrokers for whom they work. This is known as the 'sell side'. Second, there are those who work for investment management institutions. They provide ideas and information to enable their in-house fund managers to make the best decisions for their clients. This is known as the 'buy side'. The majority of investment analysts work on the 'sell side'.

Fund Manager

Investment fund managers invest the funds of other people – private clients and institutions, such as insurance companies, charities, independent schools and specialised research institutions. Managers must keep their clients' interests continually under review, offering advice on how to retain their clients' income and when to change investments. Investment fund managers may be employed by the larger institutions, or work in specialist firms that tend to serve smaller clients.

Qualifications and Training

It is becoming increasingly difficult to enter this profession without a degree. The most favoured subjects include mathematics, accountancy, economics and statistics. Some global companies like applicants to have a Masters in Business Administration.

A basic qualification for all trainees is the Investment Management Certificate (IMC) from the Society of Investment Professionals. This takes around a year to complete, and covers the regulations that investment companies and their staff must adhere to in the UK, plus statistics, maths and economics. Many analysts and managers take the Chartered Financial Analyst (CFA) qualification. This usually takes up to three years to complete.

Personal Qualities and Skills

Analyst and fund managers have to be good communicators face-to-face and on the telephone. You need to be able to work as part of a team, but also to use your own initiative and take decisions. You must be interested in current affairs and be able to make the link between these and their potential impact on financial markets and funds.

Starting Salary

Salaries for trainees range from £15,000 to £27,000, though you would have to be a pretty impressive applicant to start at the top end of this scale. Very high earnings are possible in this field.

info

Association of Private Client Investment Managers and Stockbrokers (APCIMS), 114 Middlesex Street, London E1 7JH; 020 7247 7080; www.apcims.co.uk

Chartered Financial Analyst (CFA) Institute, 29th Floor, 1 Canada Square, Canary Wharf, London E14 5DY; 020 7712 1719; www.cfainstitute.org

UK Society of Investment Professionals (UKSIP), 90 Basinghall Street, London EC2V 5AY; 020 7796 3000; www.uksip.org

Stockbroker

Stockbrokers buy and sell securities on the Stock Exchange on behalf of investors, who may be individuals but are increasingly institutions, such as banks, insurance companies, pension funds or unit trusts. They also advise clients on shares they hold and suggest good times to sell or buy. Stockbrokers work from their offices using the phone and internet to keep in touch with financial markets and news.

Qualifications and Training

A degree is desirable, but good A levels may be accepted. Before being allowed to trade, all staff must pass the Registered Representative Examination, administered by the Securities Institute. Stockbrokers train on the job, working alongside experienced brokers. Many employers expect their staff to study for the Securities Institute Diploma.

Personal Qualities and Skills

Entrants should be confident, numerate and able to express ideas clearly and concisely. Good interpersonal skills are essential, in order to ensure effective client relationships, as is the ability to work as part of a team.

Starting Salary

Depending on location, starting salaries vary from £16,000 to £25,000. Brokers' salaries depend on the amount of business carried out; top brokers can earn between £100,000 and £250,000.

Association of Private Client Investment Managers and Stockbrokers (APCIMS), 114 Middlesex Street, London E1 7JH; 020 7247 7080;www.apcims.co.uk

Financial Services Skills Council, 51 Gresham Street, London EC2V 7HQ; 020 7216 7366; www.fssc.org.uk

BEAUTY

Beauticians are predominantly, although not exclusively, female. There are a variety of occupations within the beauty sector, ranging from therapists who provide body and face treatment to make-up artists who work in film and television.

Beauty sales consultant

Working in the perfumery department of a large store, in a luxury hotel, at home and overseas, on an ocean liner or at airports, sales consultants sell and promote their firm's products, answering questions from potential buyers on skin care and make-up. They occasionally give talks at schools and colleges or to women's organisations, and may travel for their companies at home and abroad.

Beauty therapist

(*see also* Hairdresser)

Beauty therapists work in salons, health clubs and private homes and, at the glamorous end of the market, for film, television and fashion magazines. Beauty therapists offer a range of treatments to their clients, such as facials, massage, make-up, manicures, waxing and body toning and tanning treatments. Beauty therapists who visit clients in their own homes have to be good business people, keeping accounts, ordering stock and keeping up to date with the latest developments. The top end of the market is highly competitive, but it is a profession that gives you a lot of flexibility. UK hairdressers and beauty therapists are generally highly thought of.

Qualifications and Training

There are no specific entry requirements, but it is an advantage to have GCSEs in English, maths and a science and some employers may set their own entry standards. There are two ways to train: through a college course leading to a GNVQ Level 3, or through a Modern Apprenticeship, which also leads to GNVQ Level 3. The main difference is that on a Modern Apprenticeship you are based with an employer, though some college work is also included. Many people choose to do the combined hairdressing and beauty therapy Modern Apprenticeship, to give themselves a more flexible qualification. Some private beauty colleges offer training and it is very important that you check what qualifications they award before you pay for one of these courses.

Personal Qualities and Skills

You must be excellent at putting people at ease, as the work leads to a lot of close, physical contact, in massage or body waxing for example. You have to be friendly, reassuring and patient. You need good physical stamina as you are on your feet for a great deal of the time.

Starting Salary

Salaries start at around £9,000, though with experience it is possible to earn more than £20,000. One of the attractions of the job is that you can be self-employed and work the hours you choose.

Hairdressing and Beauty Industry Authority, Oxford House, Sixth Avenue Sky Business Park, Robin Hood Airport, Doncaster DN9 3GG; 08452 306080; www.habia.org.uk

British Association of Beauty Therapy and Cosmetology (BABTAC), Meteor Court, Barnett Way, Barnwood, Gloucester GL4 3GG; www.babtac.com

Local Job Centre Plus and Connexions/Careers Centres for vacancy information, local colleges for course details

Make-up artist

Make-up artists prepare and work on make-up and hair styling required for each individual such as artists, singers, dancers, actors and others appearing on television and in film production. Make-up artists also work in other environments such as on cruise liners, in beauty salons in large hotels, stage shows, fashion shows or in the medical profession, where they provide make-up to camouflage client injuries following an accident or surgery.

An experienced make-up artist will work on more versatile projects using elaborate make-up, wigs, materials to change the shape of a face or create scars and wounds for television and film productions. This will require research and design of the make-up required for a production, through to completion ready for filming. It is necessary to be able to liaise closely with producers, directors, costume designers, hairdressers and the performers.

Qualifications and Training

A minimum five GCSE (A–C)/S grades (1–3) and English literature, history and drama subjects are required to study a full-time course in beauty therapy or make-up. To become a make-up artist students must complete this full-time beauty therapy course. Some courses lead to the Hairdressing and Beauty Industry Authority (HABIA) NVQ/SVQs in beauty therapy levels 2, 3 and 4. Contact HABIA for advice on choosing the right course.

Advanced Modern Apprenticeships are available for young people in England. Skillseekers and Modern Apprenticeships (Scotland), Modern Apprenticeships (Northern Ireland) and National Traineeships and Modern Apprenticeships (Wales) may also be available. Applicants who are over 18, with an NVQ level 2 in both hairdressing and beauty therapy, can apply to FT2 which trains junior freelance make-up artists for TV and film work.

Skillset offers qualifications for people who are working in the film and television industry. Skillset professional qualifications (NVQs) are in hair and make-up at levels 2, 3 and 4.

Personal Qualities and Skills

A make-up artist should have creative imagination, a strong visual sense, manual dexterity and be able to communicate well at all levels. A good make-up artist will be able to work well under pressure and have a confident, precise and methodical approach to the work.

Starting Salary

The majority of make-up artists are self-employed, so there is not a set income for make-up artists. Rates are negotiable depending on the skills required, the type of production and its budget. Minimum rates for independent productions are set by the Broadcasting, Entertainment, Cinematograph and Theatre Union (BECTU). A freelance make-up artist can earn from around £10,000 to £20,000 or more, according to experience and reputation. Full-time make-up artists usually earn between £12,000 and £15,000 or more, especially if they have specialist skills.

info

British Association of Beauty Therapy and Cosmetology (BABTAC), Meteor Court, Barnett Way, Barnwood, Gloucester GL4 3GG; www.babtac.com

Broadcasting, Entertainment, Cinematograph and Theatre Union (BECTU), 373–377 Clapham Road, London SW9 9BT; 020 7346 0900; www.bectu.org.uk; e-mail: info@bectu.org.uk

BECTU and Skillset UK Media Careers Portal website: www.skillsformedia.com

Film and Television Freelance Training, 4th Floor, Warwick House, 9 Warwick Street, London W1B 5LY; 020 7734 5141; www.ft2.org.uk; e-mail: info@ft2.org.uk

Hairdressing and Beauty Industry Authority (HABIA), 2nd Floor, Fraser House, Nether Hall Road, Doncaster, South Yorkshire DN1 2PH; 01302 380000; www.habia.org; e-mail: enquiries@habia.org

Skillset (The Sector Skills Council for the Audio Visual Industries), Prospect House, 80–110 New Oxford Street, London WC1A 1HB; 020 7520 5757; www.skillset.org

Faceworks, International Academy of Make-Up Artistry, Cathedral Buildings, 68 Donegal Street, Belfast BT1 2GT; 028 9024 9888; e-mail: Dianne@faceworks.ssnet.co.uk

BIOLOGY

Those who work in the field of biology are concerned with the structure, processes and functions of living organisms.

Biochemist

Biochemistry is the study of chemical substances and processes in living cells and tissues. Most biochemists work in laboratories although some make their careers in education or industry, in brewing, food technology, forestry, agriculture, dietetics, pharmaceuticals, management and planning.

Many biochemists are employed in hospitals, where they manage and develop the service and carry out research into disease. Pharmaceutical firms also employ biochemists to develop new drugs and study their effects on diseases and patients. Qualified biochemists are also employed in research institutions funded by the Medical Research Council, the National Institute for Medical Research and Biotechnology, and the Biological Sciences Research Council, as well as some funded by charities such as the Imperial Cancer Research Fund (ICRF).

Qualifications and Training

Biochemists entering the professions in universities, hospitals and industry will be graduates, usually with good honours degrees in biochemistry or a related science subject. Laboratory technicians in universities and industry often join with good GCSE passes in mathematics and science subjects, or A levels or equivalent. They will usually study part-time for Edexcel (BTEC) higher certificates in appropriate subjects. Biomedical scientists in hospital laboratories can enter with either degrees (usually an accredited BSc in biomedical science) or A levels, following which they will study part-time for a degree.

Personal Qualities and Skills

It is important to be able to work independently or as part of a team in any branch of science. Patience, powers of concentration and meticulous attention to detail are also important.

Starting Salary

Salaries vary with the type of employment and the responsibility involved. Graduates entering the professions as biochemists start on £12,000–18,000. Laboratory technicians with good GCSE passes have salaries of £6,000+, and trainee biomedical scientists will start at £11,000+. Additional academic and professional qualifications attained during employment will permit career development and usually lead to positions of greater responsibility with higher salaries.

info

Association of Clinical Biochemists, 130–132 Tooley Street, London SE1 2TU; 020 7403 8001; www.acb.org.uk

The Education Officer, Biochemical Society, 59 Portland Place, London W1B 1QW; 020 7580 5530; www.biochemistry.org

BioIndustry Association, 14–15 Belgrave Square, London SW1X 8PS; 0207 565 7190; www.bioindustry.org

Biotechnology and Biological Sciences Research Council, Polaris House, North Star Avenue, Swindon SN2 1UJ; 01793 413200; www.bbsrc.ac.uk

Biomedical scientist

Biomedical scientists (including medical laboratory scientific officers in the NHS) investigate specimens of body fluids and tissues, and play an important role in the diagnosis and treatment of diseases. Most are employed in hospital laboratories and pathology departments, but many also work for the blood transfusion service, in public health laboratories, for veterinary establishments, universities, pharmaceutical and other manufacturing companies. There are sometimes opportunities to assist in research and to teach.

Qualifications and Training

The profession has all-graduate entry. A guide to courses can be obtained from the Institute of Biomedical Science. Trainees in the NHS and related bodies have to proceed to state registration and need a degree to do so.

Personal Qualities and Skills

Biomedical scientists must be able to work quickly, accurately and methodically. Complicated and new equipment must be used, so technical as well as scientific ability is needed.

Starting Salary

As a graduate trainee salaries start around £12,000 to £14,000 – there is some regional variation. On registration salaries rise to a range of £17,000 to £24,000.

info

Health Professions Council (HPC), Park House, 184 Kennington Park Road, London SE11 4BU; 020 7582 0866; www.hpc-uk.org

Health Protection Agency, 7th Floor, Holborn Gate, 330 High Holborn, London WC1V 7PP; 020 7759 2700; www.phls.co.uk

Institute of Biomedical Science (IBMS), 12 Coldbath Square, London EC1R 5HL; 020 7713 0214; www.ibms.org

Biotechnologist

Biotechnology is the application of living organisms and biological systems to industrial processes. Various aspects of biological science are involved – biochemistry, microbiology and genetics. At present, the main industrial areas in which biotechnologists are employed are fermentation, waste systems management, production of antibiotics, vaccines, hormones, and animal and human food production.

Qualifications and Training

Most new entrants are graduates. Degree entry requirements are a minimum of five GCSEs including maths, plus three A levels or equivalent including biology and chemistry.

Personal Qualities and Skills

A high degree of accuracy, thoroughness, lots of patience and the ability to check and recheck details are needed.

Starting Salary

£20,000 upwards for graduates.

info

The Education Officer, Biochemical Society, 59 Portland Place, London W1B 1QW; 020 7580 5530; www.biochemistry.org

BioIndustry Association, 14–15 Belgrave Square, London SW1X 8PS; 020 7565 7190; www.bioindustry.org

Biotechnology and Biological Sciences Research Council, Polaris House, North Star Avenue, Swindon SN2 1UJ; 01793 413 200; www.bbsrc.ac.uk

Institute of Biology, 20 Queensberry Place, London SW7 2DZ; 020 7581 8333; www.iob.org

BOOKMAKER

As a bookmaker or in betting shop management, you work with people who are placing bets on everything from horse and greyhound racing results through to whether or not there will be a white Christmas. The majority of betting shops are part of large chains, but there are a few small, independent operators. This sector has done a lot to improve its image and make its outlets more appealing to customers, especially since the advent of online gambling.

Qualifications and Training

There are no formal entry qualifications, except that trainee managers must be over 21. You are likely to face aptitude tests to check your numeracy skills as part of your application. Many trainee managers do have A levels or degrees, but all kinds of background experience are viewed as useful. Training is on the job, usually starting behind the counter. Training covers how to set bets, customer care, numerical skills and security procedures.

Personal Qualities and Skills

You need excellent customer service skills, a lot of common sense, good numerical skills and the ability to manage other people.

Starting Salary

Trainee managers start on between £14,000 and £16,000, while branch managers earn between £17,000 and £24,000.

Association of British Bookmakers (ABB), Regency House, 1–4 Warwick Street, London W1B 5LT; 020 7434 2111; www.abb.uk.com

BOOKSELLER

In a bookselling career it is essential to have in-depth product knowledge and the ability to sell. It is important to keep up to date by reading new books and reviews, in order to assist customers and to display the books to advantage. The ability to find information in catalogues and directories, both online and in hard copy, is essential. Managers are responsible for stock ordering and for giving their shops an image that will attract regular customers to help them compete with the discounts offered by supermarkets. A growing number of bookshops sell their products through the internet.

Qualifications and Training

A good general education is essential. Some bookshops require a degree. The industry-recognised qualification, the Diploma in Professional Bookselling, is available through the Booksellers Association of United Kingdom and Ireland, together with a number of comprehensive training resources. An understanding of e-commerce is an advantage.

Personal Qualities and Skills

A liking for books and people, good general knowledge and an interest in reading and handling books are necessary, as are good health and stamina for a job which involves much standing. An interest in selling and customer care is essential to create a friendly and reassuring atmosphere, where book buyers know that they are being looked after in an efficient manner by professional, knowledgeable staff.

Starting Salary

Salaries are usually negotiable in small shops, and many booksellers work part-time. Salary ranges are (with London at the top end of each range): sales assistants £9,000–12,000, senior assistants £10,000–13,000, managers £14,000–25,000. Managers of larger chains can earn up to £40,000.

Booksellers Association of United Kingdom and Ireland, Minster House, 272–274 Vauxhall Bridge Road, London SW1V 1BA; 020 7802 0802; www.booksellers.org.uk

BREWING

Brewing is the complex process of making and packaging beer. Specialist technicians are responsible for the choice of all raw materials – malt, hops, etc, and plant equipment. Brewing technicians and brewing scientists are required to maintain consistently high-quality products. There are opportunities for non-qualified people to work as plant operators.

Qualifications and Training

No formal qualifications are necessary for non-technical jobs in the brewing industry. For technical jobs the main demand is for honours graduates in science and engineering, particularly if they have specialised in brewing, biochemistry or chemical engineering. Specialist degrees in brewing are available at Heriot-Watt University and will provide exemption from the Associate Membership examination of the Institute of Brewing, which offers training and internationally recognised qualifications at various levels.

Personal Qualities and Skills

Good health is required for a job that will inevitably involve some night and shift work. The ability to organise and communicate effectively at all levels, and a keen interest in science and engineering, are the hallmarks of successful brewers and brewing scientists.

Starting Salary

Non-technical staff can earn from £13,000 to £15,000 once experienced; graduate trainees start on £15,000–22,000+.

Brewing Research International (BRi), Lyttel Hall, Coopers Hill Road, Nutfield, Surrey RH1 4HY; 01737 822272; www.brewingresearch.co.uk

Institute of Brewing and Distilling (IBD), 33 Clarges Street, London W1J 7EE; 020 7499 8144; www.ibd.org.uk/igbsite/home/index.asp

Local Job Centre Plus and Connexions/Careers Centres

BROADCASTING

Broadcast media has several aims – to inform, to entertain, to educate and to increase and retain audiences and to generate profits. The range of programmes is enormous and expanding, but this is a competitive field to enter. Relevant qualifications, training and experience are often essential. Broadcasting companies prefer individuals who are multi-skilled: digital technology and internet-related skills are in demand. It is important to demonstrate enthusiasm through practical involvement in relevant activities such as writing for a local newspaper or website, or working behind the scenes in amateur theatre. Vacancies can be found on broadcasting company websites as well as in a number of national newspapers.

Assistant floor manager and floor assistant

These people carry out a variety of tasks according to each production. They are often in charge of the prompt book.

Audio assistant

Audio assistants work on radio and television programme origination throughout the UK, doing similar jobs to sound operators and studio managers. There is a tendency now in BBC regions for the job to split into these two categories.

Broadcast engineer

Engineers are involved in maintaining and testing the equipment used in studios and in outside broadcasts in radio and television, together with operating and maintaining the transmission chain. They may also be involved in project development and research work. Recently there has been a shortage of skilled broadcast engineers owing to an ageing workforce and staff moving towards new media (internet-based media).

Camera operator

Camera operators work both in studios and on outside broadcasts. They have deep interest in subjects such as photography and lighting. An ability to establish good working relationships with other crew members and the director is necessary.

Costume designer

After gaining the relevant diplomas, costume designers should have theatrical experience. The work involves liaison with producers and make-up staff and responsibility, where necessary, for hiring and adapting costumes. They must have had basic training in pattern-making, cutting and dressmaking, and have gained practical experience in a fashion house or theatrical costumier.

Costume dressmaker

The dressmaker carries out necessary alterations and adaptations on hired or existing costumes, as well as making up new designs.

Director

The director has the responsibility of making the finished programme, and this role also requires good technical knowledge of the media as well as a strong creative ability.

Dresser

Duties involve the maintenance of costumes and the dressing of artists for performances. Requirements are sewing ability, and relevant experience in the theatre, the film industry or as a theatrical costumier.

Film editor/video editor

Film and video editors increasingly work with both formats. The editor must be able to visualise the director's/producer's ideas and make the required creative decisions. Film and video editors have usually had experience in a technical/creative capacity before moving to an editor's position.

Floor manager

Floor managers work in television doing a similar job to the stage manager in the theatre. The broadcasting floor manager's job can be strenuous – actors working on different sets cannot see each other and the floor manager's function is to cue and coordinate them all. The floor manager is also responsible for health and safety in the studio.

Journalist/reporter

(*see also* Journalism)

Journalists work in all forms of media, reporting on current affairs, events and general items of interest. They carry out research and interviews for newspapers, broadcast news programmes and online services. A candidate who is able to script, record and edit his or her own piece digitally would stand a stronger chance of gaining employment. There has been an increase in the number of journalists working for online publications.

Producer

The producer has overall responsibility for the project and may recruit all the people involved, including the director, the writer, camera staff and actors. The role requires a good technical knowledge of the media, with financial management and budgeting skills as well as the necessary creative ability.

Producer's assistant

They work for the producer, organising all the administrative work. They retype scripts to incorporate any changes that have been made, ready for the next rehearsal or performance.

Production assistant

The production assistant works as part of the production team. He or she must have good keyboard and organisational skills, be able to deal with a wide range of contacts and work to deadlines. Part of the job involves sitting in the control gallery timing the programme. In addition, PAs may do research for programmes.

Programme assistant

They work in radio and are responsible for the technical and artistic presentation of programmes. They need to be able to operate the equipment and be good at dealing with other people in the team and with the people who are interviewed or who work on the programmes.

Sound operator

They help to set up and operate sound equipment in studios and on outside broadcasts. An understanding of MD recording would be an advantage. They have a deep practical interest in subjects such as hi-fi and sound. The ability to establish good working relationships is necessary.

Studio manager

Studio managers work in radio and are responsible for all issues relating to the artistic and technical operation of a programme. They must know how to interpret the producer's ideas correctly and how to achieve the best sound effects.

Television make-up and hairdressing

(*see also* Beauty)

This is a highly skilled area of work, and competition for any vacancies is keen. It requires a thorough knowledge of period hairstyles and an understanding of the effects of lighting and camera on people's faces. In television, the make-up designer/assistant is responsible for both make-up and hair, whereas in films, the jobs are separate.

Vision mixer

Vision mixers are responsible for recording the images from different cameras under the instruction of the director. They must have strong concentration and the ability to work under pressure.

Qualifications and Training

Many companies offer in-service staff training schemes that are advertised as they occur. Competition for places on these schemes is fierce. The selection boards are impressed by good all-rounders as well as candidates with specialist knowledge.

In technical areas, engineers require, at trainee level, at least English GCSE plus A level maths and physics or a national diploma in electronics. Qualified engineers need to have a degree or HND in electronic engineering. There are a number of degree courses, including Foundation Degrees in Digital Broadcast Technology.

Technical operators require a good standard of education; at least GCSE grades A–C in English, maths and combined sciences (preferably physics). To improve their chances, candidates often progress their education further. Evidence of in-depth relevant practical involvement, often through amateur interests, always impresses. Many training courses now have an equivalent NVQ or Skillset professional qualification.

Trainee studio managers need to have knowledge of sound equipment together with practical involvement in radio. GCSEs in maths and physics are generally required. Production trainees must have practical experience of work directly related to production, either professionally or in an amateur capacity. No specific qualifications are asked for but applicants must have a wide range of interests.

Journalism training opportunities require applicants to have a demonstrable interest in news and current affairs, with evidence of practical involvement. Training schemes attract a large response and the standard is high.

Secretarial and clerical staff must have a good standard of education. Qualifications for clerical posts vary, depending on the department – for example, in finance an aptitude for figures is essential. Accurate keyboard skills are required for clerk-typist posts. Secretaries must have accurate typing; shorthand is an advantage.

Make-up trainees need to demonstrate involvement in professional or amateur theatre, and must have had formal training in make-up and hairdressing. Applicants should have A levels including art.

Personal Qualities and Skills

The qualities and skills mix required varies from a designer who must be very creative, to a sound engineer who needs excellent technical skills. There are some skills common to everyone working in this field. You have to work well as part of a team, and be capable of working under pressure and keeping calm in the face of problems. Jobs like reporting or presenting require great self-confidence and an ability to work well with a diverse mix of people.

Starting Salary

The salary range is wide, varying with the job you do and the qualifications you need to do it. Some junior jobs are relatively low paid, around £12,000, while assistant producers and editors earn close to £20,000. A lot of this work is paid on short-term contracts, per number of programmes or per individual show, for example.

BBC, Television Centre, White City, Wood Lane, London W12 7TS; 020 8752 5252; www.bbc.co.uk

BKSTS (British Kinematic, Sound and Television Society), The Moving Image Society, Pinewood Studios, Iver Heath, Bucks SL0 0NH; 01753 656656; www.bksts.com/

Channel 4 Television, 124 Horseferry Road, London SW1P 2TX; 020 7396 4444; www.channel4.com/

Five, 22 Long Acre, London WC2E 9LY; www.five.tv

FT2 – Film & Television Freelance Training, Fourth Floor, Warwick House, 9 Warwick Street, London W1B 5LY; 020 7734 5141; www.ft2.org.uk/

Independent Television Commission, 33 Foley Street, London W1P 7LB; 020 7255 3000; www.itc.org.uk

SEMTA: The Sector Skills Council for Science, Engineering and Manufacturing Technologies, Head Office, 14 Upton Road, Watford WD18 0JT; 01923 238 441; www.semta.org.uk

Skillset, Prospect House, 80–110 New Oxford Street, London WC1A 1HB; 020 7520 5757; www.skillset.org

Careers and Jobs in the Media (Kogan Page)

info

BUSINESS ADMINISTRATION

The term 'business administration' covers all of the roles required to ensure the smooth running of the day-to-day functions of a business regardless of the business purpose. 'Business' refers to any type of organisation in the public, private or voluntary sectors. The jobs range from the Company Secretary's duties (at director level) to the duties of the accounts staff and a variety in between.

Company secretary

The Company Secretary plays a major part in the organisation's governance. Duties include ensuring that the company complies with relevant legal and regulatory matters, administration of mergers and acquisitions, drafting contracts, advising the board of directors on company law and procedures and maintaining company records. Other duties can include pensions administration, personnel matters, shareholder issues, property management and finance.

Qualifications and Training

The law recognises the importance of the Company Secretary role, mandatory for every company, by requiring the Company Secretary of a public limited company (plc) to have specific knowledge and experience. Only the Institute of Chartered Secretaries and Administrators (ICSA) qualification specifically addresses the requirements of the role.

The ICSA Qualifying Scheme comprises three programmes: Foundation, Pre-Professional and Professional. Graduates and holders of recognised postgraduate qualifications are eligible for direct access onto the Professional Programme. It consists of core modules in Corporate Governance, Corporate Administration, Corporate Secretaryship, Corporate Financial Management, and top-up modules in Corporate Law, Management Accounting, Financial Accounting and Strategic Management.

Upon completion of the ICSA Qualifying Scheme, candidates become Graduates of the Institute (Grad ICSA). To become a Member, an ICSA Graduate has to demonstrate three years' relevant experience and have two sponsors of professional status to confirm his or her fitness to practise. There are two grades of Membership: Associate and Fellow.

Personal Qualities and Skills

As a company secretary you must be prepared to take responsibility and be discrete in handling confidential or sensitive information. You must be able to understand numerical information and other complex documents. You need excellent communication skills, often having to be diplomatic and tactful, and be comfortable dealing with people at all levels within an organisation.

Starting Salary

Salaries for trainees start at between £20,000 and £25,000; larger or London-based organisations pay the highest rates. With a few years experience salaries rise to £20,000 to £30,000.

Graduate Recruitment Managers, Institute of Chartered Secretaries and Administrators (ICSA), 16 Park Crescent, London W1B 1AH; Tel: Graduate Recruitment Manager, on 020 7580 4741; www.icsa.org.uk; e-mail: gradrec@icsa.co.uk

Personal assistant

(*see also* Secretary)

A senior secretary or personal assistant (PA) may work with one or more senior executives. Accurate skills in shorthand, audio typewriting, word processing and information management, and a knowledge of office-based software are desirable. The PA may also act as administrator, information centre, organiser of the manager's day, progress chaser, arranger of travel and meetings, receptionist and communicator (oral and written) internally and externally. A senior secretary or PA assumes responsibility without direct supervision and takes decisions within the scope of assigned authority.

Qualifications and Training

A minimum of GCSEs in maths and English is usually required, but it is not uncommon for people with A levels or degrees to go into this work. Any relevant IT training courses on software packages for managing data or accounts are also useful. Some colleges run full-time and part-time secretarial and administrative courses to GNVQ levels 2 and 3. Courses can also be taken through part-time study whilst working, through the London Chamber of Commerce and Industry Examination Board (LCCIEB), Oxford, Cambridge and RSA Examination Board (OCR) and Pitmans Qualifications (City & Guilds), which offer relevant qualifications that take one to two years to complete. Personal assistant work spans everything from fairly junior jobs in small companies, to extremely responsible roles working with directors or large organisations. The training courses available reflect this, and courses are offered at several different levels.

Personal Qualities and Skills

You must be friendly but discrete and diplomatic. You need to be extremely well organised and calm when you are under pressure or working to deadlines. Knowing when to use your own initiative is also important.

Starting Salary

The starting salaries for personal assistants vary enormously, from around £14,000 to £26,000. This range reflects the different levels of responsibility and experience required for the variety of posts on offer.

info

Institute of Qualified Professional Secretaries (IQPS), Suite 464, 24–28 St Leonards Road, Windsor, Berks SL4 3BB; 0844 8000 182; www.iqps.org

London Chamber of Commerce and Industry Examinations Board (LCCIEB), 112 Station Road, Sidcup, Kent DA15 7BJ; 08707 202 909; www.lccieb.com

Oxford and Cambridge and RSA Examinations (OCR), 9 Hills Road, Cambridge CB2 1PB; 01223 553311; www.ocr.org.uk

Pitman Qualifications, City & Guilds, 1 Giltspur Street, London EC1A 9DD; 020 7294 2800; www.pitmanqualifications.com

Receptionist

Receptionists work in hotels, large organisations and private firms, sometimes combining the job with the duties of telephonist. In hotels, they welcome the guests, make bookings and prepare the final accounts. They also deal with reservation correspondence and act as a general information office. In small hotels this can be handled by one person but in most, and especially the larger, hotels, they work in a team headed by the Reception Manager. In large official organisations, such as a town hall or in firms with many staff, receptionists direct visitors to the correct department. In small firms the job is often combined with answering the phone, typing and franking the mail.

Medical receptionists work in a variety of environments. They need, in addition to the standard skills of a receptionist, a full understanding of the principles of medical ethics and confidentiality, knowledge of the NHS and social services, medical terminology and clinical procedures.

Qualifications and Training

Formal educational qualifications are not necessary, but proficiency in English and maths is an advantage. For some posts knowledge of other languages is important. Many further education colleges offer one-year full-time courses and a range of part-time courses in reception skills. A range of qualifications is available, including NVQs at levels 1, 2 and 3 and Modern Apprenticeships.

The AMSPAR diploma in health service reception is a nationally recognised professional qualification. It can be achieved by examination and is available from a wide network of approved centres throughout the UK.

Personal Qualities and Skills

Receptionists should be friendly, pleasant with a good phone manner and neat appearance. They also need stamina, as they are often expected to work shifts that include evenings and weekends. They should have a real liking for people and a good memory for faces. Computer literacy is also important.

Starting Salary

Outside London salaries can start rather low at £8,500; in London, around £12,000 to £14,000. Hotel receptionists usually start on around £15,000 and some of these posts include accommodation, meals, etc.

info

People 1st, 2nd Floor, Armstrong House, 38 Market Square, Uxbridge UB8 1LX; 0870 060 2550; www.people1st.co.uk

Local Job Centre Plus and Connexions/Careers Centres

Secretary

Secretaries work in all types of organisations. Sometimes they are assigned to one person, sometimes they provide support services for several people. Most secretaries need to have well-developed ICT skills but there is still a demand for those with shorthand and audio typing. As well as producing documents, secretaries undertake a range of organisational tasks such as arranging travel and meetings. They may also work as receptionists and deal with callers and queries by phone or e-mail. Those in senior positions may make decisions on behalf of managers.

Bilingual Secretary

A bilingual secretary is fluent in a second or third language and may work in commerce, overseas or as an EU employee. The work will include composing, reading and translating documents in the foreign language. They may use speaking/listening skills in their languages for telephone work, receiving visitors and interpreting at meetings.

Farm Secretary

In addition to normal secretarial work, farm secretaries will be responsible for completing complex forms, keeping records and accounts and calculating wages. A farm secretary may work for one employer, be freelance or be sent out by an agency to smaller farms.

Legal Secretary

Accurate skills have always been paramount for legal paperwork, but word processors have made the job easier. Legal secretaries are employed by barristers and solicitors in professional practice and in large commercial organisations.

Medical Secretary

Medical secretaries are good administrators, keep records, handle correspondence and filing. They work in hospitals, for individual doctors/consultants and in health centres. Accuracy and confidentiality are essential, as is a thorough knowledge of medical terminology.

Qualifications and Training

There is a range of full- and part-time courses available. Courses usually include word processing, audio, shorthand and office procedures. There are training opportunities for young people leading to NVQ levels 1, 2 and 3 in Administration.

GCSEs are usually required to obtain a place on a full-time secretarial course. A good working knowledge of the English language is essential. Additional qualifications are needed to specialise as a legal, medical or farm secretary. There are a number of postgraduate diploma courses for graduates wishing to train as bilingual secretaries.

Personal Qualities and Skills

Good secretaries are judged by what they do, but qualities such as self-motivation, discretion, tact, loyalty, flexibility, excellent communication skills and smart appearance are expected.

Starting Salary

Varies from £8,000 to £20,000+ depending on experience, location and type of employer. Bilingual and legal secretaries are better paid.

info

Institute of Business Administration and Management, 16 Park Crescent, London W1B 1AH; 020 7580 4741; fax: 020 7323 1132; www.ibam.org; e-mail: info@ibam.org

Institute of Qualified Private Secretaries Ltd (IQPS), First Floor, 6 Bridge Avenue, Maidenhead SL6 1RR; 01628 625007; fax: 01628 624990; www.iqps.org; e-mail: office@iqps.org

Association of Medical Secretaries, Practice Managers, Administrators and Receptionists (AMSPAR), Tavistock House North, Tavistock Square, London WC1H 9LN; 020 7387 6005; www.amspar.co.uk; e-mail: amspar@atlas.co.uk

ILEX Paralegal Training, Kempston Manor, Kempston, Bedford MK42 7AB; 01234 841000; www.ilex.org.uk; e-mail: info@ilex.org.uk

Institute of Para-legal Training, The Mill, Clymping Street, Clymping, Littlehampton, West Sussex BN17 5RN; 01903 714276

Institute of Linguists, Saxon House, 48 Southwark Street, London SE1 1UN; 020 7940 3100; www.iol.org.uk; e-mail: info@iol.org.uk

CALL/CONTACT CENTRE

'Contact centre' is replacing the term 'call centre' as it more accurately describes the activities in places where customer support is provided by e-mail, fax and web chat as well as by telephone. It is an expanding industry with approximately 800,000 people working in over 5,000 contact centres in the UK. The business and organisations behind these vary from local and national government (DVLA, NHS Direct) to charities (Childline, Oxfam) through to highly technical help desk functions (Microsoft, IBM, British Telecom). The work can be sales or advice oriented, and in some centres language skills are essential as calls are taken from all over the world. The areas of growth tend to be in local government and small to medium enterprises, while some larger organisations are relocating their centres abroad.

Management

Call centre management can involve leading a small team of agents or managing a multi-site global operation which employs thousands. Managers need technical expertise and product knowledge as well as people skills. Opportunities to move into management from team leader or agent positions are common as this is a growing industry.

Call Centre Agents

The work involves dealing with queries and requests for information from the public, often in a very regulated environment with strict adherence to start, finish and break times. The role can be varied, with agents working across a number of departments to resolve the enquiry. Varied working patterns meaning the opportunity to work part-time or term-time only is common.

Qualifications and training

Keyboard skills, good communication abilities and, for e-mail and web chat, reasonable spelling and grammar. Increasingly the simpler activities in contact centres are becoming automated, leaving the human operator to deal with more complicated queries.

Many employers offer work-based training programmes in product knowledge, language skills, technical know-how and people skills and some offer

Modern Apprenticeships. There are a growing number of Certificate, Diploma and Degree-level courses in Call Centre Management. These are often available through distance or web-based learning.

Personal Qualities and Skills

This work requires you to be calm, friendly and patient, and to possess a sense of humour, a thick skin and a lot of common sense.

Starting Salary

Average wages for customer service advisers is £11,900. A fully trained agent can expect to earn between £11,200 and £15,000 per year. A call or contact centre manager's starting salary is usually between £22,000 and £32,000 depending on industry, experience and qualifications.

info

The Call Centre Management Association (CCMA), International House, 174 Three Bridges Road, Crawley, West Sussex RH10 1LE; 01293 538 400; www.ccma.org.uk/

CCA – The Professional Body for Customer Contact, 20 Newton Place, Glasgow G3 7PY; 0141 564 9010; www.cca.org.uk

e-skills UK, 1 Castle Lane, London SW1E 6DR; 020 7963 8920; www.e-skills.com

CARDIAC TECHNOLOGIST

Cardiac Clinical Scientific Officers (CCSOs) and cardiac clinical physiologists are members of the medical team responsible for the recording and analysis of different physiological data required to assist in the diagnosis and treatment of known or suspected heart disease. The CCSO is the friendly professional face in this highly technological environment, linking the patient with the diagnostic equipment. The CCSO normally works in a Cardiology Department within a hospital. The variety of procedures carried out varies from hospital to hospital. Some smaller hospitals may include procedures from other disciplines, eg respiratory function tests.

Qualifications and Training

In various parts of the UK the training schemes and courses have undergone significant changes. The profession is moving towards being graduate entry only. Degree courses in clinical physiology leading to State Registration came on stream in 2003, but at the moment there is still some flexibility within the profession. To get onto these courses you need three A levels or their equivalent, maths or physics being the preferred subjects. At present some hospitals are still operating training schemes for people with four GCSEs including maths, English and a science.

Personal Qualities and Skills

You have to be practical and confident with advanced technical equipment, but also extremely good at working closely with people. Your patients may be anxious, uncomfortable or uncertain about the procedures you are using and so will require a lot of reassurance. You also have to be attentive and meticulous in recording and observing information, and good at working as part of a team.

Starting Salary

Salaries range from £11,000 to £15,000 for new entrants. Senior staff earn between £18,000 and £32,000, but there are limited numbers of these senior posts.

info

The Society for Cardiological Science and Technology (SCST), Suite 4, Sovereign House, 22 Gate Lane, Goldmere, Sutton Coldfield B73 5TT; 0121 354 6512; www.scst.org.uk

Local Job Centre Plus and Connexions/Careers Centres and local hospital cardiology or human resource departments

CAREERS ADVISER

Careers or Personal Advisers/Careers provide information, advice and guidance to school and college students and to adults in the community. They work both inside and outside education. In England, careers advisers work mainly in the Connexions Service as personal advisers (PAs), helping young people aged 13–19 make choices about employment and further study, and helping them overcome any difficulties they face in this area. The work involves one-to-one interviews with clients, presentations to groups of clients or parents, and marketing work with local and national employers.

Outside England, careers advisers work in Careers Scotland, Careers Wales and the Training and Employment Agency in Northern Ireland. Some careers advisers also work in higher education and are employed by individual universities and colleges.

Qualifications and Training

All careers advisers working for Connexions must have the Qualification in Careers Guidance (QCG), which has replaced the Diploma in Careers Guidance. This is run at several institutions throughout the UK and can be studied full-time for one year or part-time for two. This is a mainly graduate profession, but people with a lot of other relevant experience in working with young people can get onto QCG courses without a degree.

If you work for Connexions you then have to take an NVQ level 4 in either Advice and Guidance (IAG) or Learning Development and Guidance Services (LDGS). Both of these are done mainly through portfolio work.

Personal Qualities and Skills

You need to have excellent and highly flexible communication skills, working with everyone from school students to head teachers and human resource professionals. You need to be good at working on your own, very well organised and able to analyse and suggest solutions to problems.

Starting Salary

Salaries for trainees range from £17,000 to £20,000, rising to over £23,000 when you qualify. The structure and funding of Connexions is going to change during 2006/2007 and this may affect salary structures.

info

Association of Graduate Careers Advisory Services (AGCAS), Millennium House, 30 Junction Road, Sheffield S11 8XB; 0114 251 5750; www.agcas.org.uk

Connexions, Department for Education and Skills (DfES), Supporting Children and Young People Group, W408, Moorfoot, Sheffield S1 4PQ; 0870 000 2288; www.connexions.gov.uk

Department for Education and Skills (DfES), Sanctuary Buildings, Great Smith Street, London SW1P 3BT; 0870 000 2288; www.dfes.gov.uk

Department for Employment and Learning in Northern Ireland (DELNI), Adelaide House, 39–49 Adelaide Street, Belfast BT2 8FD; 028 9025 7726; www.delni.gov.uk

The Improvement and Development Agency, Layden House, 76–86 Turnmill Street, London EC1M 5OG; 020 7296 6880; www.idea.gov.uk

Institute of Career Guidance (ICG), Third Floor, Copthall House, 1 New Road, Stourbridge, West Midlands DY8 1PH; 01384 376464; www.icg-uk.org

Learning and Skills Council, Cheylsmore House, Quinton Road, Coventry CV1 2WT; 0845 019 4170; www.lsc.gov.uk

National Assembly for Wales, Cardiff Bay, Cardiff CF99 1NA; 029 2082 5111; www.wales.gov.uk

CARPENTRY

see Construction

Cabinet maker

Cabinet makers use traditional hand skills to make, finish or restore high-quality items of wooden furniture. They may work in factories for furniture manufacturers or be self-employed in small workshops.

Qualifications and Training

A general education to secondary level is the only academic requirement, although some arithmetical ability is useful. Training is over a two- to three-year period with courses leading to NVQs.

Personal Qualities and Skills

As qualified craftspeople, carpenters and joiners must be able to work from technical drawings or notes without close supervision and to produce neat accurate work. They must be manually skilled, possessing a steady hand and a head for heights. A good eye for form is necessary, plus a willingness to work outside in all weathers.

Starting Salary

When qualified, the craftsman rate is around £230 per week; some employers pay more, offering bonuses and overtime. With experience and a good reputation, you can earn far more if you are self-employed.

info

Construction Industry Training Board, Bircham Newton, King's Lynn, Norfolk PE31 6RH; 01485 577577; fax: 01485 577802; www.citb.org.uk

Institute of Carpenters, Central Office, 35 Hayworth Road, Sandiacre, Nottingham NG10 5LL; 0115 9490641; www.central-office.co.uk/ioc/index.htm; e-mail: mail@carpenters-institute.org

A range of information leaflets is available from the Institute of Carpenters (address above)

CARPET FITTER

Carpet retailers, furniture stores and department stores all employ their own trained personnel who deliver and fit carpets and other floor coverings to customers' homes, shops, offices or hotels. Many fitters are also self-employed.

Qualifications and Training

GCSE English and maths or equivalents are usually required. Training is mainly given on the job, working with an experienced fitter, although in some firms there are possible opportunities for day-release courses leading to the examinations of the National Institute of Carpet and Floorlayers. Short one- to five-day and tailored courses are available through the Flooring Industry Training Association.

Personal Qualities and Skills

Strength and fitness are important in order to handle heavy rolls of carpet. A good head for calculations and an eye for detail (such as matching patterns) are also essential. Generally, too, it is necessary to be able to drive.

Starting Salary

Around National Minimum Wage rates. A new entrant earns between £10,500 to £12,000, and with experience can earn up to £15,000. Companies employing carpet fitters pay £18,000.

info

National Institute of Carpet and Floorlayers, 4d St Mary's Place, The Lace Market, Nottingham NG1 1PH; 0115 958 3077; fax: 0115 941 2238; www.nicfltd.org.uk;

e-mail: info@nicfltd.org.uk

Local Job Centre Plus and Careers/Connexions Centres

CARTOGRAPHY

Cartography embraces all aspects of map-making including the making of charts, globes and models of the earth or heavenly bodies.

Cartographers

Cartographers are involved primarily in the initial stages of the collection and editing of material up to the point of actual generation and production of the finished product, which is generally done by cartographic draughtsmen (and women) and assistants.

Most cartographic work is undertaken in government departments such as the Ministry of Defence, the Meteorological Office and the Department of the Environment, Transport and the Regions. The Ordnance Survey no longer employ cartographic draughtsmen or assistants as their mapping is produced digitally, but they do recruit trainee surveyors.

Vacancies sometimes occur in local authority planning departments and with specialist publishing houses or survey companies. Computers are reducing the need for manual draughtsmen, especially in repetitive work, and the increasing application of Geographical Information Systems (GIS) via a graphics workstation is significantly changing the work of professional cartographers. There is substantial growth in the number of map/chart products becoming available on CD, many of which are designed for interactive use.

Qualifications and Training

Cartographers are increasingly graduates with a relevant undergraduate or postgraduate qualification. Universities offering courses in cartography, GIS, topographic science or surveying and mapping science include Newcastle, Oxford Brookes and East London. Admission requirements vary, but are likely to include geography A level.

Personal Qualities and Skills

Neatness, precision, aesthetic appreciation and a fine attention to detail are important, as are mathematical awareness and an ability to analyse visual judgements on graphic efficiency.

Starting Salary

For a graduate, from £14,000 to £16,000; mapping and charting technicians, from £11,000; and assistants, £8,500+.

Contact: Ken Atherton, British Cartographic Society, Administration, 12 Elworthy Drive, Wellington, Somerset, TA21 9AT; tel/fax: 01823 665 775; www.cartography.org.uk; e-mail: admin@cartography.org.uk

Ordnance Survey work

The Ordnance Survey is part of the civil service and responsible to the Department of Transport, Local Government and the Regions. It produces all kinds of official maps covering the whole of Britain. Large-scale computerised Ordnance Survey mapping is used by local authorities, estate agents, solicitors, architects, civil engineers and government departments, while leisure paper maps are popular with ramblers, riders and cyclists. Other Ordnance Survey maps show historical detail, such as Roman Britain, or statistical data (for example, population density).

Job opportunities may be limited since organisations no longer employ cartographic draughtsmen or assistants as all maps are produced digitally. There are, however, sometimes opportunities for trainee surveyors. These are advertised in the locality of the vacancies. The work includes checking new features such as buildings, hedges, fences and roads and noting any alterations since the map was last printed. These are input on hand-held computers.

Increasingly, Ordnance Survey work involves the use of information technology, ranging from base data for digital atlases and computer games to complex geographical databases. Ordnance Survey's head office is in Southampton and most employees are based there. Field surveyors, however, may be posted virtually anywhere in England, Scotland or Wales.

Qualifications and Training

A good general education and five GCSE passes at grade C or above, including maths, English, geography or information technology and a minimum of 18 months' experience working in a related field. Computer literacy and a driving licence are desirable. Candidates also take an aptitude test.

Personal Qualities and Skills

A willingness to work in an outdoor environment, excellent interpersonal skills and an ability to work with all sections of the community, as well as the confidence, initiative and motivation to work alone or as part of a small team.

Starting Salary

£13,000–14,000 for trainee surveyors, £18,000–22,000 with more experience.

Ordnance Survey, Romsey Road, Southampton SO16 4GU; 08456 05 05 05; 08456 05 05 04 (dedicated Welsh language helpline); www.ordnancesurvey.co.uk

CATERING

see Hospitality and Catering

CHEMISTRY

Chemistry is the basis of a wide range of careers and is the science which deals with the composition, structure and uses of chemicals and substances.

Analysts

Analysts work in industry providing a service for research, development and production departments. They analyse the results of experiments and advise what a newly produced substance may be. An analyst may check the quality of raw materials bought in by a company and examine the quality of the company's own products. Public analysts are employed by local authorities to examine, for example, the state of the water supply; the adequacy of the sewage treatment system; toxic and suspect materials and leachate from landfill sites. They may also be asked to examine food from a suspect restaurant. Public analysts are frequently required to give witness on their findings in courts of law, and should be familiar with the law relating to goods and services.

Chemist

The majority of trained chemists work in the manufacturing industries within organisations producing such materials as foodstuffs, plastics, pharmaceuticals, cosmetics, petroleum, detergents and fertilisers. Large numbers teach in schools, colleges and universities, generally combining teaching with research work; there are also openings with local authorities, the Health Service, the civil service and the nationalised industries, as well as in marketing and sales, information and patents and specialised publishing. Chemistry is essential in many other careers such as medicine or veterinary science.

Qualifications and Training

Most professional chemists and analysts have membership of the Royal Society of Chemistry, for which a degree or equivalent qualification is necessary. Entry requirements for degree courses generally include at least two A levels or equivalent in science subjects, including chemistry and another scientific or mathematical subject. To become a public analyst it is necessary to hold the Mastership in Chemical Analysis (MChemA), a qualification awarded by the Royal Society of Chemistry.

Chemistry technicians usually need three GCSEs or equivalent for entry to a national certificate in science or chemistry – these are generally day-release courses. This can be followed by a higher certificate or degree level qualification.

Personal Qualities and Skills

Chemists usually form part of a team, so an ability to work alongside others is essential. The actual work varies enormously, but generally a chemist also needs an enquiring mind and practical experimental ability and experience. Attention to detail and a sense of responsibility are important.

Starting Salary

For new entrants, starting salaries range from £14,000 to £29,000, this broad range reflecting the different jobs, from trainee technician to research chemist.

info

Analytical Science Network (ASN), c/o Royal Society of Chemistry, Burlington House, Piccadilly, London W1J 0BA; 020 7440 3326; www.chemsoc.org

Royal Pharmaceutical Society of Great Britain (RPSGB), 1 Lambeth High Street, London SE1 7JN; 020 7735 9141; www.rpsgb.org.uk

Royal Society of Chemistry (RSC), Burlington House, Piccadilly, London W1J 0BA; 020 7437 8656; www.rsc.org

CHILD CARE

This sector covers a range of occupations, but all involve the care of children, especially pre-school children.

Childminder

A registered childminder looks after children and provides a caring environment along with stimulating play and learning activities. Childminders need to be responsible, trustworthy and affectionate. Childminders look after babies and children under five; there is a limit to the number of children of different age groups that can be cared for by a childminder.

A childminder's job needs careful planning and good organisation skills to arrange individual routines for children of different ages to include periods of play, exercise, naps and meals. It is important to keep records of payments, expenses and insurance. It is essential for the children's learning and development to include activities such as painting and drawing, reading stories and singing, playing with natural materials and construction toys in and out doors.

A childminder is expected to provide food for the children, and with babies prepare bottles, feed the babies and change nappies. Older children will require physical care, such as washing hands and going to the toilet. It is important not to discriminate against children from different ethnic groups, religious backgrounds and family types.

Qualifications and Training

All childminders must be registered with local organisations: England – OFSTED (Office for Standards in Education); Scotland – the Scottish Commission for the Regulation of Care (Care Commission); Wales – the Care Standards Inspectorate for Wales (CSIW); Northern Ireland – the local Health and Social Services Trust.

In England and Wales, childminders can work towards the CACHE level 3 Certificate in Childminding Practice (CCP). Childminders could also work towards an NVQ in early years care and education at level 3. Achieving the CCP will give most of the background and understanding needed for the NVQ. In Scotland, childminders could work towards an SVQ in early years care and education at level 3. In Northern Ireland, it is possible to work towards NVQs in early years care and education at level 2 or 3. Study is through going to a local college part-time or by distance-learning courses offered by the NICMA.

Personal Qualities and Skills

A love of children, patience and a caring nature are the key qualities for a successful career in childminding. Good communication skills, consistency and self-confidence are also essential qualities. An open-minded approach to different lifestyles and a sense of humour will help cope with unfamiliar situations. Also important is a commitment to equal opportunities and an awareness of health, safety and hygiene issues. A childminder should know about child protection issues and how to recognise and react to signs of child abuse.

Starting Salary

Childminders are self-employed and set their own fees and are responsible for their own tax and National Insurance. Most do not earn enough to be liable for either contribution. For full-time placements, these range from £2 an hour per child to £5 an hour, but are typically around £2.25 an hour, including expenses. Based on 50 weeks' work a year looking after two children, these figures mean a new entrant would get at least £7,000 a year and typically would go on to earn around £10,750. With more experience the top rate earners get £25,000.

National Childminding Association, 8 Masons Hill, Bromley, Kent BR2 9EY; information line: 0800 169 4486 (free: open Monday to Friday, 10.00 am to 4.00 pm); www.ncma.org.uk; e-mail: info@ncma.org.uk

Scottish Childminding Association, Suite 3, 7 Melville Terrace, Stirling FK8 2ND; 01786 445377; advice service: 01786 449063; www.childminding.org; e-mail: information@childminding.org

Northern Ireland Childminding Association, 16–18 Mill Street, Newtownards, Co Down BT23 4LU; 028 9181 1015; www.nicma.org

Early Years NTO, Pilgrim's Lodge, Holywell Hill, St Albans, Hertfordshire AL1 1ER; 01727 738300; www.early-years-nto.org.uk; e-mail: enquiries@early-years-nto.org.uk

Council for Awards in Children's Care and Education (CACHE), 8 Chequer Street, St Albans, Hertfordshire AL1 3XZ (please send A4 sae); 01727 847636; www.cache.org.uk; e-mail: info@cache.org.uk

ChildcareLink National Information Line: 08000 96 02 96; www.childcarelink.gov.uk

www.skillsforcare.org.uk

Nursery nurse

A nursery nurse works with babies and children under eight in the public, private and voluntary sectors. This can include schools, nurseries and hospitals. In schools, nursery nurses work in nursery, reception and infant classes alongside the teacher, providing and supervising educational and play activities. They may also be involved in providing out of school care at after-school clubs and on holiday schemes. Nursery nurses in hospitals can work in maternity and special care units, and on children's wards. Day nurseries, both private and local authority, employ nursery nurses to care for children under five whose parents are unable to care for them during the day. Nursery nurses can also be employed in clinics, residential homes, the community, family centres and private homes as nannies.

Qualifications and Training

The Council for Awards in Children's Care and Education (CACHE) level 3 Diploma in Child Care and Education (previously known as the NNEB) is a prerequisite for many jobs and can be done as a two-year full-time course or part-time up to five years. There are no minimum entry requirements, but many colleges ask for GCSEs at C or above, including English. The BTEC National Diploma in early years, a two-year course, requires four GCSEs at grade C or above. Modern Apprenticeships are available; apprentices are trained by their employers and work towards NVQ level 3 in early years care and education.

Nursery nurses in Scotland must register with the Scottish Child Care and Education Board; this requires completion of a one-year programme of SQA National Certificate units plus the one-year HNC in child care and education or a programme of SVQ level 3 units in early years and education.

Personal Qualities and Skills

A genuine love of children is essential, with the ability to work with patience, tolerance, imagination and energy. Good motivation skills and a sense of fun are important.

Starting Salary

£9,000–11,000 as a nursery assistant, £11,000–15,000 as a nursery nurse/officer, £17,000+ as a manager. Nannies working for private families can earn from £250 to £600 a week depending on location and experience. Large businesses that operate nurseries for their employees pay salaries higher than these.

info

Council for Awards in Children's Care and Education (CACHE), 8 Chequer Street, St Albans, Hertfordshire AL1 3XZ; 01727 847636; www.cache.org.uk; e-mail: info@cache.org.uk

Professional Association of Nursery Nurses, 2 St James' Court, Friar Gate, Derby DE1 1BT; 01332 372337; www.pat.org.uk; e-mail: pann@pat.org.uk

Scottish Childcare and Education Board, 01294 470380 (9.00 am to 12.30 pm weekdays)

National Day Nurseries Association (NDNA), Oak House, Woodvale Road, Brighouse, West Yorkshire HD6 4AB; 0870 774 4244; www.ndna.org.uk

www.skillsforcare.org.uk; 0113 245 1716

Local Job Centre Plus and Connexions/Careers Centres

Pre-school workers

Those working in the early years sector are committed to providing high-quality care and education for children. These include pre-school workers, who work with children every day, and pre-school managers and leaders, who have overall responsibility for the quality of their work. There are many different opportunities because different types of provision have developed to meet the varying needs of families. These include daycare nurseries where children attend all day, every week, and pre-schools and playgroups which offer morning and/or afternoon sessional care. Work in pre-schools is often part-time. However, new services are developing, for example after-school care, so there may be opportunities for work at other times and with older children. The majority of groups are registered charities, managed by parents and volunteers from the local community. Groups may also be funded by local authorities or private concerns.

Qualifications and Training

Vocational training is provided by organisations like the Pre-School Learning Alliance through classroom-based and distance-learning courses awarded by the Council for Awards in Children's Care and Education (CACHE). A Certificate at level 2 and Diploma at level 3 in Pre-School Practice are available. In Scotland, a self-study pack called 'Basic Training in Playwork' provides the basic knowledge and skills needed to work with young children in a play setting.

Personal Qualities and Skills

Pre-school workers should have a genuine interest in how children learn and develop in order to develop a coherent curriculum for the children. They also need to have the ability to work well in a team, liaising with parents, other adults and other professionals. Pre-school leaders need to have the skills necessary to lead a team.

Starting Salary

Salaries vary for pre-school workers from one area of the country to another.

info

Council for Awards in Children's Care and Education (CACHE), 8 Chequer Street, St Albans, Hertfordshire AL1 3XZ; 01727 847636; www.cache.org.uk; info@cache.org.uk

Pre-School Learning Alliance: there are 400 local branches – see website for details: www.pre-school.org.uk

Wales Pre-school Playgroup Association (Wales PPA), Ladywell House, Newtown, Powys Y16 1JB; 01686 624573; www.walesppa.co.uk; e-mail: info@walesppa.org

Northern Ireland PPA, Information Centre, 6C Flower Way, Apollo Road, Belfast BT12 6TA; 02890 662825

Scottish Pre-School Play Association (SPPA), 14 Elliot Place, Glasgow G3 8EP; 0141 221 4148; fax: 0141 221 6043

CHIROPODIST (OR PODIATRIST)

Chiropodists are also known as podiatrists; the profession is in the process of changing its name. They are concerned with the health of feet. Those working in the NHS deal with problems caused by diabetes or arthritis and may work with those suffering from sports injuries. Ailments such as corns, bunions and malformed nails are more likely to be dealt with by those in private practice.

Chiropodists perform minor operations under local anaesthetic. They may work in the NHS in hospitals, clinics or health centres, or in private practice or large organisations. Many undertake postgraduate training to specialise in areas such as sports medicine, biomechanics and podiatric surgery.

Qualifications and Training

Degrees in chiropody or podiatry are run at many institutions throughout the UK, and the only route into the profession is via one of these degrees. You then apply to the Health Professions Council for State Registration and are able to work either in the NHS or in private practice. The need for private practitioners to have an approved degree course is the result of a recent change in regulations. To get onto a degree course you need five GCSEs, including maths, English and a science. Other qualifications and experience, such as nursing, may give you some exemptions from parts of the course.

Personal Qualities and Skills

You must be calm, caring and reassuring, as well as practical, careful and patient. In the NHS you are likely to be part of a team, but you might also be visiting people in their own homes, so you must be able to work on your own and use your initiative. In private practice, you may need business skills too.

Starting Salary

In the NHS starting salaries are just over £18,000 and rise to £35,000 in senior management posts. In private practice you can earn more; the range is £25,000 to £50,000.

info

Department of Health (DH), Quarry House, Quarry Hill, Leeds LS2 7UE; 0113 254 5000; www.dh.gov.uk

Health Professions Council (HPC), Park House, 184 Kennington Park Road, London SE11 4BU; 020 7582 0866; www.hpc-uk.org

Institute of Chiropodists and Podiatrists, 27 Wright Street, Southport, Merseyside PR9 0TL; 01704 546141; www.inst-chiropodist.org.uk/

Society of Chiropodists and Podiatrists (SCP), 1 Fellmonger's Path, Tower Bridge Road, London SE1 3LY; 020 7234 8620; www.scpod.org

CIVIL AVIATION

The civil aviation sector relates to all the occupations within the world of civil aircraft flying, including passenger and goods transportation.

Aeronautical engineer

(*see also* Engineering)

Air traffic engineers are responsible for the efficient operation of the wide range of sophisticated telecommunications, electronic systems and specialist equipment needed in air traffic control centres, airports and other specialist centres.

This involves the installation, calibration and maintenance of radar, air-to-ground communication systems, navigational and landing aids, computer data and processing equipment and visual display units. Opportunities may exist for engineers to look after day-to-day maintenance and, at graduate level, for field management, installation and development work.

Air cabin crew

Flight attendants (air cabin crew) look after the safety, comfort and welfare of passengers. Before a flight they check stocks of equipment, welcome passengers on board and go through safety routines. During the flight they will serve ready-cooked meals and drinks, sell duty-free goods and deal with any problems passengers have. Flight reports are prepared by senior stewards, who also attend to first-class passengers and supervise junior staff.

Aircraft maintenance engineer

(*see also* Engineering)

Aircraft maintenance engineers make sure that aircraft are airworthy. They maintain, service and overhaul the aircraft, their engines and equipment, working to very high standards set by the Civil Aviation Authority (CAA). Every part of every job is checked and certified. Engineers usually specialise in either mechanics or avionics, and work on major overhaul or in 'turnarounds' – the work carried out after each flight. Apart from working with the airlines, other opportunities are found with firms that specialise in aircraft maintenance. There are also a few openings for professional engineers in works management, production, planning and research and development.

Air traffic control

The safe and efficient movement of all aircraft through British air space and airports is the responsibility of National Air Traffic Service (NATS) air traffic control officers and assistants. With the aid of sophisticated radio, radar and computer systems and with visual checks on visibility and weather conditions made from the control tower, they ensure that aircraft are kept a safe distance apart and that pilots are well advised as to their position and prevailing conditions, give clearance to land and directions to loading bays. Air traffic controllers mainly work for NATS, although there may be limited opportunities with other employers, such as local authorities or aircraft manufacturers. All must hold a CAA licence stipulating the service they are qualified to give and where they can operate. Some of the more routine tasks, such as checking flight plans, updating weather information, logging aircraft movements and keeping runways clear, are carried out by the air traffic control assistants. Prospects for promotion to officer level are good, but air traffic control staff are employed to work at any location within the country.

Pilot

Commercial pilots in the UK fly fixed-wing aircraft and helicopters. Before take-off the pilot must prepare a flight plan, study the weather, make sure that the craft is airworthy, check that the cargo and fuel are safely loaded and work out estimated arrival times. Little time is spent actually flying the aeroplane manually. The pilot spends most of the time carefully monitoring sophisticated computer-controlled automatic flying, navigational and communications systems. Pilots keep in touch with air traffic control and must be prepared to deal with sudden changes in weather and other conditions. Pilots work irregular hours but their actual flying time is strictly controlled.

Most UK pilots are employed by one of the major carriers of passengers and goods and when flying large aircraft they are part of a team. Opportunities for pilots of small aircraft and helicopters are to be found in flying executive jets, in the field of air taxiing (especially in the North Sea), conducting aerial surveys, or as test pilots or flying instructors.

Qualifications and Training

Air Cabin Crew

Airlines usually train their own cabin crews at special centres on courses lasting four to six weeks. Applicants should be over 18, have a good level of general education to GCSE standard, preferably including English and maths, and have conversational fluency in at least one European language. Experience in a customer care setting can be helpful.

Aircraft Maintenance Engineer

Entry to aircraft maintenance engineering is via craft, technician or student apprenticeships; entry qualifications depend upon the type of apprenticeship. The apprenticeships take the form of on-the-job training and part-time study at local colleges to prepare for aeronautical engineering/aircraft maintenance engineering qualifications offered by City and Guilds and Edexcel (BTEC)/ SQA or the CAA. Qualified aircraft engineers (including those from the armed forces) have to meet certain practical experience requirements before they can take examinations to become licensed aircraft maintenance engineers. There are some full-time courses in aeronautical engineering and aircraft maintenance, usually lasting two and a half years.

Air Traffic Control

Entrants for the NATS scheme must be eligible for work within the UK, have security clearance, be aged between 18 and 29 and pass a medical. The training lasts just under 18 months and includes practice at Bournemouth Airport. This is followed by an extensive period of practical training at a designated site.

Air Traffic Engineer

NATS runs a training scheme for graduate electrical/electronic engineers lasting a minimum of 15 months. The training is approved by the Institute of Electrical and Electronic Engineering and will lead after approximately three years to chartered engineering status.

Pilot

UK pilots are required to hold a licence issued by the Joint Aviation Authorities (JAA) which represent the civil aviation departments of a group of European states that have collaborated to set common safety standards called Joint Aviation Requirements. Licence holders can work as pilots in any of the JAA member states. Full details of licensing requirements and organisations providing approved courses can be obtained from the CAA (see further contacts). Training to be a commercial pilot costs £50,000–60,000 and may be integrated (*ab initio*) or modular. Helicopter courses tend to be more expensive. Most applicants wishing to undertake integrated courses are sponsored privately or by an airline. Such sponsorship is highly competitive and difficult to obtain. Trainees are generally expected to contribute to training costs either while training or by repaying some of the fees once in employment. An alternative entry route is via a short service flying commission with either the RAF or Royal Navy. All pilots are expected to attend retraining and refresher courses throughout their careers.

Entry requirements for sponsored pilot training vary between airlines, but most ask for a minimum of two/three A levels or equivalent, including maths and physics. Many airlines recruit graduates up to the age of 26. Eyesight must be of a very high standard. Normal colour vision and an excellent level of health and fitness are essential.

Personal Qualities and Skills

Air Cabin Crew

Air cabin crew must be reassuring and approachable, smart, have lots of energy and stamina and have the confidence and the ability to act quickly and decisively in a firm but polite and tactful manner.

Aircraft Maintenance Engineer

Maintenance engineering requires a combination of practical interest, mechanical aptitude, accuracy and manual dexterity. Engineers must be willing to adapt and to retrain. Very high standards and a responsible attitude are also most important.

Air Traffic Control Officer

The work is stressful; officers need to be able to assimilate and interpret a great deal of information and instantly act upon it. They must be able to react quickly if conditions suddenly change, be healthy, reliable and emotionally well balanced; good eyesight and colour vision are also important.

Air Traffic Engineer

Normal colour vision, great care, accuracy and a basic understanding of the practical applications of electricity and magnetism are required.

Pilot

Pilots must be very well balanced, physically fit, have stamina, be mentally and physically alert and ready to respond quickly to changing conditions. They must be unflappable, confident, self-assured leaders with considerable technical skill.

Starting Salary

The range is wide, relating to the variety of different careers. Air cabin crews start on fairly low pay – £9,500 to £13,000. Air traffic controllers start on between £20,000 and £21,000, and pilots start on around £33,000, but can earn much more. There are other benefits. Air cabin crew receive extra payments for the hours they spend flying, air traffic controllers get an accommodation allowance, and individual airlines offer various travel and other discounts to their employees.

info

Civil Aviation Authority (CAA), CAA House, 45–59 Kingsway, London WC2B 6TE; 020 7379 7311; www.caa.co.uk/

Institution of Electrical Engineers (IEE), Savoy Place, London WC2R 0BL; 020 7240 1871; www.iee.org

National Air Traffic Services (NATS), Recruitment and Selection, Mailbox 15B, LACC, Sopwith Way, Swanwick, Hampshire SO31 7AY; 01489 612157; www.nats.co.uk

The British Air Line Pilots Association (BALPA), 81 New Road, Harlington, Hayes, Middlesex UB3 5BG; 020 8476 4000; www.balpa.org/

British Women Pilots Association (BWPA), Brooklands Museum, Brooklands Road, Weybridge, Surrey KT13 0QN; www.bwpa.demon.co.uk

Royal Aeronautical Society, 22 Hamilton Place, London W1J 8BQ; 0207 670 3200; www.raes.org.uk

Go Skills: The Sector Skills Council for Passenger Transport, Concorde House, Trinity Park, Solihull, West Midlands B37 7UQ; 0121 635 5520; www.goskills.org

SEMTA: the Sector Skills Council for Science, Engineering and Manufacturing Technologies, Head Office, 14 Upton Road, Watford WD18 0JT; 01923 238 441; www.semta.org.uk

Individual airlines

CIVIL SERVICE

The civil service is a multi-million-pound business made up of many departments and agencies. Each department is responsible for a different field (for example, health or education) and together they employ around half a million people. The civil service actively recruits a diverse range of people to reflect the make-up of the country it serves and has undergone huge changes as a result of the Modernising Government initiative. Many civil servants do not work in offices but may be engineers, lawyers or scientists working anywhere from laboratories to prisons. One in five civil servants works in London, where most of the departments have their headquarters. The rest are employed in towns and cities nationwide and across the world. Some regularly travel to Brussels if their work involves business with the European Union.

Administrative staff

This is the largest group, whose members work in all departments, carrying out the work of government. At the top level it is responsible for policy and management. Many new entrants are junior staff dealing with customers and administrative work. Others join at junior manager level (sometimes known as executive officers) and may be in charge of a team of people or one particular area, such as fraud investigation. There is a Fast Stream Development Programme offering accelerated training and development to around 500 graduates a year, who are mainly recruited into positions in central government departments (for example, the Home Office, Cabinet Office or the Foreign and Commonwealth Office). It is possible to 'hop on' to this scheme (known as in-service nomination) if you enter the civil service via a different route.

Diplomatic Service

Members of the Diplomatic Service spend much of their careers living abroad as representatives of British interests in foreign countries. A diplomatic service officer works for the Foreign and Commonwealth Office (FCO), which aims to protect and enforce its foreign policy measures for the benefit of British interests overseas. A diplomat can expect to work at a British Embassy or Consulate in a foreign country, a British High Commission located in a country within the Commonwealth, or the Foreign and Commonwealth Office in London.

A diplomat works in a variety of projects to serve the British establishment at an international level. Such projects include: monitoring political and economic developments in the host country; representing Britain's views to the government of that country; informing and advising London of the local situation; and ensuring that British policy is properly explained to the government and media. Commercial projects are also part of the diplomatic brief and include the promotion of British goods and inward investment to Britain.

Diplomats based in London deal with one or more specific countries or areas by keeping in touch with associates working in those countries and with the relevant foreign or Commonwealth representatives based in London.

Qualifications and Training

This area of work is open to graduates and non-graduates with plenty of work experience, as there are different entry points: executive assistant, operational officer and policy officer. Emphasis is placed on both academic skills and previous work/life experience. You must be a British citizen and have been resident in the UK for two of the last 10 years. You must be aged between 21 and 52 and you must pass a medical and a security check. You have to be prepared to relocate anywhere in the world. Training, including intensive foreign language training, is on-the-job plus in-house courses.

Personal Qualities and Skills

Excellent interpersonal skills are essential. You must have a genuine interest in other cultures and in current and international affairs. It is important that you can adapt quickly to change, think on your feet and analyse situations quickly and accurately. You may find yourself working with anyone, from a foreign head of state to representatives of a local community, and you must be equally at home in either of these situations. There is also a lot of deskwork involved.

Starting Salary

Typical starting salaries, inclusive of London recruitment and retention allowance: executive assistant – £15,742; operational officer – £18,211; and policy officer – £20,240. These salaries are currently under review.

info

Foreign and Commonwealth Office (FCO), King Charles Street, London SW1A 2AH; 020 7008 1500; www.fco.gov.uk/

How to Pass the Civil Service Qualifying Tests (Kogan Page)

Professionally qualified staff

Professionally qualified staff (particularly in the field of technology) are employed as the government needs its own architects, accountants, computer personnel, lawyers, librarians, statisticians, photographers, surveyors, draughtsmen, valuers and veterinary surgeons in the various departments.

Scientific staff

Scientific staff are employed in government laboratories and research establishments, working in research, design and development. Most opportunities here are in physics and engineering, although there are also opportunities in maths and computing, chemical and life sciences. The majority of candidates are recruited at Scientific Officer grade (working on routine testing and analysis). Those with fewer qualifications can join as Assistant Scientific Officers.

Qualifications and Training

Requirements vary from GCSE passes or equivalent for junior posts to an honours degree for professional and higher administrative posts. For example, a good honours degree (or equivalent) is essential for the fast-stream development programme, scientific and other professional posts. Candidates with Edexcel (BTEC)/SQA higher awards may be considered for some scientific jobs. A levels or equivalent are required for executive officers. Appropriate NVQs may be acceptable for many posts. Much of the training is given on the job and supplemented by attendance at formal courses (for example, in managerial or tax skills) when necessary. A large number of in-service training courses are also available (part-time, full-time and sandwich) to assist in gaining appropriate qualifications.

Personal Qualities and Skills

Qualities required vary considerably from department to department. Much of the work of civil servants involves dealing with the public either face to face or by telephone, so good communication skills are essential. As the work is often of a confidential nature, loyalty and discretion are important.

Starting Salary

Salaries compare favourably with those for similar work in other organisations. Some departments may pay a retention and recruitment allowance.

info

Individual websites for all departments can be accessed via the Recruitment Gateway at www.civilservice.gov.uk/jobs

Jobs in the civil service are routinely advertised in both local and national press and can also be found on www.capitaras.co.uk

Government Skills SSC Secretariat, c/o Cabinet Office, Admiralty Arch, The Mall, London SW1A 2WH; 020 7276 1611, www.government-skills.gov.uk; e-mail: cgssc@cabinet-office.x.gsi.gov.uk

For further information about the fast-stream development programme, see www.faststream.gov.uk

For jobs in Europe see www.euro-staff.gov.uk

CLOTHING INDUSTRY

(*see also* Fashion)

The clothing industry is diverse and complex, with products ranging from off-the-peg garments that are turned out in thousands, to exclusive *haute couture* designs from top fashion houses. There are job opportunities in large factories, small workrooms, with large wholesaling firms, in small family businesses and on production lines. The largest sections of the industry are men's and boys' outerwear, women's and girls' outerwear, children's clothing, bespoke tailoring (made to measure) and dressmaking. More specialised areas such as millinery and glove making are relatively small. Skilled workers are generally in great demand in most areas.

The main craft jobs are pattern cutting and grading, lay making (positioning the pattern to make the most economical use of the cloth), cutting, marking or fixing (putting the different pieces of an individual garment together and marking the stitch lines), hand sewing and pressing. There are also opportunities for semi-skilled workers and operators, particularly machinists. Much of this work can be repetitive. Production lines are arranged so each machinist sews only one part of a garment. However, opportunities exist to move into more skilled work later, such as sample machining. Technology is changing the clothing industry with more advanced sewing machines, computer-controlled pattern laying and die cutting of bulk quantities. The industry needs skilled operatives and mechanics to work with, maintain and care for these increasingly sophisticated machines.

The clothing industry also employs people in its commercial sections – marketing and sales, or purchasing and supply – where there are often close links with the major textile and fibre companies. As more and more companies outsource their production overseas, the need for additional garment technologists has become apparent. This involves overseas travel and the use of a wide range of technical skills.

Qualifications and Training

Formal educational qualifications are not always needed to train for the craft skills. These are traditionally learnt by courses leading to City and Guilds and Edexcel (BTEC) examinations. The Foundation Modern Apprenticeship scheme which leads to NVQ level 2 qualifications and the Advanced Modern Apprenticeship scheme which leads to NVQ level 3 awards are available. Machinists are generally trained on the job by the employing company.

An alternative route to learn is via further and higher education. Courses are run at many colleges and universities across the UK leading to National Diplomas, Higher National Diplomas or degrees in a variety of clothing-related disciplines.

Personal Qualities and Skills

These vary according to the particular sector of the industry concerned. It is generally advantageous to have deft hands and high standards of neatness and precision. In factories, a willingness to be part of a team is needed, while in bespoke tailoring a candidate should have a pleasant manner and be able to put potential customers at their ease.

Starting Salary

Depends upon individual employers. Graduates generally start on £13,000. Many factory floor jobs are paid at minimum wage level.

Pattern cutter/grader

Pattern cutters make the patterns that enable a designer's sketch to be made into a garment. Pattern graders work from a pattern representing a basic size and create the patterns needed for a range of sizes. Jobs vary from company to company. The two ways of making patterns are by flat pattern cutting, when the cutter works from the designer's sketches or working drawings and makes a pattern for each part of a garment, or by modelling onto a stand, when the cutter works from the designer's drawings and drapes and pins fabric on to a dummy and fits it in accordance with the drawings. Computers are increasingly used to help in designing garments, creating patterns and for pattern grading.

Pattern cutter/spreader

The cutter or spreader checks that the cloth is smooth and free of wrinkles and flaws and that patterns or other features will match when it is sewn together. The laying-up process is done manually by two people or by machine. Once it is ready, the fabric can be cut using a number of methods. Hand cutting is done using shears, an electric knife or a vertical band knife. Die-cutting is done by machine. Computer-controlled cutting is also being introduced, with machines capable of cutting up to 250 inches per minute, depending on the depth of the lay. In laser cutting computer images are used to operate the cutter with great accuracy.

Qualifications and Training

Pattern Cutter/Grader

An Advanced Modern Apprenticeship in Apparel Manufacturing Technology leading to an NVQ level 3 in one of four routes (pattern cutting and grading, sample technician, garment technologist, hand craft garment making) is available. This is a work-based route providing an alternative to further and higher education.

Cutter/Spreader

Training is largely given on the job. Some employers offer the NVQ level 2 qualification for cutters or the Foundation Modern Apprenticeship route.

Personal Qualities and Skills

Pattern cutters/graders should have an interest in fashion and an appreciation of what their designers are aiming for. Numerical ability is essential for measurement and calculation. Some technical drawing skills and an aptitude for working on computers are also useful.

Spreaders/cutters need to be physically fit. They must have good eyesight and perfect colour vision. Some numerical ability is required.

Starting Salary

For a pattern cutter/grader, earnings vary tremendously, from £10,000 to £20,000, depending on qualifications and experience. Experienced cutters/spreaders are paid according to their skill and the level of responsibility in their job.

info

The British Apparel & Textile Confederation (BATC), 5 Portland Place, London W1N 3AA; 020 7636 7788; www.batc.co.uk

Skillfast, Sector Skills Council for Apparel, Footwear, Textiles and Allied Businesses, Richmond House, Lawnswood Business Park, Redvers Close, Leeds LS16 6RD; 0113 2399 800; www.skillfast-uk.org

COASTGUARD

HM Coastguard coordinates maritime search and rescue for the UK. Its area of responsibility, which covers approximately 10,500 miles of coastline and a million square miles of sea, is divided into four Search and Rescue Regions. Each is headed by a Regional Inspector, and within each Region are Maritime Rescue Coordination Centres and Sub Centres from which searches and rescues are coordinated.

At these centres, a constant watch is kept on international distress frequencies, satellite, radio and telephone communications, all of which are responded to immediately. HM Coastguard can call upon a wide range of facilities for search and rescue, including lifeboats, helicopters, tugs and local rescue organisations for rescues at sea. On-shore rescues from cliffs and mud are carried out by teams of Auxiliary Coastguards.

Qualifications and Training

Most coastguard officers are ex-seamen who have done previous marine work in services such as the Royal Navy or the Merchant Navy. Coastguard Watch Officers should have a minimum of four years' professional maritime/ navigational experience evidenced by qualifications such as laid down for Accreditation of Prior Learning for VTS (Vehicle Traffic Separation) Module 4 – Nautical Knowledge (Class 4 (Deck)), OOW (Officer of the Watch) Unlimited, Master (less than 500 grt) Near Coastal, Class 2 (fishing) or acceptable equivalent.

All candidates will require GCSE grade C or above in both English and maths. If candidates do not have these or equivalents, competency tests can be taken as part of the assessment process.

Personal Qualities and Skills

Good eyesight and hearing are essential. Candidates are expected to pass a strict medical, and must be prepared to work shifts and serve anywhere in the UK.

Starting Salary

£11,281 plus 25 per cent shift allowance.

Maritime and Coastguard Agency, MCA Infoline, Tutt Head, Mumbles, Swansea, West Glamorgan SA3 4HW; 0870 6006505; www.mcga.gov.uk

COLOUR SCIENCE AND TECHNOLOGY

Colour technologists are concerned with producing dyes and pigments that have a wide range of applications, including the textile, paint, rubber, plastics, paper, leather and foodstuffs industries. They must ensure that exact colours can be produced at an economic price and in the right quantities whenever they are needed. They are often involved in research and development projects. Technologists are also employed in sales, management, buying, development and research, quality control, customer liaison and technical services departments (depending on the industry involved and the expertise needed).

Textile technologists may work in the design, manufacture and operation of textile machinery, and in the design, production, coloration, finishing and manufacture of fibres, yarns and fabrics of all types.

Qualifications and Training

Two, preferably three, A levels or equivalents, one of which must be chemistry or a subject including chemistry, are required for entry to a degree course in colour chemistry or textile chemistry. Minimum entry requirements for part-time technician courses leading to the Edexcel (BTEC)/SQA certificate and higher certificate in textile coloration (textile dyeing) are GCSE or equivalent in maths, an appropriate science and English.

For textile technologists, the basic professional qualification is the Associateship and Chartered Textile Technologist (CText ATI) of the Textile Institute, awarded on the fulfilment of the academic and industrial/professional experience requirements. The professional qualification for a specialist in colour technology is the Associateship and Chartered Colourist of the Society of Dyers and Colourists (CCol ASDC) or the Licentiateship of the Society of Dyers and Colourists (LSDC).

Personal Qualities and Skills

Good colour vision is essential, as is scientific or technical ability and the ability to work as part of a team.

Starting Salary

£15,000+ with a degree; £9,000+ for a textile technologist.

Society of Dyers and Colourists, PO Box 244, Perkin House, 82 Grattan Road, Bradford, West Yorkshire BD1 2JB; 01274 725138; www.sdc.org.uk; e-mail: education@sdc.org.uk

COMPLEMENTARY MEDICINE

The field of complementary medicine and treatments is growing, with new therapies and treatments being added continuously. Therefore the list of occupations shown here is not exhaustive, but gives a cross-section of the more established ones.

Acupuncturist

Acupuncture is a system of treatment which involves the insertion of fine needles into one or more points of the body to restore the overall health of the person and help alleviate symptoms from which they may be suffering. Acupuncture can also be used for relieving pain, and in China is used to anaesthetise patients during operations. It has been practised in China and other Far Eastern countries for thousands of years and is a growing profession in the UK. Many health professionals, for example nurses and physiotherapists, train as acupuncturists.

Qualifications and Training

The training of acupuncturists is monitored by the British Acupuncture Accreditation Board (BAAB), an independent body which is allied to the British Acupuncture Council (BAcC). Training standards are detailed in the BAcC's Guidelines for Acupuncture Education and graduates of accredited or candidate colleges have automatic right of membership of the Council. Details of accredited, three-year full-time courses or their part-time equivalents are available from the Council.

Personal Qualities and Skills

Acupuncturists need the necessary practitioner skills, including a knowledge of Western medicine appropriate to the practice of acupuncture. They must also be able to put patients at their ease and to gain their confidence.

Starting Salary

Salaries vary depending on location, number of patients and amount charged. After qualifying, most acupuncturists will be self-employed and may practise from home, in a clinic, or occasionally within the NHS.

British Acupuncture Accreditation Board (BAAB), 63 Jeddo Road, London W12 9HQ; 020 8735 0466

British Acupuncture Council (BAcC), 63 Jeddo Road, London W12 9HQ; 020 8735 0400; www.acupuncture.org.uk

The College of Chinese Medicine, 1 Deansway, East Finchley, London N2 0NF; 020 8264 8074; www.thecollegeofchinesemedicine.com/

Foundation for Traditional Chinese Medicine, 296 Tadcaster Road, York YO24 1ET; 01904 709688; www.ftcm.org.uk/

The Acupuncture Society, 27 Cavendish Drive, Edgware, Middlesex HA8 7NR; 07734 668 402; www.accupuncture.org.uk

Aromatherapist

Aromatherapists use the organic essential oils from aromatic plants to treat a whole range of physical and emotional symptoms. Based on discussing a client's symptoms, lifestyle, diet, overall state of health, etc, the aromatherapist prescribes a combination of essential oils to treat the person. This is done either by massage, or by giving a client oils to use in their baths, on their pillows, or to scent their rooms. While aromatherapists may work in beauty salons they are also employed by healthcare organisations and often work closely with GPs, nurses and other healthcare professionals.

Qualifications and Training

There are no specific academic qualifications but certificate and diploma courses are run at a number of state and private colleges. Some courses do set particular entry requirements such as a GCSE in biology and they may also set admissions tests. The length of courses varies from a weekend to an evening a week over one or two years. The longer courses offer a much greater depth of study.

Personal Qualities and Skills

Aromatherapists must be very good at putting people at ease. They must be caring, patient and good listeners. They must be comfortable with close physical contact with other people.

Starting Salary

Aromatherapists charge between £15 and £35 an hour. They earn about £20 to £25 an hour if they are employed by health centres or other healthcare employers.

The British Complementary Medicine Association represents most aromatherapists. 0116 282 5511; www.bcma.org.uk

Chiropractor

Chiropractic is a healthcare profession concerned with, but not limited to, the diagnosis, treatment and prevention of structural and functional disorders affecting the musculo-skeletal system. Common complaints include low back and leg pain, headaches and neck and arm pain, as well as sports injuries. Working in a primary contact profession, a qualified chiropractor may be approached directly, without a medical referral, by patients seeking help.

Chiropractors are trained to utilise a wide variety of diagnostic techniques, including X-ray. Manual manipulation (adjustment) of spinal and extremity joints as well as soft-tissue structures is the most common treatment method employed. They will also offer advice on nutrition, rehabilitative exercises and modifications to activities of daily living. There is an increasing demand for chiropractic services and employment prospects are good both in the UK and in Europe.

Qualifications and Training

Chiropractors are subject to statutory regulation by the General Chiropractic Council (GCC). It is illegal for anyone to describe themselves as a chiropractor if they are not registered with the GCC. Recognised courses are provided by the Anglo-European College of Chiropractic, McTimoney College of Chiropractic and the Universities of Glamorgan and Surrey. Entry requirements vary but normally include two science A levels or equivalent. Fees for courses vary considerably because some colleges are private.

Personal Qualities and Skills

Manual dexterity and practical skills as well as a sound theoretical knowledge of the body are necessary. An ability to communicate with patients and inspire confidence is important.

info

General Chiropractic Council, 44 Wicklow Street, London WC1X 9HL; 020 7713 5155; www.gcc-uk.org; e-mail: enquiries@gcc-uk.org

British Chiropractic Association, Blagrave House, 17 Blagrave Street, Reading, Berkshire RG1 1QB; 0118 950 5950; fax: 0118 958 8946; www.chiropractic-uk.co.uk; e-mail: enquiries@chiropractic-uk.co.uk

Anglo-European College of Chiropractic, 13–15 Parkwood Road, Bournemouth, Dorset BH5 2DF; 01202 436200; fax: 01202 436312; www.aecc.ac.uk

McTimoney College of Chiropractic, Kimber House, 1 Kimber Road, Abingdon, Oxfordshire OX14 1BZ; 01235 523336; www.mctimoney-college.ac.uk; e-mail: chiropractic@mctimoney-college.ac.uk

University of Glamorgan, Chiropractic Field, School of Applied Sciences, Pontypridd, Glamorgan, CF37 1DL; 01443 482287; www.glam.ac.uk

University of Surrey, European Institute of Health and Medical Sciences, Duke of Kent Building, Stag Hill, Guildford, Surrey GU2 7TE; 01483 686700; www.eihms.surrey.ac.uk

Starting Salary

Salaries vary according to number of patients and how well established the practice is. Patients are usually charged per session at £20 to £60 per hour. A new entrant earns up to £15,000 per year. With experience it is possible to earn £30,000; a large practice will pay an experienced person up to £40,000.

Homeopath

Homeopathy is a system of healing which assists the natural tendency of the body to heal itself. There are three main principles of homeopathy. First is treating like with like – what produces the symptoms of a disease may also cure it; the patient is treated by a small amount of the substance causing the symptoms and the natural defences are stimulated. Second, the lower the dose the better the result. Third, the remedy should be unique to the particular patient at a particular time. Homeopathic remedies may be used to treat almost any reversible illness in adults, children or animals.

Many newly qualified homeopaths set up in partnership in a clinic with other homeopaths and some now work with GPs in fundholding practices. Homeopathic patients may come privately or be referred by GPs. Medical homeopaths (doctors who have trained in homeopathy) work as GPs, private practitioners or in one of the NHS homeopathic hospitals.

Qualifications and Training

Medical doctors who have been qualified for a minimum of two and a half years may take a postgraduate course at one of the five teaching centres accredited by the Faculty of Homeopathy.

Non-medically qualified candidates have a choice of institutions and courses. Several organisations register homeopaths as professionally competent. The largest, the Society of Homeopaths, is involved in developing professional education and is currently establishing a formal procedure for accrediting courses in homeopathy. There is a database of recognised courses on its website.

Personal Qualities and Skills

Homeopaths must have an interest in people, an ability to consider and interpret information and be good listeners and communicators.

Starting Salary

Because most of the work is paid for on an hourly basis, salaries range from between £5,000 and £30,000 pro rata. Homeopaths charge between £30 and £100 per hour, depending on their experience, their location and their clientele. £35 to £50 an hour is the most usual rate.

info

Alliance of Registered Homeopaths, Millbrook, Millbrook Hill, Nutley, East Sussex TN22 3PJ; 08700 736339; www.a-r-h.org

British Homeopathic Association incorporating the Homeopathic Trust, Hahnemann House, 29 Park Street West, Luton LU1 3BE; Tel: 0870 444 3950; www.trusthomeopathy.org/trust/tru_over.html

Faculty of Homeopathy, Hahnemann House, 29 Park Street West, Luton LU1 3BE; 0870 444 3950; www.trusthomeopathy.org/faculty/fac_over.html

Massage therapist

Massage is the scientific manipulation of soft tissues for a therapeutic effect, such as encouraging relaxation, relieving musculo-skeletal aches and pains or promoting healing. Massage therapists work in a range of settings such as health centres, hospitals, in professional sport, beauty clinics or as freelancers. The growth in alternative therapies has increased the demand and acceptance of massage therapy.

Qualifications and Training

There is a wide range of massage courses available and most specialise in specific types of massage, although there are some general massage courses too. Every mode of delivery is available from part and full-time, to distance learning, weekend and block courses. There are also some postgraduate courses in sports therapy, electrotherapy and manual lymphatic drainage. NVQs are available at levels 2 to 5 in a range of institutions and further education colleges.

Personal Qualities and Skills

Massage therapists must be physically strong, have good interpersonal skills and the ability to make people feel comfortable. They must also be good listeners and maintain excellent personal hygiene as the work involves close physical contact with clients.

Starting Salary

Varied, depending on employer. Freelancers charge £15–30 an hour.

info

Northern Institute of Massage, 14–16 St. Mary's Place, Bury, Lancashire BL9 0DZ; 0161 797 1800; www.nim56.co.uk; e-mail: information@nim56.co.uk

London School of Sports Massage, 28 Station Parade, Willesden Green, London NW2 4NX; 020 8452 8855; www.lssm.com; e-mail: admin@lssm.com

Naturopath

Naturopaths work in private practice since naturopathy is not offered by the NHS. They believe in treating the whole patient and in encouraging the body to cure itself, so do not generally give drugs which, they consider, often treat the symptoms without dealing with the actual cause of a problem. A naturopath uses treatments designed to correct total body chemistry; diet is seen as a major factor and patients are encouraged to eat more natural food. Hydrotherapy is often used to stimulate the blood to a specific area of the body or to draw it away from another (by applying cold packs to combat throbbing headaches, for example).

Naturopaths also need to be skilled in psychology since they recognise that physiological complaints may frequently be caused by psychological problems. Any remedies used tend to be nutritional, herbal or homeopathic, and naturopaths may also be trained in acupuncture or other systems of alternative or complementary medicine. In the UK, naturopathy is closely linked to osteopathy, and many naturopaths are qualified osteopaths using these skills in treating their patients.

Qualifications and Training

Two graduate courses are offered by the British College of Osteopathic Medicine in London: a BSc (Honours) degree in Osteopathic Medicine combined with a Naturopathic Diploma and a BSc (Honours) degree in Naturopathic Medicine.

The usual minimum entry requirements are three good A levels or equivalent, one of which should be chemistry. Mature students may be considered on an individual basis, taking into account their academic and life experiences.

Personal Qualities and Skills

Professional skills must be combined with a sympathetic and caring manner.

Starting Salary

Salaries vary depending on hours worked, number of patients and fee scales. Fees range from £25 to £100 an hour.

info

British College of Osteopathic Medicine, Lief House, 120–122 Finchley Road, London NW3 5HR; 020 7435 6464; fax: 020 7431 3630; www.bcno.ac.uk; e-mail: info@bcom.ac.uk

General Council and Register of Naturopaths, Goswell House, 2 Goswell Road, Street, Somerset BA16 0JG; 08707 456984; fax: 08707 456985; www.naturopathy.org.uk; e-mail: admin@naturopathy.org.uk

Osteopath

Osteopathy is a system of diagnosis and treatment where the main emphasis is on conditions affecting the musculo-skeletal system. Osteopaths use predominantly gentle manual and manipulative methods of treatment to restore and maintain proper body function. They work in private practice and are increasingly being asked to work as part of mainstream medicine. All osteopaths are required to register with the General Osteopathic Council (GOsC).

Qualifications and Training

Entry requirements are one of the following: a minimum of two A levels in biology and chemistry; a science access or foundation course; mature students with professional qualifications of a similar level to studying at undergraduate level, or equivalent qualifications from European and overseas applicants. Courses include the study of anatomy, physiology and biochemistry, together with a clinical course in the principles, diagnoses and techniques of osteopathy. Extensive hands-on clinical experience with patients is a key feature of any course. Studying for a degree at the British School of Osteopathy leads to a Bachelor degree in osteopathy (BOst).

Personal Qualities and Skills

Osteopaths require good manual dexterity plus a genuine desire to help and care for people. An ability to get on with and gain the confidence of their patients is also important.

Starting Salary

Within the first five years of practice new graduates can earn approximately £25,000–30,000.

info

British College of Osteopathic Medicine, Lief House, 120–122 Finchley Road, London NW3 5HR; 020 7435 6464; fax: 020 7431 3630; www.bcno.ac.uk; e-mail: info@bcom.ac.uk

British School of Osteopathy, 275 Borough High Street, London SE1 1JE; 020 7407 0222; www.bso.ac.uk; e-mail: admissions@bso.ac.uk

General Osteopathic Council, Osteopathy House, 176 Tower Bridge Road, London SE1 3LU; 020 7357 6655; fax: 020 7357 0011; www.osteopathy.org.uk

Working in Complementary and Alternative Medicine (Kogan Page)

Reflexology

A reflexologist applies pressure to the feet, or to the hands, to stimulate the reflexes which acts as a treatment to release tensions in the body, improving circulation and stimulating the body's own natural healing processes. A usual session conducted with a client involves applying pressure to the hands and feet, to clear blockages and improve circulation, easing tension and restoring the body's natural balance to all organs and parts of the body.

Qualifications and Training

Reflexology courses are available at colleges of further or higher education and private centres throughout the UK. The number of hours of study required by courses varies between 60 and 200. Most courses are private and there is a fee, but grants may be available.

Personal Qualities and Skills

A reflexologist helps people and is sensitive and sympathetic to the client's needs and condition. It is essential to have good communication skills, including listening and understanding. The work involves solving problems. Reflexologists must be logical thinkers able to offer a solution to health problems and understand when to refer patients to suitable medical practitioners.

Starting Salary

Most reflexologists are self-employed and incomes vary considerably. Each session is charged on an hourly rate, usually ranging from £20 to £60 an hour. A new entrant can earn £12,000 a year and with experience this could increase to £15,000. Working in a large practice reflexologists could earn £25,000.

info

Reflexology Forum, PO Box 2367, South Croydon, Surrey CR2 7ZE; 0800 037 0130; e-mail: reflexologyforum@aol.com

Prince of Wales's Foundation for Integrated Health, 12 Chillingworth Road, London N7 8QL; 020 7619 6140; www.fimed.org

COMPUTING

see Information and Communications Technology

CONSERVATION

Conservation falls broadly into two categories: environmental, and heritage and arts. They are each concerned with protecting and preserving – the former, the world in which we live and the latter, our cultural history.

Environmental conservation

see Environment

Heritage and arts conservation

Conservation is the ethical preservation of works of art and historic objects such as paintings and sculpture, historic buildings, furniture, textiles (such as costumes and tapestries), manuscripts, clocks and china. Some museums and art galleries employ specialist conservators who are responsible for conserving, repairing and protecting the exhibits in their charge, using the latest scientific techniques. Such work generally calls for scientific training and historical knowledge. A large number of conservators and restorers also work in the private sector, usually in small workshops of two to five people, sometimes larger units of up to 30. These serve private owners, historic house owners, dealers and auctioneers. Increasingly, museums and art galleries are sending out more of their objects to private conservators rather than taking on their own staff.

Qualifications and Training

Training courses accept students from a wide variety of backgrounds. An art, crafts or history background is a good starting point and although familiarity with a science is desirable this is often provided on the course. An important factor is to have good dexterity. The training courses for conservators, whether employed by museums or in private practice, are increasingly at degree or postgraduate level, though a number are at HND level.

Personal Qualities and Skills

Those working in this area need scientific ability, good problem-solving skills, a strong sense of ethics, meticulous attention to detail and patience.

Starting Salary

£13,000–14,000

info

Cultural Heritage National Training Organisation (CHNTO) 1st Floor, Glyde House, Glydegate, Bradford BD5 0UP; 01274 391056; fax: 01274 394890; www.chnto.co.uk

UK Institute for Conservation of Historic and Artistic Works, 702 The Chandlery, 50 Westminster Bridge, London SE1 7QY; 020 7721 8721; www.ukic.org.uk; e-mail: ukic@ukic.org.uk

Historic Scotland, Scottish Conservation Bureau, Longmore House, Salisbury Place, Edinburgh EH9 1SH; 0131 668 8600; www.historic-scotland.gov.uk

Creative and Cultural Skills, 11 Southwark Street, London SE1 1RQ; 020 7089 6866; www.ccskills.org.uk

CONSTRUCTION

The construction industry is the overarching sector for any occupation that is involved in the building and decorating of new and existing buildings. Building work involves the maintenance and construction of any structure. It is allied to civil and structural engineering, building and environmental engineering, municipal engineering, and highway and transportation engineering. There is a huge range of career options within the industry for graduates, technicians and at craft level.

Trades available include carpenters and joiners (*see also* Carpentry), formwork erectors, wood machinists, mastic asphalters, bricklayers, painters and decorators (*see also* Interior Decorator), crane drivers and mechanical equipment operators, electricians, refrigeration fitters, thermal insulators, plumbers and gas fitters, plasterers, glaziers, scaffolders, paviours, steel erectors, stonemasons, roofers, floor, ceiling and wall tilers, coiling fixers, heating and ventilation specialists. Each craftsperson is responsible for a specific part of the job but also works as part of a team whose collective responsibility is to produce high-quality work. The Construction Industry Training Board (CITB) predicts that the sector will need some 76,000 new recruits every year until 2006, to replace those leaving, and to fill new vacancies. Nearly 60 per cent of the new recruits needed are for trade occupations.

Building control surveyor

Building control is undertaken by local authorities and Approved Inspectors. The main activities involve the examination and assessment of plans, site visits to inspect work, and liaison with designers, builders and other professionals within the construction team, and the fire authorities to ensure that new building construction and alterations to existing buildings conform to building regulations. A broad knowledge of the many areas of building work and skills in dealing with people, need to be developed.

Qualifications and Training

There are two components to qualifying as a Chartered Building Control Surveyor: successful completion of a Royal Institution of Chartered Surveyors (RICS) approved degree or diploma, followed by enrolment onto the Assessment of Professional Competence (APC) which is two years' practical training while in employment, concluding with an RICS professional assessment interview. Postgraduate conversion courses are also available.

Personal Qualities and Skills

You have to be a good communicator, able to talk to property owners and builders, and you have to be firm and assertive when explaining, for example, why some work has to be redone. You have to have good technical knowledge and be able to convey this to other people. Maturity and common sense are vital.

Starting Salary

Salaries begin at around £15,000 to £19,000, sometimes more for mature applicants with a lot of relevant industry experience.

info

Association of Building Engineers (ABE), Lutyens House, Billing Brook Road, Northampton NN3 8NW; 0845 177 3411; www.abe.org.uk/siteman/index.asp?orgid=791

Construction Industry Training Board, CITB – Construction Skills, Bircham Newton, Kings Lynn, Norfolk PE31 6RH; 01485 577577; www.citb.org.uk

Royal Institution of Chartered Surveyors (RICS), RICS Contact Centre, Surveyor Court, Westwood Way, Coventry CV4 8JE; 0870 333 1600; www.rics.org

Contract manager

The contract manager is the person responsible for the overall control of a building project. This means coordinating the subcontractors and specialist firms, the technical staff and the machine operatives and making sure that the whole project is completed within the specified time limit and to budget.

Clerk of works

The clerk of works undertakes independent inspection of the works in progress to ensure that they conform to the specification so that the client obtains value for money.

CONSTRUCTION TRADES

There are many different construction trades: carpenters, painter and decorators, electricians, plasterers, plumbers and roofers. While they each have their own specialist knowledge and technical skills, much of the training and qualification route is similar for all of these trades. Have a look at the Qualifications and Training section at the end of this entry to see how to qualify and what kind of training to expect.

Carpenter

There are several different jobs covered by the general term carpenter – what they all have in common is that carpenters work with wood. They use wood to make doors, window frames, skirting boards, floorboards, cupboards and all the other woodwork you can think of in any domestic, public or commercial building. Some of the different roles include bench joiners, who prepare doors and window frames in a workshop ready for other workers to install them in properties; carpenters and joiners who work on site or inside or outside buildings, fitting cupboards, doors, window frames, etc; and wood machinists who prepare floorboards and skirting boards in the workshop ready for the carpenter and joiner to fix in place and finish.

Demolition work

Demolishing a building properly and safely is one of the most highly skilled areas in construction.

Demolition operative

Demolition operatives use heavy machinery to bring down walls, buildings and other structures. They have to be acutely aware of safety, calculating exactly how a building will collapse. They are also involved in clearance of the site once the building has been raised to the ground.

Scaffolder

Scaffolders build scaffolding that might be used in demolition, but more significantly in construction. They build scaffolding from steel tubes and wooden platforms, and it is essential they build scaffolding that is safe for other construction workers to stand on and work from.

Steeplejack

Steeplejacks work not just on steeples, but on any high structures, chimneys, clocks, etc. They have not only to work at a great height, using special safety equipment, but also have to have a good working knowledge of many different trades because they are likely to have to carry out repairs to and with many different materials: glass, wood, paint, plaster, mortar, etc.

Interior and finishing trades

Once a basic structure has been completed by bricklayers, carpenters, roofers, etc, there is still a great deal of work needed to make the building comfortable to live or work in and useful for the purpose for which it has been built. Ceiling fixers, floor layers, glaziers, painters and decorators, plasterers and plumbers are examples of some of the interior and finishing trades on offer.

Ceiling fixer

Ceiling fixers and dry liners install ceilings, especially in large modern buildings with large expanses of high ceiling. They build structures to fit large sheets of plasterboard to, and cover the whole thing with a very thin layer of plaster.

Electrician

This is a major construction industry career with many different options and pathways. You can see full details on page 135.

Glazier

Glaziers work with glass, installing glass windows, doors and glass partitions. They have to be skilled in cutting and fixing glass, from basic double-glazing to more ornate glass effects.

Painter and decorator

No building looks complete until the important finishing touches of painting, wood staining and papering have been applied. Interior decorators work inside and outside all kinds of buildings, from private houses to large warehouses, shops and offices.

Plasterer

This is a highly skilled occupation, as plasterers have to line walls or ceilings with a layer of even, smooth and attractive plaster to act as a basis for painting, wallpaper or other finishes. They have to work quickly, achieving the desired finish before the plaster dries out. Some plasterers go on to develop skills in ornamental and decorative plasterwork.

Plumber

Plumbers install and maintain all the necessary pipes, valves, tanks, boilers, etc that keep water and heating systems flowing through any building. They install and maintain drainage systems and repair flashing on roofs.

Roofers

Roofs come in many different shapes and sizes and are made from many different materials. It is the job of roofers to fix roofs onto buildings and to ensure that these roofs are safe and weatherproof. Within roofing there are several different specialist trades: felt roofing tiling and slating, lead roofing and many more. You may choose to work mainly with one of these materials, and become a specialist, or you may decide to work with all the different types of roofing material.

Trowel trades

If you work with brick or stone you will learn one of these trades. Of the many construction occupations available, these offer you the chance to be creative as well as using practical skills.

Bricklayer

Bricklayers build the external and internal walls of all kinds of buildings, from private houses to large hospitals, hotels and offices. They build garden walls and lay patios. They work mainly with ready-prepared bricks, building them up in layers, working to produce smooth and weatherproof results.

Stonemason

Stonemasons have employed their skills for hundreds of years, using natural stone as their basic building material. Today stonemasons work both restoring historic buildings and building modern structures. This is highly skilled work and a flair for design as well as practical ability is very important.

Supervisory roles

With so many different workers involved in building projects, both large and small, it is very important that there are people to take overall responsibility for employing workers, purchasing materials, health and safety, and day-to-day management.

Site technician

Site technicians get involved with the general running and safety of the site. Your role would include hiring and buying materials and machinery, and organising people and equipment. It would be your responsibility to ensure budgets and plans are followed, and that everything reaches technical requirements.

To become a site technician, you will need to have a strong knowledge of building methods and materials, and health and safety requirements, which you will have to teach workers on your site. You will need good communication and organisational skills, have a high level of competence in computing, and work well as part of a team.

There are no specific academic entry requirements to train as a site technician, although it is helpful to have GCSE/Standard Grade passes in science, maths and technology for the measurements and planning.

Site manager

Many site technicians become site managers, taking on more responsibility for larger projects and being in charge of everything that happens on the site.

Construction project manager

Construction project managers have overall responsibility for the planning, management, coordination and financial control of a construction project. It is their responsibility to see that the clients' wishes are adhered to and that the project is completed on time within the agreed budget.

Qualifications and Training

You do not need any formal qualifications to enter the building trades described above. For most trades it is a definite advantage to have GCSEs in maths, English and technology. There are several routes to entry and each route has its own specific entry requirements. Generally, training courses that do not require any formal educational qualifications lead to what are called craft level awards, and training that requires you to have four GCSEs leads to technician level awards. Many of the routes below offer both of these options. Most training takes between three and four years.

Foundation Certificates (FCs) are available at some schools and colleges in England and Wales and are really taster courses, to help you decide whether construction is for you. They are a good way of demonstrating your commitment if you are applying for further courses or traineeships in construction.

The Construction Apprenticeship Scheme (CAS) takes three to four years to complete, and you are based with an employer, earning a wage, but also receiving some structured training at your workplace and through college. At the end of your apprenticeship, if you are on a craft level scheme you will get a Construction Award (CA), and if you are on a technical level scheme you will get a National Certificate.

National Certificates (NCs) and National Diplomas (NDs) are technical qualifications available in many construction trades. You can study part-time or full-time for these awards. There are no formal entry requirements for these.

Higher National Certificates (HNCs) and Higher National Diplomas (HNDs) are one step up from NCs and NDs. You can either go from the basic level to the higher-level course or, if you have A levels, you can go straight onto a higher-level course.

National Vocational Qualifications (NVQs) are another way to combine practical on-site work and study at college, usually through day or block release.

Most construction NVQs are based with employers, but there are some full-time college courses leading to this qualification. There are no formal exams with NVQs: your on-site and college work is assessed throughout the course. For most NVQ construction courses you need four GCSEs grades A to C, and these should include English, maths and technology.

Construction Awards are available at three levels: Foundation, Intermediate and Advanced, and are available in many construction occupations. They are college-based courses that you can study full-time, or part-time while working for an employer. All your assessments are based on what you do at college.

Construction project managers and site managers often have a degree in construction, civil engineering or quantity surveying.

There are increasing numbers of short, privately run training courses in some trades, particularly plumbing, painting and decorating and plastering, but others too. These are aimed at mature applicants wishing to change career. They can be extremely expensive and it is important that you check exactly what accreditation and qualifications they lead to.

If you are trying to sift through this rather bewildering set of options, start by considering whether you want to be mainly employed as you train or mainly based at college. It is also true that not every route is always available for every trade, and employment opportunities vary in different geographical areas. The CITB-ConstructionSkills website is a very helpful and thorough starting point to help you compare trades and look at routes to qualification.

Personal Qualities and Skills

While a variety of trades have been described and each has its special requirements, there are many skills and qualities that are important for all these occupations. You need to have a special interest in and feel for the particular material you are working with – wood, metal, plaster, stone, etc. You must be good at measuring and calculating, working out how much material you will need, and measuring exactly to ensure that something fits.

For all jobs you must be physically fit, though some work, such as bricklaying, is especially demanding. You may have to climb up and down scaffolding, work outside in unpleasant weather, or work in cramped spaces such as somebody's loft.

You need to get on with people. You often work as part of a team, and if you progress to supervisory or management roles you have to be organised and be good at motivating other people. If you are working in private houses, you must be polite, pleasant and trustworthy, and good at coming up with solutions to problems. If you become self-employed you must develop good business and financial skills.

Starting Salary

Pay rates across the industry are agreed annually. First-year apprentices start on around £7,200; second-year apprentices earn around £9,000; third-year apprentices earn just under £11,000; and newly qualified apprentices earn £17,000. Salaries rise with increasing responsibility and experience, and many of these trades allow you to become self-employed, earning salaries of between £25,000 and £50,000. There is a lot of regional variation in what you can charge and therefore what you can earn.

info

CITB – Construction Skills, The Sector Skills Council for Construction, Bircham Newton, Kings Lynn, Norfolk PE31 6RH; 01485 577 577; www.CITB-ConstructionSkills.org.uk

Summit Skills, Vega House, Opal Drive, Fox Milne, Milton Keynes MK15 0DF; 01908 303960; www.summitskills.org.uk

www.bconstructive.co.uk/apprenticeships

www.apprenticeships.org.uk (England)

www.modernapprenticeships.com (Scotland)

www.elwa.org.uk (Wales)

Local Job Centre Plus and Connexions/Careers Centres

CRAFTS

There are many occupations which can come under the banner of a 'Craft' and listed below is a selection.

Cabinet maker

see Carpentry

Florist

The florist's job involves designing and creating flower arrangements and displays such as table decorations, bouquets, sprays and wreaths, as well as selling cut flowers and plants. Some florists buy from flower markets; others have stock delivered from wholesalers, local nurseries or overseas producers. The work can include providing office displays, making arrangements for banquets, functions and receptions and decorating hotels and public buildings. Florists generally work a 40-hour week, including Saturdays.

Qualifications and Training

Edexcel (BTEC) qualifications are offered by a number of colleges at First Diploma, National Diploma and HND level. The Society of Floristry offers two professional qualifications – the Intermediate Certificate (ICSF) and the National Diploma (NDSF); these are for experienced florists. NVQs in floristry are available at levels 2 and 3.

Personal Qualities and Skills

Imagination and creative flair, colour sense, organisational ability, an ability to work to deadlines, a friendly manner, patience and dexterity are necessary. Good health and stamina are essential because the work can be physically demanding.

Starting Salary

Rates of pay vary according to size and location of the business and according to the individual's own skills and qualifications, experience and seniority. Salaries are similar to those in other retail work. Part-time work may be available.

info

Lantra Connect, Lantra House, Stoneleigh, Kenilworth, Warwickshire CV8 2LG; 0845 707 8007 (Lantra Connect – Helpline); www.lantra.co.uk; e-mail: connect@lantra.co.uk

The Secretary, Society of Floristry; 0870 241 0432; fax: 01202 855520; www.societyoffloristry.org

Jewellery trade

Design

Jewellery designers craft a wide variety of items either by hand or using methods of large-scale production. These may be very expensive, traditionally styled pieces using gold or platinum, cheaper costume jewellery using synthetic stones and base metals, or fashion accessories made from beads, plastic or wood.

Although there are a few openings for designers of expensive jewellery, the more costly costume jewellery and mass-produced jewellery, there is more scope for original designers on either a freelance or artist/craftsperson basis, making fashionable ranges with semi-precious stones.

Manufacture

The jewellery, silverware and allied industries encompass a vast range of specialist skills. Apart from mounting and silversmithing, other skills needed to support these occupations include gem setting, engraving (hand and machine), enamelling, chasing, engine turning, spinning, electro-plating and polishing.

Qualifications and Training

Those wishing to follow a career in jewellery design need specialist training before looking for employment. Full-time three-year and some sandwich-based degree courses in three-dimensional design, have options in jewellery and silversmithing. The minimum entrance requirements are usually two A levels and three GCSEs or equivalents plus satisfactory completion of an art foundation course.

Manufacturing training can be by traditional trade apprenticeships, lasting between three and five years. NVQs in manufacturing jewellery and allied products are available.

The Gemmological Association and Gem Testing Laboratory (GAGTL) have two diploma qualifications – the Diploma in Gemmology (taken in two parts), and the Gem Diamond Diploma (one part). These may be studied by correspondence, or as daytime or evening courses at GAGTL and allied technology centres worldwide. There are also two examinations conducted by the British Horological Institute – the certificate for clockmakers and the diploma for salespeople.

Personal Qualities and Skills

People in the jewellery trade must have a sense of design and an appreciation of quality. Designers must be prepared to work hard and keep to a busy schedule. Self-employed or independent designers will need determination to keep going and unflagging enthusiasm to sell their products. Manufacturing employees and craftspeople must possess good manual dexterity, creativity, integrity, attention to detail, initiative and self-motivation.

Starting Salary

For shop assistants pay varies between £8,500 and £11,000. Jewellery designers and makers earn between £15,000 and £25,000. Freelance designers charge around £30 an hour for their work.

info

The Association of British Designer Silversmiths (ABDS), PO Box 42034, London E5 9WG; 07944 786 011; www.theabds.co.uk/

The Association for Contemporary Jewellery, PO Box 37807, London SE23 1XJ; 020 8291 4201; www.acj.org.uk

British Jewellers Association (BJA), 10 Vyse Street, Birmingham B18 6LT; 0121 237 1110; www.bja.org.uk

Crafts Council, 44a Pentonville Road, Islington, London N1 9BY; 020 7278 7700; www.craftscouncil.org.uk

Institute of Professional Goldsmiths, Long Cottage, 17 Acre End Street, Eynsham, Oxon OX8 1PE; 01865 464 255; www.ipgold.org.uk

Jewellery and Allied Industries Training Council (JAITC), Federation House, 10 Vyse Street, Birmingham B18 6LT; 0121 237 1111; www.jaitc.org.uk

Pottery

Employees in the pottery industry make ordinary domestic china, earthenware, vases and ornaments, fine bone china, ceramic tiles, sanitary ware, industrial and electrical porcelain and huge insulators used in distributing electricity. Although the industry is mechanised, there is still a predominant demand for skilled workers: hand painters, fettlers and spongers, casting, lithographing, binding and lining, to name a few. Some potters work individually, hand throwing or casting their own pieces and selling them personally or through a shop or gallery.

Qualifications and Training

No formal educational requirements are needed for the industry and training is mainly on the job. Craftsmen potters sometimes become apprenticed to master potters, and Foundation and Advanced Modern Apprenticeships are now available. Vocational or degree courses are also available at some art schools.

Personal Qualities and Skills

Potters need a good eye for shape and design, a steady hand and a delicate touch. Potters working for themselves must also be inventive and have business skills and marketing ability.

Starting Salary

Industry employees start at £80+ a week. Craftspeople set their own rates, and if they are selling their work through a gallery, must pay the owner a percentage.

info

Association for Ceramic Training and Development, St James House, Webberley Lane, Longton, Stoke-on-Trent ST3 1RJ; 01782 597016; www.actd.co.uk

Crafts Council, 44a Pentonville Road, London N1 9BY; 020 7278 7700; www.craftscouncil.org.uk

Craft Potters' Association, 21 Carnaby Street, London W1V 1PH; 020 7437 6781

Saddler

Saddles are still made by hand, by craftspeople of considerable experience. They usually work in one of the many small companies that specialise in saddlery, making harnesses and other leather goods such as satchels and wallets. Saddlers' shops stock all these items and may also stock suitcases and sports goods and offer a repair service.

Qualifications and Training

The Society of Master Saddlers administers a four-year apprenticeship indenture scheme leading to certification by the Worshipful Company of Saddlers. Saddlery courses of varying lengths are available at the Capel Manor College at Enfield, Middlesex, Walsall College of Arts and Technology, Cambridge Saddlery Courses in Bury St Edmunds, Suffolk, Cumbria School of Saddlery in Penrith, Cumbria and the Saddlery Training Centre in Salisbury, Wiltshire. Cordwainers at Capel Manor College offers two courses in saddlery: a diploma in saddlery studies and an HND in saddlery technology. Both courses cover many aspects of running a small business and both last for two years.

The Society of Master Saddlers administers the National Saddlery Skills Assessment Scheme by which those making saddles, bridles and harnesses may have their skills assessed and gain qualifications in each specialist area at levels 1, 2 and 3. The City and Guilds National Skill Assessment and Qualification Scheme for the Saddlery Trade is also available. These qualifications are recognised within the trade.

Personal Qualities and Skills

Painstaking attention to detail and pride in craftsmanship are needed. Owners of saddlers' shops often have a strong interest in horses too.

Starting Salary

£125–400+ per week with experience.

info

Cordwainers College at Capel Manor, Bullsmoor Lane, Enfield, Middlesex EN1 4RQ; 020 8366 4442; www.capel.ac.uk

Walsall College of Arts and Technology, Leather Department, Shelley Campus, Scarborough Road, Walsall WS1 1XN; 01922 720889; www.walcat.ac.uk

Cambridge and District Saddlery Courses (INT) Ltd, 31 St John Street, Bury St Edmunds, Suffolk IP33 1SN; 01284 700640; www.racenetservices.com/businesslinks/careers/saddlerycourses.htm

Cumbria School of Saddlery, Unit 9, Redhills Business Park, Penrith, Cumbria CA11 0DL; 01768 899919; www.saddlerycourses.com

Saddlery Training Centre, 14–17 The Malverns, Cherry Orchard Lane, Salisbury, Wiltshire SP2 7JG; 01722 341144; fax: 01722 349669; www.saddlerytraining.com; e-mail: sales@saddlerytraining.com

Society of Master Saddlers, Green Lane Farm, Stonham, Stowmarket, Suffolk IP14 5DS; 01449 711642; www.mastersaddlers.co.uk; e-mail: enquiries@mastersaddlers.co.uk

Worshipful Company of Saddlers, Saddlers' Hall, 40 Gutter Lane, London EC2V 6BR; 020 7726 8663; www.saddlersco.co.uk; e-mail: clerk@saddlersco.co.uk

Thatcher

Thatchers are self-employed craftspeople who roof, re-roof or repair thatched buildings with long straw, combed wheat straw, reed and other materials. The materials and methods they use have to preserve the building in its original form. A thatched roof gives good insulation against heat and cold and lasts 20 to 50 years. A roof is thatched by taking off the old thatch and then pegging down layers of new straw or reed.

Qualifications and Training

Academic qualifications are not essential. Thatching can be learnt on the job as an apprentice to a Master Thatcher. Training takes four to five years. The Countryside Agency runs a training scheme for people of all ages, leading to NVQ level 2 in thatching.

Personal Qualities and Skills

Thatchers need to be robust, good with their hands and not mind bad weather or heights. They also need common sense, the ability to make decisions and deal with customers.

Starting Salary

About £100 a week as an apprentice, thereafter depending on amount of work and individual charges.

info

National Society of Master Thatchers, c/o Messrs Wheelers, Vale House, Wharf Road, Ash Vale, Surrey GU12 5AR; fax: 01252 28312; www.nsmt.co.uk

The Countryside Agency, John Dower House, Crescent Place, Cheltenham GL50 3RA; 01242 533311; www.countryside.gov.uk; e-mail: info@countryside.gov.uk

CUSTOMS AND EXCISE

There is far more to this work than high profile drugs or arms seizures. Customs and excise officers carry out three main types of work. They check passengers, luggage, freight and mail at ports and airports, ensuring that people are not carrying illegal goods or items upon which appropriate tax has not been paid. They visit distilleries and oil refineries ensuring that appropriate excise duty has been paid on these items. They visit and inspect businesses to ensure that their VAT records are correct and up to date.

Qualifications and Training

There are several entry levels for this work. To start on Band 2 you must have two GCSEs grade A to C. To start on Band 3/4 you must have five GCSEs grade A to C. You can start as a junior manager (Band 5) and you will need five GCSEs grades A to C and two A levels or their equivalent. At all levels one of the GCSEs must be English language. Many successful Band 5 applicants are graduates. All the above levels are recruited directly by HM Customs and Revenue. If you apply for Fast Stream entry, you apply to Central Civil Service Recruitment then, if you join HM Customs and Revenue you become a customs officer straight away. For the Fast Stream you must have a good honours degree, either a 1st or an upper 2nd. Most of the training is on-the-job and includes appropriate short courses and sometimes opportunities to take professional qualifications.

Personal Qualities and Skills

You must be able to get on with people, being polite, tactful and able to question and listen carefully. You should be honest and fair and be able to analyse complex information. For much of the work on the excise and VAT side you must have good numeracy skills.

Starting Salary

On Bands 2 to 4 starting salaries range from £12,000 to £18,000. Junior managers (Band 5) start on salaries of £18,500 to £22,500 a year. There are additional allowances for working in and around London and for working anti-social hours. Performance-related pay has also been introduced.

info

HM Revenue and Customs; www.hmrc.gov.uk

Civil Service Fast Stream; www.faststream.gov.uk

Skills for Justice, Riverside House, Don Road, Sheffield S9 2TJ; 0114 261 1499; www.skillsforjustice.com

DENTISTRY

All professionals in dentistry in the UK must be registered with the General Dental Council. This includes dentists, dental hygienists, dental therapists, dental nurses and dental technicians.

Dentist

Dentists aim to prevent tooth decay and gum disease and to identify and treat such diseases. This involves filling, crowning and extracting teeth, scaling and cleaning teeth and gums. They design and fit dentures and plates and take corrective measures for teeth growing abnormally. They are also involved with the rectification of fractured jaws and surgery of the mouth. Much of the dentist's work today is highly technical and requires a lot of manual dexterity. There is growing emphasis on preventive work, and the dentist is expected to counsel and educate.

Opportunities exist both in the UK and abroad. In general dental practice dentists work on contract to the NHS, but growing numbers work in private clinics. Some work in hospitals, community services, school services or the armed forces. There are also opportunities for dentists to work in university dental teaching and research.

Specialist areas of dentistry include paediatric dentistry and oral and maxillofacial surgery. A number of large companies also provide dental treatment facilities for staff at work and there are some openings within occupational dentistry. The armed services also provide short service commissions or permanent careers for medical and dental staff.

Dentists need to have confidence and the ability to reassure patients as many are apprehensive about dental treatment. Team work is important as working closely with the surgery assistant and any specialists the practice employs is essential.

Qualifications and Training

To qualify, a dentist must have a degree in dental surgery. All dentists must be registered on the Dentists' Register, which is maintained by the General Dental

Council. Competition for degree course entry is stiff, requiring good A level grades in physics, chemistry and biology. Entry requirements vary: some schools have pre-dental courses for students who have not studied science A levels. All applicants are expected to have spent time work-shadowing a dentist.

The undergraduate course lasts at least five years. It incorporates a sound academic education combined with theoretical and practical training in all aspects of dental practice.

In the armed forces, dental cadetships leading to a commission are open to candidates who have completed part of their training at a dental school.

Personal Qualities and Skills

Manual and visual dexterity combined with medical knowledge and clinical skills are essential. Candidates should be equable, sympathetic and have an agreeable nature and an ability to communicate. Good administrative and managerial skills and the ability to work in a team are important.

Starting Salary

General dental practitioners and orthodontists earn the fees that they receive from patients or the NHS; these start from £24,500. Salaries for senior posts are over £50,000.

Dental hygienist

Dental hygienists clean, polish and scale teeth and in some cases prepare patients for oral operations. Through lectures and practical experience they also endeavour to educate children and adults on the importance of proper dental care. Dental hygienists work to the written prescription of a dentist.

Qualifications and Training

Applicants for the Diploma in Dental Hygiene must be over 18 with five GCSE passes, including biology and English. They also need two years' experience as a dental nurse or two A levels or equivalent. Manchester University offers a three-year BSc in oral health science. Graduates work as oral health therapists which combines the skills of a hygienist and therapist.

Personal Qualities and Skills

Manual and visual dexterity. Candidates should have an ability to communicate in order to educate patients in good dental hygiene practice. The ability to work in a team is important.

Starting Salary

Dental hygienists earn £13,500+.

Dental nurse

Dental nurses prepare the surgery and get the appropriate instruments ready. During treatment, they assist the dentist by passing instruments, mixing materials, taking notes from the dentist's dictation for records and making sure the patient is comfortable at all times. Once the patient has left, the dental nurse tidies the surgery and sterilises all the instruments. Sometimes, particularly in general practice, dental nurses also help with reception work – making appointments, taking payments, dealing with the paper work, meeting and reassuring patients.

Qualifications and Training

Many dentists like to train their own assistants and expect applicants to be educated to GCSE standard. In 2004 it became necessary for dental nurses to have obtained NVQ level 3 in oral healthcare or passed the National Certificate of the Examining Board for Dental Nurses. Preparation for this exam can be obtained either at evening or day-release classes or via full-time attendance on a course lasting between one and two years. A certificate is awarded on passing the exam and completing 24 months' practical experience. Courses are offered by colleges of further education and dental hospitals. Courses offered by dental hospitals usually require four GCSE passes, including English and biology.

Personal Qualities and Skills

Candidates should be equable, sympathetic and have an agreeable nature and an ability to communicate. Good administrative and managerial skills and the ability to work in a team are important.

Starting Salary

Salaries for dental nurses vary greatly depending on the type of practice and its location. Some employers pay around the national minimum wage; others pay more and include additional benefits. Average salaries are between £9,000 and £12,000.

Dental technician

Dental technicians design and fabricate a wide variety of different materials and equipment to make crowns, dentures, metal plates, bridges, orthodontic braces and other appliances prescribed by a dentist.

Qualifications and Training

The usual entry requirements for courses are five GCSEs or equivalents (English, maths, physics and chemistry). The Edexcel (BTEC) diploma in dental technology is a full-time three-year course but can also be studied part-time.

Personal Qualities and Skills

Good technical skills and the ability to work in a team.

Starting Salary

Dental technicians earn £7,500–9,000 while training, rising to £10,000–18,000 when qualified.

Dental therapist

Dental therapists work in local authority clinics and hospitals assisting dentists by carrying out simpler forms of treatment such as fillings and the extraction of first teeth. They also give guidance on general dental care. Dental therapists must always work to the written prescription of a dentist.

Qualifications and Training

To become a dental therapist it is necessary to take a 27-month full-time course. The minimum course entry requirement is five GCSE passes or equivalent; these should include English and biology. Applicants should also hold the National Certificate for Dental Nurses, which requires at least two years' practical experience. As competition for places is fierce, actual requirements are likely to be higher than this.

Personal Qualities and Skills

Manual and visual dexterity combined with medical knowledge and clinical skills are essential. Candidates should be equable, sympathetic and have an agreeable nature and an ability to communicate.

Starting Salary

£9,000–14,000.

Orthodontist

Orthodontists work in a specialist branch of dentistry that is concerned with the development and management of irregularities of teeth, jaws and face. The treatment is aimed at correcting dental and jaw abnormalities. Orthodontists generally (although not always) see patients for an initial assessment between the ages of 7 and 10.

Qualifications and Training

To become an orthodontist, a qualification as a dentist is required in order to gain entry to a specialised orthodontic course, which lasts three years full time and usually includes some research work, resulting in an MSc.

Personal Qualities and Skills

As with dentists, manual and visual dexterity combined with medical knowledge and clinical skills are important qualities for orthodontists. Candidates should be equable, sympathetic and have an agreeable nature and an ability to communicate. The ability to work in a team is important.

Starting Salary

Orthodontists earn the fees that they receive from patients or the NHS; these start from £24,500. Salaries for senior posts are over £50,000.

info

British Association of Dental Nurses, 11 Pharos Street, Fleetwood, Lancashire FY7 6BG; 01253 778631; www.badn.org.uk; e-mail: admin@badn.org.uk

British Dental Association, 64 Wimpole Street, London W1G 8YS; 020 7935 0875; www.bda-dentistry.org.uk

National Examining Board for Dental Nurses, 110 London Road, Fleetwood F17 6EU; 01253 778417

British Dental Hygienists' Association, 13 The Ridge, Yatton, Bristol BS19 4DQ; 01934 876389; www.bdha.org.uk

Dental Technicians' Education and Training Advisory Board (DTETAB), 64 Wimpole St, London W1M 8AL

General Dental Council, 37 Wimpole Street, London W1G 8DQ; 020 7887 3800; www.gdc-uk.org

British Orthodontic Society, BOS Office, 291 Gray's Inn Road, London WC1X 8QJ; 020 7837 2193; www.bos.org.uk

DIETITIAN

A dietitian is an authority on diet and the application of the principles of nutrition. Dietitians working in hospitals collaborate with medical staff, other healthcare professionals and catering staff in planning the correct balance of foods for all the patients, depending on their general state of health and medical requirements. Dietitians are also employed by local health authorities to work with general practitioners, in health centres and clinics dealing with infant welfare and antenatal treatment. Some dietitians may now be employed directly by fundholding GPs. They are also called upon to educate other healthcare professionals in nutrition. Other opportunities for dietitians exist in education, research, the food industry and the media. Increasingly, dietitians work in a freelance capacity.

Qualifications and Training

To become a state registered dietitian and practise in the National Health Service you must either do a four-year degree course or a two-year postgraduate course following on from a degree in another relevant subject, such as food science, medicine or nursing. Both of these include practical placements as well as academic study and some courses are developing part-time routes.

You must have three A level passes grade A to C in sciences for most degree courses; chemistry is the one most courses insist on. Advanced level GNVQ or BTEC National Diploma courses in health and science-based subjects are often accepted as alternatives to A levels. For most degree and postgraduate courses the NHS pays your fees and you can also apply for NHS grants to help support you while you are studying and training.

Personal Qualities and Skills

The complex nutritional and scientific knowledge you acquire is only useful if you can communicate it really effectively to your clients. People are often unhappy, unwilling or uncertain about how to change their diets, so you need to be able to explain scientific ideas in layman's terms, you need to be positive, encouraging and realistic and have an interest in the aesthetic as well as the nutritional properties of food. You should be able to work as part of a healthcare team, but be happy working one-to-one with patients.

Starting Salary

Salaries start at around £18,000 to £19,500, with higher salaries when qualified. Senior dietitians can become consultants earning close to £40,000.

info

British Dietetic Association (BDA), Charles House, 148/9 Charles Street, Queensway, Birmingham B3 3HT; 0121 200 8080; www.bda.uk.com

Department of Health (DH), Customer Service Centre, Richmond House, 79 Whitehall, London SW1A 2NL; 020 7210 4850; www.dh.gov.uk

Health Professions Council (HPC), Park House, 184 Kennington Park Road, London SE11 4BU; 020 7582 0866; www.hpc-uk.org

DISC JOCKEY

Disc jockeys provide music and entertainment at a range of venues such as clubs, private parties and radio stations. They use a variety of high-tech equipment for mixing, pitch control and cross-fading, and may also be responsible for lighting and multimedia effects.

Qualifications and Training

A strong interest and enjoyment of different music styles is essential, and it is useful to have an interest in technology and electronics. Some DJs specialise in specific music genres such as soul, funk, hip-hop and pop. Most are self-taught and usually begin their career by volunteering their services at clubs, radio stations or to friends. It is useful to send a tape demonstrating DJ skills when asking for work.

Personal Qualities and Skills

DJs must have a lively personality, a sense of fun and natural creativity. They need to have a good knowledge of and genuine interest in music and be able to interact effectively with an audience.

Starting Salary

This varies enormously, depending on the hours worked and the venue. Successful DJs are offered lucrative financial deals. With some experience a DJ earns up to £300 per session; a top experienced DJ earns £1,000 per session.

info

Local and national radio stations

Clubs and social venues

SKILLSET – The Sector Skills Council for the Audio Visual Industries, Prospect House, 80–110 New Oxford Street, London WC1A 1HB; 020 7520 5757; www.skillset.org

DIVING

Diver

Professional divers are mainly employed by commercial diving contractors in the North Sea, ports and docks. There are also opportunities in the armed services and police forces. The growth of diving as a popular sport has created a number of positions for instructors worldwide. Currently there are many more qualified divers looking for work than there is work available.

Qualifications and Training

Diving is potentially hazardous and it is essential for anyone who wishes to become a commercial diver to attend and satisfactorily complete a course of training at a diver training school which has been approved by the UK Health and Safety Executive (HSE). This leads to certificates of competence relevant to offshore and inland/ inshore commercial diving. All commercial offshore divers need to hold a current first aid certificate. In addition, other skills are required, including welding, cutting and underwater tools.

The Royal Navy and police forces train their own personnel. In the case of the latter, pupils must have a minimum of two years' experience as a constable. BSAC or other sport diving qualifications do not qualify divers for commercial diving.

Personal Qualities and Skills

Divers must be sound swimmers and physically fit; all professional divers have to pass a full commercial diving medical, which complies with HSE Diving Operations at Work regulations. They must be able to tolerate hard exercise, extreme conditions and recognise and work within their own personal limits. They must be very responsible and willing and able to work as part of a team. Initiative and the ability to sell their own skills to a potential employer are essential.

Starting Salary

There is no uniform pay rate for divers who work inland/inshore; it varies from £50–120 per day. Divers who work in the UK sector of the North Sea on oil- or gas-related activities are paid around £160 per day, which rises to about £260 once they have spent 300 days offshore as members of a diving team and have completed 150 'approved' dives. Sport diving instructors work largely for travel and enjoyment and pay can be low.

info

Health and Safety Executive, Magdalen House, Trinity Road, Bootle, Merseyside L20 3QZ; 08701 545500; www.hse.gov.uk

International Marine Contractors Association, Carlyle House, 235 Vauxhall Bridge Road, London SW1V 1EJ; www.imca-int.com/careers; e-mail: imca@imca-int.com

Fort Bovisand Underwater Centre, Plymouth, Devon PL9 OAB; 01752 408021; www.fortbovisand.com; e-mail: dive@fortbovisand.com

Society for Underwater Technology, 80 Coleman Street, London EC2R 5BJ; 020 7382 2601; www.sut.org.uk

Underwater Centre, Fort William, Inverness-shire, Highland PH33 6LZ; 01397 703768

British Sub Aqua Club, Telford's Quay, South Pier Road, Ellesmere Port, Cheshire CH65 4FL; 0151 350 6200; fax: 0151 350 6215; www.bsac.org

Local police forces

Royal Navy Careers Offices; Royal Navy Careers enquiries; 0845 607 5555; www.royal-navy.mod.uk

ROV pilot technician

Remotely operated vehicles (ROVs) were introduced into the military and offshore fields in the late 1970s and early 1980s and now offer a career path for well-educated technical staff. ROVs are operated by the Royal Navy, offshore companies, environmental agencies, police and salvage companies. These underwater robots carry out the work of a diver at depths where diving is impossible.

Qualifications and Training

Employers normally require ROV personnel to have a good background in electronics or hydraulics. Experience with pneumatics, plant maintenance or electrical engineering is also of interest. Candidates who do not have formal qualifications (academic, trade or in the services) in one of these areas are unlikely to be considered. Training courses are available at a number of schools which allow newcomers to the industry to learn the basics; however, none of these courses is formally required and they will not normally be accepted as a basis for employment unless the person has the right sort of background and qualifications. Details of courses are available from The International Marine Contractors Association website.

Personal Qualities and Skills

Initiative and ability to work in small close-knit teams and a willingness to work outside the UK are essential. To work offshore in any capacity it is necessary to undergo and pass a special medical examination.

Starting Salary

Starting salaries are £18,000+, rising to £28,000+.

info

International Marine Contractors Association, Carlyle House, 235 Vauxhall Bridge Road, London SW1V 1EJ; 020 7931 8171; fax: 020 7931 8935; www.imca-int.com; e-mail: imca@imca-int.com

Local Royal Navy Careers Information Offices

DOMESTIC SERVICE

The term 'domestic service' applies to those occupations such as housekeeper, maids, cooks, butlers, footmen and valets. Duties may involve the general running of a household, announcing guests, serving drinks and supervising other staff preparing food, waiting at the table, cleaning and/or looking after the employer's clothes. Some jobs can be done on a temporary basis and agencies exist to provide domestic staff for special occasions.

Qualifications and Training

While no formal qualifications are needed, catering qualifications are often extremely useful and even some management qualifications could be useful for some positions. Sometimes private training courses are an option, but check carefully what you would have to spend and what you would get for your money.

Personal Qualities and Skills

Of course you have to be very good at dealing with people, tactful, patient and sometimes quite thick-skinned. You also have to be friendly and comfortable meeting people. You need to be discrete and honest, well organised and calm. You may need a variety of practical skills associated with domestic work such as cooking, cleaning and general household tasks. Good references and personal recommendations are important in this sector.

Starting Salary

What you are paid varies according to whether food, accommodation, a car, or other benefits come with the job. For many daily or part-time domestic jobs such as cleaning and ironing you get the minimum wage. If you are aged 22 or above, this is currently £5.05 an hour, rising to £5.35 an hour from October 2006. If you are aged 18 to 21 this is currently £4.25, rising to £4.45 in October 2006.

Local Job Centre Plus and Careers/Connexions Centres

The Lady, 39–40 Bedford Street, Strand, London WC2E 9EN; 020 7379 4717; www.lady.co.uk (job advertisements)

Butler

A butler is employed to organise the domestic arrangements of the employer. This may include supervising other domestic staff, serving meals and refreshments, answering the telephone and door as well as organising social events, room settings for functions and having responsibility for the wine cellar, china and cutlery.

Butlers are employed in a range of settings: private households, five-star hotels, castles and palaces and yachts all around the world.

Qualifications and Training

No formal qualifications are required, although many butlers undertake professional training.

Personal Qualities and Skills

Butlers need to be courteous, discreet and to be motivated to provide a high standard of service to the employer.

Starting Salary

Salaries for a fully trained and experienced butler can start at £30,000+ and accommodation may also be provided.

Guild of Professional English Butlers, PO Box 32380, London SW17 9WJ; 02392 637919; www.guildofbutlers.com

Butler Bureau; www.butlerbureau.com

International Guild of Professional Butlers; www.butlersguild.com

DRESSER

Dressers may find employment in theatre, television, films and fashion houses. They prepare and maintain costumes and help the performers and models to dress, especially where quick changes are needed.

Qualifications and Training

No formal qualifications are necessary. Experience, especially in the theatre, is helpful as is sewing ability.

Personal Qualities and Skills

Calmness and speed, a soothing and sympathetic nature, discretion and tact are all helpful.

Starting Salary

Dependent on age, experience and employer, but generally relatively low.

The Stage, 47 Bermondsey Street, London SE1 3XT; 020 7403 1818; www.thestage.co.uk (job advertisements)

DRESSMAKER

see Fashion

DRIVING

Although many jobs require the ability to drive a vehicle, the occupations in this section refer to those which require professional driving skills.

Chauffeur

Chauffeurs are skilled car drivers who are employed either by one person or by companies or organisations where senior personnel need personal transport on hand at all times. Private chauffeurs may live in accommodatlon provided and have various other duties. Apart from the actual driving, the job will also involve making sure the cars are well maintained and clean. Some chauffeurs have a security role and may also act as bodyguards.

Qualifications and Training

You must be at least 21 years old, with proven driving experience. A UK driving licence, with no endorsements, is essential. Mechanical and/or geographical knowledge may be required, depending on the individual demands of the job. Some of the better-known car manufacturers run their own training schemes; Rolls-Royce, for instance, has its own driving school.

Personal Qualities and Skills

Essential attributes are a calm, unflappable nature when under pressure such as being stuck in heavy traffic when late for an appointment, patience, politeness and the discretion not to repeat confidential conversations which may well be overheard.

Starting Salary

£15,000+. Accommodation may be provided.

info

British Chauffeurs Guild, The Tower (6th Floor), 125 High Street, Colliers Wood, London SW19 2JR; 020 8544 9777; www.britishchauffeursguild.co.uk; e-mail: bcg.London@btconnect.com

The Lady, 39–40 Bedford Street, London WC2E 9ER; 020 7379 4717 (job advertisements); www.lady.co.uk

Local Job Centre Plus and Careers/Connexions centres

Courier

Couriers deliver and collect parcels, generally in larger towns and cities. Around 10,000 couriers work in Central London. Mostly the delivery or collection is in the same city, sometimes in a different one and very occasionally in another country. Most couriers use a motorbike, which they may be required to buy. Couriers carrying packages abroad travel by air.

Qualifications and Training

No formal educational qualifications are necessary. An NVQ level 2 qualification is available. Motorbike couriers must be 17 and hold a clean licence.

Personal Qualities and Skills

Couriers are generally required when speed is important or when the package cannot be entrusted to the post. Reliability is most important, as is the ability to arrive without undue delays. Common sense and initiative are also useful. It is an outdoor job so couriers must be prepared to work in all weathers.

Starting Salary

Some couriers are self-employed, with the firm paying a certain amount per mile, and the messenger being responsible for petrol, insurance and other overheads. Others are employees. Starting salaries vary, but an employed courier can earn between £180 and £350 a week.

info

Local Job Centre Plus and Careers/Connexions Centres

Camelot Training, 1st floor, Green Man Tower, 332 Goswell Road, London EC1V 7LQ; www.couriertraining.com; e-mail: mail@couriertraining.com

Driving examiner

Driving examiners must ensure that candidates are competent to drive without endangering other road users and demonstrate due consideration for other drivers and pedestrians. The examiner directs learner drivers over an approved route and asks them to carry out various exercises. While doing this, the examiner must take notes without distracting the candidate's concentration and must make a fair assessment of the learner's ability.

Qualifications and Training

Driving examiners are required to complete a strict selection process, followed by four weeks' training. They must have detailed knowledge of the *Highway Code* and road and traffic safety problems, some mechanical understanding, have held positions of responsibility and dealt with the public. Driving examiners must be over 25 and have had extensive experience of a variety of different vehicle types. Vacancies are advertised both locally and nationally by the Driving Standards Agency. Selection is dependent upon passing a special driving test and interview. For those who are successful, there are continuous checks by a supervising examiner to ensure the maintenance of a high standard.

Personal Qualities and Skills

Examiners should be fair, sympathetic, friendly, clearly spoken and have a calm, unflappable nature. The ability to work to a strict timetable is important.

Starting Salary

Varies depending on hours worked. Examiners generally have annualised hours contracts and minimum working hours are guaranteed on entry into employment.

info

Driving Standards Agency, Stanley House, 56 Talbot Street, Nottingham NG1 5GU; 0115 901 2500; www.dsa.gov.uk

Local Job Centre Plus and Careers/Connexions Centres

Driving instructor

Driving instructors teach clients how to drive in preparation for all categories of the Driving Standards Agency's theory and practical driving tests. Instructors can also provide post-test training for the Pass Plus scheme as well as prepare clients for advanced driving tests, such as the DIAmond Advanced Motorists test.

The industry is now very much structured to self-employment, with instructors either having their own business or existing as an independent operation within a franchise agreement.

Qualifications and Training

In order to be allowed by law to accept payment for teaching people to drive, car driving instructors must be either registered or licensed by the Registrar of Approved Driving Instructors (ADIs) at the Driving Standards Agency. This requires them to have passed the three-part qualifying test within the space of two years. The ADI exam consists of a written test, a practical driving test and a practical test of the ability to instruct. Training is available from any of the establishments listed in the Official Register of Driving Instructor Training (ORDIT), which is included in the starter pack (see **info** below). ORDIT establishments are regularly required to satisfy the inspection criteria under the voluntary scheme of minimum required standards set up and agreed by the Driver Training Industry and the Driving Standards Agency.

Personal Qualities and Skills

Driving instructors must have a calm and friendly nature, be very alert and quick to react, should be clearly spoken and able to express themselves well. Patience, confidence and tact are also important characteristics, as is the willingness to abide by a professional Code of Practice.

Starting Salary

Typical earnings, after business or franchise fees, will vary widely depending on tuition hours worked and operating costs.

info

Driving Instructors Association, Safety House, Beddington Farm Road, Croydon CR0 4XZ; 020 8665 5151; fax: 020 8665 5565; www.driving.org

Driving Standards Agency, Stanley House, 56 Talbot Street, Nottingham NG1 5GU; 0115 901 2500; fax: 0115 901 2940; www.dsa.gov.uk

Your Road to Becoming an Approved Driving Instructor, AD114 starter pack, including application forms, for £3.00, from DSA

www.driving-instructor-training.co.uk

Local driving schools, Job Centre Plus and Careers/Connexions centres

The Driving Instructor's Handbook (Kogan Page)

Practical Teaching Skills for Driving Instructors (Kogan Page)

Lorry driver

This work ranges from driving conventional flat-bodied lorries that can carry a variety of loads to driving lorries designed for one purpose, such as car and animal transporters and milk tankers. Drivers often take a load from A to B and then carry one back from B to A in the UK or across Europe. As well as driving, lorry drivers may have to help with the loading and unloading of goods. Drivers of potentially dangerous products must know how to handle them safely and certification is required.

Qualifications and Training

There are no formal academic entry requirements for driving work, but you must be able to read maps, handle documents and deal with people, as well as enjoying driving and already possessing a normal full, clean, driving licence. To drive vehicles of 7.5 tonnes you need a class C licence and you cannot normally apply for this until you are aged 21. To drive an articulated vehicle you need a C + E licence, which you cannot normally obtain until you are 25. Skills for Logistics, the Sector Skills Council for the Freight and Logistics Industry, has developed a range of specific qualifications. You can take NVQ level 2 in carrying and delivering goods and in goods vehicle driving. These NVQs are employment based, with some college or off-site training. You can also serve Apprenticeships in goods vehicle driving. The Young Driver Scheme (YDS), operated by Skills for Logistics, allows you to obtain a full C class driving licence at age 18 and a C + E licence at age 21.

For older entrants it is difficult to get your training funded by an employer, so you may have to consider paying for this yourself; it costs more than £2,000.

Personal Qualities and Skills

You must be a good driver with a thorough understanding of road safety, and the patience to tolerate long drives and heavy traffic. You must be happy spending many hours on your own, but also able to work with warehouse employees and customers and remain pleasant and friendly.

Starting Salary

A newly qualified driver earns between £11,000 and £12,000; the pay is less than this while you are on the Young Drivers Scheme. Experienced drivers can earn a lot more than this, especially if they are working antisocial hours.

info

Skills for Logistics: The Sector Skills Council for Freight and Logistics, 14 Warren Yard, Warren Farm Office Village, Milton Keynes MK12 5NW; 01908 313 360; www.skillsforlogistics.org

Local Job Centre Plus offices

The LGV Learner Driver's Guide (Kogan Page)

Professional LGV Driver's Handbook (Kogan Page)

Passenger transport

About 65 per cent of personnel working in passenger transport on the roads are drivers. Many work on routes within one town or city, but some are employed by coach companies taking passengers from one town to another, across the country, or on international journeys. Other staff are employed as engineers, administrators, or managers.

Engineering work includes vehicle maintenance and repair in mechanical work, electrical and electronic systems and body structures, as well as technical research and design. Increasingly, companies are looking for employees with multiple skills or the willingness to undertake training in other occupational areas.

Administration covers route planning, traffic surveys, publicity, fare scales, computer operation, legal work and financial management.

Qualifications and Training

Modern Apprenticeships are available for engineers; some formal qualifications may be required depending on the scheme offered. NVQs are available at levels 1 to 5, which provide a career pathway within the industry. Semi-skilled engineers and engineers from other occupational areas are often recruited and in-service training is provided.

There are Induction and Foundation programmes (five modules) for coach drivers. Passenger-carrying vehicle (PCV) licence driver training is provided by all major companies. This may be supported by NVQs at levels 2 and 3 in road passenger transport. Formal qualifications are not required.

School leavers and graduates are eligible for training in administration and management. In-service training is an integral part of all careers with the major bus and coach companies.

Personal Qualities and Skills

The work of bus drivers means dealing constantly with the general public, and a friendly attitude is important. Tact and good humour are essential, as well as a liking for the elderly and for young people, who form the majority of the bus-travelling public. Drivers need to be willing to work early and late shifts.

For engineering occupations, a sound mechanical ability and aptitude are preferred. A variety of skills are required within administration; information on these occupations can be obtained from individual companies.

Starting Salary

Salaries vary and applicants should enquire of the individual companies. The average for a driver is £14,500.

Local bus and coach companies

GoSkills, Concorde House, Trinity Park, Solihull B37 7UQ; 0121 635 5520; www.goskills.org.uk

Taxi driver

A 'taxi' is a traditional hackney carriage (like the black London taxis). The hackney carriage driver is allowed to 'ply for hire' – drive around the streets looking for passengers – and can be flagged down by a 'fare' (passenger). They may also operate from taxi ranks (known as 'standing for hire') in the streets. A private hire vehicle, on the other hand, has to be booked over the telephone or in person at the office from which it operates. Drivers therefore spend a good proportion of their time waiting around for passengers. Hours for both types of driver are generally long and unsocial (since there is a good deal of evening or night work, as well as weekend and public holiday work). Drivers may be owner-drivers or work for a company.

Qualifications and Training

Taxi drivers must be at least 21 years of age to be granted a licence, although in practice, because of insurance requirements, most are over 25. A valid Group A driving licence and relevant driving experience are also necessary. Hackney carriage drivers are legally bound to take the shortest or quickest route to a passenger's destination. Trainee drivers usually have to pass special tests, known as 'knowledge tests', to prove that they know their way about sufficiently well. These tests are generally oral, the most demanding being the Knowledge of London Test, which is required before drivers may operate in the capital. This usually takes some 18 months to two years to complete. Specialised training schools exist and there are also special training schemes for the disabled and for people who have been in the forces. In London, too, an additional driving test must be passed before a licence is granted.

Personal Qualities and Skills

Driving in traffic demands a calm, unflappable personality, with lots of patience. Drivers also need to have a good memory. In addition, a taxi driver must be 'of good character', as a licence will not be granted to anyone who has committed certain offences.

Starting Salary

Almost all taxi drivers are self-employed and have to pay tax and National Insurance out of their earnings. Owner-drivers generally earn more than drivers employed by a company (who are often on a fixed rate), although they must also finance the repairs and servicing costs incurred by their own vehicles. Average earnings are around £14,000.

Local taxi companies

Licensed Taxi Drivers Association, 9–11 Woodfield Road, London W9 2BA; 020 7286 1046

ECONOMIST

(*see also* Banking and Finance)

Economists study the use, organisation and distribution of the world's resources. The field of investigation is very wide, but may include the study of such topics as the reasons for balance of payments crises, the effects of different forms of taxation, international trade or business economics. Economics is not a precise science; it is only possible to forecast the degrees of probability of a particular economic model having certain results. The Government Economic Services (GES) is the largest employer of professional economists in the UK, with nearly 600 people working in 30 government departments and agencies. Economists also work in industry, teaching and research, banking and stockbroking, journalism, international organisations and independent consultancies.

Their primary task is to give advice on the probable consequences of a course of action: for example, they might advise a company on the effects of a rise in the price of its products. Economists are also concerned with collecting data, preparing reports, and, to an increasing extent, with building complex mathematical models.

Qualifications and Training

A good honours degree in economics, or in one of the specialised branches of the subject, is needed. In addition, many economists take a postgraduate qualification. Some degree courses are mathematically biased, and for these an A

info

Government Economic Service, Economist Group Management Unit, HM Treasury, 1 Horse Guards Road, London SW1A 2HQ; 020 7270 4835/4571/4581/5073; www.ges.gov.uk; e-mail: egmu.int@hm-treasury.gov.uk

HM Treasury, Correspondence & Enquiry Unit, 2/S2, HM Treasury, 1 Horse Guards Road, London SW1A 2HQ; 020 7270 4558; www.hm-treasury.gov.uk/careers

Society of Business Economists, 11 Bay Tree Walk, Watford WD17 4RX; 01923 237 287; www.sbe.co.uk

level pass in maths is essential. For most other courses, GCSEs in maths or English are required and A levels in arts subjects, such as history and modern languages, are useful.

Personal Qualities and Skills

An analytical mind, numeracy and the ability to express oneself clearly, both verbally and in writing, are required.

Starting Salary

£17,000–22,000; the average for experienced staff is £35,000 but some can earn substantially more.

ELECTRICIAN

Electricians work in domestic houses, factories and commercial buildings and on road systems, railways and vehicles. They install, service and repair every kind of electrical system, from wiring to individual pieces of equipment.

Auto electrician

Auto electricians check, repair and replace the electrical/electronic circuitry and components in cars, heavy goods vehicles, buses and other vehicles.

Highway electrician

These electricians install, maintain and replace the electrical and electronic systems that operate street lighting and road traffic management systems. They work from high, mobile platforms.

Installation electrician

Installation electricians install, inspect and test wiring systems in every kind of building. They either strip out old wiring systems and replace them, or work with other members of the construction team on new buildings, installing new wiring systems.

Instrumentation electrician

Instrumentation electricians work mainly in the manufacturing industry, installing and maintaining the electrical and electronic systems that run the manufacturing process, whether this is a conveyor belt to fill bottles of drink, build cars, or pack frozen vegetables. They are involved in measuring how efficiently electrical and electronic operations are working.

Maintenance electrician

Maintenance electricians work mainly in manufacturing, maintaining and testing electrical and electronic equipment.

Panel building electrician

Panel building electricians work from diagrams putting together complex electrical and electronic control panels. An office building could have a central panel that controls heating and air conditioning, and this is an example of the kind of panel that these electricians build.

Repair and rewind electrician

When components in pumps, compressors or transformers go wrong, it is the repair and rewind electrician who analyses what the problem is and either repairs or replaces various components. They work both in industry and in domestic properties, repairing goods such as washing machines and fridges.

Service electrician

The dividing line between repair and servicing is not always distinct. Service engineers check equipment and make minor adjustments, to minimise the risk of things going wrong. These electricians also work in industry and private homes.

Theatre electrician

Away from the world of manufacturing or faulty TV sets, theatre electricians maintain and repair all the systems that operate lighting, sound and other specialist theatrical equipment. They need to be extremely good all-rounders.

Qualifications and Training

To qualify as an electrician you must achieve an electrotechnical NVQ level 3. There are various routes to achieving this, but the most common, provided you are between the ages of 16 and 24, is to do a three to four year apprenticeship. These are mainly employer-based, but include some college work and practical and written assessments. Though it is not always essential, many employers require you to have GCSEs grades A to C in English, maths, technology and a science subject. If you are not eligible for an apprenticeship you can do college-based City & Guilds courses at GNVQ levels 2 and 3.

Electrotechnical NVQ level 3 offers several different pathways, including electrical installation, electrical maintenance, electrical instrumentation and associated equipment, installing highway electrical systems, electrical panel building and electrical machine rewind and repair. A great deal of training takes place on the job.

Recent changes to the Building Regulations have meant that many types of household electrical work must be approved either by a buildings inspector or by an electrician who has acquired an appropriate certificate. Electricians can take part in a short scheme to allow them to self-certify their work.

Personal Qualities and Skills

You must have good practical and technical skills and be able to follow technical drawings and diagrams. You should be reasonably fit, and for some jobs you need to be able to cope with heights or working in confined spaces. You should have good colour vision. You need to be able to work on your own, or as part of a team, and you must have good communication skills, able to talk to people without using a lot of technical jargon.

Starting Salary

Apprentices earn from £11,000 to £15,000 and salaries for qualified electricians range from £16,000 to £19,000. There is a lot of scope for self-employment with this work.

info

Summit Skills, Vega House, Opal Drive, Fox Milne, Milton Keynes MK15 0DF; 01908 303960; www.summitskills.org.uk

www.apprenticeships.org.uk

ENGINEERING

The British engineering industry is a major wealth producer, and almost every other industry depends upon engineering in some way. Engineering provides a challenging career for men and women, with employment offered by industry, universities and colleges, consulting engineers, contractors, local authorities and the armed forces. The Engineering Council gives a simple definition of engineering, saying that it involves 'the application of science and maths to the solving of practical problems and the making of useful things'. The variety of specialisations are covered by over 20 professional institutions. A selection are described below.

Aeronautical engineering

Aeronautical engineering is one of the most technically advanced areas of engineering. It is both exciting and rewarding, involving leading-edge technology, variety, skill and innovation. This diversity means that career opportunities can be found across the entire global aerospace spectrum, from research, design, manufacture and maintenance, through to operation and support. However, the dramatic downturn in the aeronautical industry in 2001 significantly reduced opportunities, and it may be some time before the good employment prospects once offered by the industry return.

Agricultural engineering

The main areas in which agricultural engineers are involved are: design and production of agricultural machinery; planning, design and construction of farm buildings and associated equipment; field engineering – irrigation, drainage and land resource planning and service engineering, involving the sale, servicing, repairing and installation of farm machinery. They are also involved in forestry engineering, amenity and ecological engineering, and precision farming using satellite positioning systems.

Automobile engineering

In the vehicle manufacturing industry engineers may be employed in design, development, production, operations management and maintenance activities. In motor vehicle servicing, the work tends to be at craft level, with some engineers using their technical base to develop into motor vehicle engineering management. Currently, NVQs in Vehicle Mechanical and Electronic Systems Maintenance and Repair are offered at levels 2 and 3.

Biochemical engineering

This involves the application of engineering principles to industrial processing. Biochemical engineers are involved in the research, design, construction and operation of plant used for the processing of biochemicals such as those used in effluent treatment, fermentation and the production of drugs.

Biomedical engineering

Most biomedical engineers are employed in hospitals or by companies manufacturing medical equipment. Their work involves applying engineering techniques and principles to medicine and biology.

Building services engineering

(*see also* Construction)

Building services engineers are concerned with heating and ventilation, refrigeration, lighting, air conditioning, electrical services, internal water supply, waste disposal, fire protection, lifts, and acoustic and communication systems. The work involves the planning and design of engineering systems, and supervision of contracts, working in collaboration with architects, surveyors, structural engineers and builders.

Chemical engineering

Chemical engineers are concerned with large-scale processes, not always in the chemical industry. The term 'process engineering' is often used to describe their work, as they are more interested in the physical factors involved in a process than in the chemical reaction itself. Chemical engineers are employed in the oil, chemical, pharmaceutical, food, brewing and process industries.

Civil engineering

Civil engineering plays an important part in everyday life. Civil engineers devise, plan and manage development in vital areas – the design and construction of state-of-the-art roads, dams, harbours, railroad systems, bridges and airports. Civil engineers also play an important part in the provision of electricity and water supplies, and in managing traffic and transport. Every project is unique and involves the expertise of a team of people who plan, design, build and maintain these essential assets.

Control engineering

This is a multidisciplinary field involving electrical and electronic engineering, maths, computer science, instrument and mechanical engineering. Specialisation in control engineering often follows the study of another branch of engineering.

Electrical and electronic engineering

The technology of electrical engineering deals with heavy current, while electronic engineering deals with light current. Applications of heavy current include electrical machinery of all kinds, generating stations and distribution systems. Light current is used for such products as transistors, microprocessors and telecommunications equipment. The two fields are often interdependent and training is closely related. Electronics is a rapidly developing field and offers excellent opportunities, as do the allied disciplines of computer and software engineering.

Energy engineering

This branch of engineering is concerned with the use, production, distribution, conversion and conservation of energy, with due regard to the environment. Energy engineers are employed across the whole spectrum of industry, as energy management and control are essential elements in containing costs, reducing pollution and addressing environmental concerns. The majority of openings are in major fuel industries (including renewables), consultancy and research.

Fire engineering

This involves the application of engineering principles to the assessment, prevention and inhibition of fire risk within buildings, manufacturing plant and industrial processes. The various stages include the use of mathematical principles in the assessment of fire risk, the application of scientific principles to fire safety practices and the use of management techniques for the inhibition and prevention of the onset and spread of fire.

Fire engineers are employed in the fire services, architectural and building design, project management, insurance assessment, industrial processing, the aircraft industry, environmental health and any area of safety where the possibility of fire or combustion represents a hazard.

Gas engineering

Gas engineering involves specialisation in the use, transmission and distribution of gas (natural or manufactured), or in the production of gas, or in related fields such as exploration.

Instrument engineering

Instrument engineers are concerned with the measurement of pressure, temperature, and so on, designing, installing and maintaining instrument systems. *See also* Control Engineering.

Manufacturing systems engineering

This branch of engineering deals with the skills required to operate new manufacturing systems: computerised production, computer-controlled assembly, robotic systems and flexible manufacturing systems.

Marine engineering

This discipline is related to offshore engineering under the general title of 'maritime engineering', which involves engineering systems and equipment in a maritime environment. Both marine and offshore engineers are involved in design, research, consultancy, survey, manufacture, installation and maintenance activities, the former with vessels of all sizes and types, the latter with offshore platforms, sub-sea installations and under-sea vehicles. Employment opportunities exist within firms offering design and research activities, engine- and shipbuilding firms, classification societies, government bodies, the Merchant Navy and the Royal Navy.

Mechanical engineering

Mechanical engineering is the biggest branch of the engineering industry. It involves the skills of designing, developing, producing, installing and operating machinery and mechanical products of many types. The field is enormous in scope, and most engineers specialise in a particular area. Other branches of engineering, such as electrical and civil engineering, overlap with mechanical engineering to a certain extent.

Mechanical engineers are employed in almost every sector of industry. Some of the largest areas of employment are machine tools, railway engineering, aerospace and the automobile industry.

Mining engineering

In Britain, most mining engineers are employed by companies in mining areas, working for consultants who monitor mining activity and subsidence. They need some knowledge of related disciplines such as mechanical, electrical and civil engineering, and to understand geology and surveying in relation to mining. The majority of openings in metal mining are overseas.

Municipal engineering

Municipal engineering is the application of civil engineering to the public service. Municipal engineers are employed by local authorities or other public bodies. They work on a wide range of projects concerned with public works, and in such fields as traffic engineering, environment, land reclamation, marine works (harbours and jetties), and building and infrastructure maintenance.

Nuclear engineering

Nuclear engineering involves the applications of nuclear energy and associated research and development. The work of designing and constructing nuclear reactors and the management of nuclear power stations through waste management and storage and decommissioning of plant is carried out by nuclear engineers.

Offshore engineering

Offshore engineers are concerned with the construction and operation of drilling platforms and wellheads, and other engineering problems related to the exploitation of offshore oil and gas.

Operations engineering

Operations engineers are concerned with specifying, evaluation, acquisition, commissioning, inspection, maintenance, asset management and disposal of facilities, systems, vehicles and equipment. Career opportunities exist at craft and technician level in the servicing and maintenance of a wide variety of industries, of which transport is the largest. Chartered and incorporated engineers may be engaged in asset or fleet engineering management, requiring multidisciplinary engineering, commercial and legal knowledge and encompassing health and safety, reliability, environmental and economic factors, or in specialised inspection roles. Many technicians build on their practical skills by further career development to aspire to these more senior positions.

Petroleum engineering

Petroleum engineers are concerned with exploration and drilling for oil. They obtain and interpret information – for example, the quantities and quality of oil discovered.

Production engineering

Production engineers develop and improve manufacturing techniques. They are responsible for designing production systems to ensure that products can be manufactured to the specified design, in the right quantities, at the right price and by the required date. Their work overlaps with production management.

Recording engineering

Recording engineering is a specialised branch of electronic/radio engineering. Recording engineers are mainly employed by broadcasting authorities and recording studios, and vacancies are limited. *See also* Broadcasting.

Structural engineering

Structural engineers are concerned with the design and maintenance of the framework and fabric of large structures such as bridges, motorways and office blocks.

Transport engineering

Transportation (or traffic) engineers are concerned with managing the best use of roads and related facilities, and work mainly with road traffic. Transportation planners, who are not necessarily engineers, are concerned with the provision of all types of transport. The current priority is to provide an integrated transport system.

Water engineering

Water engineers mostly work for water companies and river authorities, ensuring the supply of fresh water, and dealing with the reclamation and disposal of water which has been used.

Qualifications and Training

Professional qualifications are important throughout the industry. The Engineering Council sets standards for the registration of Chartered Engineers (CEng), Incorporated Engineers (IEng) and Engineering Technicians (EngTech) in all disciplines. There are five main categories of employment in the engineering industry, as follows:

Chartered Engineers

Chartered engineers are concerned primarily with the progress of technology through innovation, creativity and change. They develop and apply new technologies; promote advanced designs and design methods; introduce new and more efficient production techniques and marketing and construction concepts; and pioneer new engineering services and management methods. They may be involved with the management and direction of high-risk and resource-intensive projects. Professional judgement is a key feature of their role, allied to the assumption of responsibility for the direction of important tasks, including the profitable management of industrial and commercial enterprises. Entry to a career as a chartered engineer is via a four-year MEng degree accredited by one of the engineering institutions, followed by a period of initial professional development combining training and professional experience. Some disciplines specify a Professional Qualification Scheme – details are available from the engineering institutions. For those not holding a MEng, alternative routes are available. These include an honours degree followed by a Matching Section equivalent to one year of further learning and the Mature Candidate Routes offered by most engineering institutions.

Incorporated Engineers

Incorporated engineers (IEng) are specialists in the development and application of today's technology, managing and maintaining applications of current and developing technology at the highest efficiency. With their detailed knowledge and understanding of current engineering applications, they have the skills and know-how to make things happen and often have key operational management roles. They have a detailed understanding of a recognised field of technology, and exercise independent judgement and management in that field. They add substantial value to any organisation where technology is a core activity or supports the business. Entry to a career as an incorporated engineer is via a degree accredited by one of the engineering institutions. Initial professional development, combining training and professional experience, is also required. For those who do not hold a degree, alternative routes include an HND plus a Matching Section equivalent to a further year of learning and the mature candidate routes offered by most engineering institutions.

Engineering Technicians

Engineering technicians (EngTech) are creative and skilled engineering practitioners, often with responsibility for operational engineering and other staff. They apply knowledge and proven techniques and procedures to the solution of practical problems in a wide variety of contexts. They carry a measure of supervisory and technical responsibility. They make a key contribution to a range of functions, including design, development, manufacture, commissioning, operation and maintenance of products, equipment, processes and services. Engineering technicians require a National Certificate/Diploma or equivalent qualification, combined with initial professional development. This may be achieved through an Advanced Modern Apprenticeship or similar training scheme.

Craft Workers

Craft workers specialise in a particular practical skill, such as tool-making or welding. They must be able to interpret engineering drawings, and to work with a minimum of supervision. Entry is normally at 16 or 17, to an apprenticeship lasting three to four years. GCSEs in maths, science and English are an advantage, although not absolutely essential. On-the-job training, together with day or block release, leads to NVQs awarded by the City and Guilds and the Engineering Industry Training Board. With very good exam results, transfer to Technician courses is possible.

Operators

Operators are employed in a wide range of jobs, and make up about a third of the engineering industry's labour force. Their work is often simple and routine, but in some cases they may require some skill or skills similar to those of craft workers.

No specific academic requirements are needed, but aptitude in English and arithmetic and knowledge of metalwork or technical drawing are useful. Operators may work towards NVQs at an appropriate level.

Aeronautical Engineer

There are four main routes to registration as an Incorporated Engineer in aeronautical engineering: the standard route, registration for licence holders, the mature candidate route and the mature servicemen's route. Details are available from the Royal Aeronautical Society (address below).

Personal Qualities and Skills

Graduate and Chartered Engineers need academic ability, an imaginative and problem-solving approach, and social and communication skills. Incorporated Engineers and Engineering Technicians should have reasoning ability, numeracy and the ability to communicate. Craft workers, as well as manual dexterity, need basic mathematical ability, patience and self-discipline. Operators should show reliability, patience and the ability to work with others.

Starting Salary

Graduate engineers start on £18,000 to £27,000. The variation is not between the different types of engineering but rather relates to the size of employer and geographical location. Apprentices start on around £8,000 in their first year, rising in each year of training; on qualifying salaries are around £17,000. Some engineering jobs pay shift and travel allowances too.

info

Bath Institute of Medical Engineering (BIME), Wolfson Centre, Royal United Hospital, Bath BA1 3NG; 01225 824103; www.bime.org.uk

Brunel Institute for Bioengineering (BIB), Brunel University, Uxbridge, Middlesex UB8 3PH; 01895 271 206; www.brunel.ac.uk/depts/bib

Cogent: The Sector Skills Council for the Chemical, Nuclear, Oil, Gas, Petroleum and Polymer Industry, Minerva House, Bruntland Road, Portlethen, Aberdeen AB12 3QL; 01224 787 800; www.cogent.ssc.com

Chartered Institution of Building Services Engineers (CIBSE), Delta House, 222 Balham High Rd, London SW12 9BS; 020 8675 5211; www.cibse.org/

Engineering Council UK (ECUK), 10 Maltravers Street, London WC2R 3ER; 020 7240 7891; www.engc.org.uk

Institute of the Motor Industry, Fanshaws, Brickendon, Hertford SG13 8PQ; 01992 511521; www.motor.org.uk

Institution of Nuclear Engineers, Allan House, 1 Penerley Road, London SE6 2LQ; 020 8698 1500; www.inuce.org.uk/

Institution of Chemical Engineers (IChemE), Davis Building, 165–189 Railway Terrace, Rugby CV21 3HQ; 01788 578214; www.icheme.org

Institution of Civil Engineers (ICE), 1 Great George Street, London SW1P 3AA; 020 7222 7722; www.ice.org.uk

Institution of Electrical Engineers (IEE), Savoy Place, London WC2R 0BL; 020 7240 1871; www.iee.org

Institution of Mechanical Engineers (IMechE), 1 Birdcage Walk, Westminster, London SW1H 9JJ; 020 7222 7899; www.imeche.org.uk

info

Institution of Incorporated Engineers (IIE), Savoy Hill House, Savoy Hill, London WC2R 0BS; 020 7836 3357; www.iie.org.uk

Institution of Nuclear Engineers, Allan House, 1 Penerley Road, London SE6 2LQ; 020 8698 1500; www.inuce.org.uk

Institution of Structural Engineers (IStructE), 11 Upper Belgrave Street, London SW1X 8BH; 020 7235 4535; www.istructe.org.uk

Royal Aeronautical Society (RAES), 4 Hamilton Place, London W1J 7BQ; 020 7670 4300; www.raes.org.uk

SEMTA: The Sector Skills Council for Science, Engineering and Manufacturing Technologies, Head Office, 14 Upton Road, Watford WD18 0JT; 01923 238 441; www.semta.org.uk

Summit Skills, Vega House, Opal Drive, Fox Milne, Milton Keynes MK15 0DF; www.summitskills.org.uk

The Women's Engineering Society (WES), Michael Faraday House, Six Hills Way, Stevenage, Herts SG1 2AY; 01438 765506; www.wes.org.uk

ENVIRONMENT

Occupations in the environment sector are concerned with the protection and preservation of the natural world in which we live.

Energy conservation officer

An energy conservation officer works to improve the energy efficiency of domestic properties, commercial premises and public buildings. This is achieved by applying both practical solutions to energy saving and raising the profile of energy conservation and renewable energy options within an organisation or community. New legislation has meant that all kinds of organisation have to give this issue greater consideration. The major employers in this field are local authorities and organisations such as health trusts and educational institutions. Some large private companies may also employ energy conservation officers.

Qualifications and Training

You need a degree in environmental science, surveying, construction, or business studies to get into this work. Most of the training is on-the-job and there is often the need to do short updating courses, because technology and legislation are changing rapidly in this area.

Personal Qualities and Skills

You must be good at dealing with people and explaining complex information. You need to be confident and persuasive. You have to have a good understanding of energy markets and good organisational skills. You often have to work on your own and suggest solutions to problems.

Starting Salary

Salaries start at around £16,000 to £20,000. This is becoming an area of increasing interest to organisations and this may be reflected in increased salaries in the near future.

info

Association for the Conservation of Energy, Westgate House, Prebend Street, London N1 8PT; 0207 359 8000; www.ukace.org/

Building Research Establishment (BRE), Garston, Watford WD25 9XX; 01923 664000; www.bre.co.uk

Centre for Alternative Technology, Machynlleth, Powys, Wales SY20 9AZ; 01654 705950; www.cat.org.uk

Department for Environment, Food and Rural Affairs (DEFRA), Nobel House, 17 Smith Square, London SW1P 3JR; 08459 33 55 77; www.defra.gov.uk/

Environmental conservation

Environmental conservation covers a range of activities from recycling waste to habitat management. It does not just involve green issues but is about making the best use of scientific knowledge to produce solutions for a sustainable environment. Conservation includes the protection of rural and urban landscapes, plants and animals and countryside recreation. This includes protection and management of rivers, coastal zones and waterways, together with their fisheries and fish stocks.

There are opportunities in a range of organisations from government departments to the voluntary sector. Competition for jobs is high but there can be a lack of applicants with experience, which often needs to be gained through voluntary work. A large proportion of those working for conservation organisations do so on a voluntary, casual or part-time basis. It is estimated that 47,000 paid employees work in this sector alongside 200,000 volunteers. The majority of those in permanent jobs have higher education qualifications. Many of the permanent jobs are with government agencies, which include the following:

The Countryside Agency is the statutory body working for people and places in rural England. It aims to conserve and enhance the countryside, to promote social equity and economic opportunity for the people who live there, and to help everyone, wherever they live, to enjoy this national asset. This is achieved by leading via research and advice, influencing others, especially central and local government, and by demonstrating ways forward through practical projects.

English Nature, the statutory adviser to government on nature conservation in England, promotes the conservation of wildlife and natural features. Its work includes the selection, establishment and management of national nature reserves and marine nature reserves, the identification and provision of advice and information about nature conservation and the support and conduct of relevant research. **The Countryside Council for Wales** and **Scottish Natural Heritage** fulfil similar roles in those countries.

The Department of the Environment, Food and Rural Affairs (DEFRA) supervises and advises upon land reclamation and coastline protection schemes carried out by local authorities. It is also involved with national parks projects and the restoration of derelict sites.

The Natural Environment Research Council involves itself in a broad range of activities concerned with conservation (mainly involving scientists), including geological surveys, studies of the ocean, terrestrial ecology and the British Antarctic Survey, which studies atmospheric, earth and life sciences.

In addition, conservation is carried out by a large number of voluntary societies, such as the Councils for the Protection of Rural England, Wales and Scotland, the Commons Open Spaces Trust, British Trust for Conservation Volunteers and the Wildlife Trusts Partnership. Such organisations have a few full-time posts, mainly confined to administrative staff.

The National Trust is the largest single private landowner in the country. It is concerned with the conservation of places of natural beauty and historic buildings, employing land agents and various specialist staff to care for such sites and to supervise the visiting public. The Royal Society for the Protection of Birds has its own protected reserves and employs nature wardens, researchers and surveyors in reserve management, although such posts are relatively few.

Qualifications and Training

Qualifications vary, as there are many different jobs. Conservation officers and science specialists need relevant degrees or equivalent; much of the training is done on the job with the opportunity to gain related NVQs at levels 1–4 in a range of specialisms, including landscapes and ecosystems, maintaining and conserving rivers, coasts and waterways and environmental management.

Personal Qualities and Skills

Conservationists must show dedication in their chosen field and be prepared to work as part of a team.

Starting Salary

Salaries vary but are in the region of £13,000 for Assistant Ecology and Conservation Officers; scientists and engineers can earn more.

info

Lantra Connect, Lantra House, Stoneleigh, Kenilworth, Warwickshire CV8 2LG; 0845 707 8007 (Lantra Connect – Helpline); www.lantra.co.uk; e-mail: connect@lantra.co.uk

Countryside Agency, John Dower House, Crescent Place, Cheltenham GL50 3RA; 01242 531381; www.countryside.gov.uk; e-mail: info@countryside.gov.uk

Countryside Council for Wales, Maes-y-Ffynnon, Penrhargarnedd, Bangor, Gwynedd LL57 2DW; 0845 1306229; www.ccw.gov.uk

English Nature, Northminster House, Peterborough PE1 1UA; 01733 455000; www.english-nature.org.uk; e-mail: enquiries@english-nature.org.uk

National Trust, 36 Queen Anne's Gate, London SW1H 9AS; 0870 609 5380; fax: 020 7222 5097; www.nationaltrust.org.uk; e-mail: enquiries@ntrust.org.uk

Natural Environment Research Council, Polaris House, North Star Avenue, Swindon SN2 1EU; 01793 411500; www.nerc.ac.uk

Royal Society for the Protection of Birds, The Lodge, Sandy, Bedfordshire SG19 2DL; 01767 680551; www.rspb.org.uk

Scottish Natural Heritage, 12 Hope Terrace, Edinburgh EH9 2AS; 0131 447 4784; www.snh.org.uk

Environment Agency, www.environment-agency.gov.uk

BTCV, Conservation Centre, 163 Balby Road, Doncaster, South Yorkshire DN4 ORH; 01302 572 244; www.btcv.org

Wildlife Trusts Partnership; www.wildlifetrusts.org

ENVIRONMENTAL HEALTH

Environmental Health workers' aim is to protect the public from environmental health risks.

Environmental health officer

Environmental health officers are enforcers, educators and advisers, and are employed in both the public and private sectors. Their responsibilities include pollution control, including noise control, environmental protection, the inspection of food and food premises, health and safety in workplaces and in the leisure industry, and the control of housing standards, particularly in the private rented sector. Much of their time is spent out of the office, dealing with the public and visiting premises of all types.

Qualifications and Training

Training in England, Wales and Northern Ireland involves a four-year sandwich course leading to a degree in environmental health, or a two-year postgraduate sandwich course, for those with a good honours degree in a natural science. The course must be accredited by the Chartered Institution of Environmental Health (CIEH). Degree entry qualifications vary between institutions.

In Scotland, candidates for the professional qualification (Diploma in Environmental Health, awarded by REHIS) must hold a BSc honours degree in environmental health from the University of Strathclyde or Edinburgh. Currently only the University of Strathclyde offers a course for new entrants. Applicants for this four-year degree course need four H grade passes in maths, chemistry, biology or physics and one other subject. Details of current requirements should be checked with the university as there can be flexibility for mature students. Before being awarded the diploma, candidates must have undergone a minimum of 48 weeks' training with a local authority and have passed professional exams.

Personal Qualities and Skills

You have to be a very good communicator, firm and assertive, when carrying out inspections, but also encouraging and helpful, trying to work towards constructive solutions to problems. You have to be well organised, thorough and observant and able to work on your own as well as being part of a team.

Starting Salary

On qualifying, salaries range from £20,000 to £30,000. There is a shortage of employees in this work at present.

info

Chartered Institute of Environmental Health, Chadwick Court, 15 Hatfields, London SE1 8DJ; 020 7928 6006; www.cieh.org.uk; e-mail: education@cieh.org

Royal Environmental Health Institute of Scotland, 3 Manor Place, Edinburgh EH3 7DH; 0131 225 5444; www.rehis.org; e-mail: rehis@rehis.org.uk

Health and Safety Adviser

see Health and Safety Adviser

Pest controller

Pest controllers control not only mice, rats, cockroaches and ants that may be damaging foodstuffs in a factory, hotel, or private home, but also rabbits, moles, birds and foxes that attack farmers' crops. They work for local authorities and private firms. Service staff are employed to lay traps and set poison. There are also opportunities for graduates in research and management.

Qualifications and Training

Qualifications in pest control are usually preferred, although at assistant level full training is provided on the job, including day or block release to achieve a recognised qualification, such as British Pest Control Association courses. The British Pest Control Association and the Royal Society for the Promotion of Health have merged their basic pest control qualification – BPC Diploma Part 1 and RSPH Certificate in Pest Control. The examination was assessed and piloted between Autumn 2003 and Spring 2004. As part of this partnership other BPCA examinations, including the advanced level certificate (BPC Diploma Part 2), the fumigation certification scheme and the newly introduced Certificate for Surveyors – Pest Control (CSPC) will ultimately be brought under the joint BPCA/RSPH umbrella.

Personal Qualities and Skills

This is not a job for the squeamish and the work demands a mature outlook, an ability to get on with many kinds of people, to work in varying conditions and to work alone. The ability to drive is important.

Starting Salary

Salaries range from £9,000; to £19,000+ for graduates.

info

British Pest Control Association, Ground Floor, Gleneagles House, Vernongate, Derby DE1 1UP; 01332 294288; www.bpca.org.uk

Local Government Careers; www.lgcareers.com

Royal Society for the Promotion of Health, 38A St. George's Drive, London SW1V 4BH; 020 7630 0121; www.rsph.org; e-mail: rshealth@rshealth.org.uk

EVENTS ORGANISATION

Many organisations and businesses hold both internal and public events. The role of conference and events organisers is one of project management, ensuring that the event runs smoothly and efficiently.

Conference organiser

In many companies, conference organisation is combined with other promotional or administrative duties. Large organisations and industrial concerns may have their own conference departments with staff responsible for coordinating the necessary arrangements for regular sales conferences, staff conferences, product launches and special events. These will employ staff specialising in the organisation of meetings and events. Other firms employ professional conference organisers.

Conference organisers select and book the most suitable venue, organise the invitations and where necessary, accommodation for participants. They also deal with the relevant paperwork, catering and reception facilities, any specialist equipment necessary (such as video, microphones, projectors and closed-circuit television), media coverage and a host of minor details. Some firms of professional organisers have a small core staff and employ temporary freelancers.

Conference centres and hotels specialising in conference facilities have their own staff who are responsible for arrangements for conferences already booked and for advertising and encouraging further bookings.

Party/wedding organiser

Some private individuals, families or groups of friends, with special events like weddings, large parties, or other special occasions to plan, turn to professional organisers to coordinate and arrange everything. In many ways the skills are similar to those of a conference organiser, but you may be working to strict budgetary limits and you have to be sensitive and helpful when dealing with people who want occasions to be extra special. There are no specific qualifications or training for this work, but a real flair for organising, dealing with people and working well under pressure are all important. This is a recent career opening and most people who do it are self-employed, charging for individual events.

Qualifications and Training

There are no formal educational requirements, but NVQs are available. Useful experience could include sales and marketing, knowledge of hotel and venue operations, and language skills, as well as secretarial duties. Computer literacy is important.

Personal Qualities and Skills

A flair for organisation and forward planning is needed, as are tact, discretion and the ability to talk to all kinds of people and anticipate their various demands. In addition, some conference organisers should be prepared to work abroad.

Starting Salary

Large firms offer £15,000–17,000. Salaries for freelancers vary according to the type and amount of work undertaken.

info

Association for Conferences and Events, ACE International, Riverside House, High Street, Huntingdon, Cambridgeshire PE18 6SG; 01480 457595; www.marktex.co.uk/ace; e-mail: ace@martex.co.uk

How to Organise Effective Conferences and Meetings (Kogan Page)

Events organiser

Events organisers generally work for a place visited by the public such as a national park or a stately home. They may also be appointed on a temporary basis to cover a festival lasting one or two weeks.

They are responsible for organising long-standing events such as a series of waymarked walks, and activities such as a music festival or summer holiday entertainment for children. If appropriate, the organiser will be in contact with the local education department to encourage school visits. Those working for a large concern will coordinate their work with other members of staff such as information and press officers.

Qualifications and Training

Events organisers do not necessarily need formal qualifications but a background in marketing and experience at promoting events and campaigns are useful. A knowledge of simple financial planning is looked for, plus experience in preparing material for print. The ability to drive is essential.

Personal Qualities and Skills

Events officers should be energetic, sociable and adaptable, able to talk to a variety of people, and have the ability to think up new ideas and organisational skills.

Starting Salary

£12,500+.

info

Association for Conferences and Events, ACE International, Riverside House, High Street, Huntingdon, Cambridgeshire PE18 6SG; 01480 457595; www.martex.co.uk/ace; e-mail: ace@martex.co.uk

Jobs are advertised in the Monday edition of the *Guardian*; www.jobs.guardian.co.uk

Exhibition organiser

Exhibition organisers usually work for specialist companies. They plan and coordinate exhibitions, negotiating with all those concerned – managers of the exhibition, exhibitors, stand suppliers, designers and caterers. With overseas exhibitions, government departments are often involved.

Qualifications and Training

Training is usually on the job, and graduates or those with HNDs in business or marketing are preferred. CAM or Institute of Marketing qualifications are also useful. Several universities and colleges offer degree or HNDs courses in events management. NVQs at levels 2–4 are available but have no industry recognition so there has been little take-up.

Personal Qualities and Skills

Applicants should be good at dealing with people and at administration, with the ability to keep a large amount of information at their fingertips. Physical and mental stamina is essential.

Starting Salary

£12,000–16,000.

info

Association of Exhibition Organisers, 113 High Street, Berkhamsted, Hertfordshire HP4 2DJ; 01442 873331; fax: 01442 875551; www.aeo.org.uk; e-mail: info@aeo.org.uk

Chartered Institute of Marketing, Moor Hall, Cookham, Maidenhead, Berkshire SL6 9QH; 01628 427500; www.cim.co.uk

FARMING

(*see also* Agriculture)

In recent years, economic conditions and animal health crises have had significant effects on jobs in this sector. Incomes have fallen and opportunities become more limited. There is increasing mechanisation and a tendency towards greater specialisation and larger farms. Mixed farms are now in a minority, and most farmers choose to specialise in one or two areas of production. The most common of these are milk, cereals, poultry, sheep, pigs or beef. In order to survive, many farmers have to consider other activities such as leisure and recreation, niche markets, or crops for energy and raw materials. To make a farm profitable, the modern farmer needs a thorough working knowledge of the type of farming to be undertaken, an understanding of general agricultural science, and years of practical experience as well as an aptitude for farming and farm management.

Opportunities are few, land and equipment are expensive. Land prices have made the chances of a beginner becoming a tenant farmer almost impossible. Most of those who go into farming come from farming families.

Farm manager

Farm managers are employed by the landowner and are responsible for all aspects of the day-to-day working of the farm. They must plan ahead, organise the staff and work schedules, decide which crops to plant or which animals to rear, and keep a check on buildings and machinery. In addition, they must deal with the office work and accounts.

Farm worker

Specialisation and large-scale farming have led to a fall in demand for the farm worker who can turn his or her hand to anything. There is now a need for highly skilled personnel, and new entrants should aim at becoming skilled in a special area such as animal husbandry, mechanics or food, flower or fruit production.

Qualifications and Training

There is a range of qualifications related to farming, including degrees in agriculture or agricultural science, and National Diplomas in general agriculture. Various NVQ awards are available at different levels, such as crop and livestock production, levels 1, 2 and 3.

Personal Qualities and Skills

Being prepared to work outside in all conditions and to accept antisocial hours at very busy times of year is essential. Farm managers have to be able to work alone, but also to supervise other employees, have good financial and business sense and be practical and resourceful.

Starting Salary

Salaries in the agricultural industry are set by the Agricultural Wages Board, which has recently introduced a six-tier grading system for pay. Basic trainees get £5.05 an hour, standard workers get £5.58 an hour, lead workers get £5.91 an hour, craft workers get £6.58 an hour, supervisors get £6.98 an hour, and farm managers get £7.53 an hour. Many jobs also provide subsidised accommodation.

info

Lantra Connect, Lantra House, Stoneleigh Park, Kenilworth, Warwickshire CV8 2LG; 0845 707 8007 (Lantra Connect – Helpline); www.lantra.co.uk; e-mail: connect@lantra.co.uk

Royal Agricultural Society of England, National Agricultural Centre, Stoneleigh Park, Warwickshire CV8 2LZ; 02476 696969; www.rase.org.uk

Department for Environment, Food and Rural Affairs, general enquiries: Library Enquiry Desk, DEFRA, Room 320, Nobel House, 17 Smith Square, London SW1P 3JR; 08459 33 55 77; www.defra.gov.uk

Agricultural Wages Board, Nobel House, 17 Smith Square, London SW1P 3JR; Agricultural Wages Helpline: 0845 0000134; www.defra.gov.uk/farm/agwages/agwages.htm

FASHION

(*see also* Clothing Industry)

Clothing is one of the UK's largest manufacturing industries and employs over 145,000 individuals. The fashion industry covers all aspects of clothing and accessories for men, women and children, and falls into three main sectors: *haute couture* houses, where original model garments are made for individual customers; wholesale *couture*, where trends set by the *haute couture* houses are closely followed, and limited numbers of model garments in stock sizes are made for retail; and wholesale manufacture, which occupies the largest sector of the fashion industry. Here, the latest trends are adapted to styles that are attractive to the main market, and mass produced at acceptable prices.

Designer

Designers do more than produce stylish sketches. Their work will, depending on the size and organisation of the particular establishment, include a wide variety of tasks. The work of the *haute couture* designer is both highly creative and intricate. Unfortunately, there is little scope for young designers or assistants as many houses are designer owned; they are nevertheless an excellent training ground for future designers willing to work as sketchers, stylists, fitters, hands etc. In wholesale couture, designers produce original garments, but they generally follow the instructions of an employer as far as style and cost are concerned.

The wholesale manufacture designer must be able to predict future trends, combine this with the firm's own 'brand image', match it to available fabrics and produce a garment that can be produced economically and will appeal to its particular section of the market. When sketches have been drawn, it is necessary to produce working drawings and translate these into flat patterns, so sample garments can be made to show to retail buyers and garment costs in fabric and manufacturing time estimated.

Qualifications and Training

While it is possible to become a designer without a degree or HND, this is now rather difficult. Preferred subjects include fashion, textiles, knitwear, graphic design and art and design. You need to have built up a good portfolio of your work when you start applying for jobs. There is very little formal training, except in areas like computer aided design (CAD) and marketing.

Personal Qualities and Skills

As well as an interest in fashion you have to have an eye for colour and a feel for fabrics. You must be able to work under pressure, as part of a busy team. Skill in drawing either manually or with CAD is important. You have to develop market awareness and have the confidence to promote your own work.

Starting Salary

Salaries start at around £14,000 to £18,000 – often more in London – and the majority of openings are London based. It is quite common to be self-employed doing this work and you can earn £30,000 to £50,000 if you are successful.

The Chartered Society of Designers (CSD), 5 Bermondsey Exchange, 179–181 Bermondsey Street, London SE1 3UW; 020 7357 8088; www.csd.org.uk

Crafts Council, 44a Pentonville Road, Islington, London N1 9BY; 020 7278 7700; www.craftscouncil.org.uk

The Design Council, 34 Bow Street, London WC2E 7DL; 020 7420 5200; www.design-council.org.uk

Skillfast UK: The Sector Skills Council for Apparel, Footwear, Textiles and Related Businesses, Richmond House, Lawnswood Business Park, Redvers Close, Leeds LS16 6RD; 0113 2399 600; www.skillfast-uk.org

Dressmaker

Opportunities for dressmakers occur in *couture* houses which make specially designed costumes for a particular collection or customer, in wholesale fashion houses making mass-produced garments, and in theatres both making and adapting costumes. Dressmakers may also be employed by large stores to carry out alterations, or they may be self-employed making clothes either from home or from a workshop. Teachers of dressmaking are employed in schools, colleges and by adult education centres.

Qualifications and Training

No formal qualifications are necessary; but City and Guilds qualifications and NVQs are available. Some degrees and HNDs in clothing design or fashion have a dressmaking option.

Personal Qualities and Skills

Dressmakers need to combine artistic and practical skills with an ability to follow instructions and to recognise problems as they arise and make the necessary adaptations. They may have to deal with temperamental designers and their customers.

Starting Salary

Dependent on experience, practical ability and specialisations. Trainees can earn £8,000–10,000. Experienced dressmakers can earn up to £50,000 in London.

info

Skillfast UK: The Sector Skills Council for Apparel, Footwear, Textiles and Related Businesses, Richmond House, Lawnswood Business Park, Redvers Close, Leeds LS16 6RD; 0113 2399 600; www.skillfast-uk.org

Local Job Centre Plus and Connexions/Careers Centres

Leather production

Leather is produced from skins and hides to make shoes, bags, gloves, clothes, upholstery and saddlery. Modern leather production is based on up-to-date science (particularly chemistry) and technology with a responsible regard for environmental factors. There is a worldwide shortage of well-qualified leather technologists.

Qualifications and Training

Vocational qualifications are available for operatives and craftspeople through part-time, full-time and open-learning courses. Technicians require a good general education and GCSEs should include maths, science and English. Recognised qualifications include NVQs in leather production, BSc in leather technology and MSc in leather technology. Entry to a specific course is dependent on the entry requirements of the institution.

Personal Qualities and Skills

Operatives and craftspeople must be physically fit and possess stamina. Technologists must have a practical, responsible approach to their work and be prepared to travel abroad if required.

Starting Salary

The basic salary for operatives is around £140 a week and increases through piecework or incentive bonus to between £250 and £400. A leather technologist could expect an initial annual salary of approximately £16,000.

British School of Leather Technology, University College Northampton, Moulton Park, Northampton NN2 7AL; 01604 735500; fax: 01604 711183; www.northampton.ac.uk/prospective_schools_leather_intro.php; e-mail: the Admissions Tutor: gordon.paul@northampton.ac.uk

Milliner

Individual 'model' hats are designed by a milliner and made up by workers in a small retail workroom or factory attached to a boutique or fashion house. Hats for the wholesale trade are mass produced by machine, though some may be hand finished. The designs used are bought from model milliners and passed on to copyists, who work out how the hat can be adapted to machine production.

Qualifications and Training

Training as a junior in a retail workroom or factory may be supplemented by evening classes. Academic qualifications are not necessary, except for designing millinery, when a full fashion training is required. Some fashion courses include modules on hat making.

Personal Qualities and Skills

Making hats in a retail millinery workroom needs manual skill and patience – a hat may take up to three days to complete. Senior posts in wholesale production require an understanding of technology. Designers and copyists should have fashion sense and artistic creativity.

Starting Salary

Salaries start at between £8,500 and £11,500, and rise to £12,000 to £17,000 with experience. If you become well known and have famous clients, you may earn a salary that exceeds these figures, but there are only a few such opportunities.

info

British Hat Guild, PO Box 48664, London NW8 6WS; 07932 678003; www.britishhatguild.co.uk

Skillfast UK: The Sector Skills Council for Apparel, Footwear, Textiles and Related Businesses, Richmond House, Lawnswood Business Park, Redvers Close, Leeds LS16 6RD; 0113 2399 600; www.skillfast-uk.org

Model

Models work as 'live' or photographic models, generally showing clothes or accessories. Photographic and advertising models rely on an agent to get them work and handle the fees. Competition is intense and very few models get to the top of the profession.

Fashion models are employed full-time by couturiers, wholesalers or fashion stores as 'live' models. They have the garments draped and pinned on them during the design stages, and show them to the public. Live models must be tall, at least 5 ft 10 in (1.75 m). Photographic modelling involves posing in garments chosen to be illustrated in magazines, newspapers, catalogues or on advertising posters. This work is often out of season for the type of garments being modelled and some of the work is done abroad. Expenses include the provision of accessories, a good basic wardrobe and hairdressing.

Qualifications and Training

Private model schools run training courses for live and photographic modelling. Reputable schools will only take entrants whom they think will succeed, and will introduce them to agencies at the end of the training period. The London College of Fashion, a non-commercial college, offers a one-year full-time course leading to a certificate in fashion modelling. Students should have three GCSEs grades A–C or equivalent.

Personal Qualities and Skills

A model must be able to work hard, be punctual and reliable, get on well with people, and have a great deal of common sense. Competition is intense and only those who can interpret what the stylist and photographer want will get to the top. A female model should be at least 1.72 m (5 ft 8 in) tall and have body statistics of about 86–61–86 cm (34–24–34 in). A male model should be at least 1.83 m (6 ft) tall. Models should have clear skin, good hands, nails and teeth, healthy hair and attractive features.

Starting Salary

Salaries vary from £50 a day to £500+ for top models. Agencies can charge fees of 20 per cent.

info

Association of Model Agents, 122 Brompton Road, London SW3 1JD; 020 7584 6466 (send sae for information)

London College of Fashion, 20 John Princes Street, London W1M 0BJ; 020 7514 7400; www.input.demon.co.uk/careers-modelling.html

Alba Model Information, 31 The High Street, Durrington, Salisbury, Wiltshire SP4 8AE; 0871 717 7170 (calls from a UK landline cost 10p per minute); www.albamodel.info; www.albamodelinformation.com

FILM PRODUCTION

Opportunities to work in film production arise in television, film companies and advertising. Most people who work in this area are self-employed freelancers. Film production involves both studio and location work. Jobs within film production are much sought after, vacancies are few and competition is consequently fierce. Individuals who are serious about working in this area will need to develop personal marketing skills in addition to their creative craft skills.

Animation

Animation involves the design, creation and operation of animated production and effects. Much of the work is done using computer animation techniques, although there are still opportunities for traditional 'cell' animation.

Announcers

Announcers work to detailed and carefully timed scripts, communicating information to the viewer from a soundproof 'behind the scenes' office. They sometimes write or adapt their own material and need to be able to work on their own.

Archivists/librarians

(*see also* Archivist)

Archivists and librarians collect, collate, preserve and make available collections of recorded visual, sound, written and other materials for use by various productions. Archives are valuable business resources, and some archivists are now involved in selling and marketing materials.

New York Film Academy

The New York Film Academy is one of the most innovative and dynamic film schools in the world. Our programs are designed on the philosophy of "learning by doing." Every curriculum in every program stems from that belief. Our programs and workshops are the most intense, hands-on courses you can find. To support our philosophy and our curricula, we maintain an unparalleled faculty and one of the largest film school equipment inventories in the world.

Since our inception in 1992, the Film Academy has grown from offering short-term filmmaking and film production workshops to presenting students with an array of options for courses and programs ranging from one-week to one or two years in not only filmmaking, but screenwriting, 3D animation, acting, editing and new digital video technologies. The New York Film Academy is not simply a film and acting school, it is a community of artists and students who are redefining what a film school and acting school can be.

Art and Design

(*see also* Art and Design)

The art and design function is to create a visual effect to meet the needs of the production, creating manual or computer-generated graphics.

Camerawork

Workers in this area operate and assist with still, film and video cameras to record images as directed, using different techniques.

Costume/wardrobe

The wardrobe department interprets the production requirements in terms of costumes and accessories to ensure historical accuracy and an accurate portrayal of the style and ethos of the period.

Direction

The director is responsible for achieving the creative, visual and auditory effect of a production and, equally importantly, motivating a team.

Engineering

Engineers provide a design, maintenance and installation service to the production site and equipment. Research specialists are usually employed by the equipment manufacturers or design consultancies.

Film, video and audio tape editing

Raw tape or film is shaped to interpret the requirements of the director, either by physical cutting (film) or by selecting sequences and re-recording onto a master tape using sophisticated computer equipment.

IT specialists

IT specialists support many aspects of broadcasting, film and video, either within the companies or as consultants, providing and maintaining relevant systems and software.

Journalists

(*see also* Journalism)

Journalists generate and report on local, national or international stories, and research relevant background information. Bi-media (radio and television) contracts are increasing. Some journalists present their own work.

Laboratory

Lab technicians develop and process film, duplicate and check video tapes, ensuring high technical quality.

Lighting

Lighting specialists ensure that the stage or set is correctly lit to meet the needs of the production.

Make-up and hairdressing

(*see also* Beauty *and* Hair)

Make-up and hairdressing professionals interpret the requirements of the production and research to ensure accurate representation of the historical or design concept. They maintain a continuity of approach throughout the production in studio or on location.

Management

Management directs and coordinates the different elements of the industry to ensure their efficient function – ranging from commissioning a production to negotiating international rights. Specialists work in a full range of business areas.

Marketing and sales

Marketing and sales staff work in an international marketplace to raise revenue for broadcasters or film makers. Airtime is sold, sponsorship and co-production rights are negotiated and spin-off products, such as books, toys and videos, are developed.

Modelmaker

see Modelmaker

Producers

Producers perform a variety of management and operational roles to bring together the many elements of a production, either in a studio or on location. Often responsible both for the initial concept and raising the essential finance, they are the team leaders.

Production assistants

Production assistants provide high-quality administrative and secretarial support to the producer and director at every stage of production, coordinating all activities and preparing schedules and scripts.

Production managers

Production managers organise all essential support facilities for the team, from accommodation and transport to on-set catering. They will also roster crews and arrange payments.

Production operatives

Production operatives perform the operational duties of the production such as vision mixing and autocue operations.

Researchers

Researchers support the producer, helping to turn ideas into reality – providing and following up ideas, contacting and interviewing people, acquiring relevant factual material, and writing briefings for presenters.

Runners/gofers

This job is the traditional entry-level job for the industry. Bright, highly motivated – often highly qualified – people act as general assistants, taking messages, making deliveries, being indispensable, and learning the basics of the commercial business.

Setcraft/props

People working in this area construct the scenery, sets and backdrops to meet the production brief, reflecting both historical accuracy and required design and style. They also maintain sets during a production, and operate any mechanical features as directed. Props (hired or made) are used to dress the set.

Sound

Sound craftspeople interpret the requirements of a production in terms of sound collection. During post-production they may be involved in recording, editing and dubbing, using a range of sophisticated equipment.

Special effects

Special effects designers create and operate effects for a production, within technical limitations and budget, and operate the necessary machines.

Support staff

Many people working in film, video, television and radio fulfil essential support roles, including administration, catering, driving and cleaning.

Transmission

Technicians and engineers work to exhibit the production in a high-quality form, which can involve projecting images or operating transmission equipment linking electronic signals from the studios to a transmitter.

Writers

(*see also* Writer)

Writers work to produce or edit scripts for a variety of radio, television, video or film productions.

Qualifications and Training

New-entrant training is offered by Film and Television Freelance Training (FT2); competition for places is fierce. Their new entrant technical training programme covers art department assistant, props assistant, camera assistant, grips, assistant editor, sound assistant, production/continuity assistant and make-up/hair assistant. They also offer a set crafts apprenticeship training scheme for fibrous plasterers, carpenters and painters.

Skillset, the National Training Organisation for Broadcast, Film, Video and Multimedia, offers NVQs level 2–4 in areas such as camera, costume, editing, production, make-up and hair. These are available to those employed in the industry.

The National Film and Television School offers a two-year MA in film and television in 10 professional disciplines: directing (animation, documentary or fiction), screenwriting, producing, cinematography, screen design, editing, screen sound and screen music. Students specialise in one of these. NFTS courses are not for complete beginners and although many of the applicants for the 60 places available are graduates, relevant knowledge and practical experience are essential and treated as equivalent to academic study. Other institutions offering film-related courses can be found on the UCAS website.

Personal Qualities and Skills

In film work it is important to combine artistic ability with technical expertise, to pay attention to detail, to have patience, good powers of concentration and an interest in colour and design. An even-tempered, logical and visually imaginative approach is necessary. It is important to keep in touch with what is happening in the industry, and to be able to create a network of friends and contacts. Absolute reliability is essential, especially at the start of a career.

Starting Salary

Film involves so many professions that the range of starting salaries is very wide. As a rough guide, jobs in design, editing, production and sound offer starting salaries of between £10,000 and £17,000. Many people work freelance on an hourly rate of between £8 and £20.

info

Association of Motion Picture Sound, 28 Knox Street, London W1H 1FS; 020 7723 6727; www.amps.net

BKSTS (British Kinematic, Sound and Television Society), The Moving Image Society, Pinewood Studios, Iver Heath, Bucks SL0 0NH; 01753 656656; www.bksts.com/

British Film Institute (BFI), 21 Stephen Street, London W1T 1LN; 020 7255 1444; www.bfi.org.uk

Broadcasting Entertainment Cinematographic and Theatre Union (BECTU), 373–377 Clapham Road, London SW9 9BT; 020 7346 0900; www.bectu.org.uk

The National Film and Television School, Beaconsfield Studios, Station Road, Beaconsfield, Bucks HP9 1LG; 01494 731425; www.nftsfilm-tv.ac.uk

Skillset (Sector Skills Council for the Audio Visual Industries), Prospect House, 80–110 New Oxford Street, London WC1A 1HB; 020 7520 5757; www.skillset.org

Careers and Jobs in the Media (Kogan Page)

FIRE SERVICE

Firefighters save and rescue life and property in emergencies. Fighting fires is only one aspect of their work; other emergencies they deal with are tanker spillages, car, train and aeroplane crashes, flooding, building collapse, and explosions where people and animals may have to be rescued. Some firefighters specialise in particular areas such as training or communications. The Fire Service also promotes fire safety through education programmes, and advice on fire protection and prevention for existing properties and new buildings. In addition it enforces legal regulations to reduce risks of injury by fire, such as the provision of secure escape routes.

The Fire Service is administered by local authorities in the UK. Recruitment is undertaken by each local brigade which is responsible for its own recruitment procedures. The Ministry of Defence, Army, Royal Air Force, Royal Navy and the British Airports Authority all have their own brigades.

Qualifications and Training

No formal qualifications are necessary, but GCSEs in maths, English and science are useful. You must be aged 18 or over to train as a firefighter and you must pass a rigorous medical, including eyesight and hearing tests. You also have to pass a physical fitness test, and individual fire brigades set a range of aptitude tests. The training is on-the-job, with frequent courses on new risks, better procedures, etc.

Personal Qualities and Skills

As a firefighter you have to be calm and courageous, prepared to go into dangerous situations, but sensible enough to tackle things calmly. You must be good at reassuring frightened or injured people and you must be good at working as part of a team. You may also be involved in teaching about fire prevention and safety, so you must enjoy dealing with people.

info

The Chief Fire Officers Association, 10–11 Pebble Close, Amington, Tamworth B77 4RD; 01827 302 300; www.cfoa.org.uk/

Fire Brigades Union (FBU), Bradley House, 68 Coombe Road, Kingston upon Thames, Surrey KT2 7AE; 020 8541 1765; www.fbu.org.uk/

Fire Service College, Moreton in Marsh, Gloucestershire GL56 0RH; 01608 650831; www.fireservicecollege.ac.uk/

Institution of Fire Engineers (IFE), London Road, Moreton in Marsh, Gloucestershire GL56 0RH; 01608 812 580; www.ife.org.uk/

The London Fire & Emergency Planning Authority (LFEPA), 8 Albert Embankment, London SE1 7SD; 020 7587 2000; www.london-fire.gov.uk/lfepa/lfepa.asp

How to Pass the Firefighter Selection Process (Kogan Page)

Starting Salary

Salaries start at around £19,000 and you get £25,000 when you complete your training. In London you get an extra £4,500. Depending on the hours you work, you will also get shift allowances of up to 20 per cent.

FISH FARMER

In Britain around 500 fish farms produce fish, mainly rainbow trout and Atlantic salmon, for consumption and sport. Pacific oysters, mussels and scallops are also farmed. This is a growing activity and although most farms are owner-run, there are opportunities for farm managers and workers. Scientists also work in the industry, testing new methods for improving conditions, stocks and disease control. Bailiffs are employed to look after the general welfare of the fish from hatchery to harvesting. As more food manufacturers move into fish farming, there is a need for marketing staff.

Qualifications and Training

NVQs in fish husbandry at level 2 and in aquaculture at levels 2 and 3 are available. Certificates, diploma and degree courses in fish farming and agriculture are offered by universities and specialist colleges. The Institute of Fisheries Management (IFM) organises correspondence courses leading to Certificates in Fisheries Management and in Fish Farming, and run a Diploma in Fisheries Management.

No formal qualifications are required to become a bailiff, although correspondence courses are available from the IFM. Graduate and postgraduate biologists are employed on the scientific side and specialist degrees are available, as are courses dealing with the sporting aspect of fish farming.

Personal Qualities and Skills

Physical fitness, a willingness to work outside, in remote areas and in all conditions, plus an ability to think ahead and act independently are necessary.

British Trout Association, The Rural Centre, West Mains, Ingliston EH28 8NZ; 0131 472 4080; www.britishtrout.co.uk; e-mail: mail@britishtrout.co.uk

Institute of Fisheries Management (IFM), 22 Rushworth Avenue, West Bridgford, Nottingham NG2 7LF; 0115 982 2317; fax: 0115 945 5722; www.ifm.org.uk; e-mail: admin@ifm.org.uk

Lantra Connect, Lantra House, Stoneleigh, Kenilworth, Warwickshire CV8 2LG; 0845 707 8007 (Lantra Connect – Helpline); www.lantra.co.uk; e-mail: connect@lantra.co.uk

Vacancies are generally advertised in local newspapers and in the specialist magazines such as *Fish Farmer* and *Fish Farming International*.

Starting Salary

£10,000+ for technicians, £11,000+ for bailiffs, £14,000–15,000+ for scientists, and £15,000–20,000 for managers.

FISHER

Fishers perform many tasks: they cast out and haul in the nets when they are full; gut, clean and stow away the catch; mend nets; maintain the tackle and wash down the decks. Fishers may work on deep-sea trawlers in the North Sea or on 'factory' stern vessels which prepare and deep-freeze the catches of cod, haddock, plaice, halibut and sole at sea. Fishing boats operate close to shore as well as in distant fishing grounds such as Greenland, the North Atlantic and Norway. Crews may stay at sea for weeks at a time. While fishing is actually taking place, all hands must work for stretches of up to 18 hours. On the older ships all work is done on the decks but the more modern factory ships process the catch below decks. Catering staff, engineers and radio operators are also employed on these large vessels.

Fishers on drifters carry out similar tasks but these boats follow fish around the coast and land a catch every day. Small seine-net boats with a crew of only four stay at sea for two weeks. Inshore fishing boats are usually family concerns using a variety of different methods to catch white fish, herring, cod, haddock, whiting, shrimps, lobster and crab.

Although the fishing industry is in decline, there are still employment opportunities at the five main ports of Grimsby, Hull, Lowestoft, Fleetwood and Aberdeen.

Qualifications and Training

No formal education qualifications are necessary for a career in fishing, but to go to sea fishers must undertake training in basic sea survival, firefighting and first aid. Colleges generally require applicants to have spent time at sea before entry on to a pre-seagoing course. Courses are available at colleges in Hull, Fleetwood, Grimsby, Lowestoft and Aberdeen. Further training is gained in employment. NVQs in marine vessel operations are available, as is an Advanced Modern Apprenticeship in sea fishing.

Personal Qualities and Skills

Physical fitness, stamina and courage are essential for fishers, who may have to withstand terrible Arctic conditions and long periods of very hard work. They must also be good sailors, able to turn their hand to any task, react quickly to emergencies, and be able to work in a team.

Starting Salary

Fishers all take a share of the catch; the more they catch, the more they earn.

Job Centre Plus and Careers/ Connexions Centres in port towns

Sea Fish Industry Authority, Seafish House, St Andrew's Dock, Hull HU3 4QE; 01482 327837; www.seafish.org

FLORISTRY

see Crafts

FOOD SCIENCE AND TECHNOLOGY

Food scientists study the properties and behaviour of foods from raw materials through processing to the final product, using a variety of scientific disciplines, notably chemistry and biology, but also physics and nutrition. Food technologists use food science and other technological know-how to turn raw materials into finished products for the consumer in an industry that is becoming increasingly sophisticated.

The majority of those qualifying in food science or technology will readily find employment in a variety of positions in the food industry, which covers not only the manufacture of food but its ingredients, food packaging and the manufacture of food-processing machinery. Positions exist in production, quality assurance or in product or process development. The growth of 'own label' products has led to additional opportunities in the food retailing sector, where technologists are responsible for developing new products, identifying suppliers, and ensuring the quality of the product from manufacture, through distribution to the store and, ultimately, to the consumer's table. Those keen to secure a career in research will find opportunities in government service, in research associations, as well as commercial organisations and the universities. There are additional opportunities in environmental health, education, consultancy, public health laboratories and in technical publishing and journalism.

Qualifications and Training

Food science and technology qualifications may be gained via NVQs (levels 1–4), Edexcel (BTEC)/SQA national certificates and diplomas, HNC, HND and degree courses. There is also the opportunity to train while in a job. Qualifications at all levels can be taken as full-time and sandwich courses. There are also a few part-time courses. For minimum entry requirements, contact colleges directly.

Membership of the Institute of Food Science and Technology depends upon satisfying both academic qualifications (minimum HND) and having several years' experience at a responsible level for higher grades.

Personal Qualities and Skills

Food scientists and technologists require a sound theoretical knowledge and scientific ability, a practical approach, an ability to communicate with people and a willingness to work as part of a team.

Starting Salary

Graduates would expect to start at around £15,000 in a small company. A large retailer may pay up to £25,000.

info

Improve Ltd, Food & Drink Sector Skills Council (in development), 1 Green Street, London W1K 6RG; 0207 355 0830

Institute of Food Science and Technology (UK), 5 Cambridge Court, 210 Shepherds Bush Road, London W6 7NJ; 020 7603 6316; www.ifst.org; e-mail: info@ifst.org

FORENSIC SCIENTIST

The Forensic Science Service (FSS), an agency of the Home Office, employs scientists for both research and operational forensic science. Forensic scientists examine and try to identify, by means of analytical chemistry, molecular biology and microscopic analysis, samples of materials such as clothing, hair, blood, glass, paint and handwriting, in order to provide evidence to expose criminals, the location of a crime, the weapons used, and other relevant details.

Qualifications and Training

Forensic scientists are graduates; laboratory experience and postgraduate qualifications are an advantage as there is considerable competition for jobs. Relevant degrees include physical, mathematical or applied science. The universities of Bradford, Strathclyde and Cranfield offer degrees and postgraduate qualifications in forensic science but these do not guarantee a job.

Personal Qualities and Skills

Forensic scientists should be analytical, able to work as part of a team and have good communication skills. They also need to be logical and methodical, paying great attention to detail. A naturally inquisitive, unsqueamish nature and a concern for accuracy are also important.

Starting Salary

Starting salaries for graduates are around £14,000, increasing to £18,000 after a year's training and experience. There are additional allowances for those working in London.

Defence Science and Technology Laboratory (DSTL), Porton Down, Salisbury, Wiltshire SP4 0JQ; 01980 613121; www.dstl.gov.uk/about_us/index.htm

Forensic Alliance, Headquarters and Culham Laboratory, F5 Culham Science Centre, Abingdon, Oxfordshire OX14 3ED; 01235 551800; www.forensicalliance.com

Forensic Science Northern Ireland (FSNI), 151 Belfast Rd, Carrickfergus, County Antrim, Ireland BT38 8PL; 028 9036 1888; www.fsni.gov.uk/

Forensic Science Service (FSS), Trident Court, 2920 Solihull Parkway, Birmingham B37 7YN; 0121 329 5200; www.forensic.gov.uk

Forensic Science Society, Clarke House, 18a Mount Parade, Harrogate, North Yorkshire HG1 1BX; 01423 506 068; www.forensic-science-society.org.uk

Home Office, Direct Communications Unit, 2 Marsham Street, London SW1P 4DF; 0870 000 1585; www.homeoffice.gov.uk

LGC, Queens Road, Teddington, Middlesex TW11 0LY; 020 8943 7000; www.lgc.co.uk/

SEMTA: The Sector Skills Council for Science, Engineering and Manufacturing Technologies, Head Office, 14 Upton Road, Watford WD18 0JT; 01923 238 441; www.semta.org

FORESTRY

Trees, woodlands and forests cover some 13 per cent of the land area of Britain. The job of the forester is to manage this resource to achieve multiple objectives, balancing competing factors. Forests and woodlands give society many things: they create employment, give space for recreation ranging from rallying to solitary strolls in ancient woodlands while providing a home for a vast array of plants, birds and animals and producing timber for construction, paper and a multitude of other uses.

Forestry needs people with a vast range of skills and abilities ranging from manual workers who tend and manage forests by planting, fencing and felling, to machine operators who drive very sophisticated machines that fell and extract timber from woodlands. These operations are managed by supervisors and foresters who plan and oversee forests and woodlands. Their work is very varied and includes tasks such as managing habitats for bio-diversity, planning the felling and planting of forests along with the management of staff and supervision of large contracts.

Qualifications and Training

Forest workers must have nationally recognised chainsaw and pesticide application qualifications, such as those provided by the National Proficiency Tests Council (NPTC). A number of training schemes are available leading to NVQs in forestry at levels 1–3.

Foresters normally start their career with a degree or HND in forestry and then progress their career with membership of their professional body, the Institute of Chartered Foresters. Entry to courses normally requires a period of work experience in forestry as well as the relevant academic qualifications.

Personal Qualities and Skills

Forestry work requires a good standard of physical fitness, a willingness to work outside, all year round, in all weathers and in remote areas. A driving licence is usually essential. Foresters and managers should be able to organise others and be prepared to do varying amounts of office work.

Starting Salary

Trainee forest workers earn about £100 a week at 16, rising to £150–180 at 18. Forestry machine operators are normally paid on piece work but can earn in excess of £20,000. Graduate foresters are likely to start on around £15,000 which could rise to around £24,000. If further management responsibilities are taken on this could rise considerably.

info

Forestry Commission, Personnel Division, 231 Corstorphine Road, Edinburgh EH12 7AT; 0131 334 0303; www.forestry.gov.uk; e-mail: enquiries@forestry.gsi.gov.uk

Institute of Chartered Foresters, 7a St Colme Street, Edinburgh EH3 6AA; 0131 225 2705; www.charteredforesters.org; e-mail: membership@charteredforesters.org

Royal Forestry Society of England, Wales and Northern Ireland, 102 High Street, Tring, Hertfordshire HP23 4AF; 01442 822028; www.rfs.org.uk; e-mail: rfshq@rfs.org.uk

Arboricultural Association, Ampfield House, Ampfield, Nr. Romsey, Hampshire SO51 9PA; 01794 368717; fax: 01794 368978; www.trees.org.uk; e-mail: treehouse@dialpipex.com

Royal Scottish Forestry Society, Hagg-on-Esk, Canonbie, Dumfriesshire DG14 0XE; 01387 371518; fax: 01387 371418; www.rsfs.org; e-mail: rsfs@ednet.co.uk

National Proficiency Tests Council, Avenue 'J' , National Agricultural Centre, Stoneleigh, Warwickshire CV8 2LG; 024 7669 6553; www.nptc.org.uk; e-mail: information@nptc.org.uk

Lantra Connect, Lantra House, Stoneleigh, Kenilworth, Warwickshire CV8 2LG; 0845 707 8007 (Lantra Connect – Helpline); www.lantra.co.uk; e-mail: connect@lantra.co.uk

Forestry Contracting Association, Dalfling, Blairdaff, Inverurie, Aberdeenshire AB51 5LA; 01467 651368; www.fcauk.com

FOUNDRY WORK

Foundry work is craft-based. The industry provides for a wide range of industries, metal-cast components such as propellers, turbines, crankshafts, all types of machinery, and domestic items such as fireplaces.

Craftspeople are employed in foundry work as pattern, mould and model makers and to maintain the equipment. The introduction of computerised processes means foundries also employ machine operators with a range of different skills. Technical engineering staff are concerned with estimating, inspection and laboratory work. There are many opportunities for operatives in foundry work as die casters, dressers, finishers, moulders, coremakers and in metal melting.

There are also limited openings for foundry technologists, metallurgists, chemists and engineers in research and development. Graduate trainees are recruited to production and administrative management posts.

Qualifications and Training

Craftspeople and operatives do not require formal qualifications. Foundation and Advanced Modern Apprenticeships are available and training is work based, leading to NVQs level 1–3. Technicians study on a day-release or full-time basis for the Higher National Certificate/Diploma, in cast metals technology, mechanical or electrical engineering. Management trainees need HNDs or degrees in a relevant subject.

Personal Qualities and Skills

Workers in the foundry industry must be fit and strong as the work is heavy. They should have good eyesight and be skilful in the use of tools. They must be willing to work in noisy conditions and to work shifts.

Starting Salary

Operatives earn £10,000–12,500; craftsmen, once trained, earn £15,000+; technicians start at around £14,000.

info

Institute of Cast Metal Engineers, National Metalforming Centre, 47 Birmingham Road, West Bromwich, West Midlands B70 6PY; 0121 601 6979; fax: 0121 601 6981; www.icme.org.uk; e-mail: info@icme.org.uk

Local Job Centre Plus and Careers/Connexions Centres

Cast Metals Federation, National Metalforming Centre, 47 Birmingham Road, West Bromwich B70 6PY; 0121 601 6390; www.castmetalsfederation.com; e-mail: admin@cmfed.co.uk

FUNDRAISING

Fundraising managers work mainly for charities, but sometimes for pressure groups, community projects and other organisations. They are responsible for overseeing all those activities that help their organisations to generate income. Their varied activities include working with advertisers and marketing specialists to decide how to target a particular audience; working with businesses to obtain corporate funding such as the sponsoring of a project; and organising special fundraising events. They are also responsible for managing trading through charity shops or mail order catalogues; keeping in touch with donors; and organising and supervising the work of volunteers. The particular mix of tasks varies greatly. Large charities may employ fundraising managers who specialise in just one of the above areas. Working for a small charity, you may have to turn your hand to anything and everything.

Qualifications and Training

While there may be no specific entry qualifications, many fundraisers are graduates with degrees in business studies or marketing. This work is now highly competitive and organisations have to consider who will really be able to help them generate income. A background in advertising, public relations, finance or marketing is ideal. Having done some voluntary work for your chosen charity, or for something similar, can also strengthen your application.

The Institute of Fundraising offers a part-time foundation course in the basics of fundraising, for people who have just embarked on this career. They also offer a certificate in fundraising management, which is equivalent to GNVQ level 4. A great deal of training is informal and on-the-job.

Personal Qualities and Skills

A full range of excellent interpersonal skills is essential. You must be persuasive, good at negotiating and able to speak confidently to groups of people. You need good business sense, IT skills and numeracy, and the knack of spotting an imaginative solution or coming up with an appealing idea.

Starting Salary

Fundraising managers earn between £17,000 and £25,000. With experience and working for a large organisation it is possible to earn far more than this. Some vacancies with small organisations or community groups will be less well paid and many may be part-time with pro rata pay for hours worked.

Institute of Fundraising, Park Place, 12 Lawn Lane, London SW8 1UD; 020 7840 1000; www.institute-of-fundraising.org.uk

Working for a Charity, NCVO, Regent's Wharf, 8 All Saints Street, London NW1 2DP; 020 7250 2512; www.workingforacharity.org.uk

FUNERAL DIRECTOR

Funeral directors collect the deceased from hospital or their residence and prepare them for burial or cremation, which may include embalming. Most funeral premises include private viewing rooms for family visitations. The funeral director often makes all the funeral arrangements on behalf of the family, such as the date, time and place of any ceremony and interment or cremation. The funeral director places the relevant notice of death and acknowledgement of thanks for sympathy in newspapers, pays all the fees, arranges flowers, transports the coffin and mourners to and from church, and will act as a collection point for flowers, or donations in lieu, if desired.

Funeral directors may be employed by large firms such as cooperative societies, or by small family-run concerns. In remote rural areas, a local carpenter or other craftsperson may also work as a funeral director.

Qualifications and Training

Those wishing to obtain the Diploma in Funeral Directing must register with the National Association of Funeral Directors (NAFD) and will also have student membership of the British Institute of Funeral Directors (BIFD). Full details of the diploma course are forwarded to each student. Every student must follow the foundation module – there are no exceptions.

A satisfactory standard must be reached in the foundation module before proceeding to the diploma. A student will be required to have 24 months' experience and have arranged 25 funerals before the diploma is awarded. NVQs levels 2 and 3 in Funeral Services are available for those employed within the profession.

Personal Qualities and Skills

Tact, sympathy and a reassuring, helpful nature are essential to funeral directors when they are advising the bereaved. They also need to combine administrative ability with technical expertise in the varied preparations of funeral arrangements. On-call and out-of-hours work is an integral part of the job and an ability to adapt to irregular hours is essential.

Starting Salary

Salaries vary greatly depending on size of firm, many of which are family concerns.

British Institute of Embalmers, Anubis House, 21c Station Road, Knowle, Solihull, West Midlands B93 0HL; 01564 778991; www.bioe.co.uk; e-mail: enquiry@bioe.org.uk

National Association of Funeral Directors, 618 Warwick Road, Solihull, West Midlands B91 1AA; 0845 230 1343; www.nafd.org.uk; e-mail: info@nafd.org.uk

Institute of Burial and Cremation Administration, 107 Parlaunt Road, Langley, Slough, Berks SL3 8BE; 01753 771518; fax: 01753 770518

FURNITURE AND FURNISHING

Furniture manufacture

Furniture manufacturing and repair companies exist in all parts of the country. The industry maintains much of its craft base, with skilled people carrying out many of the tasks needed to create a piece of furniture. Within larger factories some of this has been mechanised, making use of computerised production methods. At the other end of the scale many small designer/makers bring together the designs, materials, machinery and knowledge of today coupled with the skills from a previous age.

Modern furniture is made from timber, textiles, steel, glass, plastics, stone and a range of polymers. Skilled frame makers provide frames to be filled, sprung and covered by upholsterers. The machining part is increasingly done by use of IT-driven processes, but other work is still done by hand.

There are opportunities to work on a freelance or self-employed basis, or for one of the many manufacturing units which specialise in particular items, or materials, or in certain types of furniture such as school, office or domestic furniture. In the design of furniture, carpets, fabrics, curtaining and wall coverings, opportunities exist to work freelance, in studios and in the retail trade. There are also a number of openings for teachers; craft, design and technology teachers are in short supply.

Qualifications and Training

Craft training is generally gained through a three- to four-year Modern Apprenticeship including NVQs at level 3. Other training is available, from beginner-level courses (City and Guilds/OCN Craft Certificates) through more advanced knowledge-based programmes (City and Guilds Progression Awards) to HND/Cs, foundation and full degrees. Entry to many of these courses is dependent on practical ability, although some courses do have specific academic requirements.

Personal Qualities and Skills

Furniture craftspeople must be neat, accurate and able to follow drawings exactly. They must be interested in practical work which requires great precision, have care and patience, and sufficient strength to lift heavy furniture. Good eyesight is an advantage. Designers are required to work as part of a team to a busy schedule and present their work well; a sound knowledge of how furniture is made is valuable.

Starting Salary

Salary rates vary but pay is generally good with apprentices at 16 earning £70+ a week. By 19 many are earning in excess of £300 a week. Qualified and experienced staff can earn a lot more. Individual craftspeople working for themselves set their own rates.

info

Furniture, Furnishings and Interiors National Training Organisation (FFINTO), 67 Wollaton Road, Beeston, Nottingham NG9 2NG; 0115 9221200; fax: 0115 9223833; www.ffinto.org; e-mail: info@ffinto.org

Upholstery

The upholstery industry in the UK has a long tradition of supplying and repairing seating. While competition from cheap imports is fierce, the UK's reputation for quality has helped sustain the industry. Companies range from small businesses supplying a local market to large undertakings making suites for the major retailers. The job may entail anything from providing modern chairs and sofas for large hotel chains to the restoration of antique furniture in private homes or museums.

There are three main roles within the sector: the cutter, the sewer and the upholsterer. Often within smaller companies all three roles are carried out by all staff but with some specialisation. Upholsterers measure up, prepare and fit the fabric components in all kinds of furniture. It is highly skilled work and includes not only the visible top coverings (which can vary from velvet to leather), but also the preparation and supports below, such as padding, stuffing, springing or webbing.

Qualifications and Training

Craft training is generally gained through a three- to four-year Modern Apprenticeship including NVQs at level 3. Other training is available, from beginner-level courses (City and Guilds/OCN Craft Certificates) through more advanced knowledge-based programmes (City and Guilds Progression Awards) to HNDs, foundation and full degrees.

Personal Qualities and Skills

Upholsterers need to have nimble fingers, good eyesight and infinite patience, and must enjoy working on individual projects.

Starting Salary

Salary rates vary but pay is generally good, with apprentices at 16 earning £70+ a week. By 19 many are earning in excess of £300 a week. Qualified and experienced staff can earn a lot more. Individual craftspeople working for themselves set their own rates.

info

FFINTO, 67 Wollaton Road, Beeston, Nottingham NG9 2NG; 0115 9221200; fax: 0115 9223833; www.ffinto.org; e-mail: info@ffinto.org

GARDENING

Gardening, also known as amenity horticulture, involves not only planting and caring for flowers, trees and shrubs, but also the routine jobs of cleaning out flower beds, sweeping leaves and, in the winter, shovelling snow.

Gardener

(*see also* Landscape Architecture)

Gardeners may be employed by local authorities to care for parks, school and hospital grounds, work for a garden centre or landscape contractor, or be self-employed. Heritage gardening is a growth area and involves working for organisations such as the National Trust, English Heritage, and other private gardens.

Qualifications and Training

It is desirable but not always necessary to have formal qualifications to become a gardener. Training is given on the job, often as part of an apprenticeship; NVQ levels 1–3 are available. Full-time training courses in horticulture are available at colleges throughout the country, from first diploma level. The Royal Horticultural Society offers a limited number of opportunities for practical training and plantsmanship at its gardens at Wisley, Rosemoor and Hyde Hall.

info

Local Job Centre Plus and Careers/Connexions Centres

Agricultural Wages Helpline; 0845 0000134; www.defra.gov.uk/farm/agwages/agwages.htm

Institute of Horticulture, 14–15 Belgrave Square, London SW1X 8PS; 020 7245 6943; www.horticulture.org.uk; e-mail: ioh@horticulture.org.uk

Royal Horticultural Society, 80 Vincent Square, London SW1P 2PE; 020 7834 4333; www.rhs.org.uk; e-mail: info@rhs.org.uk

Writtle College, Chelmsford CM1 3RR; 01245 424200; www.growing-careers.com

Careers Working Outdoors (Kogan Page)

Voluntary Internships for four or more weeks are available for those studying horticulture at college, and at a number of schools work experience placements are available for secondary pupils.

Personal Qualities and Skills

You must have a real interest in the plants you work with, whether they are commercial fruit and vegetables or ornamental flowers and shrubs. You should be very practical and happy to work in all weathers and you must be patient – some of your work takes a long time to come to fruition. For some gardening jobs you need an eye for design and colour. You should be comfortable working on your own, but able to talk to people about their gardens, their crops and their ideas.

Starting Salary

Salaries in commercial horticulture are set by the Agricultural Wages Board, which has just introduced a six-tier grading system for pay. Basic trainees get £5.05 an hour, standard workers get £5.58 an hour, lead workers get £5.91 an hour, craft workers get £6.58 an hour, supervisors get £6.98 an hour and managers get £7.53 an hour. Very many gardeners are self-employed and the hourly rate they can charge varies with different geographical location; they can earn up to £25,000, but earnings in winter may be very sparse.

GAS SERVICE ENGINEER

Gas service engineers, also known as gas service technicians or gas service fitters, work in people's homes and on business premises, installing, servicing and repairing appliances and systems such as cookers, boilers and central heating systems. They test controls and safety devices to ensure that they are working and they locate and repair gas leaks. Often they specialise either in installation, servicing or repair, but some gas service engineers will work in all three areas.

Qualifications and Training

The usual route to qualification is through a technician-level apprenticeship lasting between three and four years. You need four GCSEs grades A to C including English, maths and science, and you must have perfect colour vision. Most apprentices start at age 16, but you can start up to the age of 24. Successful completion of the apprenticeship also leads to an NVQ level 3 award.

To work as a gas fitter, installer or service engineer, you must register with the Council for Registered Gas Installers, which will check your qualifications and ascertain that you have had suitable training and work experience before allowing you to register.

Personal Qualities and Skills

You must be practical, able to handle tools and instruments, and you must be able to apply technical knowledge to practical problems. You have to be able to work on your own or as part of a team, and it is important that you are polite and friendly and enjoy meeting and dealing with people. Having an acute awareness of safety issues is essential.

Starting Salary

During training salaries are from £8,000, going up during each year of training. On qualifying as a technician, salaries range from £16,000 to £19,500. There are plenty of opportunities for overtime and shift work bonuses with this work.

info

Ambition Energy, Energy and Utility Skills: The Sector Skills Council for Electricity, Gas and Water, Friars Gate Two, 1011 Stratford Road, Shirley, Solihull B90 4BN; 0845 077 9922; www.euskills.co.uk

British Gas Recruitment Centre, The Harrow Way, Basingstoke, Hampshire RG22 4AR; www.britishgasacademy.co.uk

The Council for Registered Gas Installers, 1 Elmswood, Chineham Business Park, Crockford Lane, Basingstoke, Hampshire RG24 8WG; 0870 401 2300; www.corgi-gas-safety.com

GEOLOGIST

Geoscience is essential to the understanding of the natural resources contained in earth and rocks, oil, water, minerals and precious metals. Geologists also contribute to an understanding of the earth's history and the scientific study of natural phenomena like volcanoes and earthquakes. Since geoscience encompasses so many different areas of expertise, there are many specialist occupations within this field.

Geologists study the earth's crust, its materials, their origin, formation and composition. The work involves examining rocks and mineral deposits; some deposits (for example, coal) are assessed for their value. Specimens of rock, soil, water, fossils and minerals are collected for laboratory analysis and preserved for future reference. Geology includes not only fieldwork but much laboratory work, testing and analysing, often using computers. Geologists work mainly for oil, mining, quarrying or engineering firms and government establishments, and are becoming increasingly involved in environmental issues.

Closely allied to the work of the geologist is that of the geophysicist (*see* Oil/Gas Rig Work), geochemist and hydrogeologist, who use field and laboratory-based techniques to better understand the earth's physical and chemical properties and its underground water supplies. Hence, most of their work is related to the resources and the environment.

Qualifications and Training

The common route for entry into a professional geoscience career is a first degree (BSc/BA) in one of the geosciences. Such a degree also forms the basic qualification for Fellowship of the Geological Society of London, and for becoming a Chartered Geologist.

Personal Qualities and Skills

Geologists must be fit, as they are often required to work in difficult climatic conditions or even underground. They must be able to work both as team members and as team organisers when required. Relevant foreign languages are useful.

Starting Salary

£15,500+ to £23,000+; higher abroad.

For careers information: British Geological Survey, BGS Personnel, British Geological Survey, Keyworth, Nottingham NG12 5GG; 0 115 936 3209; 0 115 936 3537; www.bgs.ac.uk; e-mail: enquiries@bgs.ac.uk

Geological Society, Burlington House, Piccadilly, London W1J 0BG; 020 7434 9944; www.geolsoc.org.uk; e-mail: enquiries@geolsoc.org.uk

HAIR

Hairdresser

Hairdressers offer a variety of services involving hair, such as cutting, styling, perming and colouring. Salons or individual stylists may specialise in male or female hairdressing, or a niche market such as specialist colouring, Afro-Caribbean or ethnic hairstyles. Hairdressers may also be responsible for answering the telephone, making appointments, serving drinks to clients, cleaning and stock control. They work in salons, hotels, airports, cruise liners, hospitals and prisons. Some hairdressers work as freelancers. There are over 170,000 hairdressers in the UK.

Qualifications and Training

Most trainees combine on-the-job training with part-time study at a college or training centre towards an NVQ in hairdressing at levels 1, 2 and 3. Salons may offer a three-year apprenticeship which includes training alongside experienced stylists and day release at college. Some colleges also offer full-time NVQs and full- or part-time BTEC courses in design, fashion styling for hair and make-up. Full-time courses usually last for two years and include work experience in a college and external salon. Colleges may also offer the National Diploma of Hairdressing, awarded by the Guild of Hairdressers.

After training, hairdressers are expected to work for at least a year as an improver before being considered experienced. Hairdressers who want to enter salon management, become self-employed or teach hairdressing may need further qualifications in business studies or teaching. It may become necessary for all hairdressers to be state registered with the Hairdressing Council at some time in the future.

Personal Qualities and Skills

Hairdressers should have a genuine interest in people, a natural friendliness, the ability to stay calm under pressure, creative ability and an eye for detail. A presentable personal appearance is also essential. Hairdressers must not have skin conditions that can be affected by chemicals.

Starting Salary

Trainees earn around £2,300, which rises according to qualifications obtained. Experienced hairdressers earn £8,000–12,000, although some may earn considerably more. Hairdressers may be paid commission for selling hair products and some receive tips from clients. Hairdressing offers good opportunities for self-employment and for working at home.

Hairdressing Council, 12 David Street, 45 High Street, South Norwood, London SE25 6HJ; 020 8771 6205; www.haircouncil.org.uk; e-mail: registrar@haircouncil.org.uk

Hairdressing and Beauty Industry Authority (HABIA), Fraser House, Nether Hall Road, Doncaster DN1 2PH; 01302 380000; www.habia.org.uk; e-mail: enquiries@habia.org.uk

National Hairdressers Federation, One Abbey Court, Fraser Road, Priory Business Park, Bedford MK44 3WH; 0845 345 6500; www.nhfuk.com; e-mail: nhf@tgis.co.uk

Guild of Hairdressers, Unit 1E, Redbrook Business Park, Wilthorpe Road, Barnsley S75 1JN; 01226 786555; fax: 01226 208300

Careers in Hairdressing and Beauty (Kogan Page)

Trichologist

Trichologists treat hair and scalp disorders, the most common being hair loss. Electrical and heat treatments, massage and special lotions and ointments are used. Trichologists practise on their own behalf; some of their patients are referred to them from doctors, but trichology is not available on the NHS.

Qualifications and Training

Basic academic qualifications are necessary. Training may be by a three-year pupillage with a practising trichologist. The necessary theoretical instruction is available at technical colleges, evening classes or by correspondence. It is also necessary to have some practical experience of working in a recognised clinic.

Personal Qualities and Skills

Trichologists must understand the necessary biological principles and have a knowledge of nutrition, plus an interest in helping people. They must have high standards of personal hygiene.

Starting Salary

This is dependent upon number of patients, hours worked and fees charged.

Institute of Trichologists, 08706 070602; www.trichologists.org.uk

HEALTH AND SAFETY

Health and safety adviser

Health and safety advisers work for every kind or organisation, from multinationals and government agencies to small businesses. Advisers work in partnership with employers, employees, directors and trade unions, and are responsible for ensuring that all safety legislation is adhered to and that suitable policies and practices are put in place. They help organisations minimise safety risks and they are often involved in staff training.

Health and safety inspector

Health and safety inspectors work to assess and improve every kind of work practice and the health and safety applications attached to it. In the UK one person is killed every day at work, and inspectors working for the Health and Safety Executive (HSE), which is a government agency, are constantly working to try to reduce this statistic. Inspectors check work premises, from building sites to farms and factories, and they have legal powers to demand changes. They are also called in to investigate when accidents do occur.

Qualifications and Training

It is possible to become an adviser without a degree, if you have plenty of work experience in management, engineering, science or health, but there is a move towards making this a graduate entry profession. Degrees in occupational health, engineering, health science and management are the most favoured, and these each have their own entry requirements. Graduates or HND holders of any subject can become Health and Safety Inspectors, but again there is a preference for subjects such as engineering, environmental health or physics.

Personal Qualities and Skills

To be an adviser or an inspector you have to be an excellent and persuasive communicator and negotiator. You must be good at understanding and interpreting legal or technical documents and prepared to keep abreast of changes in legislation. You must be keenly observant, spotting potential problems, but also able to suggest solutions. You must be able to write reports and have the confidence to talk to large groups of people. To be an inspector you must be practical enough to use measurement equipment of various kinds and you need numerical skills to make calculations.

Starting Salary

As an adviser at the start of your career you can expect between £20,000 and £26,000 depending on whether you have had useful work experience as well as offering a relevant qualification. At a senior level salaries rise to around £40,000. Trainee inspectors with the Health and Safety Executive start on £20,000.

British Safety Council, National Safety Centre, 70 Chancellor's Road, London W6 9RS; 020 8741 1231; www.britishsafetycouncil.co.uk

Department for Environment, Food and Rural Affairs (DEFRA), Nobel House, 17 Smith Square, London SW1P 3JR; 08459 33 55 77; www.defra.gov.uk/

The Health and Safety Executive (HSE), Magdalen House, Trinity Road, Bootle, Merseyside L20 3QZ; 0845 345 0055; www.hse.gov.uk/

Institution of Occupational Safety and Health (IOSH), Membership Department, The Grange, Highfield Drive, Wigston, Leics LE18 1NN; 0116 257 3100; www.iosh.co.uk

National Examination Board for Occupational Safety and Health (NEBOSH), Dominus Way, Meridian Business Park, Leicester LE19 1QW; 0116 263 4700; www.nebosh.org.uk

Royal Society for the Prevention of Accidents (ROSPA), Head Office, Edgbaston Park, 353 Bristol Road, Edgbaston, Birmingham B5 7ST; 0121 248 2000; www.rospa.com/index

HEALTH SERVICE (NON-MEDICAL)

There are over 70 non-medical career options within the health service, employing a wide range of skills.

Ancillary staff

Includes porters, who move supplies and people around the hospital, general building maintenance staff, and ambulance services.

Catering

In hospitals, ordinary meals are provided for both patients and staff, as well as special diets. The catering officer supervises the kitchen, plans menus in consultation with the dietitian, and is in control of ordering the food as well as its preparation.

Domestic services

This covers all grades from basic domestic cleaner level to domestic supervisors and housekeepers. This section is responsible for cleaning beds and areas within the hospital under the charge of the domestic superintendent. It includes district and area domestic managers who coordinate the hospital domestic services.

Laundry

This department deals with the supply of sterilised sheets, towels, blankets and overalls; the number of items handled weekly within one hospital may run into millions.

Management

Health service managers work with professional staff, patients and the public to ensure efficiency and cost-effectiveness at all levels of the health service. This involves forward planning, finance, personnel management, purchasing and supply, building maintenance, and the organisation of laundry, catering and cleaning. At district and regional health authority levels, the responsibilities are for ascertaining the health needs of the local population and monitoring the quality of provision.

Patient services

Clerks arrange appointments, patients' registration, maintain waiting lists and filing systems, keep patients' records and maintain statistical data. The medical records officer may work within the hospital, in charge of the clerks and medical secretaries, or may work at regional or district authority level.

Qualifications and Training

Staff are recruited and trained by the hospitals and health authorities. Some may work towards NVQs levels 1–4. Graduates are eligible to apply for two-year General and three-year Financial Management Training Schemes.

Personal Qualities and Skills

Working for the health service requires a real and sympathetic concern for people. Management trainees need good organisational, administrative and IT skills.

Starting Salary

Salaries for some non-medical posts start at National Minimum Wage levels but increase according to responsibility and experience. Graduate management trainees start on £19,000 + London allowance.

info

NHS Careers; Careers Helpline: 0845 6060 655; www.nhscareers.nhs.uk; www.futureleaders.nhs.uk (for graduate management training)

Institute of Healthcare Management, 18–21 Morley Street, London SE1 7QZ; 020 7620 1030; www.ihm.org.uk

Local Job Centre Plus and Careers/Connexions Centres

HEALTH VISITOR

see Nursing, Health Visiting and Midwifery

HEALTHCARE ASSISTANT

see Nursing, Health Visiting and Midwifery

HOME ECONOMICS

Home economics covers a variety of subjects connected with the home, family life and consumer issues. This includes nutrition and health, the preparation of food, equipment used in the home, home management and budgeting.

Demonstrator

Home economists demonstrate products for manufacturers in shops or exhibitions, organise exhibitions and train demonstrators. Their work can include giving talks to institutions or in the home on products or services, or giving advice on home management.

Home economist

Home economists prepare written instructions for new food products, recipe leaflets and cookery books, or deal with consumer affairs. There are several levels of training, from certificate to degree courses.

Industry

Many home economists are employed in the food industry in marketing and/or the research and development of new products to supply retailers. Their counterparts in retailing are the home economists who, as buyers/selectors, choose the products to be stocked. Home economists are similarly employed in the domestic appliance manufacturing industry and with those retailers.

Local authorities

Home economists are used by local authorities in the social services, housing departments, consumer services and health promotion units.

Teaching

A knowledge of science, particularly chemistry, is advisable for teaching. There are openings for teachers in colleges and universities, as well as in schools. Food and textiles are taught under technology.

The media

Some home economists work for magazines, journals, radio and television, where they are concerned with fact-finding and assessment, answering enquiries and preparing articles for publication or broadcast.

Qualifications and Training

Degree courses and HNDs available in this area have a range of titles, for example home economics, consumer studies and applied consumer sciences. Entry to these is with two A levels or equivalent. For those interested in teaching, a one-year Postgraduate Certificate in Education (PGCE) in home economics is available to graduates. Some food science and food technology degrees are also acceptable.

Personal Qualities and Skills

Home economists care about people and their quality of life, and need therefore to have an interest in the quality, performance and safety of goods and services related to the people who use these products. Much of the work involves communicating with the general public on the one hand and specialists on the other, so home economists must be confident and have the ability to express themselves verbally and in writing. Good self-management and interpersonal skills are needed.

Starting Salary

From £14,000–15,000 for those with a degree.

info

Institute of Consumer Sciences incorporating Home Economics, Lonsdale House, 52 Blucher Street, Birmingham B1 1QU; tel/fax: 0121 616 5188, www.institute-consumer-sciences.co.uk; e-mail: icsc-office@btconnect.com

National Association of Teachers of Home Economics and Technology, Hamilton House, Mabledon Place, London WC1H 9BJ; 020 7387 1441; e-mail: nathe@globalnet.co.uk

HORTICULTURE

Horticulture is the science of growing fruits, vegetable and flowers and there are a variety of occupations to choose from in this sector.

Advisory work

The adviser provides a link between research workers and the grower, to pass on the result of experimental work. The commercial and consultancy firms and producer organisations provide opportunities for advisers. A degree plus practical experience is necessary.

Amenity horticulture

(*see also* Landscape Architecture)

Landscape architects, parks directors, landscape gardeners and groundspeople maintain public and private gardens and parks, sport and recreational facilities, industrial and residential areas, and landscape and plant roadsides. Employers may be local authority public parks and recreation departments, commercial landscaping, contract garden maintenance firms, or owners of major gardens.

Arboriculturist

(*see also* Forestry)

Arboriculturists care for and maintain trees and are mainly employed by local authorities, although there are some opportunities in private firms. The term 'tree surgeon' is often used for a commercial arboriculturist.

Commercial horticulture

Commercial horticulturists grow crops, such as vegetables, on open land, and tomatoes, lettuce and cucumbers in glasshouses. Both orchard and soft fruits account for over one-fifth of the value of all horticultural production. Commercial horticulture also covers the growing of flowers and ornamental plants, including chrysanthemums, roses and carnations under glass, and for the gardening market, nurseries, landscaping and seeds.

Market gardening

Crops grown in market gardens are vegetables, salad crops – such as lettuces and tomatoes – and flowers and ornamental plants. The work consists of preparing the soil, and working by hand on such jobs as transplanting young plants, thinning growing plants, and grading, washing and packing the produce after harvesting so that it can be sold.

Research

Horticultural scientists work on pests and diseases and general research to produce better and healthier plants, in industrial and government organisations and in universities and colleges. There is a wide range of prospects for graduates.

Teaching

Opportunities for teaching in horticulture occur in universities, colleges and schools. A degree or diploma is required.

Qualifications and Training

There are openings in horticulture for people from a variety of educational backgrounds. No GCSEs are required for part- or full-time initial training courses, although beginners should be competent in biology, chemistry and maths. Applicants may work towards NVQs levels 1 to 4.

Those with five GCSEs, including science and maths plus one A level pass or equivalent, and one year's experience can study for the Higher National Diploma, specialising in commercial or amenity horticulture. Two A levels or equivalent are necessary to study for a degree in horticulture.

info

Institute of Horticulture, 14–15 Belgrave Square, London SW1X 8PS; 020 7245 6943; www.horticulture.org.uk; e-mail: ioh@horticulture.org.uk

Royal Horticultural Society, 80 Vincent Square, London SW1P 2PE; 020 7834 4333; www.rhs.org.uk; e-mail: info@rhs.org.uk

Lantra Connect, Lantra House, Stoneleigh Park, Kenilworth, Warwickshire CV8 2LG; 0845 707 8007 (Lantra Connect – Helpline); www.lantra.co.uk; e-mail: connect@lantra.co.uk

Royal Agricultural Society of England, National Agricultural Centre, Stoneleigh Park, Warwickshire CV8 2LZ; 01476 696969; www.rase.org.uk

Department for Environment, Food and Rural Affairs: general enquiries: Library Enquiry Desk, DEFRA, Room 320, Nobel House, 17 Smith Square, London SW1P 3JR; 08459 33 55 77; www.defra.gov.uk

Agricultural Wages Board, Nobel House, 17 Smith Square, London SW1P 3JR; Agricultural Wages Helpline: 0845 0000134; www.defra.gov.uk/farm/agwages/agwages.htm

Local Job Centre Plus and Careers/Connexions Centres

'Come into Horticulture' and 'Education and Training Courses in Horticulture' (available free from the Institute of Horticulture).

The Royal Horticultural Society offers a limited number of opportunities for practical training and plantsmanship at its gardens at Wisley, Rosemoor and Hyde Hall. Committed gardeners aged between the ages of 19 and 35 can apply for the two-year Wisley Diploma in Practical Horticulture and the one-year certificate course. Students receive £10,300 per year and accommodation.

Voluntary Internships for four or more weeks are available for those studying horticulture at college, and at a number of schools work experience placements are available for secondary pupils.

Personal Qualities and Skills

A real enthusiasm for plants and an interest in how to provide the ideal conditions for growing them is essential. You have to be prepared to work in all weathers, to be patient when awaiting the results of your work, and you should be observant – quick to note changes or potential problems. Good commercial and marketing awareness is often useful. You should be able to work as part of a team, as well as feeling comfortable working on your own.

Starting Salary

Salaries in commercial horticulture are set by the Agricultural Wages Board, which has recently introduced a six-tier grading system for pay. Basic trainees get £5.05 an hour, standard workers get £5.58 an hour, lead workers get £5.91 an hour, craft workers get £6.58 an hour, supervisors get £6.98 an hour and managers get £7.53 an hour. There are sometimes different rates for seasonal work and some of this work may also include accommodation and food.

HOSPITALITY AND CATERING

There is a wide variety of job opportunities in this category at all levels, from managers and supervisors to craft workers. Sometimes the dividing lines are not clear-cut, and it is quite usual for individuals to move up from one to another.

Chef/cook

In addition to creating and supervising the preparation of all kinds of different dishes, a head chef/cook has to be trained in the management of a kitchen, being responsible for the staff and the organisation of their workload, planning the menus, budgeting, ordering and approving the necessary ingredients and maintaining high standards of efficiency and hygiene. Chefs are employed in hotels, restaurants, industrial organisations (such as offices or factories), institutions (such as hospitals, schools and universities or colleges) and in the armed forces. In large establishments the chef de cuisine is in overall charge while there may be a number of chefs de partie (in charge of their part of the kitchen) and a number of commis chefs (still learning the trade).

Qualifications and Training

No formal qualifications are necessary, but depending on what training route your employer wishes to put you through, you may need four GCSEs including English and maths. If you want to study full or part-time at college before you start training with an employer, you can study for BTEC National Certificates and Diplomas in hospitality and catering; you need four GCSEs grades A to C to get a place on one of these courses. You can study for NVQ courses to level 1, 2 and 3, either full-time before you start work or part-time while you are training in a kitchen. There are also apprenticeships (leading to NVQ level 2) and Advanced Apprenticeships (leading to NVQ level 3) available in food preparation and cookery. These last 12 and 24 months respectively. There are also some GNVQ level 4 courses available in kitchen and larder, confectionery and patisserie.

If you have five GCSEs and two A levels, there are several foundation degree courses available in food preparation, including professional cookery, professional patisserie, culinary arts, culinary creativity and hospitality.

Personal Qualities and Skills

You must have a real interest in food, and understand how to be imaginative and creative producing appetising food. You must be able to work under pressure, and be part of, or ultimately lead, a team. You must have a sense of what things cost and you must be well organised and able to cope with several tasks at the same time.

Starting Salary

As a junior chef you can earn between £9,000 and £11,000. A chef in charge of a section of a kitchen earns around £16,000.

Food service assistants

Waiters and waitresses, as well as serving, may cook special dishes at table or specialise in particular skills such as wine-waiting. As well as serving food and drink, they have to maintain contact with their customers; unfriendly staff may ruin the reputation of a restaurant. Promotion is to head waiter/waitress.

Hotel housekeeping

Room staff, cleaners and other support staff keep the hotel clean and comfortable. The head housekeeper is in charge of this aspect of hotel life.

Hotel reception

Receptionists receive guests, handle reservations and perform bookkeeping duties, so it is important to be good at figures, able to handle cash and use computers. Languages are an advantage. Working hours are arranged to deal with early and late arrivals and departures, so may entail shift and weekend work.

Kitchen staff

In the kitchen there are opportunities at all levels, from the chef in charge of a select restaurant to the dishwasher in a snack bar. There are also opportunities for freelance work – catering for directors' dining rooms, private parties and business lunches, for instance. It is demanding work, often in 'unsocial hours', when most people are out enjoying themselves. Some cooking can be repetitious (such as take-away menus), some creatively satisfying.

Management

Catering management can cover work in a roadside or motorway restaurant, a luxury restaurant, a hospital meals service, a snack bar, a take-away service, university and college restaurants, the armed forces, outdoor events or contract catering (providing meals and snacks to the management and staff of the contractor, for example a bank or insurance company). The manager in charge is normally responsible for budgeting, menu planning, stock monitoring, seeing that good food is served as and when it is required, often round the clock, keeping customers satisfied and supervising staff.

Large hotels have a general manager, food and beverage manager, personnel and training manager and house manager, and there may also be heads of departments or sections. There are specialised opportunities in the fields of finance, administration, food and beverage operations, accommodation services, sales and marketing product development, public relations, personnel and training.

Accommodation management is concerned with the domestic side of colleges and universities (where managers are sometimes known as bursars), hospitals, local authority day centres and residential homes, for the aged or disabled, for instance. The demanding duties of such managers include responsibility for accommodation and catering, particularly in halls of residence, which may be used as conference centres during the vacation. The work can involve personal contact with the residents (in homes, for instance, where the population is fairly permanent), or be more in the nature of housekeeping, as in hospitals where the patients are constantly changing and are not the direct concern of the domestic staff.

Qualifications and Training

There are two main routes to qualification: attending a college or university as a full-time student, or joining a training programme operated by an employer or an organisation that works with employers to provide training, such as the Hotel and Catering Training Company (HCTC). In the latter case, entrants learn on the job and attend college or a training centre on a short-course or day-release basis. Recruits on the work-based training programme will generally acquire NVQ awards. An increasing number of employers are offering Modern Apprenticeships which provide a route to higher-level technical or supervisory posts and NVQs at level 3.

Full-time courses are available in hospitality-related subjects, including HNDs, Foundation Degrees and degree courses.

Personal Qualities and Skills

Craft workers usually need physical fitness and stamina as well as high standards of personal hygiene. Skin complaints may disqualify entrants. Managers need to be well motivated with good interpersonal and team skills. All staff have to be prepared to work split shifts and antisocial hours.

Starting Salary

Average wages for qualified hotel and restaurant staff are £14,500. Salaries for managers start around £16,000 but vary depending on the size of the business. Many employees live in hotel accommodation and have food provided.

info

British Hospitality Association, Queens House, 55–56 Lincoln's Inn Fields, London WC2A 3BH; 020 7404 7744; www.bha-online.org.uk

Hotel and Catering Training Company (HCTC), HCTC Limited, 2nd Floor, South Wing, 26–28 Hammersmith Grove, London W6 7HT; 020 8735 9700; www.hctc.co.uk

Hotel and Catering International Management Association (HCIMA), Trinity Court, 34 West Street, Sutton, Surrey SM1 1SH; 020 8661 4900; www.hcima.org.uk

People 1st: The Sector Skills Council for the Hospitality, Leisure, Travel and Tourism Industries, 2nd Floor, Armstrong House, 38 Market Square, Uxbridge, Middlesex UB8 1LH; 0870 060 2550; www.people1st.co.uk

Publican

The licensee of a pub may be a manager who is paid a salary, a lessee or tenant who rents the property from a brewer, a pub company or a free trader who owns the premises. As well as the ever-popular traditional town and country pubs there is now a wide variety of pubs ranging from theme pubs, café bars and steak bars to pubs with gourmet restaurants and full entertainment facilities. Nearly all pubs serve food and an increasing number also offer accommodation.

Qualifications and Training

To hold a licence individuals generally need a National Licensee's Certificate – an entry-level qualification available from the British Institute of Innkeeping (BII), which also offers a number of other relevant qualifications. NVQs, diplomas and degrees are available in hotel, catering and licensed retail management. Brewery companies put their managers through a comprehensive training programme. Licensees could well be running businesses grossing more than half a million pounds a year. They must know how to market their services and devise new ideas to attract customers. They must also have a good knowledge of subjects such as bookkeeping, licensing laws, hygiene, staff motivation, customer care and cellar management.

Personal Qualities and Skills

Publicans should be ambitious and able to take responsibility. They should enjoy working with people, have a customer-care focus and good interpersonal skills.

Starting Salary

Salaries range from £18,500+ with participation in bonus schemes, to £35,500+. Accommodation, lighting and heating are normally provided.

info

British Beer and Pub Association, Market Towers, 1 Nine Elms Lane, London SW8 5NQ; 020 7627 9191; www.beerandpub.com; e-mail: enquiries@beerandpub.com

British Institute of Innkeeping, Wessex House, 80 Park Street, Camberley, Surrey GU15 3PL; 01276 684449; fax: 01276 23045; www.bii.org or www.Barzone.co.uk (dedicated website for careers in licensed retailing); e-mail: Careers@bii.org

Pubs, Bars and Clubs Handbook, Danny Blyth (Kogan Page)

HOUSING OFFICER/MANAGER

Housing officers work mainly for local authorities and housing associations, but there are also opportunities in voluntary and private housing concerns. The work covers a broad range of areas that will vary by organisation and sector. In catering for the demand for rented accommodation, the housing officer will manage and maintain properties, which includes dealing with rent arrears, reporting repairs, applications, allocations and arranging property exchanges and transfers. Housing officers often work with social and welfare agencies, and need to have a basic understanding of the different welfare benefits.

Qualifications and Training

The basic qualifications needed for professional training in housing are three GCSEs and one A level or equivalent. Students over the age of 21 who do not meet these requirements but have relevant work experience may be considered as exceptional entrants. Contact local colleges to discuss this in more detail.

Those employed in housing follow a day-release or distance-learning course to study for the Chartered Institute of Housing's professional qualification (PQ). NVQs levels 2, 3 and 4 in housing are available, and anyone working in housing is eligible to do these; NVQ level 4 allows candidates to proceed to stage 2 of the Chartered Institute of Housing's PQ.

In addition to the course, candidates also need to do the work-based Test of Professional Practice (TPP), normally completed within two years. The PQ can take three or four years to complete, depending on whether the graduate or non-graduate route is taken.

Graduates or mature entrant candidates are required to study a one-year graduate foundation course followed by a two-year professional diploma. Non-graduates are required to complete an Edexcel (BTEC)/SQA HNC in housing studies followed by a two-year professional diploma. There are also full-time degree courses and full- and part-time postgraduate diplomas. The Test of Professional Practice will still need to be undertaken with these alternative routes.

Personal Qualities and Skills

An interest in improving people's living conditions, good interpersonal skills, effective organisation skills, sensitivity to an individual's needs and flexibility are all important.

Starting Salary

Trainee posts and general enquiries and customer service jobs pay between £10,000 and £13,000. Housing officer/manager posts pay from £16,000 to £23,000 according to experience and the kind of organisation you are working for. Local authorities may pay more than employers in the voluntary sector.

info

Chartered Institute of Housing, Octavia House, Westwood Business Park, Westwood Way, Coventry CV4 8JP; 024 7685 1700; www.cih.org; e-mail: careers@cih.org

Chartered Institute of Housing in Scotland, 6 Palmerston Place, Edinburgh EH12 5AA; 0131 225 4544; www.cih.org/scotland; e-mail: scotland@cih.org

Chartered Institute of Housing Cymru, 4 Purbeck House, Lambourne Crescent, Cardiff Business Park, Llanishen, Cardiff CF14 5GJ; 029 2076 5760; www.cih.org/home_cymru/; e-mail: cymru@cih.org

Chartered Institute of Housing in Northern Ireland, Carnmoney House, Edgewater Office Park, Dargan Road, Belfast BT3 9JQ; 028 9077 8222; www.cih.org/home_ni/; e-mail: ni@cih.org

Asset Skills, 2 The Courtyard, 48 New North Road, Exeter EX4 4EP; 01392 423 399; www.assetskills.org.uk

HUMAN RESOURCES

The field of human resources (HR) deals with all the functions in a business or organisation that relate to staff issues, such as recruitment, training and development and employment. In some businesses the term 'personnel' is used, although human resources is more commonly used now.

Human resources adviser/manager

The role of an HR professional can vary and is largely dependent on the individual organisation's needs and the value that the organisation's senior managers place on the HR function. It can include working at a strategic level on a range of HR policies, processes and practices in relation to the business needs of the organisation. More commonly, however, HR advisers work on day-to-day issues such as recruitment, contracts of employment, payroll, training, induction, disciplinary and grievance procedures, redundancy programmes, equal opportunities policies and setting up staff support systems. In large organisations, individuals may specialise in one of these areas, but in smaller companies they will deal with all aspects of the job.

Qualifications and Training

A good general education is essential, and most HR professionals will have NVQ at level 3 or above, or a first degree in an appropriate area. A range of appropriate qualifications includes NVQs in training and development, management or administration, and postgraduate qualifications are also increasingly available. The Chartered Institute of Personnel and Development (CIPD) provide a range of professional qualifications.

Personal Qualities and Skills

You must be highly organised with at least basic computer skills and the ability to interpret and produce statistics. You must have excellent 'people' skills since staff at all levels need to be able to approach and trust you. Sometimes you may have to use negotiating and persuading skills. You need to understand the business or organisation you work for at a strategic level.

Starting Salary

Salaries start at between £19,000 and £25,000, but many human resource staff attain senior management positions in their organisations.

Chartered Institute of Personnel and Development (CIPD), 151 The Broadway, London SW19 1JQ; 020 8612 6200; www.cipd.co.uk

Training officer/manager

Training officers work in medium-sized and large firms and organisations, national and local government, emergency services and voluntary organisations. They are responsible for identifying training requirements, designing training programmes, delivering training to individuals or groups and evaluating the success of training.

Qualifications and Training

This is an area of work that people move into after gaining experience in other posts or following general personnel experience. A professional qualification is advisable. The Chartered Institute of Personnel and Development (CIPD) offers a certificate in training practice for those new to the profession or with limited experience. NVQs in training and development at levels 3–5 are available.

Personal Qualities and Skills

You need to be happy and confident presenting to or facilitating groups of people. You need to be a good problem solver able to get people to change their attitudes. You must also be well organised, positive and enthusiastic. Sometimes you will have to be creative and imaginative, developing your own training materials.

Starting Salary

Salaries start at between £17,000 and £19,000, sometimes a little more in London.

info

Chartered Institute of Personnel and Development (CIPD), 151 The Broadway, London SW19 1JQ; 020 8612 6208; www.cipd.co.uk

Department for Education and Skills (DfES), Sanctuary Buildings, Great Smith Street, London SW1P 3BT; 0870 000 2288; www.dfes.gov.uk

Employment National Training Organisation (ENTO), Head Office, 4th Floor, Kimberley House, 47 Vaughan Way, Leicester LE1 4SG; 0116 251 7979; www.ento.co.uk/

I

ILLUSTRATION

see Art and Design

Medical illustrator

see Medical Illustration

INDEXER

see Publishing

INFORMATION SCIENCE

Information science is the collection, classification, storage and retrieval of information and knowledge, and the main occupations relating to this are outlined below.

Information scientist

Rather like librarians, information scientists organise, manage and develop information systems. Working with IT and paper-based systems, they store, analyse and retrieve information and distribute it to interested clients. They work for many types of organisation and with all kinds of information, including scientific, technical, legal, commercial, financial and economic. As well as cataloguing and indexing information and dealing with enquiries, information scientists often have to analyse statistics or write reports summarising highly technical or specialised information.

Qualifications and Training

This is a graduate profession and unless your degree is in librarianship or information science/management, you also have to do a one-year postgraduate qualification. Competition for places on these courses is fierce, and you need a year's experience in a library or information centre of some kind before you start your course.

Personal Qualities and Skills

You must be able to get on well with people and enjoy dealing with enquiries. It is important for you to have good IT skills: experience of handling databases is particularly useful. You should have a good memory and either a breadth of knowledge or highly specialist knowledge in a particular field such as law or science.

Starting Salary

Salaries start at between £16,000 and £21,000. You may be eligible for funding from the Arts and Humanities Research Council during your postgraduate studies.

info

ASLIB, The Association for Information Management, Temple Chambers, 3–7 Temple Avenue, London EC4Y 0HP; 020 7583 8900; www.aslib.co.uk

Chartered Institute of Library and Information Professionals (CILIP), 7 Ridgmount Street, London WC1E 7AE; 020 7255 0500; www.cilip.org.uk

Institute of Information Scientists, 39–41 North Road, London N7 9DP; 020 7619 0624/0625; www.iis.org.uk

Librarian/information manager

Librarians and information managers anticipate the information needs of their clients, acquire that information by the most efficient means possible on behalf of their clients, and may well analyse it and repackage it for the client. Information may come in the form of a book or journal, or may be extracted from databases in-house, on CD ROM or online. Librarians and information managers need to be able to use the internet themselves and show others how to do so.

Information needs to be organised to make it accessible to users by indexing, cataloguing and classifying. Librarians and information managers promote and exploit the library's collection to the library or information source users and assist them with any enquiries. They work in public libraries and schools, universities and colleges, in government, in the law, in hospitals, business and industry, and also in accountancy, engineering, professional and learned societies and in virtually all areas of economic activity.

Qualifications and Training

Library assistants are usually required to have four to five GCSEs or equivalent, to include English language; training is on the job. Part-time or distance-learning vocational courses leading to City and Guilds and SQA qualifications are available to library assistants in post. NVQs levels 2–4 in information and library services are also available. To qualify as a professional librarian or information officer and gain Chartered Membership of the Library Association, a degree or postgraduate qualification accredited by the association is necessary.

First degree courses, postgraduate diplomas and Master's are jointly accredited by the Library Association and the Institute of Information Scientists. A full list of the courses offered by 17 universities is available through the Library Association website. The Library Association and Institute of Information Scientists have joined together to create a new organisation, the Chartered Institute of Library and Information Professionals.

Personal Qualities and Skills

Librarians and information managers need to be well educated, with an outgoing personality, and able to communicate with people at all levels with clarity, accuracy and tact. They need intellectual curiosity, breadth of knowledge and a logical and methodical approach to seeking out, organising and presenting information. A good memory is also useful. Management skills and an interest in working with computers are important assets.

Starting Salary

Depending on age and experience, library assistants' salaries range from £9,000 to £16,500; newly qualified librarians earn from £11,900 to £16,500, and middle managers from about £17,000 to £27,000. The most senior qualified library managers of large services can earn above £32,000.

Chartered Institute of Library and Information Professionals, CILIP, 7 Ridgmount Street, London WC1E 7AE; 020 7255 0500; fax: 020 7255 0501; www.cilip.org.uk; e-mail: info@cilip.org.uk

Aslib, Association for Information Management, Temple Chambers, 3–7 Temple Ave, London EC4Y 0HP; 020 7583 8900; fax: 020 7583 8401; www.aslib.co.uk/info/careershome.htm

INFORMATION AND COMMUNICATION TECHNOLOGY

Information and communication technology (ICT) has an effect on all aspects of our lives. Almost all businesses and services make use of ICT to reach more customers, offer better services, reduce costs and improve efficiency. In the airline industry, for example, ICT underpins everything from selling and allocating seats to calculating fuel and filing flight plans. In the UK alone, 1 million people work as ICT professionals: 45 per cent in the ICT industry itself, and 55

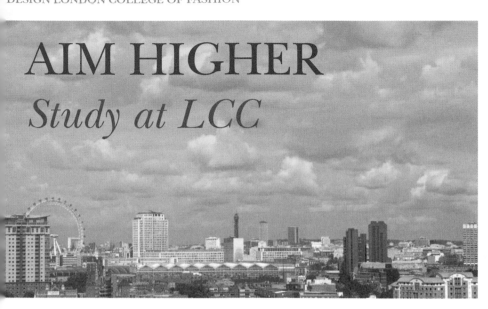

As the largest college of the University of the Arts London, the London College of Communications offers its students top class equipment across media and design areas. LCC film and TV students work in the only widescreen digital studio installed in a UK university while publishing and printing students have access to industry technology. The College has 500-plus computers on campus, an impressive new library and learning resource areas with open access ICT.

In many ways for LCC students, London is also their campus. Links with the Tate Modern have been in place for sometime and former students are really making their mark on the arts front. Currently, one of our graduates – Tom Hunter – has become the first ever photographer to have an exhibition in the National Gallery. Eddie Otchere, also a photographer, has become one of the five founding fellows chosen by the Arts Council to bring a young black viewpoint into arts management.

There are a number of areas in which LCC and its students have recently won major awards and national recognition. The UK Film Council and employers' body, Skillset, have named LCC as one of only two university-led National Screen Academies in England.

A wonderful collection of film memorabilia, the Stanley Kubrick Archives – 400 boxes of film history are going to be housed soon at LCC. Stephen Spielberg, pleased that the archives are coming to the University of the Arts London said, "His work will inspire future film-makers to push the boundaries of film." Last year, LCC students watched Stephen Poliakoff and playwright, Kwame Kei Armah – familiar to millions as a paramedic in *Casualty*, discuss the creation of compelling drama. Similarly in printing, LCC has been selected by the industry leader – Heidelberg – to become a Print Media Academy offering their worldwide Masters Programme.

per cent working in an ICT role in other industries. The e-skills National Training Organisation (NTO) estimates that around 150,000 to 200,000 additional ICT professionals are needed every year. A career in ICT can mean working in any industry – from the media to healthcare, education to financial services. Most jobs need a combination of technical, business and personal skills and can be divided into the following categories.

This is such a significant, growing and developing employment sector, that it is only possible to cover some of the major job titles and work areas in the sections that follow. When looking for work in this field it is important to read job specs and adverts carefully and to avoid a narrow approach to looking for highly specific job titles.

Computer service technician

Technicians are employed by retailers, manufacturers and organisations that make extensive use of computers in their business. Regular upgrading of office systems means a substantial amount of time is spent on installing and checking new systems, the rest being spent on diagnosing and correcting faults.

Database administration

Organisations obtain and store information about their customers, accounts, orders or stock levels on computers. The database manager takes responsibility for maintaining these and for security, access and the legal use of information held.

Hardware engineer

Engineers design, develop and undertake research into computers and the computerised components of cars and appliances. They are involved in manufacture, installation and testing. As well as dealing with engineering issues they need to be aware of safety, efficiency and environmental factors.

IT operations

This involves working in an IT department, running the computer systems. The work could include making sure the IT system is working properly, solving problems with it, helping those having trouble using the IT system, upgrading to add new functions and deciding how best to use IT to meet your organisation's goals or enhance their business. Job titles include applications programmer, systems analyst, network manager and database administrator.

IT research and development

Those who work in this sector create new technologies or new products. This could mean researching new approaches to mobile communications, or developing software packages. Job titles in this area include software developer, product tester and technical author.

IT sales and marketing

This covers promoting or selling products, services and IT solutions. You may be assigned to a particular customer or group of customers, or specialise in particular products or services.

IT services

This covers a range of customer-facing roles and could include developing websites, designing and installing IT systems for customers, supporting customers with software or hardware problems, and managing projects. Job titles include software support professional, technical architect and hardware engineer.

Multimedia programmer

Multimedia programmers write computer programs that draw together text, sound, graphics, digital/analogue photographs, 2D/3D modelling, animation, video, information and virtual reality in order to produce a multimedia product. Multimedia products are designed to work with the internet, interactive TV, CD ROMs, information kiosks, DVDs, computer games consoles and WAP mobile phones.

Network engineer

A network is a system of computers and other communication equipment linked to exchange information. This could be used to enable staff to share information through a company intranet or for global communication via the internet. Network engineers advise clients on options and benefits, as well as installing and testing equipment. They also diagnose faults and maintain the hardware, software and cabling systems.

Programmers

These are the people who write software such as operating systems. They may be employed by software manufacturers or in the computer departments of large organisations. As well as creating new programs they can be involved in identifying bugs in existing programs, modifying them, testing new programs and preparing user manuals.

Software engineers

They have a similar role to that of programmers but use this in technical and engineering settings. They may, for example, work on systems for contact centres or air traffic control. Most have a degree in software engineering or a related computer science. Many universities ask for maths A level or equivalent for entry to such courses. As most commercial and manufacturing functions now have established IT systems, the work undertaken by software engineers has shifted emphasis from creating new systems to using existing software and devising appropriate interfaces to integrate it with new products.

Systems analysts

Systems analysts work on delivering the best IT solutions for an organisation's needs. They examine how and where computerised systems would be of benefit, assess the hardware needed and look at the most cost-effective solutions. Systems analysts then work with programmers and supervise software production.

Systems support staff

Systems support staff work for suppliers of software and hardware, internet service providers or the computer departments of large companies. They provide technical support to users, often via the phone or e-mail. The work involves establishing what the problem is, helping the client put things right or deciding to refer the problem to other specialists. It requires detailed product knowledge as well as extreme patience and excellent communication skills. Training is often on the job, with entrants coming from a variety of backgrounds in which they have been able to demonstrate high levels of computer literacy.

Trainers

Software packages are increasingly complex and users require training to get the best out of them. Trainers are employed by software vendors, training consultancies and user companies for their own staff. Trainers need to be familiar with the packages at all levels, and have excellent communication and teaching skills. They may also be required to develop and write materials.

Web designers

(*see also* Art and Design)

Web designers design and plan websites either for their own company or for clients. The complexity of the task varies according to the nature of the site, and can include extensive use of multimedia or implementing secure systems for financial transactions. A considerable amount of time is spent testing sites and checking they are user-friendly. Once the site is working properly, designers upload it to a server and may be responsible for registering it with search engines in terms of both content and design.

Designers need an in-depth knowledge of the internet and must be up to date with technological developments. Many designers work on a freelance basis. The availability of jobs in this area is decreasing as increasingly sophisticated software packages are making web design less of a specialist area.

Qualifications and Training

Many employers set their own entry requirements, but are increasingly asking for academic or vocational qualifications from NVQs to degrees. Applicants for posts may be asked to take aptitude tests to assess their numeracy, logic, accuracy, thinking speed and verbal reasoning. Systems analysts and programmers are generally expected to be graduates. Entry to computer science degrees is normally with 2–3 A levels or equivalent, including maths. Web designers need knowledge of HTML and Java as well as familiarity with web design software such as Dreamweaver and Flash. Technicians and network engineers usually have a related National Diploma or vendor qualifications.

There are a large number of computer-related courses, and entry requirements vary according to the nature of the course. A growing number of Foundation degrees with flexible entry requirements are becoming available. Product-specific and professional qualifications are offered by companies such as Microsoft, Cisco and Novell and by professional bodies such as the British Computer Society, the Help Desk Institute and the Institute for the Management of Information Systems.

Employment-based training opportunities include Modern Apprenticeships for school leavers and Graduate Apprenticeships for those from non-IT disciplines. Many companies run their own programmes as well as sending trainees on relevant external courses.

Personal Qualities and Skills

The balance of skills that are most important varies between some of the above roles, but excellent problem solving, analytical and technical expertise and the willingness to develop with technological advances are all essential, though to different degrees. Being able to work under pressure, be part of a team and communicate well, especially to less technically trained colleagues, are equally important.

Starting Salary

An industry that encompasses so many jobs offers a wide range of starting salaries, reflecting qualifications, experience and market needs. Database managers start on between £15,000 and £21,000, database support staff around £15,000 to £18.000. Programmers start on between £19,000 and £27,000. Network engineers and systems administrators start on a similar range. Sales jobs often include an element of commission, and some roles offer overtime, shift allowances and extra payment for working at weekends.

info

e-skills UK, 1 Castle Lane, London SW1E 6DR; 020 7963 8920; fax: 0207 592 9138; www.e-skills.com; e-mail: info@e-skills.com

British Computer Society, 1st Floor, Block D, North Star House, North Star Avenue, Swindon, Wiltshire SN2 1FA; 0845 300 4417; www.bcs.org; e-mail: bcshq@hq.bcs.org.uk

Help Desk Institute, 21 High Street, Green Street Green, Orpington, Kent BR6 6BG; 01689 889 100; fax: 01689 889 227; www.hdi-europe.com; e-mail: support@hdi-europe.com

Institute of Analysts and Programmers, Charles House, 36 Culmington Road, Ealing, London W13 9NH; 020 8567 2118; www.iap.org.uk; e-mail: dg@iap.org.uk

Institute for the Management of Information Systems, 5 Kingfisher House, New Mill Road, Orpington, Kent BR5 3QG; 0700 00 23456; fax: 0700 00 23023; www.imis.org.uk; e-mail: central@imis.org.uk

British Interactive Media Association, Briarlea House, Southend Road, South Green, Billericay CM11 2PR; 020 7436 8250; www.bima.co.uk

Careers and Jobs in IT (Kogan Page)

INSURANCE

Apart from statutory obligations, insurance is a way of covering the costs arising from disasters of various kinds. Many people pay into a common pool, and those who incur losses can draw money from the pool. The four main areas are personal lines (motor, household, travel), commercial lines (fire, liability, goods in transit), life assurance and reinsurance. Work undertaken in the office includes assessing risks, policy drafting, underwriting (the acceptance and rating of business) and claims settling, and often involves computers. Sales staff work outside the office, as do surveyors and claims inspectors who assess losses on site. Other aspects of insurance include investment, legal and accountancy work. Insurance companies also operate pension funds for businesses. Lloyd's of London is a group of private insurers and is traditionally connected with international insurance, offering all types of cover.

Agents and inspectors

Agents call on people in their homes, selling insurance and collecting premiums; inspectors are salespeople and may also supervise agents and areas. The increase in internet and contact centre insurance sales means many companies have reduced the number of traditional sales staff they employ. Opportunities in contact centres are increasing.

Broker

As the link between client and insurer, the broker advises on and arranges policies for a wide range of businesses.

Loss adjuster

They work independently, and are appointed by insurers to negotiate settlement of insurance claims. Most chartered loss adjusters used to operate in private practice, 'adjusting' claims to ascertain the proper liability of an insurer. Increasingly, loss-adjusting companies are just as likely to provide cost-effective claims and risk-management services to large corporations, local authorities, health services or brokers.

Qualifications and Training

It is getting harder to enter this profession without either a degree or other professional qualifications in law, accountancy or engineering, but it is still possible to train straight from school or college if you have two A levels. If you already have a background in law, accountancy, etc, you have to work for an independent loss adjuster for two years before you can take the examinations of the Chartered Institute of Loss Adjusters (CILA). New entrants without approved background experience must take Chartered Insurance Institute (CII) exams before they can work towards their loss adjuster exams. To achieve chartered status takes three to four years for people with relevant experience, and six to seven years for new graduates.

Personal Qualities and Skills

You need to be a good communicator both on paper and face to face. You must have extreme integrity, be good at taking decisions and be very self-reliant.

Starting Salary

Salaries start at between £15,000 and £21,000, depending on whether you have relevant professional experience and the size of the company you work for.

info

Chartered Institute of Loss Adjusters, Peninsular House, 36 Monument Street, London EC3R 8LJ; 020 7337 9960; fax: 020 7929 3082; www.cila.co.uk; e-mail: info@cila.co.uk

Society of Claims Technicians, Peninsular House, 36 Monument Street, London EC3R 8LJ; 020 7337 9960; fax: 020 7929 3082; www.soct.co.uk; e-mail: info@soct.co.uk

Chartered Insurance Institute (CII), Training Advisory Service, 42–48 High Road, South Woodford, London E18 2JP; 020 8989 8464; www.cii.co.uk; e-mail: is@cii.co.uk

Underwriter

An underwriter works in one type of insurance such as motor, life or household and is responsible for assessing the extent of a risk, deciding whether to offer insurance cover and if any special terms or conditions are due. Underwriters calculate how much the individual or organisation should pay in insurance premium. They also answer enquiries and negotiate with clients and brokers, and communicate regularly with other professionals, such as doctors, to gather information.

A trainee insurance underwriter will study the proposal form for a request for insurance from a broker or potential customer, and may gather further information, for example from a person's doctor to ask for their medical history. The underwriter will then have to assess the risk and decide whether the company is going to insure against that risk.

Personal Qualities and Skills

An insurance underwriter is able to think clearly and have an analytical mind. He or she is confident at making decisions and always pays attention to detail. Underwriters are creative and like to solve problems; they have excellent communication skills which help when dealing with clients, negotiating and explaining complex details with brokers. A high level of numerical skills is required to understand and work with statistics.

Qualifications and Training

Although there are no formal entry requirements for insurance underwriters, many companies require entry qualifications equivalent to those required for the Associateship examination of the Chartered Insurance Institute (CII). These include: two A levels plus two GCSEs (A–C) including English; three A levels or vocational A levels; BTEC (Edexcel); CII Certificate of Insurance Practice; relevant NVQ; Advanced Financial Planning Certificate (AFPC).

Training is usually in-house in most insurance companies but external training courses also take place. The work takes place in different departments such as claims, accounts and investment. An experienced underwriter will provide hands-on training and work as a mentor for the trainee. The training takes 12–18 months to complete and is followed by up to five years of training in a specialist area of risk.

It is possible to train to become an Associate of the Chartered Insurance Institute; obtaining this qualification will improve career promotion and prospects.

To work as an underwriter for a Lloyd's company or Lloyd's broker it is compulsory to pass the Lloyd's Introductory Test. Applicants for the test must be already working for a Lloyd's company or broker. Study routes for the test can be through in-house or public courses.

Underwriters can work towards NVQs/SVQs levels 2, 3 and 4 in insurance.

Starting Salary

Income depends on the area of the country and the employer. New entrants with A levels/H grades may earn around £10,000–12,000. Graduate entrants may earn between £13,000–16,000. Senior underwriters earn between £40,000–60,000. Lloyd's underwriters earn up to £300,000. Underwriters working in the City of London earn considerably more. A few companies' salary scales are performance-based and include medical insurance and life insurance benefits.

info

Chartered Insurance Institute (CII), Training Advisory Service, 42–48 High Road, South Woodford, London E18 2JP; 020 8989 8464; www.cii.co.uk

Financial Services NTO, 51 Gresham Street, London EC2V 7HQ; 020 7216 7366; fax: 020 7216 7370; www.fsnto.org.uk

Society of Technicians in Insurance, Chartered Insurance Institute (CII), 20 Aldermanbury, London EC2V 7HY; 020 7417 4434; www.cii.co.uk/qualifications/societies/st

General Insurance Standards Council, 110 Cannon Street, London EC4N 6EU; 020 7648 7800; www.gisc.co.uk

INTERIOR DECORATOR

see Construction

CITB-Construction Skills, Bircham Newton, King's Lynn, Norfolk PE31 6RH; 01485 577577; fax: 01485 577793; www.constructionskills.net

INTERIOR DESIGNER/INSCAPE DESIGNER

Interior designers work for commercial organisations as well as undertaking private commissions. They are responsible for the interiors of buildings (whereas an architect is responsible for its shell). Interior design can cover materials for floors and ceilings, fitments and fittings, and colour schemes, along with electrical and spatial planning. The commercial organisations may be offices, hotels, pubs, stores or banks. Interior designers may work with architects, have their own consultancies, or work in design units within large organisations.

Qualifications and Training

Most interior designers have a degree in one of the following subjects: fine art, fashion and textile design, product design, interior design or graphic design. It is possible to get into this work without a degree if you have really demonstrable creative flair or a lot of relevant experience. Most training is on-the-job, working closely with more experienced and established designers. It can be valuable to do short courses on photography, desktop publishing and new product knowledge, in order to remain current.

Personal Qualities and Skills

As well as an eye for colour and a feel for fabric, you need considerable technical and product knowledge and technical drawing skills, either on paper or with computer aided design (CAD). You need to be able to work closely with other people and, if you work freelance, you should be confident enough to promote your own work.

Starting Salary

Salaries start at between £16,000 and £21,000. but can go much higher if you have established your reputation. If you work freelance you can charge £30 or more an hour. What you can charge depends upon geographical location and upon personal recommendations of your work.

The Chartered Society of Designers (CSD), 5 Bermondsey Exchange, 179–181 Bermondsey Street, London SE1 3UW; 020 7357 8088; www.csd.org.uk

Crafts Council, 44a Pentonville Road, Islington, London N1 9BY; 020 7278 7700; www.craftscouncil.org.uk

The Design Trust, 9 Burgess Hill, London NW2 2BY; 020 7435 4348; www.thedesigntrust.co.uk

The British Interior Design Association (BIDA), 3/18 Chelsea Harbour Design Centre, Lots Road, London SW10 0XE; www.bida.org

JEWELLERY

see Crafts

JOURNALISM

Journalism is the profession that writes and produces material for print, broadcast and digital media. Newspapers, magazines, television, radio and the internet offer myriad opportunities for journalists. Journalists can develop specialist fields or work in a general capacity. They can work as salaried employees or as freelancers, for national or local press.

Editor

The editor of a publication is responsible for its policy, content and the appointment and organisation of staff. An editor will prepare schedules for content and will build up key relationships with external bodies. An editor of a publication will become the spokesperson for the title and will be expected to speak at conferences and to comment publicly on issues of importance. The editor works closely with the different groups within the team including writers, production staff, advertising sales team, marketing and the publisher (*see also* Publishing). The editor will hold regular editorial meetings to discuss current work and to plan forthcoming features. The editor will also oversee the editorial budget. Section editors (newspapers and magazines) specialise in specific areas and run their own teams of journalists and commission articles for their sections. Typical newspaper sections include home affairs, foreign affairs, health, media, education and travel.

Qualifications and Training

Most editors have come from a background in journalism and have worked their way up to the job, and so may have journalism qualifications.

Personal Qualities and Skills

Editors coordinate the editorial team and need to have good leadership and managerial skills. Financial planning is also a key element to the job and being able to manage financial resources is important. The editor's role as a spokesperson for the publication requires confident communication skills and the ability to speak in public and in the media.

Starting Salary

Editors of trade magazines will earn £20,000 rising to £80,000+ for national newspapers.

info

Association of British Editors, 49 Frederick Road, Birmingham B15 1HN; 0121 455 7949; fax: 0121 454 6187

Newspaper Society, 74–77 Great Russell Street, London WC1B 3DA; 020 7636 7014; fax: 020 7631 5119; www.newspapersoc.org.uk

National Union of Journalists, Headland House, 308–312 Gray's Inn Road, London WC1X 8DP; 020 7278 7916; www.nujtraining.org.uk

Careers and Jobs in the Media (Kogan Page)

Journalist

Reporters find, research and write news articles and features for newspapers, magazines, special-interest periodicals, news agencies, radio, television and the internet (*see* Broadcast Journalist). Most reporters start out on local papers where they cover a mix of stories from weddings to council meetings. Local reporters are generally expected to multi-skill and might be expected to write the local news or features, sub-edit or take photographs. They work irregular hours and must be able to produce accurate, interesting and readable copy quickly, often in noisy offices or even public places. Editors look for trainees with an interest in current affairs and events, an accessible writing style and a good use of grammar, and an understanding of the role of local newspaper within its community. Good time management and being able to work under pressure are also important qualities as journalists have to work to strict deadlines.

Inexperienced journalists are expected to work their way up, starting with more routine jobs. Regional and local newspapers recruit trainee reporters and photographers under a training contract and some newspaper groups run trainee schemes. These schemes are open to school or college leavers who have not taken a specialist university or college course. Applications should be made direct to the editor for traineeships. Direct entrants to these schemes will be expected to attend block release or day release courses and to sit the National Council for the Training of Journalists (NCTJ) National Certificate or a National (Scottish) Vocational Qualification.

National papers generally employ reporters with some experience, and will look to journalists who have had experience on local newspapers. Trade magazine experience, where a knowledge of a specialist area has been developed, is also a route to entry in the national press. Occasionally national newspapers do advertise for trainee recruits but these opportunities are rare.

Trade magazines are also a route into the industry. Many magazines are produced on a monthly or fortnightly basis and specialise in particular subjects. Reporters on trade magazines are able to develop a specialist subject that can then be used to transfer to writing for national newspapers or to develop into a freelance career.

Experienced journalists have the opportunity to become feature writers or columnists for national newspapers. Feature writers suggest subjects for research, and produce longer than average articles dealing with topics not necessarily of current news value but of general interest. Feature writers will have developed an expertise or specialism within the subject they write about, and may have come originally not from a journalistic background but from the specialist area on which they write. Columnists often write about subjects from a personal point of view. Feature writers and columnists tend to be freelance writers working for a number of different newspapers, magazines and publishers, and will also work in broadcast media.

Qualifications and Training

Most journalists begin their career by serving for two or three years on a provincial newspaper. Minimum entry requirements are five GCSEs and two A level passes, but more than 65 per cent of all entrants are now graduates. There are also a number of degree courses in journalism, but many entrants have a degree in other disciplines plus on-the-job or postgraduate training.

Approximately 1,000 school/college leavers undertake NCTJ pre-entry courses each year at some 30 colleges/universities accredited by the NCTJ. Direct entrants must complete a two-year on-the-job training period that includes either a 12-week block release or day release to an approved course.

Personal Qualities and Skills

Journalists must possess powers of self-expression, observation, accuracy, patience and tact. They must take pride in their work, be resourceful, willing to

info

British Association of Journalists, 89 Fleet Street, London EC4Y 1DH; 020 7353 3003; www.bajunion.org.uk

National Council for the Training of Journalists (NCTJ), NCTJ Training Ltd, Latton Bush Centre, Southern Way, Harlow, Essex CM18 7BL; 01279 430009; fax: 01279 430008; www.nctj.com; e-mail: info@nctj.com

National Union of Journalists, Headland House, 308–312 Gray's Inn Road, London WC1X 8DP; 020 7278 7916; www.nujtraining.org.uk

www.newspapersoc.org.uk

Newspaper Society, 74–77 Great Russell Street, London WC1B 3DA; 020 7636 7014; fax: 020 7631 5119; www.newspapersoc.org.uk

Periodicals Training Council, Periodical Publishers Association, Queens House, 28 Kingsway, London WC2B 6JR; 020 7404 4166; fax: 020 7404 4167; www.ppa.co.uk; e-mail: info@ppa.co.uk

Careers and Jobs in the Media (Kogan Page)

travel and to work under pressure and irregular hours; stamina is required, as is confidence, great curiosity and the ability to put people at their ease. It helps to be able to write fast in longhand; word processing and internet research skills are also important.

Starting Salary

Salaries vary greatly. Trainees on a small weekly paper earn about £10,000, more in London. Experienced journalists earn £18,000–23,000+.

Broadcast journalist

Broadcast journalists work in radio, television and online. Unlike print journalists, almost all broadcast journalists take a postgraduate pre-entry course. Some journalists still make the transition to broadcasting from newspapers but it is increasingly regarded as a specialist branch of the profession in its own right. As in print, broadcast journalists will need to have good communication skills, an enquiring mind, a knowledge of current events and a sense of what makes a news story. The ability to speak clear, standard English is important. Both the BBC and ITN run traineeships for entrants into broadcast journalism.

Experience in radio journalism can be found in hospital, community and college radio. This can be used as evidence of interest and experience when applying to courses – many postgraduate courses will require a recorded news story as part of their application procedure.

Qualifications and Training

Broadcast journalists tend to be graduates or postgraduates in broadcast, bi-media, multimedia TV or online journalism. The Broadcast Journalism Training Council accredits courses that cover radio, television and online journalism.

info

BBC Training; 0870 122 0216; fax: 0870 122 0145; www.bbctraining.co.uk; e-mail: training@bbc.co.uk

BECTU (the independent union for those working in broadcasting), 373–377 Clapham Road, London SW9 9BT; 020 7346 0900; www.bectu.org.uk; e-mail: info@bectu.org.uk

Broadcast Journalism Training Council, www.bjtc.org.uk

CSV Training, 237 Pentonville Road, London N1 9NJ; 020 7278 6601; www.csv.org.uk/csv/Media; e-mail: info@csv.org.uk

Skillset (The Sector Skills Council for the Audio Visual Industries), Prospect House, 80–110 New Oxford Street, London WC1A 1HB; 020 7520 5757; www.skillset.org; e-mail: info@skillset.org

UK Association of Online Publishers, Queens House, 28 Kingsway, London WC2B 6JR; 020 7400 7510; fax: 020 7404 4167; www.ukaop.org.uk

Careers and Jobs in the Media (Kogan Page)

The BBC and ITN courses are fiercely competitive but will cover key aspects of broadcast journalism.

Personal Qualities and Skills

You need a real interest in and good knowledge of current affairs or particular topics such as sport or economics, depending what you are talking about. You have to be able to analyse information and present it in a way that can be clearly understood. Your speaking voice should be clear and authoritative, though regional accents are perfectly acceptable. You should be able to keep calm and think on your feet.

Starting Salary

Starting salaries range from £12,000 to £20,000; this wide range reflects the difference between working for a small local radio station or one of the large news and broadcasting organisations. With experience you can earn up to £45,000.

Press photographer

A small number of trainee photographers are recruited into the press each year. Press photographers work in newspapers, magazines and online, although many now work in a freelance capacity. Press photographers can specialise in areas such as sport or fashion. News photographers will work closely with journalists and editors.

Qualifications and Training

Trainee photographers are expected to gain a National or Scottish Vocation Qualification or national Certificate in Press Photography during work experience. Direct entrants are expected to have two years' relevant experience or taken an education course in photography.

Personal Qualities and Skills

Press photographers work under pressure and independently. They need good physical health and the ability to work unsocial hours, as well as technical and creative skills.

info

Association of Photographers, 81 Leonard Street, London EC2A 4QS; 020 7739 6669; fax: 020 7739 8787; www.the-aop.org; e-mail: general@aophoto.co.uk

British Institute of Professional Photography, Fox Talbot House, Ware, Herts SG12 9HN; 01920 464011; fax: 01920 487056; www.bipp.com

Newspaper Society, 74–77 Great Russell Street, London WC1B 3DA; 020 7636 7014; fax: 020 7631 5119; www.newspapersoc.org.uk

National Union of Journalists, Headland House, 308–312 Gray's Inn Road, London WC1X 8DP; 020 7278 7916; www.nujtraining.org.uk

Careers and Jobs in the Media (Kogan Page)

Starting Salary

£12,000 rising to £40,000+ for experienced photographers.

Sub-editor

Sub-editors are journalists who work for national daily or weekly newspapers, local and regional newspapers and magazines of every kind. They process all the copy that will appear in their publication to ensure that copy is accurate, free of typographical errors and spelling mistakes, makes sense and reads well. Sub-editors take the stories written by journalists and reporters and rewrite copy to make it fit the 'house-style', adhere to word counts and remain within the law. The sub-editor is responsible for putting the story on the page and is often responsible for designing and laying out pages. Sub-editors write headlines, picture captions and summaries.

Qualifications and Training

Many sub-editors will have been trained as journalists and then specialised. The NCTJ runs short courses and distance learning qualifications for sub-editors. The Periodical Publishers Association also runs courses for sub-editors.

Personal Qualities and Skills

Sub-editors must be meticulous in their work. They are required to make quick decisions and to have the confidence to rewrite or cut the work of others. They must be able to work under pressure and to meet deadlines.

Starting Salary

Starting salaries in local or regional press from £12,000 rising to £35,000 for senior sub-editors.

info

National Council for the Training of Journalists, Latton Bush Centre, Southern Way, Harlow, Essex CM18 7BL; 01279 430009; www.nctj.com; e-mail: info@nctj.com

National Union of Journalists, Headland House, 308–312 Gray's Inn Road, London WC1X 8DP; 020 7278 7916; www.nujtraining.org.uk

Periodicals Training Council, http://www.ppa.co.uk Periodicals Training Council, Periodical Publishers Association, Queens House, 28 Kingsway, London WC2B 6JR; 020 7404 4166; fax: 020 7404 4167; www.ppa.co.uk; e-mail: info@ppa.co.uk

Society for Editors and Proofreaders, Riverbank House, 1 Putney Bridge Approach, Fulham, London SW6 3JD; 020 7736 3278; fax: 020 7736 3318; www.sfep.org.uk; e-mail: administration@sfep.org.uk

Careers and Jobs in the Media (Kogan Page)

LABORATORY TECHNICIAN

Assisting with research, helping to diagnose diseases, measuring pollution levels and developing new products – these are some of the tasks laboratory technicians help to undertake. Laboratory assistants ensure that equipment is clean and in working order. They set up experiments and investigations and record data. They may also be involved in stock control, monitoring and ordering chemicals, equipment and other supplies. Laboratory technicians working in education help school and college students to use equipment safely and record results correctly, and they may be involved in demonstrating how to conduct experiments. Laboratory technicians work in education, in medicine, in the pharmaceutical industry, in food science and in research laboratories of every kind.

Qualifications and Training

Most employers expect you to have at least four GCSEs grades A to C including science, maths and English. A BTEC qualification in science or applied science is also an accepted entry qualification. There is a trend towards employers taking on more applicants with A levels and degrees. Most training is on the job, but many employers provide the opportunity for technicians to attain NVQ levels 2, 3 and 4 in laboratory science. Employers also send technicians on regular updating courses on health and safety, risk assessment and on learning to use specific pieces of equipment or computer systems.

Personal Qualities and Skills

As a laboratory assistant you need to have good practical skills, including manual dexterity, and you need to pay great attention to detail, adopting a methodical approach to your work. You should enjoy working in a team, but also be prepared to take on particular responsibility. In education, there is a lot of contact with teachers and students, so you need to be a good communicator.

Starting Salary

Salaries for new technicians range from £13,000 to £16,000; £20,000 to £22,000 for a senior technician. Salaries tend to be higher in the private sector, particularly in the pharmaceutical industry.

The Association for Science Education, College Lane, Hatfield, Hertfordshire AL10 9AA; 01727 283000; www.ase.org.uk

CLEAPSS School Science Services, Brunel University, Uxbridge UB8 3PH; 01895 251496; www.cleapss.org.uk

SEMTA: The Sector Skills Council for Science, 14 Upton Road, Watford, Hertfordshire WD18 0JT; 01923 238 441; www.semta.org.uk

LAND AND PROPERTY

The land and property sector covers a wide range of occupations all to do with the management, sale and purchase of land and buildings.

Estate agent

Estate agents are responsible for the sale, letting and management of any kind of property – factories, shops, offices and farms as well as residential property. In many cases, they also deal with valuation and survey work, and offer other services such as auctioneering and financial services advice. Large firms provide a wide range of these services through specialist departments employing qualified professionals, particularly in the area of surveying and valuation. Dedicated sales staff fulfil the role of property negotiators, and in the majority of smaller firms with just one or two branches, a combination of these functions will be found.

Qualifications and Training

The principal professional bodies are the National Association of Estate Agents (NAEA) and the Royal Institution of Chartered Surveyors (RICS). Membership of RICS is normally attained through graduate entry coupled with a period of accredited practical training. NVQs in Residential Estate Agency and Lettings and Management are available through the NAEA's National Assessment Centre. The NAEA also offers examination-based, nationally recognised qualifications in Residential Sales (CREA), Lettings and Management (CRLM) and Commercial and Business Transfer (CCBT). These qualifications also provide the route to membership of the Association at the senior level of Fellow.

Professional qualifications are an asset and becoming more sought-after by employers. However, anyone can set up in business as an estate agent unless they have been banned from doing so by the Director General of Fair Trading, are bankrupt or guilty of a range of other criminal offences proscribed under the 1979 Estate Agents Act.

Established firms will very often provide opportunities for unqualified beginners within the field of property negotiation, but at the same time encourage the attainment of a more formal qualification.

Personal Qualities and Skills

For most people the purchase or sale of a house is the biggest financial transaction they will ever make, and there are bound to be attendant worries and problems. Estate agents must be able to deal with their clients' problems sympathetically, but in a businesslike way. In addition to being numerate and literate, they should possess an outgoing personality, coupled with the energy and enthusiasm to work in a competitive, fast-moving environment where customer care is of paramount importance.

Starting Salary

School leavers with A levels start on £10,000 to £12,000 – graduates or mature entrants on between £14,000 and £20,000. A substantial part of your salary is made up from commission on sales or lettings of property. A basic income is often guaranteed for the first six months of employment, but after this you have to meet specific sales targets to achieve your predicted salary. Performance-related pay is very much the norm in this profession.

info

National Association of Estate Agents, Arbon House, 21 Jury Street, Warwick CV34 4EH; 01926 496800; fax: 01926 400953; www.naea.co.uk; e-mail: info@naea.co.uk

Royal Institution of Chartered Surveyors, Surveyor Court, Westwood Way, Coventry, West Midlands CV4 8JE; 0870 333 1600; www.rics.org/com; e-mail: contactrics@rics.org

Gamekeeper

Gamekeepers work on large country estates for private landlords, management firms and private syndicates who wish to organise a shoot. They rear the game birds and fish, and protect them from poachers and predators. They must ensure that the proper environment for the game is maintained, and on shooting days, organise the beaters.

Qualifications and Training

There are no formal entry qualifications, but gamekeepers must have a driving licence, be good at handling a dog, and suitable to apply for a shotgun licence. There are part-time and full-time City & Guilds and BTEC courses in gamekeeping, and gamekeeping and countryside management. Some of these courses may set specific entry requirements. The training is on the job and most gamekeepers start as an assistant or under keeper.

Personal Qualities and Skills

You have to love being outside in all weathers and have a real interest in nature. You need to be very practical, good with your hands and physically fit. It is important that you are very observant, both of animal and plant life and of safety issues. You are on your own for a great deal of the time, but you must be able to communicate well with other people when shoots or other events are taking place.

Starting Salary

Salaries start at between £13,000 and £16,500. Many jobs include free or subsidised accommodation, and clothing allowances or other benefits.

info

Game Conservancy Trust, Fordingbridge, Hampshire SP6 1EF; 01425 652381; www.gct.org.uk

British Deer Society, Fordingbridge, Hampshire SP6 1EF; 01425 655434; www.bds.org.uk

Lantra, Lantra House, Stoneleigh Park, Coventry, Warwickshire CV8 2LG; 0845 707 8007; www.lantra.co.uk

Land agent

Land agents work for estate owners and for large institutional owners. Their work overlaps to some extent with that of agricultural surveyors in that they are both concerned with the use and development of land, and may advise owners on agricultural methods, forestry, accountancy, building or improving of farm buildings. In addition the land agent may be responsible for stocking and for employing estate staff, as well as attending to the owner's personal business matters.

Qualifications and Training

Formal qualifications are not always necessary for a land agent who is employed by a private owner. However, it is advisable to become professionally qualified as a surveyor (*see* Surveying).

Personal Qualities and Skills

Necessary requirements include a love of the land and being out of doors, a practical approach and the ability to direct one's own work.

Starting Salary

A school leaver could expect about £8,000, whereas a newly qualified surveyor with professional competence would receive about £15,000–20,000.

Royal Institution of Chartered Surveyors, 12 Great George Street, London SW1P 3AD; 0870 333 1600; www.rics.org.uk

Valuer

(*see also* Auctioneer, Estate Agent, Land Agent, Surveying)

Valuers are employed by a wide variety of firms to assess the worth of goods and property (including land, buildings, fine arts, chattels, machinery and livestock). They may work for building societies, estate agents, insurance companies, property companies or any commercial, financial or industrial organisation that has to know true commercial values for selling, renting, investment or taxation purposes. Some valuers are also surveyors, auctioneers or land agents.

Qualifications and Training

There are two components to qualifying as a Chartered Surveyor or Valuer. First is successful completion of a degree or diploma approved by the Royal Institution of Chartered Surveyors (RICS), followed by enrolment onto the Assessment of Professional Competence (APC). This is two years' practical training while in employment, concluding with an RICS professional assessment interview. Postgraduate conversion courses are also available.

Professional qualifications in rating and valuations are awarded by the Institute of Revenues, Rating and Valuation (IRRV). Courses leading to IRRV examinations are available on day release or block release and by distance learning.

Personal Qualities and Skills

A valuer needs discretion combined with aptitude to understand the various economic factors involved in commerce.

Starting Salary

Trainees £10,000–13,000 depending on age and qualifications, with higher salaries in London; £13,000–19,000 when qualified.

info

Institute of Revenues, Rating and Valuation, 41 Doughty Street, London WC1N 2LF; 0207 831 3505; fax: 0207 831 2048; www.irrv.org.uk

Royal Institution of Chartered Surveyors (RICS), 12 Great George Street, Parliament Square, London SW1P 3AD; 0870 333 1600; www.rics.org/afa

LANDSCAPE ARCHITECTURE

see Gardening

LANDSCAPE ARCHITECT

Landscape Architecture as a profession covers the three divisions of design, management and science.

Landscape designer

Designers are trained in the planning and design of all types of outdoor spaces. They use design techniques based on their knowledge of the functional and aesthetic characteristics of landscape materials, and of the organisation of landscape elements, external spaces and activities. Their work ranges from large-scale landscape planning to the preparation of schemes for the short- and long-term development of individual sites. It also includes preparing detailed designs, specifications, contract drawings and letting and supervising contracts. Some practitioners are also qualified in other disciplines such as planning and architecture, and the landscape designer draws on many fields in order to promote new landscapes, and sustain existing ones.

Landscape manager

Landscape managers employ management techniques in the long-term care and development of new and existing landscapes, and also in determining policy and planning for future landscape management and use. They have particular expertise in the management and maintenance of landscape materials, both hard and soft, based on established principles of construction, horticulture and ecology. In addition, the landscape manager will have a thorough knowledge of budgetary control procedures, property and resource management, especially related to labour requirements and machinery, and the letting and administration of contracts.

Landscape scientist

Landscape scientists have a specific understanding of the principles and process of natural biological and physical systems. They relate their training and experience in subjects such as ecology, conservation, biology, soil science and botany to the solution of practical landscape problems, providing both traditional and innovative input to landscape design, planning and management work. Evaluation of the significance and effects of planning proposals, along with creating new habitats and environments in association with mineral workings, forestry and agriculture, make up a considerable amount of the work of landscape scientists. Smaller-scale ecological and habitat surveys, species assessments, wildlife management plans and the appraisal and preparation of conservation schemes are frequent tasks. Some landscape scientists are involved in research and teaching.

Qualifications and Training

The recognised professional qualification for those working in all aspects of landscape architecture is Member of the Landscape Institute (MLI), which entitles the use of the title Chartered Landscape Architect. There are three divisions: Design, Management and Science. Associate Membership, the first step towards achieving this, is gained after completing an accredited degree. Two years' relevant work is required as an Associate Member before taking the Institute's Professional Practice Examination and progressing to full Professional Membership. A list of accredited courses is available from the Landscape Institute.

Personal Qualities and Skills

Those working in design need creativity, imagination, a practical outlook, interest in the landscape and an enthusiasm for working outdoors. Those in management require good organisational and interpersonal skills, consistent application and a practical outlook. Scientists need enthusiasm for the subject, technical commitment and good communication skills.

Starting Salary

A recent graduate could expect to earn around £20,000. A fully qualified chartered member could expect to start on approximately £23,000.

info

British Association of Landscape Industries (BALI), Landscape House, Stoneleigh Park, Warwickshire CV8 2LG; 0870 770 4972; www.bali.co.uk

Landscape Design Trust, Bank Chambers, 1 London Road, Redhill, Surrey RH1 1LY; 01737 779 257; www.landscape.co.uk

The Landscape Institute (LI), 33 Great Portland Street, London W1W 8QG; 020 7299 4500; www.L-i.org.uk

LAW

The legal profession has many occupations within it, but all are based on upholding the laws of the land and dealing with those who contravene the laws. The word 'lawyer' is a blanket term that covers both solicitors and barristers. Solicitors advise clients and operate in the lower courts. Barristers are instructed by solicitors to act for clients, and work in the higher courts. Opportunities for lawyers can be found in the public and private sector as well as within the legal system. The legal profession also offers careers for those who have not trained as lawyers, such as legal clerks and executives.

Advocate/barrister

The services of a barrister are required by solicitors (*see also* Solicitor) who deal with the clients and then 'brief' the barrister. Barristers give specialised advice on the law and plead counsel in the higher court. They may also appear in the lower courts, where they usually begin their careers. Some are employed in the Army Legal Services, giving advice on all aspects of service and civil law that may affect the Army.

In Scotland, an advocate is the equivalent of a barrister. Advocates may not select their clients. Provided that a reasonable fee is tendered they may not, without good cause, refuse instructions to act in litigation. Advocates also work in the public sector, Crown Prosecution Service, the legal section of a government department or as Parliamentary drafters.

Barristers specialise in arguing a case in court and offer a legal opinion for solicitors when asked to consider a particular question of law. Barristers are instructed by solicitors on behalf of clients and never directly employed by clients.

The majority of barristers work independently through sets of 'chambers' (which are a collective organisation of barristers), and tend to be self-employed. Once established within chambers, barristers can advertise for work.

Qualifications and Training

Full details of qualifications required for admission are available from the General Council of the Bar, but generally students are expected to hold a UK law degree with second-class honours or better, or a non-law degree at the same standard plus a pass in a special one-year course known as the Common Professional Examination/Postgraduate Diploma in Law.

Every intending barrister must join one of the four Inns of Court. Students intending to practise must also attend a one-year full-time vocational course. A list of institutions offering this is available from the Bar Council. This is followed by a one-year pupillage under the personal instruction and guidance of a barrister. Pupillage may involve researching relevant details of a case, setting them out in detail and drafting documents. During the first six months, pupils may attend court but may not accept briefs.

After completing pupillage a barrister has to find a 'seat' in an existing set of barristers' chambers. Some may choose to work as employed barristers and enter the civil service, local government or commerce and industry. About 15 years after being established at the Bar, a barrister may apply for a 'patent' as a Queen's Counsel. Although 'taking silk', as it is known, is usual (but not obligatory) if a barrister wishes to become a High Court Judge, it can have financial penalties and some barristers stay 'juniors' throughout their career at the Bar.

Full details of the qualifications and training required for advocacy in Scotland are available from the Clerk of Faculty. Generally speaking, applicants require a Scottish law degree with second-class honours or better, or a degree in Scottish law together with an Honours degree, second-class or better, from a university in the UK in another subject. In addition, they will have obtained a Diploma in Legal Practice from a Scottish university and served at least 12 months' traineeship in a solicitor's office in Scotland.

Personal Qualities and Skills

As it will be necessary to understand and interpret complex legal wording into clear basic English, barristers must have an excellent command of the English language and a meticulous understanding of the use of words. Barristers must understand and talk knowledgeably about technical matters in order to be able to cross-examine the most expert witness, for example, on complex aspects of technology. It is also useful if barristers present a highly confident and self-assured manner and can put on a 'good performance' in court. Since the work is confidential, a barrister needs to be trustworthy and discreet.

Starting Salary

Barristers' earnings relate to the amount and type of their work, their reputation, and, if they share chambers, the apportionment and value of briefs. Barristers may find it a struggle to make a living at the beginning of their profession, but the rewards for those who succeed can be high.

info

General Council of the Bar, 2/3 Cursitor Street, London EC4A 1NE; 020 7440 4000; www.barcouncil.org.uk

Details of education and training at the Bar: www.legaleducation.org.uk

Faculty of Advocates, Advocates Library, Parliament House, 11 Parliament Square, Edinburgh EH1 1RF; 0131 226 5071; www.advocates.org.uk

Barrister's clerk/advocate's clerk

The barrister's clerk is the administrator or manager of the business chambers, deciding which briefs to accept, which of the barristers in the chamber to give them to, and negotiating the fees with the solicitor. The accounts, the barristers' appointment books and the efficient day-to-day running of the office are all part of the job of an experienced clerk.

Qualifications and Training

The minimum qualification is four GCSE pass grades at A, B or C in academic subjects. Training is on the job and juniors can apply through the Institute of Barristers' Clerks to attend a two-year part-time Edexcel (BTEC) national certificate course studying organisation, finance, management, law, marketing and chambers administration. On obtaining the certificate, juniors may apply, after five years' service, for qualified Membership of the Institute of Barristers' Clerks.

The Bar in Scotland is divided into 10 'stables', each of which is served by an advocate's clerk and a deputy clerk employed by Faculty Services Ltd. Training is provided in service. The job of advocate's clerk is very similar to that of barrister's clerk in England and Wales. Their rates of pay are linked to the civil service scale on a level that roughly relates to a comparable post within the courts' administration. The 10 advocate clerks have clerical and secretarial staff to provide them with administrative support.

Personal Qualities and Skills

In order to manage efficient chambers and the barristers who work from them, a barrister's clerk needs good organisational skills, the ability to lead a team as well as be part of a team, and to get on with the general public. A good command of written and spoken English and an appreciation of the necessity for absolute confidentiality at all times are vital to success in this career.

Starting Salary

Starting salaries are in the region of £10,000. Junior clerks with two or three years' experience receive £13,500–18,000, going up to £28,000 for very experienced juniors. Senior clerks may earn £60,000–75,000 plus a performance-related bonus. Senior clerks were traditionally paid a fee which was a percentage of the barrister's own earnings. Some are still paid in this way, and the fee is usually around 5 per cent.

The Bar Council, 289–293 High Holborn, London WC1V 7HZ; 020 7242 0082; www.barcouncil.org.uk/

Institute of Barristers' Clerks (IBC), 289–293 High Holborn, London WC1 7HZ; 020 7831 7144; www.barristersclerks.com

Court staff

Court clerk

Court clerks are legal advisers who give advice to unpaid (non-stipendiary) magistrates who are trying cases in the magistrate's courts. They are qualified lawyers, but they do not take part in the decision making about judgements and sentencing. As magistrates do not have to be legally qualified, it is the court clerks who ensure that magistrates interpret and apply the law correctly.

Qualifications and Training

Court clerks have to be either qualified solicitors or barristers, who themselves must have either a law degree or an approved postgraduate legal qualification. Court clerks follow a set training programme and also learn by working with more experienced clerks, finding out about the many different areas of work – road traffic, licensing, fines enforcement, sentencing, etc.

Personal Qualities and Skills

As well as a real interest in and broad knowledge of the law, court clerks must be logical thinkers, capable of undertaking fairly detailed research. They must be discreet, sensitive and calm, but also able to remain detached when dealing with stressful and upsetting situations.

Starting Salary

Salaries start at £19,000 to £20,000. Experienced court clerks earn around £30,000.

info

Her Majesty's Court Service, 5th Floor, Clive House, Petty France, London SW1H 9HD; 0845 456 8770; www.hmcourts-service.gov.uk

Scottish Court Service, Hayweight House, 23 Lauriston Street, Edinburgh, EH3 9DQ; 0131 229 9200; www.scotcourts.gov.uk

Skills for Justice, 9 & 10 Riverside Court, Don Road, Sheffield S9 2TJ; 0114 261 1994; www.skillsforjustice.com

Court Reporter

Court reporters attend court sittings and take down a complete report of all the evidence, the summing-up or judgment and, on occasions, the speeches of counsel in the various cases. Formerly, the proceedings were taken down in shorthand; now a palantype or stenograph is used. This is a typewriter-like machine that enables the reporter to achieve 200 words per minute. In addition, computers may be used to prepare transcripts, with all the advantages of on-screen editing and speed of preparation. The work sometimes involves travelling to a number of different courts. The majority of verbatim reporters begin their careers in the courts but can also work for Hansard, producing reports of proceedings in the House of Commons and the House of Lords. Television subtitlers also use the skills of verbatim reporting.

Justices' Clerks' Assistant

Administrative assistants and administrative officers assist Justices' Clerks in the administration of the magistrates' courts. Their work involves the preparing of summonses and warrants, the issuing of licences and fine notices, and seeing that correct court procedures are followed.

In Scotland, the administration of the court comes under the province of the Scottish Court Administration, which is part of the civil service. This includes staff who do a similar job to Justices' Clerks' assistants.

Qualifications and Training

No specific academic qualifications are demanded for court reporters, although GCSE and A level passes can be an advantage. Applicants need to have proven ability in shorthand or steno-typing (usually over 150 words per minute), good typing speeds, and a thorough knowledge of grammar and punctuation. Legal experience can also be an asset. Details of full-time, part-time and distance learning courses are available from the British Institute of Verbatim Reporters. In Scotland, there are no college courses but training is provided on the job by working alongside an experienced reporter.

Administrative Officers need five GCSE passes (grade C or above), one of which must be English. The Scottish Court Service looks for applicants with Highers. Training lasts for two to three years, during which time trainees work and undertake courses run by the Court Service.

Personal Qualities and Skills

Anyone concerned with the courts must be discreet, honest and trustworthy, as most of the work is confidential. Reporters must show a high degree of accuracy.

Starting Salary

Qualified court reporters earn around £13,000. Freelancers can earn £140+ a day.

info

British Institute of Verbatim Reporters, Cliffords Inn, Fetter Lane, London EC4A 1LD; 020 8907 8249; www.bivr.org.uk

Individual Courts of Law

Northern Ireland Court Service, Windsor House, Bedford Street, Belfast BT2 7LT; 028 9032 8594; www.nics.gov.uk/pubsec/courts/courts.htm

Law Society of Scotland, 26 Drumsheugh Gardens, Edinburgh EH3 7YR; 0131 226 7411; fax: 0131 225 2934; www.lawscot.org.uk; e-mail: legaleduc@lawscot.org.uk

Careers in the Law (Kogan Page)

Legal services commission research assistant

The statutory government advisory body on law reform, the Law Commission, is currently working on projects in a variety of fields including common law, company and commercial law, crime and property law, and on general revision of statute law. The work is carried out in small teams, each under the direction of a Commissioner, consisting of qualified lawyers and research assistants. Law graduates and graduates of other disciplines who have completed the Legal Practice Course or the Bar Vocational Course are recruited annually to work as research asslstants. The work offers the opportunity to take part in the creation of new legislative measures, as well as the in-depth development of skills in a particular area of law. Extensive consultation and investigation takes place before proposals are formulated; a sizeable proportion result in legislation. Projects range from major investigations of controversial areas of law to the consideration of a specific problem.

Qualifications and Training

The **minimum academic standard** required is a first or high upper second-class (or equivalent) degree achieved in legal studies (based on the law of England and Wales) of at least two years' duration.

Personal Qualities and Skills

You need a genuine interest in, as well as a thorough knowledge of the law and legal issues. You must have excellent research skills, including the use of databases. You must be able to think and write articulately, be good at solving problems and be able to communicate well.

Starting Salary

Starting salaries range from £20,000 to £29,000. The highest salaries include London Weighting and are also paid to entrants with good postgraduate qualifications as well as a high class of degree.

info

Legal Services Commission, Legal Services Research Centre, 85 Gray's Inn Road, London WC1X 8TX; 020 7759 0000; www.legalservices.gov.uk

Law costs draftsman

Legal costs are a complex and developing subject. The costs that may be charged by a solicitor or recovered against an unsuccessful party in litigation depend on many different factors. Frequently the amount of costs payable is disputed.

Many solicitors employ law costs draftsmen to prepare their bills, to justify the costs claimed or to challenge the amount of costs payable by their client to another party to litigation. Some law costs draftsmen are employed in solicitors' offices while others work independently.

Qualifications and Training

To become a student with the Association of Law Costs Draftsmen an applicant must have a minimum of four GCSEs at Grade C or higher, including English and maths, be in employment predominantly concerning law costs, and able to provide employment and character references. Students are required to enrol on the Association's training course. Exemptions may apply to parts of the course for those with legal qualifications.

Personal Qualities and Skills

Law costs draftsmen need to be patient, able to cope with detail, and be methodical and careful in their work.

Starting Salary

From £11,000–16,000, but in this work there is a range of payments and some people may earn much more than this.

info

Association of Law Costs Draftsmen, c/o S A Chapman, Church Cottage, Church Lane, Stuston, Diss, Norfolk IP21 4AG; 01379 741404; fax: 01379 742702; www.alcd.org.uk; e-mail: enquiries@alcd.org.uk

Legal cashier/administrator

Legal cashiers and administrators work in solicitors' offices and are responsible for dealing with the accounts and finance function of a solicitor's practice. Legal cashiers may work as the sole bookkeeper, administrator or manager or, in a big firm, be responsible for a large number of staff. The Institute of Legal Cashiers and Administrators keeps a register of vacancies, providing a free service to solicitors and members.

Qualifications and Training

The Institute of Legal Cashiers and Administrators has three levels of qualification: Diploma, Associateship and Fellowship. It offers correspondence courses leading to the Diploma and Associateship examinations. Formal academic qualifications are not required to take these. The diploma is a qualification in its own right and covers the maintenance of a solicitor's internal financial records. It is particularly aimed at those without bookkeeping knowledge. The Associateship is for those who wish to make a career as a legal cashier or administrator, and enables them to advise and manage financial and administrative affairs in any solicitor's office. The Fellowship, available to Associates, is the highest qualification, offering a deeper insight into the profession.

Personal Qualities and Skills

Entrants must have a high standard of integrity and reliability and be very discreet.

Starting Salary

£11,000–16,000

Institute of Legal Cashiers and Administrators, 146–148 Eltham Hill, Eltham, London SE9 5DX; 020 8294 2887; www.ilca.org.uk; e-mail: info@ilca.org.uk

Legal executive

A legal executive is a professional lawyer employed in a solicitor's office or in the legal departments of commerce and central and local government. The training and academic requirements in a specified area of law are at the same level as those required of a solicitor. Consequently, with few exceptions, a legal executive is able to carry out tasks that are similar to those undertaken by solicitors. The main areas of specialisation are conveyancing, civil litigation, criminal law, family law and probate. In addition to providing a worthwhile career in its own right, the legal executive qualification provides access to those wishing to qualify as solicitors via the Institute route. In Scotland, the term 'legal executive' is not used, but solicitors engage assistants to do similar work.

Qualifications and Training

The minimum entry requirement is four GCSEs to include English, but A level students and graduates are welcome. As an alternative, the Institute accepts a qualification in vocational legal studies, and has special arrangements for students who are over 21. In the main, training is on a part-time basis so that there is potential for trainees to 'learn while they earn'. For those already working in a legal environment, but with no formal legal qualifications, an NVQ (level 4) in legal practice is available, and the Institute of Legal Executives (ILEX) is the awarding body.

Personal Qualities and Skills

An ability to communicate, both verbally and in writing, with people at all levels, absolute discretion and trustworthiness, together with meticulous attention to detail, are essential.

Starting Salary

Varies according to age and qualification, and the type of work undertaken. The average starting salary is around £12,000. Many established legal executives earn £60,000+.

Institute of Legal Executives, Kempston Manor, Kempston, Bedford MK42 7AB; 01234 841000; www.ilex.org.uk; e-mail: info@ilex.org.uk

Notary public

A notary public is an international lawyer, whose main duty it is to prepare and verify legal documents for use abroad. These can be certified translations, powers of attorney and all manner of mercantile documents. There are two types of notaries: general notaries who are usually full-time solicitors with a part-time notarial practice, or scrivener notaries who are full-time notaries with linguistic skills. The latter are usually to be found in central London, the former anywhere in the UK. Although nearly all the work of scrivener notaries is of an international nature, they are competent to advise on certain domestic matters as well.

Qualifications and Training

Qualification as a notary is open to solicitors, barristers and graduates, whose degree need not necessarily be in law. There is a unified system for the initial stage of qualification for both branches of the profession. This consists of a diploma course administered by Cambridge University. A general notary, having obtained this diploma, can then apply for a faculty to practise to the Faculty Office of the Archbishop of Canterbury. A scrivener notary, however, would need to take additional examinations such as those testing knowledge of two languages and the law of the country of one such language, with a requirement also to spend two years in a scrivener notary's office.

Personal Qualities and Skills

A notary public should be discreet, meticulous and knowledgable.

Starting Salary

A general notary will receive not only the remuneration earned as a notary but also any income earned as a solicitor. A scrivener notary, on the other hand, will only receive notarial income, and a starting salary upon qualification will be about £30,000.

info

Notaries Society, Administration Dept, PO Box 226, Melton Woodbridge, Suffolk IP12 1WX; Fax: 01394 383772; www.thenotariessociety.org.uk; e-mail: NotariesSociety@compuserve.com

Society of Scrivener Notaries; www.scrivener-notaries.org.uk

Worshipful Company of Scriveners, HQS Wellington, Temple Stairs, Victoria Embankment, London WC2R 2PN; 020 7240 0529; fax: 020 7497 0645; www.scriveners.org.uk; e-mail: clerk@scriveners.org.uk

Solicitor

The role of the solicitor is to provide clients with skilled legal representation and advice. The clients can be individual people or companies, or any type of organisation or group. A solicitor may work on all kinds of legal matters, from house purchases to defence of people accused of crimes; from selling a corporation to drafting a complicated will or trust. Solicitors may also represent clients in all courts, but will often brief a barrister (*see* Barrister) to represent the client, and then act as a liaison between them.

Scottish solicitors can appear in all courts and tribunals in Scotland up to and including the Sheriff Court. They can also gain rights of audience enabling them to appear in the higher courts by becoming a solicitor-advocate, or may brief an advocate to represent their clients.

While some solicitors may deal with a variety of legal problems, others specialise in a particular area such as shipping, planning and construction, financial services or social security. Specialisation within the profession is increasing. The majority of solicitors work in private practice, with firms made up of several partners. Many others work as employed solicitors in commerce, industry, local and central government and other organisations.

Solicitors are instructed directly by clients and have a lot of contact with them. They have rights of audience in the magistrates' court and the county court. Unlike barristers, solicitors do not wear wigs but do wear gowns if they appear in county court. Solicitors are governed by a professional body called the Law Society.

Qualifications and Training

England and Wales: the Law Society governs the training of solicitors in England and Wales, which takes place in two stages – the academic and the professional. Most, but not all, entrants to the profession are graduates. Fellows of the Institute of Legal Executives over the age of 25 with five years' qualifying experience do not need to complete the academic stage. Non-law graduates take the Common Professional Examination (CPE) or a Postgraduate Diploma in Law; those with the qualifying law degrees are exempt from this. The next stage, the vocational stage, is taken via the legal practice course, available at a number of colleges or universities. It is a one-year full-time or two-year part-time course. The trainee solicitor then has to undertake a two-year training contract with an authorised firm or organisation. During the course of this, a 20-day professional skills course is undertaken, usually on a modular basis.

Scotland: the Law Society of Scotland governs the training of solicitors in Scotland. It is possible to study for a Bachelor of Laws degree at five Scottish universities: Aberdeen, Dundee, Edinburgh, Glasgow and Strathclyde. Alternatively, it is possible to take the Law Society's own examinations by finding employment as a pre-diploma trainee. After completion of the LLB degree or professional examinations, all graduates who would like to become solicitors must take the diploma in legal practice – a 26-week postgraduate course, which also offers training in office and business skills. After successful completion of the degree and the diploma, those who wish to become solicitors then serve a two-year training contract with a Scottish solicitor. Trainees must undertake a further two-week course of study, keep training records, which will be examined and monitored by the Society, and take a test of professional competence. The trainees can then apply to the Law Society of Scotland for a practising certificate. All Scottish solicitors must hold a Law Society of Scotland practising certificate.

Personal Qualities and Skills

A high level of academic achievement, integrity, good communication skills, patience, discretion, a good command of language and problem-solving skills are all required.

Starting Salary

Salaries vary but graduate trainees can receive up to about £20,000 in London, and newly qualified solicitors can earn considerably more than this. Those working for provincial solicitors and for small firms may find the salaries slightly lower. The Law Society lays down minimum salaries below which trainees cannot be paid. On average, qualified solicitors earn £28,000–30,000.

In Scotland the Law Society does not lay down salaries, but recommends minimum salary rates for trainees, which are currently £10,300 for trainees in their first year and £13,905 for trainees in their second year.

info

Law Society, 113 Chancery Lane, London WC2A 1PL; 020 7242 1222; fax: 020 7831 0344; Legal Education Line: 0870 606 2555; www.lawsociety.org.uk; e-mail: legaled@lawsociety.org.uk

Law Society of Scotland, 26 Drumsheugh Gardens, Edinburgh EH3 7YR; 0131 226 7411; fax: 0131 225 2934; www.lawscot.org.uk; e-mail: legaleduc@lawscot.org.uk

So... you want to be a lawyer? (Kogan Page)

Careers in the Law (Kogan Page)

LEISURE AND AMENITY MANAGEMENT

People employed in this field may work in leisure centres, Outward Bound centres, theatres and arts centres, historic houses and ancient monuments, country areas offering nature trails, fishing and camping facilities to the public, or even be in charge of bingo or dance halls. Managers, as well as being interested in their particular leisure activity, are responsible for the administrative and financial running of the enterprise. Many in this field are employed in local government, but there are also opportunities in private sports centres, health and fitness clubs and tourist attractions.

Qualifications and Training

The Institute of Leisure and Amenity Management (ILAM) offers five levels of qualification based upon the completion of work-based projects: the ILAM first award for candidates who are new to the industry and who hold junior positions within leisure organisations; the ILAM Certificate in Leisure Operations, for candidates who have a working knowledge of the industry and hold junior supervisory positions; the ILAM Certificate in Leisure Management for candidates with a good understanding of the industry and who hold junior or middle management jobs; the ILAM Diploma in Leisure Management for candidates who have successfully demonstrated their managerial ability at a senior level; and the Advanced Diploma in Leisure Management for those with substantial experience.

HND courses and a range of degree courses, including foundation degrees in leisure studies/recreation management and sports sciences, are available.

Personal Qualities and Skills

A strong interest in the particular area of leisure is necessary, as is the ability to organise, administer and manage people, and be an all-round good communicator.

Starting Salary

Assistant managers earn £15,000–20,000, depending on the size and type of establishment.

info

Institute of Leisure and Amenity Management, ILAM House, Lower Basildon, Reading, Berkshire RG8 9NE; 01491 874800; fax: 01491 874801; www.ilam.co.uk; e-mail: education@ilam.co.uk

See the ILAM website for downloadable documents on careers in the industry.

Institute of Sport and Recreation Management, Gifford House, 36–38 Sherrard Street, Melton Mowbray, Leics LE13 1XJ; 01644 565531; www.isrm.co.uk; e-mail: info@isrm.co.uk

Fitness Industry Association, 115 Eastbourne Mews, London W2 6LQ; 020 7298 6730; fax: 020 7298 6731; www.fia.org.uk; e-mail: info@fia.org.uk

SkillsActive, Castlewood House, 77–91 New Oxford Street, London WC1A 1PX; 020 7632 2000; www.activeskills.com

LINGUISTICS, LANGUAGES AND TRANSLATION

Interpreter

Interpreters communicate between people who do not share a common language. They use two main techniques: simultaneous and consecutive interpreting. Conference interpreters usually work using the simultaneous method in a booth with headphones and communicative technology, allowing them to hear the speaker and interpret to their audience.

Very few openings are available for interpreters, even worldwide. Conference interpreters work at international conferences such as the United Nations or the European Commission and at the International Court of Justice, using simultaneous or consecutive interpreting. Some work for international agencies; others are freelance. Demand for conference interpreters in particular languages may fluctuate depending on the political and economic requirements of the day.

Interpreters with specialist knowledge, such as engineering or economics, may have the chance to work at conferences on their subject. Interpreters may also work as guides in tourist centres, and to do this they must usually be accredited and trained as guides.

Demand for interpreting in the public services (police, courts, public health and local government) has led to the creation of the National Register of Public Service Interpreters covering a wide range of African, Asian, European and Far Eastern languages. This register is supported by the Home Office and the UK legal agencies. The Institute of Translation and Interpreting (ITI) can also help source qualified public service interpreters from its membership, as can numerous other commercial agencies.

Qualifications and Training

To take a degree course, two A levels or equivalent, including a foreign language, are normally required. At the newer universities and colleges, training in interpreting and translating is offered, combined with regional studies or technological or business studies, aimed at industry, commerce and international organisations. A list of these courses is offered by the Institute of Linguists and the Institute of Translation and Interpreting (ITI). Such degree courses usually involve work or study abroad. The Institute of Linguists Educational Trust also offers the only qualification in public service interpreting – the Diploma in Public Service Interpreting, which is mapped at between NVQ level 4 and 5.

Personal Qualities and Skills

Fluency in two or more languages should be allied with a natural feeling for words and phrases and a good ear. It is necessary to be able to think quickly, to remain alert for long periods, and to be socially confident. Subject knowledge is essential, especially for simultaneous interpreting, which requires a degree of understanding and anticipation of subject matter and context.

Starting Salary

Starting salaries are between £19,000 and £25,000 – a little less in the civil service and for other public services. Freelance interpreters can earn between £200 and £350 a day.

Institute of Linguists, Saxon House, 48 Southwark Street, London SE11 1UN; 020 7940 3100; fax: 020 7940 3101; www.iol.org.uk; e-mail: info@iol.org.uk

Institute of Translation and Interpreting (ITI), Fortuna House, South Fifth Street, Milton Keynes MK9 2EU; 01908 325250; fax: 01908 325259; www.iti.org.uk; e-mail: info@iti.org.uk

Translator

Translators work freelance from home or as staff translators, within a commercial organisation whose main business is not translation, or within a translation agency. Normally, they only translate from another language into their mother tongue. The work translated varies from whole books to business letters and documents. Translators, especially those who specialise in work for publication, must be able to express themselves very well. In areas where the subject matter of the text is specialised, for example computing, maths or mountaineering, expert knowledge is required of the translator. A broad-based general knowledge is always an advantage. Translators may be responsible for finding their own work but may also be registered with a translation company or agency.

Qualifications and Training

Proficiency in a foreign language is obviously necessary, as is the ability to write well in the target language. An understanding of the culture of the relevant countries is important. Increasingly, there is a need to be computer-literate. Most translators have a postgraduate qualification or a diploma in translation. First degree courses in translation are available at a number of universities and diplomas are available via the Institute of Linguists.

Personal Qualities and Skills

Translators must be meticulous, conscientious, creative and persistent. The ability to carry out research as and when necessary, and good interpersonal skills are also required.

Starting Salary

There is a wide range of starting salaries with the lowest being £16,500–18,000 depending on qualifications and work experience; £75–120 per 1,000 words depending on language combinations. The rate goes up for translating Chinese characters. Some translators own copyright of their translations and can make money by selling this, or through royalty payments, but these are less common sources of income.

info

Institute of Linguists, Saxon House, 48 Southwark Street, London SE11 1UN; 020 7940 3100; fax: 020 7940 3101; www.iol.org.uk; e-mail: info@iol.org.uk

Institute of Translation and Interpreting (ITI), Fortuna House, South Fifth Street, Milton Keynes MK9 2EU; 01908 325250; fax: 01908 325259; www.iti.org.uk; e-mail: info@iti.org.uk

A variety of downloadable documents relating to linguistic careers are available from the ITI website.

LITERARY AGENT

Literary agents act as negotiators between authors and publishers, film producers and theatre managements. Initially they read authors' manuscripts and decide whether or not to accept an author as a client. Once accepted, an author may be guided by an agent about ideas for books and changes to existing manuscripts. The agent then finds a publisher or producer for the author's work and negotiates the best possible terms. The agent deals with the publisher on all matters that will affect the client, including the contract, manuscript delivery, follow-up titles, advertising, publicity, paperback, television and film rights, and obtaining payments when due.

Some literary agents also act for foreign publishers attempting to find British publishers who will bring out an English edition of a book already published abroad. Like publishers, agents tend to specialise in areas such as fiction, general non-fiction and specialist publishing.

Qualifications and Training

No particular educational qualifications are necessary. Experience of the book trade is the most important factor, and most literary agents have gained this by working in a publishing house. Foreign languages are an asset, particularly in the international field.

Personal Qualities and Skills

Agents need shrewd literary judgement and a knowledge of worldwide market conditions, negotiating and legal skills, business and financial ability. They must be hard working, persistent, adaptable and sympathetic towards their authors.

Starting Salary

Agencies receive a percentage of the money earned by the author – usually 10–20 per cent. Literary agents working for these companies would receive a salary plus annual bonuses related to the level of commission they bring in.

Association of Authors' Agents;
www.agentsassoc.co.uk

The Writers' and Artists' Handbook,
A&C Black (annual publication)

LOCAL GOVERNMENT

The public sector is now the largest employer within the United Kingdom and has seen a rapid growth in job opportunities and employment. Local authorities provide a range of services that affect the daily lives of people living in their area, from sports centres to refuse collection, schools to homes for the elderly, fire services to libraries. They also have responsibility for ensuring that food sold in shops and restaurants is fit to eat; that streets are lit; that land is developed with environmental considerations and the needs of the local population in mind. All of these services rely on the collection of local revenues, and for the less well off, the efficient administration of housing and Council Tax benefits is essential. Consequently there are many varied areas of work to consider and over 500 different careers to choose from, some of which can be found elsewhere in this publication.

Local government employs over 2 million staff in England, Scotland and Wales, some of whom are administrators who supervise, coordinate and organise the provision of services to the community. It also employs professional and technical staff: for instance, architects, accountants, engineers and electricians.

Qualifications and Training

There are a variety of paths to follow to obtain a position in local government, because of the range of careers on offer. GCSE and A level passes may be necessary, or a degree, with some posts requiring professional qualifications. Training is seen as an important commodity in local government, and as such is available through both internal and external courses.

Personal Qualities and Skills

These vary according to the job to be performed, but in general local government employees should be able to communicate effectively both with colleagues and with the community at large, work well in a team, be professional in their approach and have good customer service skills.

Starting Salary

Salaries in local government can be competitive. There may also be a variety of benefits, including relocation packages, as well as flexible working arrangements.

info

Institute of Revenues, Rating and Valuation, 41 Doughty Street, London WC1N 2LF; 020 7691 8980; www.irrv.org.uk/education/index.asp (for information on qualifications in revenues and benefits administration)

Local Government Careers; www.LGcareers.com – for further careers information; www.LGjobs.com – for current job vacancy adverts in local councils all over the country

Personnel officers of individual local authorities

LOGISTICS

(*see also* Road Transport)

Logistics is the management of the moving of goods or materials from one place to another.

Freight forwarding

A freight forwarding firm will arrange for the most efficient means of the international transport of goods, and will ensure that all documentation, legal and insurance requirements are met, and customs duties paid. Freight forwarders may be individuals or firms; they may specialise in a particular method of transportation, certain goods or countries. They may arrange for a number of different shipments to be grouped together for more economical transport. Some very large organisations have their own freight forwarding department or a subsidiary company.

Freight forwarders are usually located near ports or airports and in provincial centres. They employ people to deal with a wide range of clerical and administrative tasks such as sales, personnel, timetabling, accounting and computer work.

Qualifications and Training

School leavers can enter the industry through the Modern Apprenticeship route. NVQs are available in International Trade and Services, Distribution and Warehousing Operations and Organising Road Transport. There are several degree courses in international trade, logistics, supply chain management, transport, export studies and overseas business. Large companies may offer graduate training schemes for those with relevant degrees.

The Institute of Freight Forwarders offers an Advanced Certificate in International Trade that can be studied full- or part-time or by correspondence. The Institute of Logistics and Transport offers a range of professional qualifications from introductory to MSc level which can be studied by distance learning.

Personal Qualities and Skills

People working in freight forwarding need excellent problem-solving and communication skills. Accuracy and clarity are essential, as misunderstandings can cause major problems. IT skills are essential with a growth in internet trading and greater use of technology such as global position satellite systems to plan and manage journeys. Geographical, cultural and religious awareness are also important.

info

British International Freight Association, Institute of Freight Forwarders, Redfern House, Browells Lane, Feltham, Middlesex TW13 7EP; 020 8844 2266; fax: 020 8890 5596; www.bifa.org; e-mail: bifa@bifa.org

Institute of Logistics and Transport, Logistics and Transport Centre, Earlstrees Court, Earlstrees Road, Corby, Northants NN17 4AX; www.iolt.org.uk; e-mail: careers@iolt.org.uk

Institute of Transport Administration, IoTA House, 7B St Leonards Road, Horsham, West Sussex RH13 6EH; 01402 242412; fax: 01403 242413; www.iota.org.uk

Logistics and Transport Management Careers Guide available for download from www.insidecareers.co.uk

Starting Salary

Clerical salaries are similar to those in other industries. Graduate salaries can be between £17,000 and £25,000, and increase significantly with experience.

Logistics

When a customer places an order, a chain reaction – the supply chain – is started. The supply chain ensures that the product that has been ordered, whether it is a car for an individual, or a thousand bars of chocolate for a retailer, reaches the customer who placed the order.

Logistics is the management of the supply chain. The professionals working in logistics are responsible for warehouse management, distribution and transport management, inventory (stock) control, information systems, transport, logistics planning and analysis, and supply-chain management.

Qualifications and Training

Entry with GCSEs or A levels is still possible but many new entrants to managerial posts now have a degree or professional qualification. There are several degree courses in international trade, logistics, supply-chain management, export studies and overseas business. Large companies may offer graduate training schemes for those with relevant degrees. The Institute of Freight Forwarders offers an Advanced Certificate in International Trade that can be studied full- or part-time or by correspondence.

An MSc in logistics or supply-chain management may be an advantage when seeking progression into senior management positions in some organisations. The Institute of Logistics and Transport offers a range of professional qualifications from entry level upwards, which includes a distance-learning MSc offered in conjunction with Aston University.

info

British International Freight Association, Institute of Freight Forwarders, Redfern House, Browells Lane, Feltham, Middlesex TW13 7EP; 020 8844 2266; fax: 020 8890 5546; www.bifa.org; e-mail: bifa@bifa.org

Institute of Logistics and Transport, Logistics and Transport Centre, Earlstrees Court, Earlstrees Road, Corby, Northants NN17 4AX; 01536 740100; fax: 01536 740101; www.iolt.org.uk; e-mail: careers@iolt.org.uk

Institute of Transport Administration, IoTA House, 7 St Leonards Road, Horsham, West Sussex RH13 6EH; 01403 242412; fax: 01403 242413; www.iota.org.uk

Logistics and Transport Management Careers Guide downloaded from www.insidecareers.co.uk

Personal Qualities and Skills

Logistics can offer early responsibility, so trainee managers should be responsible, able to motivate others and enjoy a challenge. Organisational, numeracy and people management skills are essential. Foreign language skills are an advantage. The ability to use IT packages and electronic communication has become increasingly important with the growing use of the internet. The supply chain is at the centre of many e-commerce developments.

Starting Salaries

Graduate management trainees start between £18,000 and £22,000. Managers' salaries are variable and can reach £60,000, rising as high as £100,000 for directors with board-level responsibility in large organisations.

MANAGEMENT CONSULTANT

Management has been defined as the art of getting results through other people, and consultancy as giving professional advice. Management consultants are employed to provide a higher degree of expertise than is available in a particular company; to recommend business solutions and assist in their implementation; to assist in cultural change and to provide expertise to solve specific business issues.

Firms of management consultants specialise, tending to divide their activities into the following areas: organisation, development and policy formation – long-range planning and reorganisation of a company's structure; production management – production control arrangements; marketing, sales and distribution; finance and administration – installation of budgetary control systems; personnel management selection; management of information systems – the provision of software, systems analysis; economic and environmental studies – urban and regional development planning, work for overseas organisations. With the growth in e-commerce many consultancies are providing advice on e-business solutions.

Management coach

This is a relatively new career and management coaches work far more with individuals than with whole organisations or departments. They work mostly with managers at a senior level in all kinds of organisation, helping them to work more efficiently and effectively and working on any problem areas, for example presenting in public, interpreting data, and team leadership.

Qualifications and Training

Management consultancy is a graduate-only profession and preferred degree subjects include business, management, IT, economics and psychology. If you specialise in a particular area of consultancy such as marketing or human resources, a relevant degree is helpful. You should have a 2.1 and an A level points tariff of 320 points. Training is on the job, but many consulting firms provide extensive in-house courses. After about two years in the profession you are likely to have the option either to take a Masters in Business Administration (MBA) or a professional qualification linked to your area of expertise, for example, finance, marketing or personnel. Management coaches have often worked as management consultants and developed a special interest in personal coaching and one-to-one work.

Personal Qualities and Skills

You need to be an excellent communicator, one-to-one, with groups and on paper. You should have good IT and numerical skills and the ability to analyse problems and suggest solutions. You should have a broad knowledge of business issues. If you are working as a management coach, you need to be very good at working one-to-one, good at motivating people and accurate in analysing their problems.

Starting Salary

Graduate entrant management consultants starting salaries range from £20,000 to £35,000. At a senior level you can earn £100,000+ in this work. Management coaches tend to work freelance and may charge £100 per hour, or more.

info

Chartered Institute of Personnel and Development (CIPD),151 The Broadway, London SW19 1JQ; 020 8612 6200; www.cipd.co.uk

Chartered Management Institute (CMI), Management House, Cottingham Road, Corby, Northants NN17 1TT; 01536 204 222; www.managers.org.uk

Institute of Management Consultancy (IMC), 3rd Floor, 17–18 Hayward's Place, London EC1R 0EQ; 020 7566 5220; www.imc.co.uk

Management Consultancies Association (MCA), 49 Whitehall, London SW1A 2BX; 020 7321 3990; www.mca.org.uk/

MANUFACTURING

Manufacturing encompasses many occupations, all of which are concerned with the large-scale production of goods and packaging.

Factory worker

Factory work is all about the manufacturing of products of every kind: food, furniture, cars, clothing, electronic equipment, etc, in fact, everything that we use. A whole range of jobs support any manufacturing process: administration, research, engineering and marketing, but they are covered elsewhere.

The term 'factory worker' refers to workers who are involved in the production process – and specific tasks and duties vary depending on what is being produced. Workers may operate special machinery for building cars, work on a conveyor belt filling cans of drink, wash and grade raw fruit and vegetables to be processed, assemble complete items by putting components together, or monitor for quality and consistency of any product. The range is really very wide.

Qualifications and Training

For most jobs there are no specific academic requirements, although some employers may like you to have GCSEs in maths, English and technology. Many employers set their own entry tests to measure how well you are likely to perform the tasks you will be expected to do. There are now some GNVQs level 2 available in Performing Manufacturing Operations, and if you are under 24 years old there may be opportunities to do an apprenticeship in electrical, electronic or mechanical engineering.

Personal Qualities and Skills

You need to be good at practical work and quick with your hands. It is important that you don't mind carrying out repetitive tasks and that you can keep your concentration while doing this. You must be able to follow instructions, pay close attention to safety and work well as part of a team.

Starting Salary

Starting salaries range from £11,000 to £15,000, and if you take on some supervisory responsibility they can rise to £20,000. Many jobs include shift work allowances.

info

Local Job Centre Plus and Careers/Connexions Centres

SEMTA (Science Engineering and Manufacturing Technologies Alliance), 14 Upton Road, Watford, Hertfordshire WD18 0JT; 0808 100 3682; www.semta.org.uk

Improve (Food and Drink Sector Skills Council), 1 Green Street, London W1K 6RG; 020 7355 0830; www.improvefdssc.org

Cogent (Sector Skills Council for the Oil and Gas Extraction, Chemicals Manufacturing and Petroleum Industries), Minerva House, Bruntland Road, Portlethen, Aberdeen AB12 4QL; 01224 787800; www.cogent-ssc.com

Packaging technologist

The purpose of packaging is to protect, preserve, contain and present its contents. It also has a vital function in branding and brand awareness. Opportunities for work exist with manufacturers of raw packaging materials, with companies that produce packaging and companies that have a product to be packed. Many small firms do not have their own packaging adviser/ technologist, and hire a consultant when the need arises.

Work opportunities exist in developing materials for packaging purposes, for designing equipment to manufacture or fill packaging, for structural design of parts, for graphic design on packs, for physical and chemical testing and quality assurance.

Qualifications and Training

Packaging modules are available in some first degree courses, and two universities offer the MSc in Packaging Technology. The Diploma in Packaging Technology from the Institute of Packaging is internally recognised as a qualification of excellence. It can be studied in three ways: residential, part-time and by distance learning.

Personal Qualities and Skills

Technologists and scientists must be able to look at problems in a practical way and have the ability to communicate their ideas to others both verbally and on paper.

Starting Salary

This varies according to age and qualifications but falls in the region of £15,000 to £20,000.

info

The Head of Training, Institute of Packaging, Sysonby Lodge, Nottingham Road, Melton Mowbray, Leicestershire LE13 0NU; 01664 500055; fax: 01664 564164 (for details of available training and careers advice); www.iop.co.uk; e-mail: training@iop.co.uk

Brunel University, Department of Design and Systems Engineering, Brunel University, Uxbridge, Middlesex UB8 3PH; 01895 203059; fax: 01895 812556; www.brunel.ac.uk

Sheet-metal worker/plater

Sheet-metal workers/platers are engaged in shaping, cutting and joining together pieces of metal. Sheet-metal workers work with thin metal sheet up to 3 mm thick, using a wide range of hand and power tools. They make such items as aircraft sections and car prototypes. Platers work with metal plates from 3 mm thick upwards. As well as hand and power tools, heavy presses are needed to bend the plate. Products include ship and submarine parts and industrial boilers.

Qualifications and Training

If you are between 16 and 24 years old and want to join a National Apprenticeship Scheme for Engineering Construction (NASEC), you need GCSEs (A–C)/S grades (1–3) in maths, English and a science. If you have engineering drawing, metalwork or other practical subjects as well you may have an advantage. Applicants without the required entry grades may also be considered. These apprenticeships take up to three years and you train on-the-job, working alongside experienced sheet metal workers. This apprenticeship leads to an NVQ level 3 award in engineering production. Older applicants can get into this work without GCSEs, but won't get the opportunity to do a full apprenticeship.

Personal Qualities and Skills

You must have good manual dexterity and be able to concentrate for long periods of time. You should be good at following instructions, but able to work without direct supervision. Normal eyesight is essential and good colour vision is important.

Starting Salary

Salaries range from £12,000 to £16,000, but can go up to £20,000 to £22,000. There are often opportunities for shift work payments.

info

SEMTA (Science Engineering and Manufacturing Technologies Alliance), 14 Upton Road, Watford, Hertfordshire WD18 0JT; 0808 100 3682; www.semta.org.uk

Local Job Centre Plus and Connexions/Careers Centres

Toolmaker

Toolmakers work in engineering making a wide range of jigs, used to guide cutting tools and to hold the work in position; fixtures, to hold metal for bending or welding or to hold parts together; press tools in different shapes and sizes for cutting parts; mould tools to make items such as fridge interiors or mobile phone cases and measuring gauges. Toolmakers are often involved in making small quantities of a new product when it is at the design and development stage. Toolmaker machinists make the tools, often specialising in just one kind. Toolmaker fitters work on large structures that are constructed from many parts. They check all the parts, number them and then fit them together.

Qualifications and Training

If you are between 16 and 24 years old and want to do a National Apprenticeship Scheme for Engineering Construction (NASEC) apprenticeship, you need GCSEs (A–C)/S grades in maths, English and a science. If you have engineering drawing, metalwork or other practical subjects as well you may have an advantage. Applicants without the required entry grades may also be considered. These apprenticeships take up to three years and you train on-the-job, working alongside experienced toolmakers. This apprenticeship leads to an NVQ level 3 award in engineering production. Older applicants can do BTEC Certificates in manufacturing engineering.

Personal Qualities and Skills

You must have good manual dexterity and be able to understand engineering drawings. You should be good at following instructions, but able to work without direct supervision. Normal eyesight is essential and good colour vision is important.

Starting Salary

Salaries range from £12,000 to £16,000, but can go up to £20,000 to £22,000. There are often opportunities for shift work payments.

info

SEMTA (Science Engineering and Manufacturing Technologies Alliance), 14 Upton Road, Watford, Hertfordshire WD18 0JT; 0808 100 3682; www.semta.org.uk

Local Job Centre Plus and Connexions/Careers Centres

Welder

Welders join pieces of metal together by applying intense heat and melting the edges so that two pieces become one. The sorts of items welded are metal sections of aeroplanes, ships, oil rigs, cars and power turbines. Welders work in light and heavy engineering firms, in foundry work and in shipbuilding. Some plastics are also welded.

Welders work on all types of fabrication from the manufacture of metal-frame chairs, to high-quality, complex applications such as building a submarine.

Qualifications and Training

If you are aged between 16 and 24 you can do an Engineering Apprenticeship. There are no set entry qualifications for this, but many employers do prefer you to have GCSEs in English, maths, technology and a science subject. If you have these GCSEs, this also offers a wider range of further qualifications you can take part time or full time at college. These qualifications are also open to people of any age. There are several different NVQ awards related to welding, including fabrication and welding, performing engineering operations and welding with pipe work.

Personal Qualities and Skills

You must have good practical and technical skills and be able to concentrate for long periods of time. You should be good at following instructions, but able to work without direct supervision. Normal eyesight is essential and good near vision is important.

Starting Salary

Salaries range from £12,000 to £16,000, but can go up to £20,000 to £22,000. There are often opportunities for shift work payments.

info

SEMTA (Science Engineering and Manufacturing Technologies Alliance), 14 Upton Road, Watford, Hertfordshire WD18 0JT; 0808 100 3682; www.semta.org.uk

Local Job Centre Plus and Connexions/Careers Centres

MARINE SCIENTIST

Marine scientists are drawn from various academic disciplines, mainly biology, geology and oceanography. This is a small but developing profession concerned with a detailed study of plant and animal life in the oceans and along coastlines. Its main purpose, as well as expanding our knowledge and understanding, is to research the food chains and levels of fish stocks in the oceans and to analyse the impact of pollution and other human activity on the ecology of the water. Marine scientists are employed by governments, research organisations, pressure groups and the marine laboratories of private organisations.

info

Institute of Biology, 20 Queensberry Place, London SW7 2DZ; 020 7581 8333; fax: 020 7823 9409; www.iob.org; e-mail: info@iob.org

Marine Biological Association of UK, The Laboratory, Citadel Hill, Plymouth PL1 2PB; 01752 633207; fax: 01752 633102; www.mba.ac.uk

Scottish Association for Marine Science, Dunstaffnage Marine Laboratory, Oban, Argyll, PA37 1QA; 01631 559 000; fax: 01631 559 001; www.sams.ac.uk; e-mail: mail@dml.ac.uk

Southampton Oceanography Centre, University of Southampton, European Way, Southampton SO14 3ZH; 023 8059 6666; www.soc.soto.ac.uk

Society for Underwater Technology, 80 Coleman Street, London EC2R 5BJ; 020 7382 2601; www.sut.org.uk

Qualifications and Training

Two or three A levels or equivalents in biology, chemistry and maths or another science, plus GCSE level or equivalent in maths and physics are necessary for entry to a first degree course in biology. Some universities offer degrees in marine biology, but it may be advisable to take a broader degree in applied biology first.

Personal Qualities and Skills

Biologists need the same characteristics as all scientists: patience and the willingness to repeat experimental work and measurements to check results, a methodical way of working, good observation and accuracy.

Starting Salary

£13,000–16,000 on entry, £18,000–26,000 for high-level research work.

MARKETING

Marketing is concerned with undertaking research, identifying consumer needs and demands relative to product or service, price, place and time, organising their production and promoting them to the appropriate customer segment. It includes new product development, packaging, advertising, pricing, sales, distribution and after-sales service. It is often claimed that advertising, PR, market research and the like all come under the umbrella of marketing.

Marketing executive

People usually come into marketing either from sales or from the market research side, or they may have worked for an advertising agency before joining the marketing team of a manufacturing company. Some enter as graduate trainees. There are a growing number of posts in e-marketing.

The responsibilities of a marketing executive vary according to the size of the organisation and the importance marketing takes within the company. In a large firm, for example, the marketing director will have a say in all the company's activities and be involved in product development. Marketing executives will handle products or ranges, and organise advertising, public relations and sales promotion activities for that product.

The increased sophistication of databases has led to the growth of niche marketing known as direct marketing. Information gathered is used, subject to industry codes of practice, to make direct contact between companies and prospective customers. Direct marketing is based on providing relevant, timely products and services and then developing an ongoing relationship with customers and encouraging loyalty. The industry makes use of all communications channels, including mail; telephone; door-drops; fax; field marketing; direct response television, radio and press advertisements and inserts; the internet; mobile phone SMS and interactive television.

Job roles within the industry include creative/copy writing, production,

account planning, data planning, and account handling (also known as client service). The most frequently chosen path for people with good marketing qualifications (see below under Qualifications and Training) is account handling. New entrants tend to be graduates, with some work experience in a marketing or sales-led organisation.

Other career opportunities include specialist areas such as field marketing (demonstrations, merchandising; road shows), telemarketing, mailing, e-mail and SMS marketing which can require some technical ability and knowledge.

Qualifications and Training

While there are no specific qualifications to get into marketing, it has become very much a graduate-entry profession. Some people with A levels, HNDs or relevant work experience in a sales or other 'people' environment can get into this sector. Preferred degree subjects include business, marketing and statistics. The Chartered Institute of Marketing (CIM) awards Marketing Diplomas run by the Communications and Marketing Foundation (CAM). You normally do this course part-time and it is a highly practical course, taught by people who work in marketing. The Institute of Direct Marketing also offers a diploma course.

Personal Qualities and Skills

You need a broad mix of skills to be successful in marketing, be confident in dealing with people and possessing good written communication skills. You need to be numerate, have good IT skills and be able to work under pressure. You should be a good negotiator, able to be persuasive and encouraging. It is helpful if you can think creatively and come up with imaginative solutions to problems.

Starting Salary

Salaries start at between £16,000 and £24,000. There is very strong competition for the best paid jobs with large companies or marketing consultants. A successful marketing executive can earn up to £50,000.

info

Chartered Institute of Marketing (CIM), Moor Hall, Cookham, Maidenhead, Berks SL6 9QH; 01628 427500; www.cim.co.uk

The Communication Advertising and Marketing Education Foundation (CAM), Moor Hall, Cookham, Maidenhead, Berkshire SL6 9QH; 01628 427120; www.camfoundation.com

The Institute of Direct Marketing (IDM), 1 Park Road, Teddington, Middlesex TW11 0AR; 020 8977 5705; www.theidm.co.uk

How to get on in Marketing, Advertising and Public Relations (Kogan Page)

MARKET RESEARCHER

Market research is the collection and analysis of information about markets, organisations and people to support better business decisions. It is used to discover gaps in the market, to ensure customer satisfaction and to plan effective marketing campaigns. In a competitive environment, the more knowledge a business has about its customers, the more likely it is to succeed.

Over the past few decades, market research techniques have developed significantly, making it a more precise science. Methods used depend on the requirements of the business and the budget available, and include interviews with individuals, surveys by telephone, post and via the internet, and increasingly using mobile phone text messaging. These are used to gather quantitative (numerical) data. Qualitative research by face-to-face interviews with individuals or groups is geared to providing insight into why people hold the views they do, and provides greater understanding of customers. Interviewers are known as field workers, and their work, and that of the analysis personnel, is organised by the research executive, who is in overall charge of the project for a marketing executive or client, and is responsible for interpreting the results.

Every year, the Market Research Society (MRS) publishes the *Research Buyer's Guide*, which lists the majority of market research agencies in the UK and outlines the size of each agency, together with their areas of specialisation. The guide also details other organisations that can offer advice on getting started in market research; the online version of the guide is free at www.rbg.org.uk.

Qualifications and Training

Field workers do not need qualifications but must be articulate, persuasive and presentable. Applicants for research and executive positions will be expected to hold a degree. The majority of market research graduates are drawn from disciplines that require strong communication or analytical skills, such as languages, English literature, maths, psychology, geography, history, politics, science and IT. However, graduates with degrees as contrasting as zoology and theatre studies are also welcomed by the industry.

The Market Research Society offers a range of qualifications that are linked to the UK's National Qualifications Framework and are designed to suit a wide range of candidates, from those with no experience to practitioners seeking continuous professional development.

Personal Qualities and Skills

Excellent communication skills and ability to get on with people of all types. Analytical skills, numeracy and data interpretation are important.

Starting Salary

Market research interviewers are paid between £35 and £50 for a six to seven hour day, and for some their pay is linked to target numbers of interviews, or questionnaires completed. Permanent staff who analyse data, plan research strategies and liaise with clients are paid between £16,000 and £20,000 a year.

info

British Market Research Association (BMRA), Devonshire House, 60 Goswell Road, London EC1M 7AD; 020 7566 3636; www.bmra.org.uk/

The Market Research Society (MRS), 15 Northburgh Street, London EC1V 0JR; 020 7490 4911; www.mrs.org.uk/

The Social Research Association (SRA), PO Box 33660, London N16 6WE; 020 8880 5684; www.sra.org.uk

MEAT INDUSTRY

As well as retail and supermarket work as a butcher, or working for large organisations such as hotels, there are other openings in the meat industry. Some wholesale establishments selling pre-packed meat need teams of butchers for boning, cutting and packing the meat, or processing it into pies. Wholesale butchers do not meet the general public but deal with other butchers and retailers. Workers are also needed in abattoirs, to handle and kill the animals, and to inspect and deal with the meat.

Butcher

Career prospects are varied in the meat industry, extending from work in a small retail shop through to supermarkets; from meat buying for large organisations such as hotels and caterers, to the manufacture of meat and poultry products.

Qualifications and Training

A good general education is necessary but there are no formal educational requirements. Training is on the job and courses are available at further education establishments and technical colleges, leading to examinations of the Meat Training Council. NVQs are available at levels 1–4, and higher national diploma/certificate qualifications. Modern Apprenticeships are available. Further training, appropriate to the relevant sector of the industry, in management, meat technology, or small business ownership, may follow an apprenticeship.

info

Meat Training Council, PO Box 141, Winterhill House, Snowdon Drive, Milton Keynes MK6 1YY; 01908 231062; www.meattraining.org.uk

Scottish Meat Training, 8–10 Needless Road, Perth PH2 0JW; 01738 637785; www.foodtraining.net

Improve Ltd, Sector Skills Council for Food and Drink Manufacturing and Processing, Providence House, 2 Innovation Lane, Heslington, York YO10 52F; 0845 644 0448; www.improveltd.co.uk

Personal Qualities and Skills

Butchers need to be very practical, with good manual dexterity, and not squeamish. They must ensure that they and their work environments are really clean and hygienic and they must enjoy talking to people and giving advice. A good business sense is also useful.

Starting Salary

Trainee butchers earn around £12,000 a year, skilled butchers earn around £16,000 and butcher managers earn £16,000 to £21,000. Some supermarkets offer bonuses and other staff benefit schemes.

MEDICAL ILLUSTRATION

A career in medical illustration involves recording medical conditions precisely for the medical profession and related sectors. The profession provides specialist photographic, graphic design, art and video services tailored to patient care, pre/postgraduate medical education, research and medico-legal needs. As a collective body, medical illustrators form an integral part of the clinical healthcare team. Members of the profession include the following.

Graphic designers

(*see also* Art and Design)

They specialise in the design, layout and production of artwork, brochures, scientific posters and other visual material, primarily for patient information or marketing.

Medical artists

Medical artists produce highest quality artwork for publication and medical education purposes.

Medical photographers

They are responsible for recording clinical conditions, working within the studio, clinic, ward and operating theatre environments. Specialised areas include diagnostic services within ophthalmology and planning images for craniofacial surgery.

Medical videographers

Medical videographers produce high-quality programmes for teaching and research purposes.

Qualifications and Training

Many trusts and health authorities now ask for a BSc in Medical Illustration. A prospective candidate may, however, be working towards the BSc, or commit to undertake the BSc upon commencement of employment. Trainees need at least a media qualification to HND level (or equivalent) in photography, video or graphic design.

The Glasgow Caledonian University/Institute of Medical Illustrators (GCU/IMI) BSc in Medical Illustration can be taken as a full-time course or as a three-year distance-learning course. With a first degree in photography, video, graphics, art or media studies, such graduates may apply to undertake the IMI Post Experience Certificate (PEC). Other degree courses available nationally are an MSc in Medical Illustration at the University of Wales College of Medicine and a BSc (Hons) in Biomedical Imaging at the University of Derby.

The Institute of Medical Illustrators is the leading professional body. Members qualify at degree level with the BSc in Medical Illustration, are actively involved in continuing professional development and are registered with the National Board of Registration of Medical Illustrators (NBRMI). They are governed by a Code of Conduct, a Code of Responsible Practice and relevant law, for example the Data Protection Act. These measures cover legal and ethical aspects such as consent, confidentiality and copyright, and are designed to protect both patients and healthcare organisations from the misuse of medical images.

Personal Qualities and Skills

As well as natural artistic ability and an eye for fine detail, you have to have a very good, reassuring manner with people. You also have to be prepared to draw, photograph, etc any part of the human body in any condition of disease, injury or trauma. You have to work quietly and calmly, without getting in anyone's way.

Starting Salary

Trainees start on between £9,000 and £11,500. Once you have completed your training your salary rises to between £12,000 and £22,000.

MEDICINE

Most doctors work for the NHS in some capacity, in hospital services, general practice or in public health medicine and community health. Some doctors work exclusively in private practice. All doctors, whether GPs or hospital consultants, will have completed a degree at medical school. The specialisms described below are taken up once a Bachelor's degree in medicine has been gained.

General practitioner

Family doctors, or GPs, may form long-standing relationships with their patients. They must be able to diagnose and deal with a broad spectrum of illnesses and disorders, mainly those common within the community, but also to recognise those that are rare. Increasingly, doctors are asked to help their patients to cope with personal and emotional problems. They have to be aware of and take into account physical, psychological and social factors when looking after their patients About 90 per cent of GPs now work together in group practices, allowing some specialisation.

For doctors who work in the community, people are of prime importance. GPs are involved with individuals' problems, whether personal, social, organisational or environmental. General practice is the most personalised of all the health services, based close to patients' homes and with opportunities for long-term relationships between doctor and patient. Within this context, it is the doctor's job to give early treatment and continuing care for the great variety of problems and disorders presented by patients. GPs have to deal with many moral decisions, and much of the work is challenging because of its unpredictability.

General practice differs from all other areas of medicine in that it is not salaried and GPs are technically self-employed. The government sets an average amount that GPs are supposed to earn, and basic pay is based on the number of patients on a GP's list.

Hospital doctor

A doctor who wishes to work in hospital medicine as a consultant will apply for a post as a specialist registrar (SpR) on completion of general professional training. All SpRs are issued with a national training number (NTN) which helps postgraduate deans keep track of trainees and guarantees them a continued place in a Certificate of Completion of Specialist Training (CCST) training programme. In addition, it ensures that both nationally and within specialities the right number of doctors are being trained to meet the demand for consultants. Once SpRs are awarded completion of the CCST they can be included on the specialist register and apply for consultant posts.

If a doctor is unable or unwilling to become a consultant but wishes to remain in hospital medicine he or she is able to apply for a Staff Grade post on completion of the SHO post (see qualifications). Staff Grades are responsible to a consultant and have intermediate responsibility for patients.

Occupational physician

Occupational physicians identify and investigate health problems at work, and advise both management and employees on the prevention of hazards of occupations and the effects of work on health. Occupational physicians are usually employed by small to medium-sized companies at a grade equivalent to that of hospital consultant.

Public health and community health medicine

Public health medicine is concerned with preventive medicine, environmental health, the prolongation of life and the promotion of health. Public health physicians generally work in health authorities. Community health doctors deal with child health, family planning, social services, special hostels and day centres, and other roles as advisers to the authority. The career structure is similar to that within a hospital.

Research and teaching

Research work is carried out in universities, hospitals, public health laboratories, and other research establishments and pharmaceutical manufacturing companies. There are opportunities too for teaching in universities. Teaching may involve very little or no contact with patients, or it may be similar in content to hospital doctors' work. An academic career in medicine either through teaching or research is possible in practically all hospital specialities, general practice and public health medicine.

Qualifications and Training

Medical training in the UK is designed to meet the needs of the NHS, and its length and structure may differ from those in countries with different healthcare systems.

A minimum age of 18 and excellent A level passes in chemistry and two other science subjects (biology, physics or maths) are necessary for entry to medical school. Most medical school courses last five years. Some, however, offer a six-year course, which includes a pre-medical year. This year, intended as a foundation year in basic sciences, gives students with good non-science grades and some non-science graduates a way into the medicine degree course. Medical schools now run accelerated four-year graduate entry courses for both science and arts graduates. Once a medical student graduates, he or she must apply to the General Medical Council for provisional registration.

All (not just hospital) doctors then begin their career in medicine as pre-registration house officers (PRHOs) to complete their general clinical training. The PRHO year is generally split into two six-month periods of surgical disciplines and medical disciplines. Once doctors successfully complete their PRHO year they are fully registered with the GMC. They then progress to senior house officer (SHO). This two- to three-year period is called general professional training, and aims to equip doctors with the knowledge, skills and aptitudes required for entering a range of speciality training programmes. A large part of this training can be spent in the speciality of the doctor's choice. Doctors wishing to become GPs undertake a GP vocational training scheme, where they spend two years as an SHO in selected specialities, followed by one year as a GP registrar within general practice. On completion they will become a GP principal – the career post for general practice.

Personal Qualities and Skills

With so many different paths open to medical professionals, the skills mix for different roles varies somewhat, but there are qualities and abilities that are important for everyone working in this sector. Doctors must be able to listen respectfully to their patients and be good at explaining medical information to non-medical people. They must have a strong interest in science and in problem solving; this is especially true in research. They must be understanding, but be able to avoid becoming emotionally involved in difficult situations. These days, they must also be good resource managers, budgeting both time and money.

Starting Salary

Junior hospital doctors start on between £19,500 and £22,000, and senior hospital doctors earn between £22,000 and £30,000. GPs start on £60,000, but they will already have spent time as hospital doctors and doing additional GP training. These figures do not include any additional payments from private patients, on-call fees or London Weighting. In industry and research, salaries may be higher, depending on the kind of organisation you are working for.

info

British Medical Association (BMA), BMA House, Tavistock Square, London WC1H 9JP; 020 7387 4499; www.bma.org.uk

Department of Health (DH), Customer Service Centre, Richmond House, 79 Whitehall, London SW1A 2NL; 020 7210 4850; www.dh.gov.uk

General Medical Council (GMC), Regent's Place, 350 Euston Road, London NW1 3JN; 0845 357 8001; www.gmc-uk.org

The National Health Service (NHS), PO Box 376, Bristol BS99 3EY; 020 7210 4850; www.nhs.uk/

Royal College of General Practitioners, 14 Princes Gate, Hyde Park, London SW7 1PU; 020 7581 3232; www.rcgp.org.uk

MERCHANT NAVY

The 'Merchant Navy' is the collective term for the British shipping industry, which operates worldwide and includes the ferry sector, containership companies, cruise companies, oil, gas and chemical tankers, bulk carriers of ores, grain and coal, and support vessels for the offshore exploration industry.

Communications

Electro-technical officers are responsible for the maintenance and efficient operation of complex electrical, electronic and control systems on board ship.

Deck staff

Deck officers are responsible for controlling the navigation of the ship, communications, cargo handling and ship stability. A deck officer is a step on the way to becoming captain (master). Deck ratings assist in the navigation of the ship, are involved in operating deck machinery such as winches and cranes, and carry out maintenance tasks. There are also some dual officer roles, covering both deck and engineering departments.

Engineering staff

Engineer officers are responsible for the provision and maintenance of all technical services on board, including the propulsion and auxiliary machinery in the engine room. They are responsible for the work of engine-room staff, so managing people is part of the job, as with all ships' officers. An engineer officer is a step on the way to becoming chief engineer officer.

Engineer ratings are involved in routine maintenance, engine operation and repairs.

Hotel and entertainment services on cruise ships and ferries

This includes pursers/receptionists, restaurant and bar staff, chefs, housekeepers, cruise directors, entertainments team, hairdressers, beauticians, photographers and retail staff. Those recruited are qualified and experienced within their own specialism.

Qualifications and Training

Training for careers at sea is provided by shipping companies or group training organisations. It usually consists of programmes of learning and experience based on a sandwich pattern of alternating periods at college and at sea, leading to nationally recognised qualifications and professional maritime certificates of competency. There are four main entry routes, each with deck and engineering options. Each provides progression opportunities to the next stage and, through the ranks, to captain (master) or chief engineer officer depending on ability and ambition. The routes are:

- Marine Traineeship: structured training for seafarers employed, usually, as ratings, in the deck or engineering departments in support of the officers of the watch. Entrants must show an aptitude to succeed to at least NVQ level 2. As a guide, they are expected to have attained three GCSEs or equivalent.

- Marine Apprenticeship: provides an enhanced level of training for those employed initially as ratings in the deck or engineering departments while following a programme of learning leading to NVQ level 3 and qualification as officer of the watch. As a guide, entrants are expected to have attained a minimum of four GCSEs, including English, mathematics and science (or equivalents).
- Officer cadet: provides structured learning for those aiming to progress to captain (master) or chief engineer officer, and achieve qualifications at HND or degree level in addition to professional certificates of competency. Entry standards may vary from company to company, and according to whether the degree or HND option is chosen. As a guide, candidates are expected to have attained A levels and a minimum of four GCSEs at grades A–C, or equivalents, including mathematics, English and science. Entry with GCSEs only may be possible for suitably motivated candidates.
- Postgraduate entry: accelerated programmes have been developed for new entrants with suitable science-based degrees. This is similar to the cadet programme but recognises prior qualification and maturity of applicants.

Personal Qualities and Skills

All candidates must be in good health and pass a statutory medical examination, with a good standard of eyesight required for prospective deck personnel. The ability to get on well with other people and adapt to new conditions is also important.

Starting Salary

Starting salaries vary between sponsoring companies. Food, accommodation and other allowances often go with the job.

info

Careers in Shipping, Carthusian Court, 12 Carthusian Street, London EC1M 6EZ; general information on all Merchant Navy careers and list of shipping companies providing sponsorship; 0800 085 0973; www.gotosea.org.uk; e-mail: careers@gotosea.org.uk

Marine Society, 202 Lambeth Road, London SE1 7JW; 020 7261 9535; fax: 020 7401 2537; www.marine-society.org; e-mail: enq@marine-society.org

Merchant Navy Training Board (MNTB), Carthusian Court, 12 Carthusian Street, London EC1M 6EZ; 020 7417 2800; fax: 020 7726 2030; www.mntb.org.uk; e-mail: enquiry@mntb.org.uk. For careers information pack call 0800 085 0973.

Listings of individual shipping companies

METALLURGIST

Metallurgists are involved with the extraction of metals from ores, their purification, and with reclaiming them from scrap. They are also concerned with developing new alloys and processing metals during manufacture.

Qualifications and Training

GCSE passes in a science subject, maths and English or equivalent are required for entry to Edexcel (BTEC) and SQA two-year courses for a certificate or diploma in metallurgical studies. Candidates who have successfully completed the two-year course and those with A levels or equivalent in maths, physics or chemistry may study for the Edexcel (BTEC)/SQA Higher Certificates and diplomas, or qualify for entry to full-time, sandwich or part-time courses leading to degrees in metallurgy.

Personal Qualities and Skills

Metallurgy demands an interest in scientific and technological subjects, an ability to solve practical problems and work with other people on specific projects.

Starting Salary

Salaries vary, but newly qualified graduates can expect £15,000–18,000, and earn over £30,000 once experienced.

Institute of Materials, Minerals and Mining, 1 Carlton House Terrace, London SW1Y 5DB; 020 7451 7300; fax: 020 7839 1702; www.iom3.org/; www.materials-careers.org.uk

METEOROLOGIST

The Meteorological Office is an executive agency within the Ministry of Defence. It is a centre of excellence for the production of numerical weather forecasts, climate prediction and related studies. It serves the different and varying needs of defence, other areas of government, civil aviation, industry, commerce and the general public. A wide range of jobs is available such as researching, developing and delivering weather and environmental information.

Qualifications and Training

From time to time there are vacancies in administration, for which a minimum of five GCSEs to include English are required. Most vacancies arise in the forecasting, research and IT areas, for which a first or upper second-class degree is necessary in maths, one of the physical sciences, computer science or meteorology.

Personal Qualities and Skills

Candidates need to be adaptable and prepared to work in more than one specialist area. Good communication and computing skills are necessary.

Starting Salary

Graduates can earn between £15,500 and £24,000.

info

Local Job Centre Plus and Careers/Connexions Centres

Meteorological Office, FitzRoy Road, Exeter, Devon EX1 3PB; 0870 900 0100; fax: 0870 900 5050; www.metoffice.com; e-mail: enquiries@metoffice.gov.uk

Royal Meteorological Society, 104 Oxford Road, Reading RG1 7LL; 0118 9568500; fax: 0118 9568571; www.royal-met-soc.org.uk

A list of relevant courses at UK universities is available by post from the Royal Meteorological Society.

MICROBIOLOGIST

Microbiology is the study of tiny living organisms (bacteria, viruses, fungi, protozoa and algae) and the massive impact they have on almost every aspect of our lives. There are good job opportunities for microbiologists in the human and animal healthcare sector, medical research, and the food production and agricultural industries. Microbiologists are employed in hospitals, research institutes, industrial research and development and manufacturing sites, universities and environmental companies. Their skills and knowledge are vital to the rapidly growing biotechnology industry, where gene technology, fermentation and bioprocessing play an important part in developing products of the future.

Qualifications and Training

Minimum requirements for entry to a full-time first degree course are five GCSE passes (grades A–C) and two A level science passes. Some courses concentrate on specific areas of microbiology, others are more general and allow specialisation at a later stage. Some courses offer a period of industrial training. It is also possible to obtain qualifications via part-time study while working in a laboratory.

Personal Qualities and Skills

Microbiologists have enquiring minds, are good problem solvers and can work accurately. Good communication skills are vital as microbiologists have to describe their work to other people. Most scientists work in a multidisciplinary group so it helps to be a good team worker.

Starting Salary

Graduate starting salaries are usually in the range of £13,000 to £19,000, depending on the area chosen.

info

Society for General Microbiology, Marlborough House, Basingstoke Road, Spencers Wood, Reading RG7 1AG; 0118 988 1800; fax: 0118 988 5656; www.socgenmicrobiol.org.uk; e-mail: careers@sgm.ac.uk

www.microbiologyonline.org.uk

'Microbiologists make a difference' (free leaflet from the above)

'Your career in microbiology' (free booklet from the above)

MILK ROUNDSPERSON

see Roundsperson

MODELMAKER

Models can be made to represent almost anything: towns, office blocks, oil terminals, shopping centres, motorways, houses, cars and planes. They are often scaled-down versions of the real thing, but sometimes they can be enlargements. They are used to show what the real thing will look like, and if they are working models, may be used as testers. Models are often used too in television and films. Modelmakers work for firms specialising in such work, or sometimes branch out on their own.

Qualifications and Training

Formal academic qualifications are not necessary. Modelmakers may teach themselves or learn at evening class; some large firms offer apprenticeships. Edexcel (BTEC) courses in modelmaking are available at some FE colleges and some art colleges.

Personal Qualities and Skills

Patience, manual dexterity, a good sense of design, shape and colour are necessary. Modelmakers must be prepared to do one job for a considerable length of time; a project such as a model town could take up to a year to complete.

Starting Salary

Low when training; with experience £200+ a week; good modelmakers may earn much more.

Local Job Centre Plus and Careers/Connexions Centres

MOTOR INDUSTRY

The motor industry – or automotive sector as it is also known – has many occupations within it, from the design and production of vehicles to their retailing and maintenance.

Garage work

This involves selling and buying cars, supplying car parts, repairing and maintaining cars and other vehicles, and overall management of the garage. Selling petrol, car accessories and other consumables such as food and drink, is actually more closely related to other retail work, though of course if you do this work, you will be based at a garage retail outlet.

Qualifications and Training

No specific educational qualifications are necessary for people working on a petrol forecourt as training is given on the job, but an aptitude in dealing with cash transactions and good numeracy skills are generally required. Technicians generally need to have at least three GCSEs (grade C or above) preferably in maths, science or a craft subject. Training via Apprenticeship usually leads to NVQ level 3. Preferred qualifications for salespeople and parts people are four GCSEs (grade C or above). A range of NVQs is available as qualifications in these areas. Managers are recruited with varying qualifications, and some have degrees. Membership of the Institute of the Motor Industry is encouraged.

Personal Qualities and Skills

Mechanics must have strong analytical and manual skills and get on well with people. Salespeople need to be friendly, polite and have a good sense of humour. Parts people need to be well organised with good administrative skills. Managers need to have all the above qualities plus good people management skills and the ability to inspire confidence and gain respect.

Starting Salary

Varies across the country and is dependent on experience and level of responsibility.

Motor vehicle body repairer

Motor vehicle body repairers repair damage to vehicles caused by accidents or general wear and tear. As well as work on the actual vehicle body, they fit replacement windscreens and other glass. Much of the work involves hammering out dents and removing patches of rust, filling damaged areas with resin and preparing the vehicle for painting.

Qualifications and Training

To undertake an apprenticeship in this area, you need to have GCSEs in English, maths and technology. If you are aged 16 to 24 you are eligible for a relevant apprenticeship, lasting three to four years, and again some employers will only consider you if you have GCSEs. If you aren't able to do an apprenticeship, qualifications that may be useful include City & Guilds Automotive Vehicle Servicing and Repair (4100) and BTEC First Diploma in Vehicle Service and Technology (Body and Paint). Most training is on-the-job, learning from more experienced workers.

Personal Qualities and Skills

A real interest in cars and good practical and technical skills are important. You must be reasonably fit with good eyesight. You should be able to work as part of a team, but also get on with your own work unsupervised. A driving licence is usually necessary.

Motor vehicle technician

Motor vehicle technicians (often referred to as mechanics) repair, maintain and test motor vehicles of every kind, from motorcycles and cars, to heavy goods vehicles and high performance sports cars. Technicians work in garages and fast repair centres, at dealerships, breakdown and recovery services, public transport and freight vehicle operators. Technicians work on all a vehicle's systems – engine, gearbox, steering, electronics, etc. They diagnose faults and either repair or replace parts, and then test to ensure that the vehicle is now running efficiently and safely.

Technicians train to work on particular groups of vehicles: light vehicles, which include vans and cars; or heavy vehicles such as trucks, buses, tractors and diggers. Some technicians specialise in repairing and maintaining motorcycles. It is also possible to work with vehicles that have broken down or been involved in accidents. These technicians learn particular skills in roadside repair and recovery, and customer skills, for example, are very important

For anyone interested in a vehicle's electrical and electronic systems, there is the option to train as an auto electrician. Auto electricians find and repair electrical faults in vehicles.

There are also increasing opportunities for converting cars with petrol engines to enable them to run on LPG (liquefied petroleum gas), though this requires specific training.

Qualifications and Training

You need to train and qualify to become a motor vehicle technician. It is sometimes essential and always an advantage to have GCSEs grades A to C in English, maths and technology. If you are aged between 16 and 24, you are eligible for an apprenticeship. These last between three and four years and may lead to NVQ awards levels 1, 2 and 3 in many different aspects of vehicle repair and maintenance.

If you are not eligible for an apprenticeship it is possible to take other relevant City & Guilds or BTEC qualifications. These can either be done as day-release courses, while you are working for an employer, or as full-time, college-based courses. Many City & Guilds and BTEC courses also require you to have three or four GCSEs at grades A to C including English, maths and technology. For both body repair and technician work there are also degree-level courses available.

All these training routes offer a range of different units and options according to the types of vehicle on which you are learning to work and the types of faults and systems upon which you work.

If you want to become an MOT tester, ensuring that a vehicle is properly roadworthy and safe, and issuing MOT certificates, you must have a relevant qualification equivalent to NVQ level 3 and at least four years' experience as a mechanic.

Personal Qualities and Skills

A real interest in cars or other vehicles, as well as good practical and technical skills, are important. You should be good at solving problems and be able to work quickly but carefully. You must be reasonably fit with good eyesight. You should be able to work as part of a team, but also get on with your own work unsupervised. A driving licence appropriate to the kinds of vehicle you are working on is usually necessary. You may have dealings with customers, and colleagues within the workplace, so you should enjoy working with people and be polite and pleasant. ICT skills and an understanding of technology is very important in this role.

Motor vehicle valeter

Valeters ensure that cars and other vehicles are thoroughly cleaned both inside and out. This includes cleaning the bodywork, glass, wheels and interior. This work suits anyone who loves the idea of working with cars and enjoys dealing with people, but does not have or wish to develop some of the technical knowledge and skill required for technician work. Vehicle valeters work for car showrooms, in garages and in specialist car cleaning outlets, or they may work for themselves.

Qualifications and Training

There are no specific entry qualifications to do this work, but there are some relevant NVQ units that you may be able to take while you are working.

Personal Qualities and Skills

You have to have a good eye for details and enjoy taking a pride in your work. You must be practical and sensible, able to work quickly, and to fit in as part of a team or get on with work on your own.

Starting Salary

Starting salaries range from £8,000 to £11,000 at the start of an apprenticeship, £16,000+ when qualified. With experience you can earn £18,000 to £25,000, though not many body repairers achieve the top end of this range. Car valeters don't earn as much as technicians, but there is the potential to earn some money from tips if you do this work.

info

Automotive Skills: The Sector Skills Council for the Automotive Industry, 93 Newman Street, London W1T 3DT; 0800 093 1777; www.automotiveskills.org.uk/careers

The Sector Skills Council for the retail motor industry, who supply impartial careers information for the entire sector.

Automotive Distribution Federation, www.adf.org.uk

British Vehicle Rental and Leasing Association, www.bvrla.co.uk

City and Guilds, www.city-and-guilds.co.uk

The Institute of the Motor Industry, Fanshaws, Brickendon, Hertford SG13 8PQ; 01992 511 521; www.motor.org.uk

Society of Motor Manufacturers and Traders, www.smmt.co.uk

Vehicle Builders and Repairers Association, Belmont House, 102 Finkle Lane, Gildersome, Leeds LS27 7TW; 0113 253 8333; www.vbra.co.uk

MUSIC

(*see also* Performing Arts)

Occupations in music range from composing and performing, to making and repairing instruments, to teaching.

Incorporated Society of Musicians, 10 Stratford Place, London W1C 1AA; 020 7629 4413; fax: 020 7408 1538; www.ism.org.uk; e-mail: membership@ism.org.uk

Composer

Very few composers earn a living solely by composition; most also perform or teach. The most lucrative area of composition is writing music for television, films, videos and the commercial market, but some composers also find time to write their own music and get it performed. Professional advice on copyright (from a solicitor or professional association) is essential.

Musical instrument technologist

The instrument technologist is concerned with making and repairing instruments of all kinds, from pianos to guitars. Good training and practical skill are essential and ensure plenty of work for the technologist.

Qualifications and Training

The Department of Communications and Music Technology at the London Guildhall University offers courses in almost every aspect of instrument technology through its City and Guilds Certificate, BTEC National Diploma, HND and degree courses. Full- and part-time courses are also offered by Leeds College of Music, Morley College, West Dean College, Merton Technical College and Newark Technical College. The Institute of Musical Instrument Technology awards a diploma and can provide further advice and information.

Personal Qualities and Skills

Instrument technologists need some musical ability, at least an ear for tuning, and relevant technical skills – woodwork, electronics and metalwork.

Starting Salary

Salaries vary greatly: the average is £250–300 a week when trained, but lower without experience.

info

Incorporated Society of Musicians (ISM), 10 Stratford Place, London W1A 1AA; 020 7629 4413; www.ism.org

Society for the Promotion of the New Music, Francis House, Francis Street, London SW1P 1DE; 020 7828 9696; www.spnm.org.uk

National Association of Musical Instrument Repairers; www.namir.org.uk

Skillset, Sector Skills Council for Advertising, Culture and the Arts, Prospect House, 80–110 New Oxford Street, London WC1A 1HB; 020 7520 5757; www.skillset.org

Musician

see Performing Arts

Music teacher

With music now placed as one of the foundation subjects in the National Curriculum there is an increasing demand for music teachers. Opportunities range from private instrumental teaching to class teaching at primary, secondary and tertiary levels. Class teachers and some visiting instrumental teachers working in state schools require Qualified Teacher status.

Private teachers set up and develop their own independent, studio-based business. The Incorporated Society of Musicians (ISM) sets professional standards for members who are listed in their Register of Professional Private Music Teachers. They set minimum hourly tuition fees, so that a reasonable income can be assured, and advise on business matters such as tuition contracts.

Qualifications and Training

Entry to undergraduate courses of study usually requires a minimum of five GCSEs and one or more A levels, preferably including music. Full-time courses of study over three or four years, usually leading to a degree, are available at conservatoires (performance-based), universities (more academic) and colleges of higher education (more broad spectrum). Singers require a longer training, often over six years. Conservatoires and universities also offer a range of postgraduate courses. Teachers require an appropriate teaching qualification, such as a PGCE (Postgraduate Certificate in Education). Details of courses in performance, composition, musicology and teaching are available from the Incorporated Society of Musicians' website. The government has introduced a training scheme for the music industry under the 'New Deal' initiative; details are available from Job Centre Plus centres.

Personal Qualities and Skills

A love of music, a positive and persuasive personality, robust physical and mental health, stamina, patience and excellent communication skills are essential for any career in music. Competition is fierce for performers, and only a very few talented musicians can establish a successful solo career. The ability to get on well with others helps to ensure good relationships with colleagues, managers and promoters to support career development.

Starting Salary

Salaries vary enormously. Guidance on rates of pay is available from the Incorporated Society of Musicians. Hourly rates of £16–20 are usual.

Music therapist

see Therapy

Piano tuner

Piano tuners or technicians are able both to tune a piano evenly throughout the scale, and to discover and put right any fault. They work with a kit of specialised tools, and are employed in piano factories and by piano dealers. Some also work for themselves.

Qualifications and Training

Courses are available at three institutions: London Guildhall University, Newark and Sherwood College and the Royal National College for the Blind, Hereford. No formal entry qualifications are required. The Piano Tuners' Association will accept a candidate for membership after five years from the start of training – at least two years training and at least two years working as a piano tuner.

Personal Qualities and Skills

Musical ability, while not essential, is an advantage. Patience and deftness are required, together with an aptitude to be able to use woodworking, home-improvement and DIY tools. As tuners are mostly self-employed, the ability to work alone, competence in managing a small business and self-motivation are also important.

Starting Salary

Salaries vary greatly: the average is £250–300 a week when trained but lower without experience. Established, self-employed piano tuners may earn up to £800 a week.

Pianoforte Tuners' Association, www.pianotuner.org.uk; e-mail: enquiries@pianotuner.org.uk

NAVAL ARCHITECT

Naval architects are professional engineers who play a key role as project leaders and specialists in the design, building and marketing of all systems that have to move just above, on or under the sea, including merchant ships, warships, offshore structures, submarines, hovercraft, yachts and other small craft. They also have to ensure that a safe, economic and seaworthy design is produced. The workplace may be a large company, a small group, a consultancy or a government department.

Qualifications and Training

Naval architects who meet the education, training and experience requirements may become members of the Royal Institution of Naval Architects (RINA), the professional institution for all qualified naval architects. They need to have had an aggregate of at least seven years' engineering education, training and responsible experience. Students and graduates working towards meeting these requirements may also become members. It is possible to register with the UK Engineering Council as a Chartered Engineer (CEng), an Incorporated Engineer (IEng) or as an Engineering Technician (EngTech) through RINA.

Personal Qualities and Skills

A naval architect requires a creative, enquiring and logical mind; the ability to communicate clearly in speech and writing with others inside and outside the engineering profession; sound judgement and qualities of leadership, and the ability to work as a part of a team.

Starting Salary

£25,000–30,000 per year, five years after qualifying.

info

Royal Institution of Naval Architects (RINA), 10 Upper Belgrave Street, London SW1X 8BQ; 020 7235 4622; fax: 020 7259 5912; www.rina.org.uk; e-mail: hq@rina.org.uk

The RINA publishes a booklet 'Careers in naval architecture' which is available online.

NEUROPHYSIOLOGY TECHNOLOGIST

A more familiar name for the neurophysiology technologist is the EEG (electro-encephalography) technologist, who is responsible for setting up and operating electronic equipment that records electrical activity in the brain and nervous system. These tests often include visual, auditory or other types of evoked potentials (EPs), which are the responses of the brain to specific stimuli. EEG and EP tests are performed to help in the diagnosis of patients with epilepsy, cerebral tumours, strokes, dementias or multiple sclerosis.

In many departments, the technologist is also required to assist the clinician with electromyography (EMG) and nerve conduction studies (NCS). These tests look at the way in which nerves and muscles in the body are working, and help in the diagnosis of diseases such as dystrophies and nerve dysfunction. All these procedures are carried out either in the department, wards, intensive care units or operating theatres. Both outpatients and in-patients come to the department, and the tests are performed on all ages. Heart rate and respiration may also be recorded. The neurophysiology technologist works as part of the hospital team in the surgical, neurological or psychiatric department.

Qualifications and Training

Five GCSEs, grade C or above, are normally required, including maths, English and combined science. Many entrants have A levels or equivalent. There are two main ways of entering the profession: as a student technologist employed by a hospital in an EEG clinical neurophysiology department; or as a student supernumerary technologist employed by a regional health authority. Training takes place mostly on the job with day-release facilities to study for an Edexcel (BTEC) qualification/NVQ award, level 3.

Personal Qualities and Skills

A medical technologist needs to be willing to take responsibility, able to keep calm under pressure and must be meticulous. In addition, a pleasant manner to put patients at their ease is essential.

Starting Salary

Trainee £9,600+ plus London allowance where appropriate; once qualified £12,400–16,900, potentially rising to £35,000+ for senior posts.

www.nhscareers.nhs.uk/nhs-knowledge_base/data/4861.html

Electrophysiological Technologists' Association, c/o EEG Department, Staffordshire General Hospital, Weston Road, Stafford ST16 3SA (enclose sae)

British Society for Clinical Neurophysiology, Middlesex Hospital, Mortimer Street, London W1T 3AA; www.bscn.org.uk; e-mail: bscn@bscn.org.uk

NURSING, HEALTH VISITING AND MIDWIFERY

Nurses are employed in a wide variety of settings in hospitals, institutions (such as prisons and colleges), the armed forces, schools, industry and private organisations. There are four specialisms or 'branches' within nursing: adult nursing, children's nursing, mental health nursing and learning disability nursing. Midwifery and health visiting are regarded as separate professions although still part of the nursing family. Healthcare assistants now work with nurses and other healthcare professionals.

Applicants must decide which branch of nursing they want to qualify in before training. Specialist training within community nursing or other areas of nursing can be pursued once registration as a general nurse has been achieved. Specialist qualifications in district nursing, health visiting, community psychiatric nursing, learning disability nursing (community practice), occupational health nursing, school nursing and practice nursing can be taken at degree or diploma level.

Nurses working in the 'adult nursing' branch spend time not only working on hospital wards but also in outpatient departments, operating theatres, intensive care and with elderly patients. They also work in the community under the supervision of district nurses, health visitors and community midwives. A qualification in adult nursing could lead to specialising in areas such as accident and emergency, practice nursing or health visiting.

Children's nursing, usually referred to as 'paediatric nursing', covers community care, surgical nursing, medical nursing and caring for children with physical and learning disabilities. Children's nurses need to be able to deal with the fears and anxieties of sick children and provide support for their family. Communication skills are very important in this branch of nursing. A children's nurse will care for newborn babies and teenagers, support the child's family and help them care for the child, work with the family to plan care, and work within the paediatric team. Specialisms following on from qualification in children's nursing might be in intensive care, child protection or cancer care.

The mental health nurse will care for people who are mentally ill. Mentally ill people are increasingly being cared for at home or in homes within the community setting. Mental health nurses care for patients suffering from a wide range of illnesses. Some patients simply require help, counselling and support from the nurse. Others with more serious mental health illnesses will require monitoring and help with medication. The mental health nurse assesses individual needs and works with the patient to develop a plan of care; monitors the effectiveness of planned care; administers and monitors the dosage of prescribed medicine; and explains the effects of medication to the individual. He or she works as part of a team of professionals and acts as 'key worker' coordinating the care of an individual. The mental health nurse will require skill, tact and patience in caring for people.

A nurse working within the learning disability branch of nursing assesses each individual and works with the person to develop a plan of care. Some people need to be taught basic skills such as bathing, and the nurse breaks each skill into a series of small tasks and works with the individuals. People with learning disabilities often have physical handicaps, and nurses work with other professionals such as physiotherapists, occupational therapists and doctors in providing care and promoting independence. More people with learning disabilities are cared for at home and in the community than ever before, and increasing numbers of nurses are undergoing specialist training to offer care in the community.

Qualifications and Training

Courses are offered at degree and diploma level. Entry to degree courses is through UCAS. For the diploma, entry is directly to the Colleges of Nursing and Midwifery in Northern Ireland and Wales and through central clearing houses in England (NMAS) and Scotland (CATCH). A minimum of five GCSEs or equivalent are required, but candidates without such qualifications may sit an education test known as the DC test. The minimum age of entry to programmes is 17 and a half (17 in Scotland).

Courses are offered in colleges of nursing and midwifery (except for Northern Ireland – see **info** below), which may be linked with a university or college of higher education. The 18-month Common Foundation Programme gives a general introduction to nursing, followed by 18 months in one of four branches, chosen before the course begins: adult nursing, mental health nursing, nursing people with a mental handicap or children's nursing. The focus of the course is equally split between theory and practice. Students spend time in the hospital and the community, gaining experience.

Once registered, nurses practise in a wide variety of settings. Some take further courses to gain specialist knowledge in meeting the needs of patients in differing clinical specialities. Others may choose nurse teaching or management within the health services. Whatever the area chosen, the initial nursing qualification will be the first step in a lifetime of professional education.

Personal Qualities and Skills

Nursing is always about people: patients, their families, their friends and the team of colleagues working to deliver nursing care. The ability to get on with others and good communication skills are essential. As nursing is physically demanding, candidates need to be fit. Nurses must be committed to developing their knowledge and skills throughout their careers, enhancing their ability to care.

Starting Salary

Since September 2005 the grading system and pay for nurses has been completely restructured under the 'Agenda for Change'. Each post is evaluated in terms of skills, effort and knowledge needed, with extra money for extra responsibilities and demonstrable knowledge and skills. Newly qualified nurses working in the NHS earn between £17,600 and £19,500 a year, sisters and charge nurses earn between £24,000 and £29,000, and nurse specialists are paid from £26,600 to £31,000. A limited number of nurse consultants can earn between £37,000 and £51,000. Nurses are entitled to overtime payments for any hours they work over a 37.5-hour week.

Healthcare assistant

Healthcare assistants work alongside nurses and provide basic care for patients. They help with treatments, keep wards tidy and complete basic paperwork. They work on general hospital wards, in clinics and outpatient departments, psychiatric hospitals, hospices and care homes. There are also opportunities for community-based work, providing physical care to individuals who might otherwise have needed to go into hospital or residential care homes.

Qualifications and Training

No prior qualifications are needed to start work as a healthcare assistant, but hospitals, care homes and other organisations do provide training and there is currently a drive to ensure that everyone doing this work will achieve at least NVQ level 2.

Personal Qualities and Skills

Like qualified nurses, healthcare assistants must have patience, tact, tolerance and an ability to communicate with the patients in their charge. Physical fitness is essential as the job sometimes involves heavy work (such as lifting and turning patients).

Starting Salary

Health care assistants in the NHS aged 18 or over start on a salary of between £11,100 and £13,300. More experienced staff with a relevant NVQ level 2 or 3 can earn up to £17,000. There are also allowances for antisocial hours, and some overtime payments are possible.

info

NHS Careers, PO Box 376, Bristol BS99 3EY; 0845 606 0655; www.nhscareers.nhs.uk

Skills for Care, Sector Skills Council for Social Care, Albion Court, 5 Albion Place, Leeds LS1 6JP; 0113 245 1716; www.skillsforcare.org.uk

Skills for Health, 1st Floor, Goldsmiths House, Broad Plain, Bristol BS2 0JP; 0117 922 1155; www.skillsforhealth.org.uk

Careers and Jobs in Nursing (Kogan Page)

Health visitors

Health visitors promote health and contribute to the prevention of mental, physical and social ill health in the community. This involves educating people in ways of healthy living and making positive changes in the environment. Education may be achieved by teaching individuals or families in their own homes, in health centres, clinics, in informal groups, or through campaigns for the promotion of good health practices through local or national mass media.

The health visitor may work with people who are registered with a GP or who live within a defined geographical area. The work includes collaboration with a wide range of voluntary and statutory organisations.

Qualifications and Training

Applicants must hold a first-level nurse or midwifery qualification with post-registration experience. One-year health visitor courses are provided at institutions of higher education.

All approved programmes now lead to the award of Specialist Practitioner (Public Health Visiting/Health Visiting). These programmes are at a minimum of first degree level.

Personal Qualities and Skills

Health visitors must be excellent communicators, able to convey information to all types of people without being patronising. They must have self-confidence, tact and a lot of common sense. They must be able to work alone, yet know when to seek advice. They should be confident, articulate public speakers.

Starting Salary

Approximately £18,000, rising to £25,000.

info

NHS Careers; Careers Helpline: 0845 6060 655; www.nhscareers.nhs.uk

Community Practitioners and Health Visitors Association, 40 Bermondsey Street, London SE1 3UD; 020 7939 7000; fax: 020 7403 2976; www.msfcphva.org; e-mail: infocphva@amicustheunion.org

Midwifery

Midwives (who may be female or male) provide care and advice to mothers and fathers before, during and after birth; they are either employed by the NHS in hospital and/or community settings, including home births, by private hospitals, or work independently. The midwife provides care during normal pregnancy and birth, and up to 28 days following the birth. The midwife will also care for women who have complications. The midwife is an integral part of the multidisciplinary team responsible for delivering care, working closely with obstetricians and other health professionals in ensuring the wellbeing of mothers and babies.

Qualifications and Training

A three-year diploma or degree programme of midwifery education leading to qualification as a registered midwife (RM) is available at various centres nationwide. Candidates need to have a minimum of five GCSEs (grades A–C), or equivalent, including English and a science subject, and must be at least 17 and a half years old (17 in Scotland). Programmes are also available for those with general nursing qualifications. Both courses include theory and practical components. Students spend time on a variety of placements in hospitals and the community.

Personal Qualities and Skills

Midwives must engage in continuous professional development throughout their career to be able to provide safe and effective care to mothers and their babies.

Starting Salary

Midwives in the NHS earn between £16,000 and £25,000.

info

Nursing and Midwifery Admissions Service (NMAS), Rosehill, New Barn Lane, Cheltenham, Gloucestershire GL52 3LZ; 0870 1122206; www.nmas.ac.uk

National Board for Nursing, Midwifery and Health Visiting for Scotland, 22 Queen Street, Edinburgh EH2 1NT; 0131 226 7371; fax: 0131 225 9970; www.nes.scot.nhs.uk/nursing

Careers Information Service, NHS for Scotland, 66 Rose Street, Edinburgh EH2 2NN; 0131 220 8660; e-mail: careers@nes.scot.nhs.uk

Northern Ireland: School of Nursing and Midwifery, Queen's University Belfast, Medical Biology Centre, 97 Lisburn Road, Belfast BT9 7BL; 028 9097 2233; fax: 028 9027 2328; www.qub.ac.uk/nur; e-mail: nursing@qub.ac.uk

NHS Careers, PO Box 376, Bristol BS99 3EY; 0845 6060 655; www.nhscareers.nhs.uk

Nursing and Midwifery Council, 23 Portland Place, London W1B 1PZ; 020 7637 7181; www.nmc-uk.org

Careers and Jobs in Nursing (Kogan Page)

OIL/GAS RIG WORK

There are various openings for personnel working on oil or gas drilling rigs, both onshore (on land) and offshore (such as in the North Sea). Opportunities in all fields are generally limited to experienced and/or highly qualified applicants. An offshore rig has to be self-sufficient and is a combination of a factory, hotel and heliport. The catering and accommodation are similar to the provision onshore. Many of the routine factory tasks (such as cleaning and maintenance) are carried out by outside contractors and service companies.

Divers

(*see also* Diver)

Divers are employed in exploration and production work, as well as underwater repair work such as welding.

Drilling crew

The drilling crew is responsible for the drilling of wells, and the operation and maintenance of a variety of heavy machinery. The crew consists of a toolpusher who manages the team and is responsible for the safety and integrity of the operation, and a team of people including a driller, assistant driller, derrickman, roughnecks and roustabouts. A typical drill crew will number around 10 people. Progression to the role of driller is hierarchical, with people working through general labouring jobs (roustabouts), working on the drill floor (roughnecks) or at the top of the derrick (derrickman). The work is physical, from the operation of the drilling equipment to the cleaning and maintenance of pumps and equipment. A graduate drilling engineer and a range of other specialists such as logging engineers, directional drilling specialists and mudloggers will also work with the drill crew.

Engineers

(*see also* Engineering)

A production engineer supervises activities ranging from production and storage, gas compression and injection (to assist in the recovery of the oil), to tanker loading. The reservoir engineer is concerned with the behaviour of the oil accumulation or reservoir, and has to attempt to discover how much oil remains below ground and what are the most effective methods of recovery. Economics plays an important role. The maintenance engineer must ensure that all equipment is functioning properly, selecting and monitoring the companies under contract.

Geologist

(*see also* Geologist)

The oil companies employ technical experts such as geologists, geophysicists and drilling and petroleum engineers. Geologists collect and analyse data from a variety of sources to determine whether drilling might prove successful at a particular site, and to optimise production from existing oilfields. There are opportunities around the world.

Geophysicist

Geophysicists use remote sensing to study the composition and structure of the sub-surface. A major element of this is computer-aided analysis of seismic data.

Qualifications and Training

Geologist: a good honours degree is the minimum required; many companies prefer postgraduate training. Geophysicist: an honours degree in geology or geophysics or other numerate discipline, such as maths or physics. Postgraduate training may be an advantage. Drilling crew: trainees are normally sponsored by drilling companies. Roughneck courses last four weeks. Drillers, toolpushers and drilling engineers will receive further training, including statutory well-control, safety and emergency response training. Divers: must be trained on courses approved by the Health and Safety Executive. Training is expensive; candidates may be sponsored by employers. Engineers: oil companies recruit engineering graduates for trainee posts.

Personal Qualities and Skills

Geophysicists need scientific aptitude, numeracy, a good eye for detail, an enquiring mind and the ability to work in a team under pressure. Drilling crew members must be physically fit, as the work is arduous. Good team-work skills are essential. Divers must be physically fit and able to stay calm in a crisis. Everyone must be able to cope with harsh environments and long periods away from home.

info

Cogent, the Sector Skills Council for the oil and gas extraction, chemicals manufacturing and petroleum industries; www.cogent-ssc.com

Institute of Petroleum, 61 New Cavendish Street, London W1G 7AR; 020 7467 7100; www.petroleum.co.uk; e-mail: ip@petroleum.co.uk; *Energy: Careers in the oil and gas industry* available from website

Institute of Materials, Minerals and Mining, 1 Carlton House Terrace, London SW1Y 5DB; 020 7451 7300; www.iom3.org; www.materials-careers.org.uk

Engineering Careers Information Service, SEMTA, 14 Upton Road, Watford, Hertfordshire WD1 7EP; 0800 282 167; www.semta.org.uk/enginuity; e-mail: ecis@emta.org.uk

Starting Salary

New members of a drilling crew earn around £20,000 and this rises quickly to around £25,000. Periods of leave are also quite generous. Engineers start on between £20,000 and £30,000, and the range is similar for geologists and geophysicists.

OPTOMETRY

Dispensing optician

Dispensing opticians do not examine eyes or test sight, but supply and fit spectacles and other aids prescribed by an optometrist. They usually work in general practice, including independent businesses, partnership, as an employee of corporate bodies or as a franchisee. There are also job opportunities in hospitals and clinics. Once registered, dispensing opticians can undertake further training to enable them to fit contact lenses.

Qualifications and Training

To practise as a dispensing optician, you must complete a training course approved by the General Optical Council (GOC) and pass a professional examination administered by the British Association of Dispensing Opticians (BADO). There is a choice of four methods to achieve this: a two-year full-time diploma; a three-year day-release course; a three-year distance learning course; or a three-year full-time degree course in dispensing optics or ophthalmic dispensing management. Degree courses require you to have five GCSEs and two A levels, but entry requirements are a little more flexible if you choose the other routes. From 2007 dispensing opticians will have to demonstrate to the BADO that they have undertaken appropriate continuing education and will have to register annually. There is a lot of on-the-job training, academic study and practical placements involved in qualifying for this profession.

Personal Qualities and Skills

You must be pleasant, friendly, approachable and patient. You must also be good at handling delicate equipment and have reasonable mathematical skills for taking measurements and making calculations. It is also useful to have a grasp of fashion and style, since this is very important to many of your clients when they choose spectacles or lenses.

Starting Salary

On registration you will earn around £16,000 to £17,000; with a few years experience this rises to £18,000 to £29,000.

info

Association of British Dispensing Opticians, 199 Gloucester Terrace, London W2 6LD, 020 7298 5100; fax: 020 7298 5111; www.abdo.org.uk; e-mail: general@abdo.org.uk

ABDO College of Education, Godmersham Park Mansion, Godmersham, Canterbury, Kent CT4 7DT; 01227 738829; www.abdo.org.uk; e-mail: education@abdo.org.uk

General Optical Council, 41 Harley Street, London W1G 8DJ; 020 7580 3898; www.optical.org

A Career in Vision Care is available for download from www.college_optometrists.org

Optometrist

Optometrists are trained to examine eyes and test sight, detect and measure defects in healthy eyes and prescribe spectacles, contact lenses or other appliances to correct or improve vision. They must carry out whatever tests are clinically necessary to detect signs of injury or disease to the eye or elsewhere, and must refer these patients to a medical practitioner. Most optometrists work in general practice in a variety of arrangements, including independent businesses, partnership, as an employee of corporate bodies, as a franchisee or in the hospital eye service. There are also job opportunities in research organisations, academic departments, ophthalmic hospitals and clinics.

Qualifications and Training

Optometrists must be registered with the General Optical Council before being permitted to practise in the UK. To obtain registration they must pass the professional qualifying exam run by the College of Optometrists. The exam is in two parts. For Part I the candidate must gain a BSc honours degree in optometry after three years of study at an accredited institution (or four years in Scotland). Part II is taken after the candidate has completed a pre-registration year of supervised practice. The professional qualifying exam combines practical and oral assessment of the candidate's ability to manage patients and practise safely as an independent optometrist.

For acceptance on to a university course students normally need three A levels, two of which must be maths or science. GCSEs should include English and physics if not gained at A level. Average entry grades vary but are usually 320 A level points.

Personal Qualities and Skills

Opticians need mathematical and scientific skills to make accurate observations and calculations. They also need an ability to get on with and communicate effectively with patients of all ages and backgrounds and to be able to put them at their ease.

Starting Salary

Pre-registration salaries are £8,000–9,000; post-registration: £25,000–35,000.

info

College of Optometrists, 42 Craven Street, London WC2N 5NG; 020 7839 6000; fax: 020 7839 6800; www.college-optometrists.org; e-mail: optometry@college-optometrists.org

General Optical Council, 41 Harley Street, London W1G 8DJ; 020 7580 3898; fax: 020 7436 3525; www.optical.org

Scottish Committee of Optometrists, 7 Queens Buildings, Queensferry Road, Rosyth, Fife KY11 2RA; 01383 419444; www.scottishoptometry.co.uk; e-mail: secretarysco@aol.com

A Career in Vision Care available for download from www.college-optometrists.org

Orthoptist

Orthoptists diagnose and treat various abnormalities and weaknesses in the eye, such as a squint or double vision. Many patients are children, and special equipment and exercises are used to help correct any defects while they are still young. They work closely with medical eye specialists and, where operations are necessary, with ophthalmic surgeons. Most orthoptists work within the NHS, in hospitals and clinics (including school clinics). There are also opportunities in private practice and teaching.

Qualifications and Training

Qualification is via a degree; courses are available at the universities of Sheffield and Liverpool. Applicants must have five GCSEs to include at least one science, English language and maths, plus three A levels or equivalent.

Personal Qualities and Skills

Orthoptists have to be able to win the confidence of their patients (who are often very young), so need a sympathetic manner and a good deal of patience. Some mathematical and scientific ability is also called for.

Starting Salary

From £15,920 in the NHS, slightly more in private practice.

British and Irish Orthoptic Society, Tavistock House North, Tavistock Square, London WC1H 9HX; 020 7387 7992 (information pack available); fax: 020 7387 2584; www.orthoptics.org.uk; e-mail: bos@orthoptics.org.uk

PAINTER AND DECORATOR

see Construction

PATENTS

A patent is a legal document that gives an inventor the right to claim an invention as his or her own work and to produce, sell or make the invention. It also protects the inventor from having his or her work and/or ideas copied by others.

Patent agent/patent attorney

Patent agents/patent attorneys (these terms are interchangeable) have expertise in the area of intellectual property, advise individual clients and companies on matters relating to patent law, and act on their behalf if they wish to patent an invention, or to register a trademark or a design in the UK or abroad. First, records are searched to gauge the likelihood of a patent being granted. The patent agent then draws up the particulars of the client's invention clearly and concisely, ensuring it neither infringes another patent nor is liable to be copied without infringing its own patent. In cases where a client's patent has been infringed, the agent advises as to the best course of action. Patent agents are employed by private practice firms of patent agencies, industrial companies with a patent department and the government.

Patent examiner

These are civil servants who examine the applications for patents submitted by patent agents and others. The principal task is to establish the originality or otherwise of the invention and whether or not the applicant is entitled to the protection claimed. There is some opportunity to work abroad in the European Patent Office.

Patent officer

These are civil servants employed in protecting Crown rights in new inventions and developments, compensating the owners of patents used by the Crown and generally advising government departments on matters relating to patents.

Qualifications and Training

The minimum educational requirement for an agent is a degree in a science or a technology-related subject. It is usually necessary to register as a patent agent in the European Patent Office. This involves taking the European qualifying exams, for which a degree is necessary.

Patent examiners and officers need a first or second-class honours degree in engineering, physics, chemistry, maths or an equivalent professional qualification.

Personal Qualities and Skills

Curiosity, the ability to assimilate new ideas, good analytical and critical skills, clear and concise thinking and the capacity for logical and clear expression both in speech and writing are all essential.

Starting Salary

Trainees (no examinations passed) £15,000–25,000; technical assistants (close to qualification) £25,000–45,000; newly-qualified attorneys £50,000–70,000; attorneys with three to five years' post-qualification experience £65,000–90,000.

info

Chartered Institute of Patent Agents, 95 Chancery Lane, London WC2A 1DT; 020 7405 9450; www.cipa.org.uk; e-mail: mail@cipa.org.uk

Patent Office, Concept House, Cardiff Road, Newport, South Wales NP10 8QQ; 0845 9 500 505; fax: 01633 813600; www.patent.gov.uk

Inside Careers, Unit 3, The Quadrangle, 49 Atalanta Street, London SW6 6TR; 020 7565 7900; fax: 020 7565 7938; www.insidecareers.co.uk – downloadable guide to becoming a patent attorney

PERFORMING ARTS

Performing arts cover the range of occupations that is in the world of entertainment.

Actor

Acting mainly involves the interpretation of someone else's work and the communication of it to an audience, although there are opportunities for actors to write their own material. Actors are employed in various types of theatre (commercial, subsidised, community, fringe theatre and theatre-in-education), and also in television, film, radio, and television and radio commercials.

Competition is keen and, because it is such a precarious profession, those entering it must be prepared for long periods of unemployment.

Qualifications and Training

Most potential actors attend drama school. The National Council for Drama Training is a useful source for information on accredited courses. A good general education is important, and some schools require GCSEs and A levels or equivalent. Training courses at established schools usually last two or three years. Entrance is by audition and is competitive. Further experience may be gained from working in a repertory company or in fringe theatre. This may be an alternative way of entering the profession, but it is becoming increasingly difficult to enter solely by this method.

Personal Qualities and Skills

Acting requires a combination of intelligence, sensitivity and imagination, together with a good memory, determination and physical stamina.

Starting Salary

Comparatively low: minimum weekly salaries are set by theatre employers after negotiations with Equity, which has a number of different agreements for theatre, television and film work. Actors often need to take on other work to make a living, especially while they are getting established.

Creative and Cultural Skills: Sector Skills Council for Advertising, Culture and the Arts, 11 Southwark Street, London SE1 1RQ; 020 7089 5866; www.ccskills.org.uk

Equity – The British Actors Union, Guild House, Upper St Martins Lane, London WC2H 9EG; 020 7379 6000; www.equity.org.uk

National Association of Youth Theatres, Arts Centre, Vane Terrace, Darlington DL3 7AX; 01325 363330; www.nayt.org.uk

National Council for Drama Training, 1–7 Woburn Walk, Bloomsbury, London WC1H 0JJ; 020 7387 3650; www.ncdt.org.uk

Dancing

Dance can be divided into the two main categories of theatre dance (ballet, modern and contemporary dance, jazz and tap) and social dance (ballroom, folk dance and disco). However, there are no hard and fast divisions between the different forms. The profession of dancing consists of two main areas: performing and teaching. Choreography, notation, dance animation and dance therapy are related areas of work.

Choreographer

Choreographers create and plan dance routines and oversee the execution of their plans by the dancers. Choreographers are often former dancers.

Dance animateur

Dance animateurs work in the community or education to encourage participation and involvement and to raise the profile of dance activity locally. Their precise role is dependent on the funding organisation and the needs of the community in which they work. Animateurs are often qualified dance teachers.

Dance notator

Notators are employed by dance companies to record their repertoire, and assist choreographers and rehearsal staff in the revival of choreographic works. Most notators are graduates of vocational dance schools or ex-professional dancers, as the work involves close and informed observation of the choreography, the ability to demonstrate the movement accurately and the ability to work effectively with professional dancers.

Dance performer

Many of those who wish to perform have had early training in ballet and/or other forms of theatre dance. Opportunities in ballet and contemporary companies are limited, and many dancers find their first employment in companies abroad. Dancers also work in pantomimes, shows and musicals, and on cruise ships. Professional performers find it useful to be members of the British Actors' Equity Association.

Dance teacher

Teachers of dance can specialise in one area of dance teaching or teach in a variety of areas. The demand for teachers is high, especially as dance is now seen as a form of recreation. Teachers may work in commercial dance studios and professional dance schools both in the UK and abroad.

Qualifications and Training

Ideally, ballet students should attend a recognised residential establishment such as the Royal Ballet School from the age of 11 to 18. Means-tested financial assistance may be available to UK students. Dancers who want to become teachers must obtain the relevant qualifications, for which full-time or part-time courses are available. These generally have an entry requirement of four to five GCSEs at grade C and above. The Royal Academy of Dancing offers certificates, diplomas and degrees in classical ballet teaching. The courses are available on a part-time and full-time basis.

Personal Qualities and Skills

Dancers need to be hard working, self-disciplined both physically and mentally, dedicated and determined. They must be imaginative, able to express themselves artistically, have a good sense of timing and an ear for music.

Starting Salary

Dancers who belong to equity earn a minimum of £285 per week. Non-equity members earn much less and some dancers will work voluntarily to help gain contracts. Teachers earn £18,000+ and possibly more in the private sector. Choreographers and notators are reasonably well paid. You can only work as a dancer for a limited period of time, while you are at the peak of physical fitness, so this can affect your long-term income.

info

British Association of Teachers of Dance, 23 Marywood Square, Glasgow G41 2BP; 0141 423 4029; www.batd.co.uk

British Dance Council, Terpsichore House, 240 Merton Road, South Wimbledon, London SW19 1EQ; www.british-dance-council.org

Council for Dance Education & Training (CDET), Toynbee Hall, 28 Commercial Street, London E1 6LS; 020 7247 4030; www.cdet.org.uk

Dance UK, Battersea Arts Centre, Lavender Hill, London SW11 5TF; 020 7228 4990; www.danceuk.org

Laban Centre for Movement and Dance, Creekside, London SE8 3DZ; 020 8691 8600; www.laban.org

National Dance Teachers Association, 47 Grove Hill Road, London SE5 8DF; www.ndta.org.uk

Royal Academy of Dance, 36 Battersea Square, London SW11 3RA; 020 7326 8000; www.rad.org.uk

Musician

(*see also* Music)

A musical training, leading to a degree or equivalent qualification, opens the door to a wide range of careers in music, including performing, teaching, administration, management, broadcasting, recording, journalism, publishing, promotion, librarianship and the retail trade.

Many professional musicians work on a freelance basis as soloists, orchestral players, commercial session musicians and in a variety of chamber music ensembles including classical, rock, dance and jazz groups. A performer's working life often includes some teaching, master classes or community education work alongside regular and vital practice.

Some musicians arrange their own engagements, others have agents or use a diary service to find work. For all performers, membership of a professional association or union is desirable.

There are opportunities, particularly for those who already play an instrument, to join the Army, the RAF or Royal Marines as a bandsman.

Qualifications and Training

Entry to undergraduate courses of study usually requires a minimum of five GCSEs and one or more A levels, preferably including music. Full-time courses of study over three or four years, usually leading to a degree, are available at conservatoires (performance-based), universities (more academic) and colleges of higher education (more broad spectrum). Singers require a longer training, often over six years. Conservatoires and universities also offer a range of postgraduate courses. Details of courses in performance, composition, musicology and teaching are available from the Incorporated Society of Musicians' website. The government has introduced a training scheme for the music industry under the 'New Deal' initiative; details are available from Job Centre Plus centres.

Personal Qualities and Skills

A love of music, a positive and persuasive personality, robust physical and mental health, stamina, patience and excellent communication skills are essential for any career in music. Competition is fierce for performers, and only a very few talented musicians can establish a successful solo career. The ability to get on well with others helps to ensure good relationships with colleagues, managers and promoters to support career development.

Starting Salary

Salaries vary enormously. Guidance on rates of pay is available from the Incorporated Society of Musicians.

info

Incorporated Society of Musicians, 10 Stratford Place, London W1C 1AA; 020 7629 4413; fax: 020 7408 1538; www.ism.org; e-mail: membership@ism.org

Local Job Centre Plus and Careers/Connexions Centres

Singer

Singers are performers that use certain styles of music, such as pop, rock, jazz, folk, country and western, world or 'easy listening' music. Singers sometimes play musical instruments, record music in a studio, for albums or 'session' work, work as a solo artist or as part of a duo or group, and write songs for themselves or other musical artists.

Singers need to practise for many hours at a time and attend regular rehearsals. They enjoy listening to as much varied music as possible, at gigs, concerts and clubs and on the radio, Internet and CD.

Some singers include dance and movement as part of their performance. If a singer is successful, it is possible to appear in videos or on television. To be a successful singer really depends on an individual's talent, determination and hard work.

Personal Qualities and Skills

Success depends largely on musical talent and individuality. A passion for music and the ability to perform to an audience are good qualities for a singer. A certain level of discipline, focus and determination is required.

Qualifications and Training

The more experience of performing the better; a singer can start at parties and public events. If a singer is then spotted by a recording company it could be possible to get a recording contract. Alternatively, singers can contact record and music publishing companies directly by sending them a 'demo' tape recording. BTEC and SNCC courses in music are available, as are degrees in popular music. In addition, HND and HNC courses are also available in a wide range of relevant subjects. Entry requirements usually start with one A level/H grade or equivalent. Strong evidence of ability and interest in music are normally required.

There are many other full-time and part-time courses, both privately and state funded, and popular music courses offered by adult education institutes and local community organisations.

info

Brit School for Performing Arts and Technology, 60 The Crescent, Croydon CR0 2HN; 020 8665 5242; fax: 020 8665 5197; www.brit.croydon.sch.uk

British Phonographic Institute (BPI), Riverside Building, County Hall, Westminster Bridge Road, London SE1 7JA; 020 7803 1300; fax: 020 7803 1310; www.bpi.co.uk

Equity, Guild House, Upper St Martins Lane, London WC2H 9EG; 020 7379 6000; fax: 020 7379 7001; www.equity.org.uk; e-mail: info@equity.org.uk

Incorporated Society of Musicians, 10 Stratford Place, London W1C 1AA; 0207 629 4413; fax: 020 7408 1538; www.ism.org; e-mail: membership@ism.org

Musicians Union, 60/62 Clapham Road, London SW9 OJJ; 020 7582 5566; fax: 020 7582 9805; www.musiciansunion.org.uk

Rockschool, 245 Sandycombe Road, Kew TW9 2EW; 020 8332 6303; fax: 020 8332 6297; www.rockschool.co.uk

Scottish Arts Council, 12 Manor Place, Edinburgh EH3 7DD; 0131 226 6051; fax: 0131 225 9833; www.scottisharts.org.uk

Starting Salary

Only a small minority of singers earn high incomes. Many singers supplement their earnings with full-time work because they often earn less than the national average wage. The Musicians Union sets minimum rates for musicians. Singers performing live often earn the national minimum rate of £47.50 for up to two hours before midnight. A very experienced singer making backing tracks on an album might earn about £350 per three-hour session.

A solo musician on tour could earn between £500 and £2,000 per week, depending on experience. Equity (the performers' union) sets minimum rates for singers appearing in stage or television productions. The minimum rate for performances in London's West End is £320 per week for eight shows.

PHARMACY

Pharmacists are involved in the dispensing of medicinal drugs, usually prescribed by doctors. There are three branches of the profession: community pharmacists, hospital pharmacists, and industrial and research pharmacists.

Community pharmacist

Community pharmacists work from the high street, health centre and rural pharmacies as part of the NHS. They dispense prescriptions and ensure that medicines ordered on prescription or bought over the counter are correctly and safely supplied, with all necessary advice on their use. They keep a poisons register, and act as a link between the doctor and the pharmaceutical manufacturer, being prepared to discuss developments with both. They are readily accessible health advisers to the public. In addition, they sell a wide range of non-pharmaceutical articles.

Hospital pharmacist

They dispense drugs for hospital in- and outpatients and work side by side with nurses, doctors and other health professionals to ensure NHS patients receive the most appropriate medicines in the most effective way. In addition, in some hospitals, pharmacists manufacture their own products, take part in research work and come into direct contact with in-patients by accompanying medical staff on their ward rounds.

Industrial and research pharmacist

They work as part of a team of scientists researching diseases, developing new drugs and carrying out clinical trials. Industrial pharmacists are also recruited to work in the areas of manufacturing, regulatory and medical affairs, sales and marketing and computer science/information technology.

Qualifications and Training

Pharmacists must complete a four-year Master of Pharmacy degree, followed by one year's paid competency-based training and a registration examination. Entry to degree courses is with A level chemistry plus two other A levels or equivalent; maths and biology are preferred.

Personal Qualities and Skills

On top of excellent relevant medical knowledge and the need to be very careful and accurate, it is also important that you get on well with people and can be patient and understanding. Pharmacists already have responsibility for handling dangerous drugs, and it seems likely that they will be given greater prescribing rights in the near future, when responsibility and decision making will be extremely important aspects of their skills mix.

Starting Salary

In hospitals newly qualified pharmacists start on a range of between £18,000 and £22,000. Community (retail) pharmacists earn between £25,000 and £33,000. The highest salaries are paid in geographical locations where there is a recruitment problem. Industrial pharmacists start on between £20,000 and £30,000.

info

Association of the British Pharmaceutical Industry, 12 Whitehall, London SW1A 2DY; 020 7930 3477; fax: 020 7747 1414; www.abpi.org.uk; www.abpi-careers.org.uk

Guild of Healthcare Pharmacists, 40 Bermondsey Street, London SE1 3UD; 020 7939 7042; www.ghp.org.uk

National Pharmaceutical Association (trade association for community pharmacists), Mallinson House, 38–42 St Peter's Street, St Albans, Hertfordshire AL1 3NP; 01727 832161; fax: 01727 840858; www.npa.co.uk; e-mail: npa@npa.co.uk

Royal Pharmaceutical Society of Great Britain, 1 Lambeth High Street, London SE1 7JN; 020 7735 9141; fax: 020 7735 7629; www.rpsgb.org.uk; e-mail: careers@rpsgb.org.uk; Scottish Department, 36 York Place, Edinburgh EH1 3HU; www.rpsgb.org.uk/scotland/index.html; e-mail: info@rpsis.com

NHS Careers, 0845 60 60 655; www.nhscareers.nhs.uk

A Future in Pharmacy (Royal Pharmaceutical Society of Great Britain)

Pharmacy technician

Pharmacy technicians work as part of the pharmacy team and are supervised by a pharmacist. Their duties can include the dispensing of medicines from prescriptions, preparing sterile medicines, assessing stocks of drugs, patient counselling, advising on health promotion issues and collecting and collating information on drugs from a variety of sources. Pharmacy technicians can work in chemists, hospitals, the armed forces, the prison service, or within the pharmaceutical industry.

Qualifications and Training

A nationally recognised qualification is the NVQ Pharmacy Services at level 3 which is available from approved centres. Entry requirements for this are generally four GCSEs at grade C or above, including English, mathematics and chemistry plus one other science. Mature applicants are welcome, and previous education and work experience are considered.

Personal Qualities and Skills

As a pharmacy technician you should have a real interest in science and the ability to be accurate and careful. You should be able to deal sensitively and tactfully with people, be good at working as part of a team, and in some posts you may have to use sales skills as well.

Starting Salary

The starting salary for a pharmacy technician is around £11,000 to £13,000 a year. Technicians with experience are likely to earn around £15,000 to £16,000 a year.

info

Association of Pharmacy Technicians; www.aptuk.org

Royal Pharmaceutical Society of Great Britain, 1 Lambeth High Street, London SE1 7JN; 020 7735 9141; fax: 020 7735 7629; www.rpsgb.org.uk; e-mail: careers@rpsgb.org.uk; Scottish Department, 36 York Place, Edinburgh EH1 3HU; www.rpsgb.org.uk/scotland/index.html; e-mail: info@rpsis.com

NHS Careers, 0845 60 60 655; www.nhscareers.nhs.uk

PHOTOGRAPHY

Photography is an international means of communication. Its great advantage over the written word is that it does not need to be translated for use in a different country. The uses of photography range from commercial and press to medicine and crime detection. The use of digital equipment is changing the way photographs are taken, edited and stored. Photography is also a popular hobby, providing jobs for many in the photographic manufacturing, retailing, servicing and photo-finishing trades.

Commercial photographer

This work includes advertising, fashion, industrial and general practice photography. Photographers in advertising, editorial and fashion are nearly always freelance, employed for a particular campaign or job. Industrial photographers may be freelance or employed by large organisations, where they take photographs for brochures, catalogues, instruction manuals and in-house magazines. General practice photographers are mainly involved in wedding photography, family and animal portraits, and may do some work for local papers that don't employ press photographers.

Institutional and specialist photography

Scientific photographers are used to provide information essential for research in a scientific or engineering field. This work may include aerial photography as well as the use of techniques such as holography, photomicrography and macrophotography. The main employers are the civil service, private industries and universities. The main uses for photography in hospitals are to satisfy clinical, research, publication and teaching requirements. Clinical photography in particular demands the use of specialist techniques: photomicroscopy, macrophotography, endoscopic photography and the use of infra-red and ultraviolet light sources.

Photojournalism and press photographer

(*see also* Journalism)

Press photographers work for newspapers, magazines, periodicals and technical journals. All these media, particularly the last three, employ freelance as well as in-house staff. Photojournalists are photographers who are able to tell a story with pictures. They are almost always freelance, and the main market for their work is Sunday colour supplements.

Institutions that require photographers include museums, trade associations, national parks departments, charities, advisory councils, education authorities, libraries, auction houses and national galleries.

Photographers are also employed to teach photography in colleges and schools run by manufacturers and major retailers. There are opportunities to teach part-time photographic courses in many schools and colleges.

There are also opportunities to be a photographer in the Army, Royal Navy and Royal Air Force, but no one can join the Army or Royal Navy solely to be a photographer. The RAF alone recruits directly into ground photography. In police forces, most photographers are civilian employees.

Qualifications and Training

Formal educational qualifications are not always required but for a place on a course, four to five GCSEs or equivalent are usually necessary. (*See* Medical Illustrator for the requirements for medical photography.) To be a trainee press photographer, five GCSEs at grades A, B or C are necessary, or four GCSEs and one A level, or two GCSEs and two A levels. English language is necessary. There are a number of HND and degree courses available, and for entry to these five GCSEs plus two A levels or equivalent are necessary. Some establishments will accept individuals with a good portfolio of work.

The Royal Navy requires a good general education to GCSE level with particular attention to maths and English. In the police force requirements vary: some ask for City and Guilds qualifications and some for three GCSEs, including English, maths and a science.

Training is often on the job in photography, in a junior position; for example, a messenger or general assistant in an advertising studio or as a trainee assistant photographer in the police force. NVQs in photography at levels 3 and 4 are available.

Personal Qualities and Skills

Photographers generally require a blend of artistic and technical skills, the ability to deal with people and to put them at their ease, and good eyesight and colour vision. Medical and police photographers must have the ability to

info

Association of Photographers Ltd, 81 Leonard Street, London EC2A 4QS; 020 7739 6669; fax: 020 7739 8787; www.the-aop.org; e-mail: general@aophoto.co.uk; see Web site for downloadable careers information pack

British Institute of Professional Photography, Fox Talbot House, Amwell End, Ware, Hertfordshire SG12 9HN; 01920 464011; fax: 01920 487056; www.bipp.com; e-mail: BIPPWare@aol.com

British Kinematograph Sound and Television Society, The Moving Image Society, Pinewood Studios, Iver Heath, Bucks SL0 0NH; 01753 656656; fax: 01753 657016; www.bksts.com; e-mail: info@bksts.com

National Council for the Training of Journalists, Latton Bush Centre, Southern Way, Harlow, Essex CM18 7BL; 01279 430009; fax: 01279 438008; www.nctj.org.uk; e-mail: info@nctj.com

Great Careers in Video, Film and Photography (Kogan Page)

remain 'outside' their work and not be too squeamish. All photographers should have some IT skills and experience in digital imaging.

Starting Salary

Salaries vary enormously but the following are intended to give some indication: assistant photographers earn around £9,000; established photographers £20,000+. Medical photographers start around £13,500; social and wedding photographers are generally self-employed and earnings vary depending on number and type of clients.

Photographic production

There is a range of jobs associated with the production of photographs and images.

Manufacturing, retailing and service trades

Large quantities of film, photographic and non-photographic papers and chemicals are manufactured in the UK. Opportunities exist for technicians to research and develop new products; this sector of the industry also employs engineers and sales personnel.

Photographic laboratories/imaging centres

Professional laboratories/imaging centres can be divided into two major segments: social and commercial. The social laboratories cover printing (hand and machine), processing (paper and film), colour negative/colour transparency, and black and white photography, and mostly deal with wedding photographs and portraits. Digital imaging techniques have had a significant effect on the work of commercial laboratories, and use of imaging software is now common.

Photographic laboratory technician

Photographic laboratory technicians work in one of three areas: film processing, digital imaging or print finishing. They work for processing laboratories and imaging centres, which specialise either in commercial or social photography. Film processing technicians process films to produce either prints or images on a disk; they can adjust lighting, colour, etc, to produce the best possible results. Digital imaging technicians acquire specialised knowledge and skill in layout and design of pictures. They use computer software to enhance images, change colours, move subjects, blend two pictures into one, etc. Print finishers learn to finish prints well and show them off to best effect; they become skilled at using precise cutting equipment and laminating machines. They prepare large prints for exhibitions, for example.

Qualifications and Training

In most instances, an interest in photography is more important than formal qualifications, though a good general education including GCSEs in maths and a science can be useful, and larger professional laboratories may set their own entry requirements. Anyone interested in digital imaging should have some experience of desktop publishing. Macintosh (Mac) computers, rather than PCs, are the industry standard. It is possible to take NVQs levels 2 and 3 in photo processing, photo imaging, mini-lab processing and laboratory operations. An apprenticeship in photo laboratory work is sometimes an option, if you are aged between 16 and 24, but these are not all that widely available in this profession. There are also design courses available at every level, from BTEC certificate to a university degree. Most of the training for this work is on-the-job, with frequent requirements to update on new techniques and new equipment.

Personal Qualities and Skills

You should have a genuine interest in photography and design and some creative flair. You need to work with great accuracy and be able to pay attention to small detail. You should be practical and interested in using computers or other professional equipment. You also need good communication skills and you should enjoy working in a team.

Starting Salary

Salaries start between £9,000 and £15,000, rising to £16,000 to £25,000 with three or four years' experience. Digital imaging work offers the highest salaries and good, experienced operators can earn up to £35,000.

info

Skillet, Prospect House, 80–110 New Oxford Street, London WC1A 1HB; 020 7520 5757; www.skillset.org

British Institute of Professional Photographers (BIPP), Fox Talbot House, 2 Amwell End, Ware, Hertfordshire SG12 9HN; 01920 464011; www.bipp.com

PHYSICIST

Physics deals with the interrelation of matter and energy. Physicists are needed wherever the physical properties of materials have to be studied. They are employed in the fields of electronics, nuclear power, computing, aerospace, optics, telecommunications, engineering and instrument manufacture. In addition, hospitals employ medical physicists whose work includes support for medical use of radiation, and design and implementation of new equipment for diagnosis and treatment of disease. Some physicists lecture in universities or teach in schools. Physics technicians assist fully qualified physicists.

About one-third of all physicists work in public service industries, one-third in private industry and one-third in secondary and higher education. Some physicists work on problems at the frontiers of knowledge; others tackle the problems which arise in the application of physical ideas to industrial and engineering problems. Physics graduates also find themselves employed in occupations such as medicine, computing and even finance.

Qualifications and Training

To continue with science at A level, students must choose either a double award in science (England, Wales and Northern Ireland), which combines the three subjects and leads to two science GCSE qualifications, or a combination of the individual sciences (biology, chemistry, physics), at GCSE or equivalent.

Entry to most degree courses requires two or three A levels (or a suitable combination of A and AS levels) or equivalent, including maths and physics. Since there is a shortage of applicants, grade requirements in some universities are not high, but all departments will consider good grades in maths to be equally as important as good grades in physics. A National Diploma with several merits and distinctions may be considered if it has suitable maths and physics content.

Junior technicians need a good education to GCSE level with particular attention to maths, a science and a subject showing the use of English in order to take an Edexcel (BTEC)/SQA national certificate. There are special certificate courses for medical junior physics technicians. For senior technicians an Edexcel (BTEC)/SQA HND award is available; the requirements are an A level in physics and GCSE maths, chemistry and English. An Edexcel (BTEC)/SQA NC or ND award is acceptable in place of A/H levels. Training for technicians is generally on the job, such as Modern Apprenticeships, with time off to attend courses.

Personal Qualities and Skills

Those working in physics must be able to recognise a problem and plan an experiment or set of experiments to solve it. They should be imaginative, persevering, have good powers of concentration and adopt a sound, logical approach. Technicians should have the practical skills necessary to carry out experiments, be responsible, accurate and caring in their attitude to work.

Starting Salary

Trainee technicians start between £8,000 and £10,000; the majority of senior technicians earn £12,000–18,000. Salaries for new graduates are variable, averaging £18,000. Civil service researchers and teachers start on a salary of around £17,000.

Institute of Physics, 76 Portland Place, London W1B 1NT; 020 7470 4800; fax: 020 7470 4848; www.iop.org; e-mail: physics@iop.org

Institute of Physics and Engineering in Medicine, Fairmount House, 230 Tadcaster Road, York YO24 1ES; 01904 610821; fax: 01904 612279; www.ipem.ac.uk; e-mail: office@ipem.ac.uk

PHYSIOTHERAPIST

Physiotherapists treat patients suffering from a wide variety of diseases, conditions or injuries by physical means. They help people who have had strokes to regain the use of lost functions, treat sports injuries and people with arthritis, and help children with cerebral palsy to learn to walk. The techniques used include massage and manipulation, exercise, electrotherapy and hydrotherapy. Most physiotherapists work in the Health Service but there are many opportunities now for employment in industry, sports clinics, schools and private practice.

Qualifications and Training

A minimum of five GCSEs and three A levels or equivalent are normally required for a place on a three- or four-year course leading to a degree; entry to these courses is very competitive. Subjects at GCSE should ideally include English and two sciences, and A levels should include a biological science.

Personal Qualities and Skills

Physiotherapists must be caring, patient, reasonably fit, good communicators, and have the ability to inspire confidence in their patients.

Starting Salary

On joining the NHS, starting salaries range from £18,000 to £24,000 – senior physiotherapists earn from £24,000 to £35,000. Pay varies between health trusts and is also linked to knowledge, skills and responsibilities. There are plenty of opportunities to be self-employed as a physiotherapist, where fees range from £30 to £50 an hour.

Chartered Society of Physiotherapy, 14 Bedford Row, London WC1R 4ED; 020 7306 6666; fax: 020 7306 6611; www.csp.org.uk

NHS Careers: Careers helpline 0845 60 60 655; www.nhscareers.nhs.uk

Careers in Nursing and Related Professions (Kogan Page)

PLUMBER

see Construction

POLICE SERVICE

Police Community Support Officer

Police Community Support Officers (PCSOs) are a recent introduction to the Police Service. This work is done by civilians, rather than serving police officers, but they support and report to local police. They patrol public areas, providing a visible presence to reassure the public. In some areas they have powers to direct traffic or issue arrest warrants, and they often work at events such as football matches or public demonstrations.

Qualifications and Training

As long as you are 18 years old, there are no specific entry requirements, though you must be physically fit with good eyesight. Some police forces set their own entry criteria or selection tests.

Personal Qualities and Skills

You must have excellent people skills, be able to calm down situations, but also be capable of being firm when necessary. You must be able to use your initiative, but know when to seek advice. You should be able to take decisions in difficult circumstances and keep calm under pressure.

Starting Salary

The basic salary for PCSOs is between £16,000 and £19,000. Shift allowances are paid in addition to the basic salary.

Police officer

Police officers are recruited as trainee police constables (PCs). PCs work in all aspects of policing, including preventing and investigating crime, maintaining public order and protecting people and property. PCs work from police stations or out on the beat, either on foot or in patrol cars. There are many opportunities to specialise in particular areas of police work once you have completed your probationary period.

There is a separate British Transport Police Force, which operates on passenger transport services to prevent crime, protect public safety and maintain public order.

Qualifications and Training

There are no specific entry requirements, though a good standard of education is expected, and police forces throughout the UK set rigorous selection tests, which cover literacy, numeracy, information handling and reasoning (thinking) skills. Applicants also face psychological, physical and medical assessments.

There are fast-track training schemes open to graduate applicants, but these are highly competitive and many graduates join via the standard selection and training route. In England, Scotland, Northern Ireland and Wales the graduate entry route is called the High Potential Development Scheme; in Scotland it is termed the Accelerated Promotion Scheme. The normal training (probationary period) lasts for two years and a great deal of what police officers learn comes from working on-the-job and learning from other officers.

Personal Qualities and Skills

You need excellent communication skills, since you are likely to be dealing with people who may be angry, frightened, distressed or violent. You should be good at taking decisions and acting responsibly, and you should be very good at working as part of a team. You must have honesty and integrity and you need a socially tolerant attitude, able to accept and deal with very diverse individuals and groups of people. You should be well organised with good administration and basic IT skills.

Starting Salary

Salaries start at just under £19,000 a year and rise to £22,000 once you have completed your probationary period. There are often opportunities to get overtime payments, and police officers in London get a cost of living allowance.

info

Police Recruitment, www.policecouldyou.co.uk

Skills for Justice, 9 Riverside Court, Don Road, Sheffield S9 2TJ; 0114 261 1499; www.skillsforjustice.com

British Transport Police, 15 Tavistock Place, London WC1H 9SJ; 020 7830 8800; www.btp.police.uk

Central Police Training and Development Authority (CENTREX), Bramshill, Hook, Hampshire RG27 0JW; 01256 602100; www.centrex.police.uk

The High Potential Development Scheme, Home Office, Police Leadership and Powers Unit, 5th Floor, 50 Queen Anne's Gate, London SW1H 9AT; 020 7273 3374/3353; www.policecouldyou.co.uk

Home Office, Direct Communications Unit, 2 Marsham Street, London SW1P 4DF; 0870 000 1585; www.homeoffice.gov.uk

Scottish Executive Justice Department, The Scottish Executive, Regent Road, Edinburgh EH1 3DG; 0131 556 8400; www.scotland.gov.uk

Careers and Jobs in the Police Service (Kogan Page)

How to Pass the New Police Selection System (Kogan Page)

POLITICAL WORK

Though politics offers relatively few career opportunities, there are a number of jobs in politics associated with supporting political parties, undertaking political research and lobbying political bodies on behalf of interest groups.

Politician

Politicians for the House of Commons, the Scottish Parliament, the Welsh Assembly and the European Parliament are all elected, so they don't 'apply' for their jobs in the traditional sense. Their work involves representing the concerns of their constituents and contributing to the process of decision making by joining in debates, asking questions and voting.

Political party agent

Only large political parties employ full-time agents. The agents are responsible for organising and motivating party activity at a local level, whether this is training volunteers, organising meetings or maintaining contact between local party members and their MP.

Political researcher

Many different kinds of organisations employ political researchers; MPs, political parties, trade unions, public relations consultancies and non-government organisations are the most likely employers. The work involves detailed research, by monitoring the media, the daily work of both Houses of Parliament and the institutions of the European Union. Researchers also provide detailed answers to questions on almost every topic imaginable.

Public affairs consultant/lobbyist

This very specialised field of public relations employs researchers and lobbyists to monitor political information and to lobby government on behalf of their clients. Clients may be businesses, trade unions or pressure groups, or any organisations that wish to influence the decision-making processes of government.

Qualifications and Training

Politicians do not need specific qualifications and come from many different career backgrounds; law is one of the more common. Other political jobs require at least a good 2.1 degree in a relevant subject, such as economics, law, politics or social policy. Many successful applicants also have postgraduate qualifications.

Personal Qualities and Skills

Politicians have to be good communicators who are well organised and able to balance the needs of their constituency work with demands in Westminster, or wherever they are based. Good organisational and interpersonal skills as well as a rigorous attitude to information research are essential for other political jobs.

Starting Salary

MPs earn £55,000 with various additional allowances. Salaries for other political work are more wide ranging. Junior research jobs pay £10,000+; an experienced lobbyist can earn £25,000 to £30,000.

info

Local constituency parties

Conservative Central Office, 32 Smith Square, London SW1P 3HH; 020 7222 9000; www.conservatives.com

Labour Party, Millbank Tower, Millbank, London SW1P 4GT; 08705 900200; www.labour.org.uk

Liberal Democrats, 4 Cowley Street, London SW1P 3NB; 020 7222 7999; www.libdems.org.uk; e-mail: info@libdems.org.uk

A list of all other UK political parties is available from http://bubl.ac.uk/uk/parties.htm

Association of Professional Political Consultants (APPC), c/o Citigate Public Affairs, 26 Grosvenor Gardens, London SW1Y 0GT; 020 7838 4883; www.appc.org.uk

Parli-training, Suite 49, 34 Buckingham Palace Road, Belgravia, London SW1W 0RD; 020 7898 1103; www.parli-training.co.uk; e-mail: enquiries@parli-training.co.uk

Parliamentary Communications Ltd, 14 Great George Street, Westminster, London SW1P 3RX; 020 7878 1576

POST OFFICE

Royal Mail Group plc has three major brands: Post Office, Royal Mail and Parcelforce Worldwide. Opportunities for school leavers include administration, secretarial, postman/woman, counter clerk and retail assistant. For graduates there may be opportunities in commercial management, information technology, finance, logistics, marketing, human resources and e-business.

Qualifications and Training

No formal educational qualifications are necessary for the school-leaver jobs, but applicants are required to take an aptitude test. Training is provided for postmen/women, counter clerks and retail assistants, and NVQs are available.

Graduate entrants should have studied a relevant degree. Useful subjects include business studies, information technology, maths, geography, transport and planning or engineering.

Personal Qualities and Skills

All public-facing employees need to be good communicators, patient and prepared to help. Counter clerks and retail assistants should be numerate and have good interpersonal skills. Graduates should be numerate and possess good interpersonal and organisational skills.

Starting Salary

Starting salaries for postmen and women are £9,900 at age 16, £11,500 at 17 and, at 18, the salary is £15,000 for the first six months, rising to £15,700 during the next six months. The salary for postmen/women aged 18 or over with 12 months service is £16,500 a year. There are supplementary payments for unsocial hours, driving duties and other responsibilities. There is also London Weighting.

info

Royal Mail Group plc, 148 Old Street, London EC1V 9HQ; 08457 850 850 www.royalmailgroup.com

School leavers should apply to the Human Resources manager at the local Royal Mail, Parcelforce Worldwide or Post Office (address and telephone number in local telephone directory)

PRINTING

The purpose of printing is communication, whether the printed matter is books, magazines, newspapers, security documents or bank cards. Printers are also involved in other products, from wallpaper and floor coverings to advertising slogans on milk cartons. The printing industry covers a wide range of jobs in both factories and offices. The printing industry employs 200,000 people in 12,000 companies.

Camera/scanner operator

The reproduction of colour photographs is largely done by electronic scanners, requiring technical ability rather than the craft skills of the past.

Finishing department

Printed products are usually produced in large flat sheets or reels. To convert and finish sheets or reels into books, brochures or magazines, the material must be folded, stitched, sewn and trimmed. A range of specialised machinery is used to produce the finished product at high speed. Great care is needed at this stage to avoid faults, which could result in scrapping the product and financial loss to the company.

Graphic design

(*see also* Art and Design)

This is the most artistic job in the printing industry. Designers liaise with clients, understand their needs and transform ideas into high-quality printed products. A mastery of computers, complete understanding of processes, techniques, typography and colour is required. Applicants normally enter the industry after a National Certificate diploma or higher-level course in graphic design.

Office jobs

Account executives look after individual printing jobs; they write instructions for each department and check the product's arrival into and departure from each section. Estimators work out how much a job will cost. Cost clerks go through the costs item by item and discover where and why the money was spent. Sales staff find customers.

In large companies production controllers manage a team of estimators and production control staff. They interpret sales orders, estimate costs, plan materials purchase, arrange time on appropriate machines, set priorities and advise customers on the progress of their order.

Pre-press department

Most setting is via electronic transfer or CD. The pre-press operator uses a computer keyboard and mouse to set type and arrange the page, which is output to film or direct to the printing plate. An error in the pre-press department could result in the scrapping of thousands of books or products.

Printing department

This is where ink is applied to paper or other materials, by a variety of large and small printing machines. Such machines are complex and often computer controlled. They are managed by one or more craftspeople who control the physics and chemistry of the press to ensure that each copy produced is perfect.

Proofreader

Proofreaders check customers' proofs for spelling mistakes and incorrect typefaces before returning them. When setting to disk, proofreading is done automatically.

Qualifications and Training

Academic qualifications are not mandatory for craft workers but the following subjects studied to GCSE level are preferred: English, maths, computer studies and science. Training is to NVQ levels 2 and 3, with time off to attend courses.

Office staff have qualifications ranging from GCSEs to a degree. GCSEs are preferred for junior clerks and there are opportunities to gain further qualifications through Edexcel (BTEC)/SQA or City and Guilds awards. To take the higher diploma in printing on a two- or three-year basis, four GCSEs to include English, maths and a science plus one A level are necessary, or an Edexcel (BTEC)/SQA or NC/ND in printing. There are in addition three print-related degree courses, for which two A levels are necessary.

NVQs at levels 2 and 3 are available in print production and print administration. Modern Apprenticeships are available for production and office trainees.

Personal Qualities and Skills

A responsible attitude and a pride in what is being produced are necessary. Production workers need good colour vision and manual dexterity. Applicants must provide evidence of careful work and attention to detail. They must possess dexterity and normal colour vision. The work requires images to be manually or computer manipulated to a high degree of accuracy. Applicants for jobs in the finishing department need physical strength, an affinity with machinery, concentration and the ability to work as a team.

Starting Salary

The range of starting salaries is very wide, but many production jobs start at between £12,000 and £17,000. It is possible to earn more than this with payments for shift work and if you develop highly specialised technical knowledge. Management jobs pay up to £23,000.

info

British Printing Industries Federation (BPIF), Farringdon Point, 29–35 Farringdon Road, London EC1M 3JF; 0870 240 4085; www.britishprint.com

Institute of Printing, The Mews, Hill House, Clanricarde Road, Tunbridge Wells, Kent TN1 1PJ; 01892 538118; fax: 01892 518028; www.instituteofprinting.org; e-mail: admin@instituteofprinting.org

Scottish Print Employers Federation, 48 Palmerston Place, Edinburgh EH12 5DE; 0131 220 4353; fax: 0131 220 4344; www.spef.org.uk; e-mail: info@spef.org.uk

Print Education Forum, 962 Alum Rock Road, Ward End, Birmingham B8 2NS; 0121 789 5100; fax: 0121 789 5101; www.printnto.org; e-mail: info@printnto.org

PRISON OFFICER

Prison officers are employed in prisons, detention centres, young offender institutions and remand centres. The work involves supervising prisoners inside the place of detention, escorting them to courts and other prisons and, if relevant, teaching a skill or trade. Officers also deliver programmes that help prisoners address their offending behaviour. Some specialist prison officers are employed as hospital officers, dog handlers, security experts and caterers.

Qualifications and Training

Five GCSEs, including maths and English, are required and applicants must pass an aptitude test and an interview. Training is a mixture of time spent at a local prison and residential courses at an officers' training school. In Scotland, the requirement is five standard grades (1, 2 or 3) or equivalent (including maths and English) or three years' experience managing people. A good level of physical fitness is required. NVQs in custodial care are available at levels 2 and 3, as is custodial healthcare level 3 and youth justice levels 3 and 4. There is special training for caterers, dog handlers, physical education instructors and medical staff. An accelerated promotions scheme exists for graduate entrants.

Personal Qualities and Skills

Officers should be positive thinkers with humanity and common sense; they must be good listeners, assertive, have excellent communication skills and the ability to mix with a wide range of people.

Starting Salary

Salaries in England and Wales are between £17,500 and £25,500. This can be increased by local allowances ranging from £1,000 to £4,000 depending on location. There are also long-service payments for anyone who has worked in the service for 12 years or more. Starting salaries in Scotland are between £12,000 and £14,000.

info

HM Prison Service, Headquarters, Cleland House, Page Street, London SW1P 4LN; 020 7217 3000; www.hmprisonservice.gov.uk

Home Office, Direct Communications Unit, 2 Marsham Street, London SW1P 4DF; 0870 000 1585; www.homeoffice.gov.uk

Prison Officers Association, Cronin House, 245 Church Street, London N9 9HW; 020 8803 0255; www.poauk.org.uk

Scottish Prison Service, Calton House, 5 Redheughs Rigg, Edinburgh EH12 9HW; 0131 244 8745; www.sps.gov.uk

Skills for Justice, 9 Riverside Court, Don Road, Sheffield S9 2TJ; 0114 261 1499; www.skillsforjustice.org.uk

PRIVATE INVESTIGATOR/DETECTIVE

A private detective can either be self-employed or work as part of an agency. The investigation profession has a diverse workload and it is therefore difficult to generalise. A small cross-section of the subjects that an investigator may be instructed to assist with are tracing missing persons and debtors; finding witnesses and taking statements; undertaking video and photographic surveillance for matrimonial cases or insurance company fraud investigations; process serving (the correct delivery of legal documents); pre sue and means enquiries; verification of credit worthiness; road traffic and industrial accident investigations involving sketch plans and photographs; land registry searches; land and property repossession and test purchases.

Qualifications and Training

No formal qualifications are necessary but a good standard of education will be an advantage in the preparation of reports and the taking of statements. Training seminars are run by the Association of British Investigators. A sound knowledge of computers, experience in credit control or in a service industry providing direct contact with the public is useful. NVQs level 3 and 4 are available in investigation techniques.

A private detective needs personal indemnity and public liability insurance, and should also register with the Office of Fair Trading and the Data Protection Registrar. It is also advisable to obtain membership of a recognised association.

Personal Qualities and Skills

Honesty, integrity, and discretion are vital. Patience, perseverance, self-motivation, ability to work on one's own initiative, adaptability and a good outgoing personality are all useful qualities.

Starting Salary

This depends upon experience and location. An agency charges £20+ per hour but pays lower rates to staff. The self-employed may be able to charge similar rates.

info

Association of British Investigators, 48 Queens Road, Basingstoke, Hampshire RG21 7RE (the General Secretary can assist with finding a local agency that may offer further information.); www.assoc-britishinvestigators.org.uk

Local Job Centre Plus and Careers/Connexions Centres

Libraries hold directories of investigators

PSYCHOLOGY

Psychologists study people: how they think, act, react and interact. They are concerned with all aspects of behaviour and the thoughts, feelings and motivation underlying such behaviour. The profession has many different specialities, from clinical psychology, concerned with reducing psychological distress and promoting psychological wellbeing, to market research where psychologists may research why and how consumers prefer one product to another. Psychologists work in the NHS, private hospitals, industry, for government and local authorities, in schools and in private practice.

The British Psychological Society maintains the Register of Chartered Psychologists, which has stringent entry requirements. Anyone who wishes to become a Chartered Psychologist should ensure that their degree is accredited by the society as conferring the Graduate Basis for Registration (GBR). This is required for all BPS-accredited postgraduate training courses in applied psychology.

Clinical psychology

Clinical psychologists use their knowledge of psychology when working with people with health problems or severe learning difficulties. They work alongside professionals such as doctors, nurses, social workers and counselling psychologists within NHS trusts, hospitals, clinics, children's homes, and other community or related settings. They also work in private practice or research and academic institutions.

Qualifications and Training

Applicants must have an accredited psychology degree and some work or research experience, which should have clinical relevance. To register as a Chartered Clinical Psychologist candidates must obtain GBR and complete an accredited postgraduate training course in clinical psychology.

Starting Salary

A typical starting salary is around £25,000 to £26,000, but the starting range is from around £18,000 to £29,000. Senior clinical psychologists earn up to £45,000 if they have management responsibility, as well as casework.

Counselling psychologists

Counselling psychologists work with individuals, couples, families and groups such as people with disabilities or those who are discriminated against. They work to improve their client's sense of wellbeing, reduce stress and to help them resolve crises. They help people understand their problems and develop coping strategies and solutions. Counselling psychologists work in GPs' surgeries, NHS trusts and hospitals, business institutions or specialist agencies.

Qualifications and Training

A degree in psychology and postgraduate professional training in counselling psychology is necessary for Chartered Counselling Psychologist status.

Starting Salary

This is based upon nationally agreed scales and should range between £15,000 and £60,000, depending on experience and level of responsibility.

Educational psychologists

Educational psychologists work primarily in schools and colleges with teachers and lecturers, and with parents. They can work directly with a child or young person (up to the age of 19) or indirectly via parents and teachers. Educational psychologists are often involved in policy planning within the education departments of local authorities.

Qualifications and Training

An appropriate qualification in psychology, a teacher training qualification, teaching experience and a postgraduate qualification are all necessary to become registered as a Chartered Educational Psychologist in England, Wales and Northern Ireland. Teachers can retrain by undertaking an accredited qualification in psychology, postgraduate training and supervised experience. In Scotland, there is no requirement to become a fully qualified teacher.

Starting Salary

Educational psychologists in Britain are usually employed by LEAs as part of the psychological service. In Northern Ireland they are appointed by the Education and Library Boards. Main grade educational psychologists earn between £22,000 and £33,000. Senior principal educational psychologists earn £35,000 to £45,000.

Forensic psychology

This is one of the fastest-growing areas of employment for psychology graduates. Work can be found in academic institutions, prison services, the National Health Service, probation services and social services. Forensic psychologists undertake their work in the criminal and civil justice field.

Qualifications and Training

To register as a Chartered Forensic Psychologist an accredited degree must be followed by either successful completion of Stages 1 and 2 of the British Psychological Society's Diploma in Forensic Psychology or successful completion of a Society-accredited training course in forensic psychology followed by successful completion of Stage 2 of the Society's Diploma in Forensic Psychology.

Personal Qualities and Skills

All psychologists should have a genuine interest in people, their behaviour, and have an empathy for their problems. They also need to be excellent communicators and have the skills to work with people from different backgrounds and social groupings. In addition, they need to have a scientific approach and in branches such as educational and occupational psychology, must have a good grasp of statistics.

Starting Salary

As for clinical psychologists.

Health psychology

This is an evolving area, which applies psychological methods to the study of behaviour relevant to health, illness and healthcare. Health psychologists may study why and when people seek professional advice about their health, how patients adapt to illness and how they interact with healthcare professionals.

Qualifications and Training

To register as a Chartered Health Psychologist, an accredited degree must be followed by a one-year accredited postgraduate course in health psychology, followed by a minimum of two years' appropriate practice as a health psychologist under the supervision of a Chartered Health Psychologist.

Starting Salary

As for clinical psychologists.

Occupational psychologists

Occupational psychologists focus on the performance of people at work and in training, how organisations function and how individuals and groups behave in the work environment. The services of occupational psychologists are increasingly in demand, and this area of psychology is broader in scope and less formalised than others. The work of an occupational psychologist can include work with individuals, organisational consultancy, assessment and training, vocational guidance and counselling, ergonomics and health and safety.

Qualifications and Training

To register as a Chartered Occupational Psychologist it is necessary to obtain GBR, plus an accredited postgraduate course in occupational psychology, and to complete two to three years' supervised practice.

Starting Salary

Salaries vary enormously. The range for those in government departments is as follows: graduates £12,500–14,000, senior psychologist £19,000–23,000.

Private sector and industry salaries can vary from £15,000 to £100,000, depending on experience and expertise.

Teaching and research

There are no formal qualifications that are a preparation for teaching at university, although most universities encourage newly appointed staff to take a postgraduate certificate in higher education. All university lecturers are expected to be involved in developing their subject via research projects. For example, an educational psychologist may undertake research on how to teach concepts to blind children and an occupational psychologist may research the relationship of stress to work conditions.

Qualifications and Training

A degree in psychology is acceptable for teaching in further education but most individuals involved in teaching and research in higher education will have a PhD or have held a research post. A teaching qualification such as the Postgraduate Certificate in Education (PGCE) is also increasingly required.

Starting Salary

Salaries at further and higher education institutions range from £17,000 to £37,000 for lecturers, to £27,000 to £37,000 for senior lecturers and professors.

info

British Psychological Society, St Andrews House, 48 Princess Road East, Leicester LE1 7DR; 0116 254 9568; fax: 0116 247 0787; www.bps.org.uk (the Society publishes free information leaflets on its website); e-mail: enquiry@bps.org.uk

Association of Educational Psychologists, 26 The Avenue, Durham DH1 4ED; 0191 384 9512; fax: 0191 386 5287; www.aep.org.uk; the Association produces a Careers Information booklet which can be obtained from the Association's head office (please send an A4 size stamped-addressed envelope), or downloaded from its website.

PSYCHOTHERAPIST

Psychotherapy is a generic term, within which there are many specialist disciplines. People may practise as psychoanalytic psychotherapists, as cognitive or behavioural psychotherapists, or as counsellors, with varying degrees of training and experience; however, there are plans to introduce greater regulation.

Psychotherapists may work with individuals of any age, couples and families, or groups resolving problems such as over-shyness, over-aggression, sleeping disorders, separation difficulties, behavioural problems, eating difficulties, self-harm and depression. They work in hospitals, in- and out-patient clinics, child and family consultation centres, GPs' surgeries, special schools for disturbed children and in private practice.

Qualifications and Training

Psychotherapists come from varying professional backgrounds, but will usually have a degree in medicine, psychology, social sciences or a qualification in one of the core professions of the Health Service plus appropriate experience of working with people with mental health problems. Training then takes a further four years and involves academic study, personal analysis, workshops and supervised therapeutic treatment. There are several different training organisations. Most courses lead to national registration with either the British Confederation of Psychotherapists (BCP) or the UK Council for Psychotherapy.

Personal Qualities and Skills

Psychotherapists must have a genuine interest in the problems of children and adults, and a desire to help. They must themselves be emotionally well balanced.

Starting Salary

Salaries vary depending on the experience and professional background of the individual therapist. Self-employed therapists charge between £30 and £100 an hour.

info

British Association of Psychotherapists, 37 Mapesbury Road, London NW2 4HJ; 020 8452 9823; fax: 020 8452 0310; www.bap-psychotherapy.org; e-mail: mail@bap-psychotherapy.org

British Confederation of Psychotherapists, West Hill House, 6 Swains Lane, London N6 6QS; 020 7267 3626; fax: 020 7267 4772; www.bcp.org.uk; e-mail: mail@bcp.org.uk

UK Council for Psychotherapy (UKCP), 2nd Floor, Edward House, 2 Wakley Street, London EC1V 7LT 020 7014 9955; fax: 020 7014 9977; www.psychotherapy.org.uk; e-mail: info@psychotheraphy.org.uk

NHS Careers, Careers helpline: 0845 60 60 655; www.nhscareers.nhs.uk

PUBLIC RELATIONS OFFICER

The chief aim of the public relations (PR) officer/executive is to ensure that the correct information about his or her employer or client is made known to the right people in order to establish and maintain goodwill and mutual understanding between an organisation and its public. This is done by a variety of means, including media relations, internal and external communication, company literature, exhibitions and events. Corporate PR work is concerned with effectively putting across an organisation's policy and activities to a variety of people, including government departments, employees, shareholders and other stakeholders. Consumer PR is concerned with giving information about a product; it is closely allied with marketing and advertising. Other areas of PR include community relations, sponsorship and financial PR. PR executives are employed by organisations, PR consultancies, or work as freelance consultants.

Qualifications and Training

Most entrants to the profession are graduates. The Institute of Public Relations (IPR) has approved 15 courses at various levels as qualifications for associate membership. Entry requirements for degree courses vary according to the institution, but most require five GCSEs and A levels or equivalents. The IPR runs its own postgraduate foundation and diploma courses, available at eight centres across Britain.

Personal Qualities and Skills

Public relations officers must understand people and what motivates them, and have the ability to get on well with people from different backgrounds. They must be imaginative, creative, reliable and have good managerial skills. Excellent written and oral communication skills are essential.

Starting Salary

Trainees in PR earn around £15,000. Salaries vary across the business sectors but the average for a PR account executive is £23,000+.

info

Institute of Public Relations, The Old Trading House, 15 Northburgh Street, London EC1V 0PR; 020 7253 5151; fax: 020 7490 0588; www.ipr.org.uk; e-mail: info@ipr.org.uk

Public Relations Consultants Association (PRCA), Willow House, Willow Place, London SW1P 1JH; 020 7233 6026; fax: 020 7828 4797; www.prca.org.uk

Careers in Marketing, Advertising and Public Relations (Kogan Page)

PUBLISHING

Publishing houses differ in their structure, but most have three main departments: editorial, production/design, and sales and marketing. Additionally, there are the service departments found in most commercial offices: accounts, reception, personnel, warehousing and distribution.

Book publishing: editorial

This is the department which attracts the most applicants although editors are a very small percentage of the total publishing labour force. Editors liaise with those Involved in the design, planning and production of each book. They read and edit the manuscript, prepare it for the typesetter, check the proofs and are responsible for assembling all the various parts, paginated in the correct order, for the printer. There is no automatic promotion system or salary structure. In a small company the only way to move up may be to move out.

The editorial director or managing editor runs a centralised copy-editing department, and commissions and supervises freelance editorial workers.

Acquisitions or commissioning editors (also known as publishers) build lists and find authors and books of quality. They may have specialist knowledge or contacts. They buy book rights, commission translations, find new authors, read and report on commissioned and unsolicited manuscripts and proposals, keep established authors happy and negotiate with literary agents. They must manage the editorial team and deliver books within budget and on time. They are also responsible for spotting and capitalising on new buying trends and markets.

Desk editors, also known as sub-editors or copy editors, read a manuscript several times, check it for copyright material and prepare it for the printer. They check references and facts, correct grammar, spelling and punctuation, discuss revisions with the author, decide picture content, design and produce schedules, choose the illustrations, and draft the jacket blurb and catalogue copy. They hand the edited manuscript to the design department for production. Once the manuscript has been set in type, they send a set of proofs to the author, proofread one themselves, collate the two sets of corrections and return the proofs (via the production department) to the printer.

Editorial assistants are publishing novices. Most of them have secretarial skills and, under the guidance of a senior editor, perform basic editorial tasks such as preparing captions for illustrations, researching bibliographic information, obtaining pictures and so on.

The copyright/permissions editor deals with requests from individuals and other publishers to reproduce passages or illustrations from its copyright works.

Picture researchers are briefed on the pictures needed for a book and asked to acquire them within a set budget. Picture researchers need to have an eye for detail and good negotiation skills.

Training and Qualifications

Editorial entrants will normally be expected to have degrees. Work experience and/or postgraduate vocational qualifications are also desirable. Specialist titles, such as science and technical publishing, will require appropriate degrees.

Personal Qualities and Skills

Commissioning editors will need to have good communication skills and exercise tact and diplomacy when dealing with authors. They will need to have an enquiring mind and a good knowledge of the field in which they specialise. Good management and team leader skills are also important.

Desk editors will need to be meticulous and have a good eye for detail. They will be expected to have excellent literacy skills and be able to communicate well with both authors and other members of the publishing team.

Editorial assistants should have good secretarial and organisational skills.

Starting Salary

Editorial assistants start on around £16,000 to £19,000, and after this you are likely to take on a different editorial role, rather than get a higher salary as an assistant. Commissioning editors get between £20,000 and £26,000 and salaries can be higher than this for anyone with wide commissioning responsibilities. Picture researchers/editors get between £16,000 and £22,000. Publishing is a field where there are many opportunities for short-term contracts, where you receive a fixed sum per contract.

Production controller: books

The production controller draws up an accurate specification for the book and invites tenders from typesetters, printers, paper suppliers and binders. When all the estimates have been received, the production controller places orders and ensures that all the production stages are carried out to the required standard, and on schedule. Undemanding production work on, for example, leaflets or reprints, is often given to a production assistant, who is regarded as a trainee.

Designer: books

(*see also* Art and Design)

Designers prepare layouts, sketches, specimen pages and dummies, and mark up all the manuscripts for the typesetter after they have been edited. All the activities of the design department are managed by the design director. Directors discuss illustrated or complicated technical books with the author and the editor, commission freelance artwork, arrange the in-house preparation of artwork and impose a visual style on the company product.

Training and Qualifications

Production and design staff tend to be graduates and will be expected to have a vocational diploma or relevant qualification.

Personal Qualities and Skills

Production and design professionals will need to be able to work under pressure and to tight deadlines. Being able to work well in a team and to interpret editorial briefs is also a quality expected in this area. Good planning skills are also essential. Production staff will also be expected to negotiate with printers and freelance designers for good deals.

Starting Salary

Production assistant £14,000+, production controller £18,000+, production manager £25,000+.

Sales, marketing and publicity executives: books

(*see also* Marketing, Public Relations Officer and Sales Representative)

Depending on the size of the company, there will be one, two or three departments working on the promotion and selling of the books. Applicants are usually graduates and should be creative and write lively and informative copy.

Sales representatives will spend a considerable amount of time travelling to booksellers both in the UK and abroad. They will present details of new publications in order to secure orders for the books, and continue to present the back catalogue to potential purchasers.

Training and Qualifications

Marketing and publicity executives are expected to have good literacy skills and are normally graduates. A postgraduate marketing qualification is also expected in more experienced marketing professionals. Sales representatives are also expected to have had experience within the book trade, and international sales representatives are expected to have a language degree or equivalent qualification.

Personal Qualities and Skills

Staff in this field need to be able to work in a team, and to develop and stick to marketing plans and budgets. They should have an interest in the field and the ability to pick up leads, and require good communication and literacy skills.

Starting Salary

Sales and marketing assistant £14,000+, marketing executive £18,000+, publicity manager £22,000+, sales representatives £20,000+, marketing manager £24,000+.

Indexers: books

Indexers provide a systematic arrangement of the terms appearing in a book, journal or other publication, which could be electronic or paper-based. They also work with page numbers or other locators in order to ensure the information can be easily found. Indexers are generally employed by publishers or authors. Most are freelancers working from home.

Qualifications and Training

No formal qualifications are required but a good education, normally to degree level, is necessary plus subject knowledge in the case of specialist books. Training is by open-learning course leading to accreditation. Registered indexers prove their experience and competence through an assessment procedure and admission to the Register of Indexers.

Personal Qualities and Skills

An ability to analyse a text and meticulous attention to detail are essential, plus the ability to work to set requirements and time limits.

Starting Salary

Payment may be per contract or by the hour. The Society of Indexers recommends rates of £16–30 per hour or £1.20–5.00 per page.

info

Society of Indexers, Blades Enterprise Centre, John Street, Sheffield S2 4SU; 0114 292 2350; fax: 0114 292 2350; www.socind.demon.co.uk; e-mail: admin@indexers.org.uk

Careers and Jobs in the Media (Kogan Page)

Magazines and newspapers

(*see also* Journalism)

The organisation of periodical publishing differs from that of book publishing and has much in common with newspapers. The main areas of activity outside the service departments are editorial, advertisement sales and circulation. Editorial jobs within the magazine and newspaper industry are covered in 'Journalism'.

However, in addition to editorial opportunities a number of alternative career paths can be found in magazine and newspaper publishing. Advertising sales are crucial to the majority of magazines and newspapers, and represent just one of the opportunities available to those who wish to work in these fields of publishing but are not seeking a job as a journalist.

Design: magazines

(*see also* Art and Design)

The range of work includes cover design, typographical design, layout, design of advertisements and direct mail material. Entrants will need a design qualification. Entrants need to have a good working knowledge of current design software used within the industry.

Production manager: magazines

Production staff are trained in the printing trade. It is their responsibility to see the magazine is available at point of sale on publication day, and this involves meticulous planning and a tolerance of stress.

Training and Qualifications

Production and design staff tend to be graduates and are expected to have a vocational diploma or relevant qualification.

Personal Qualities and Skills

Production and design professionals need to be able to work under pressure and to tight deadlines. Being able to work well in a team and to interpret editorial briefs is also a quality expected in this area. Good planning skills are also essential.

Starting Salaries

Production assistant £15,000+, designers £18,000+.

Advertisement sales representatives: magazines

Commercial magazines depend on advertising revenue for survival. Graduates are often recruited straight from university to sales posts and are trained on the job. Sales staff must know the magazine's readership and build up advantageous contacts with potential advertisers. They spend a lot of time researching, analysing and planning, and need a persuasive manner and numerical skills.

Qualifications and Training

Requirements for trainees vary and many sales reps learn through work experience.

Personal Qualities and Skills

Sales staff need an outgoing personality and good communication skills, the ability to work under pressure and to meet deadlines.

Starting Salary

Many advertising reps earn a basic salary of approximately £12,000 and then are expected to earn the rest on commission. Successful advertising sales reps can earn £40,000+.

info

BookCareers.com, PO Box 1441, Ilford, Essex IG4 5AW; 020 8550 8023; www.bookcareers.com/

The Booksellers Association of The United Kingdom and Ireland Ltd (BA), Minster House, 272 Vauxhall Bridge Road, London SW1V 1BA; 020 7834 5477; www.booksellers.org.uk

The London School of Publishing, David Game House, 69 Notting Hill Gate, London W11 3JS; 020 7221 3399; www.publishing-school.co.uk/

The Periodical Publishers Association (PPA), Queens House, 28 Kingsway, London WC2B 6JR; 020 7404 4166; www.ppa.co.uk

Publishers Association (PA), 29b Montague Street, London WC1B 5BW; 020 7691 9191; www.publishers.org.uk

Publishing Training Centre, Book House, 45 East Hill, Wandsworth, London SW18 2QZ; 020 8874 2718; www.train4publishing.co.uk/

Scottish Publishers Association, Scottish Book Centre, 137 Dundee Street, Edinburgh EH11 1BG; 0131 228 6866; www.scottishbooks.org

The Society for Editors and Proofreaders (SfEP), Riverbank House, 1 Putney Bridge Approach, Fulham, London SW6 3JD; 020 7736 3278; www.sfep.org.uk

The Society of Young Publishers, Endeavour House, 189 Shaftesbury Avenue, London WC2H 3TJ; www.thesyp.org.uk

Women in Publishing, 1 York Villa, York Road, West Byfleet KT14 7ZF; 07985 792 542; www.wipub.org.uk

Careers and Jobs in the Media (Kogan Page)

PURCHASING OFFICER/INDUSTRIAL BUYER

Purchasing careers exist in all large organisations, whether profit-making or not. Essentially, purchasing and supply management involves identifying the requirements of the company's internal customers and then obtaining the necessary products and services by negotiation and agreement with suppliers. The primary objective is to obtain value for money. This does not always mean achieving the very lowest price – sometimes other commercial considerations are more important. For example, the flexibility and speed of response of the supplier might be the deciding factor, or the need to minimise risk by choosing a vendor with a good business record.

In a manufacturing environment such as a car plant, the purchaser is directly involved in buying components such as wheels, lights and shock absorbers for the production line. In a financial services company, purchases might well be for telecommunications systems, catering services and marketing services, including advertising and design. In retail purchasing the role is slightly different as buyers are more involved in merchandising, selecting product lines which appeal to the consumer and sell quickly.

Qualifications and Training

Most companies require a minimum of four or five GSCE passes. Graduates or individuals with A levels usually enter as trainee buyers, working with experienced personnel and continuing their training in the workplace. The minimum requirement for individuals wishing to study for the Foundation Stage of the CIPS Graduate Diploma is two A levels and three GCSEs (or equivalent). The Certificate in Purchasing and Supply Management is offered to those with no A levels.

Personal Qualities and Skills

You need good written and spoken communication skills and a high level of numeracy. You have to have the confidence to negotiate firmly and the temperament to take risks at times. You should be able to build good relationships with people and you need a good all round business awareness.

Starting Salary

Salaries start between £19,000 and £26,000, but senior purchasing managers will earn between £30,000 and £45,000.

info

Account Planning Group, 16 Creighton Avenue, London N10 1NV; 020 8444 3692; www.apg.org.uk

Chartered Institute of Purchasing and Supply (CIPS), Easton House, Easton on the Hill, Stamford, Lincs PE9 3NZ; 01780 756777; www.cips.org

Skillsmart Retail: The Sector Skills Council for Retail, 40 Duke Street, London W1A 1AB; 020 7399 3450; www.skillsmartretail.com

QUARRYING

Quarrying is opencast mining for clay, sand, limestone, slate and other materials that are just below the layer of topsoil. Quarry workers or quarry operatives are involved in the operations connected with this extraction process. Modern quarrying involves using very heavy machinery to excavate, transport, cut and crush the different products, and quarry workers operate this machinery.

Qualifications and Training

There are no specific academic entry qualifications, but you must be fit, and having an LGV (light goods vehicle) driving licence or experience of using heavy plant and machinery can be an advantage. If you are between 16 and 24 years old, you may be able to do an apprenticeship; availability of these varies according to locality. Some employers will expect you to have four GCSEs to do an apprenticeship; these should include, English, maths and technology. The industry offers the chance to do NVQs at levels 2 and 3 in drilling operations, plant operations and process operations. There is also an NVQ level 3 in working with explosives, and there are higher-level courses in sampling. The majority of training is on-the-job.

Personal Qualities and Skills

You need to be physically fit and confident in handling highly specialised technical equipment. You should have good numeracy skills for calculating quantities and you must be able to work as part of a team. You should have an acute awareness of health and safety issues.

Starting Salary

New entrants start on around £12,000; this rises to £17,000 after two or three years' experience. Senior quarry workers earn between £20,000 and £25,000. There are often opportunities to increase earnings with overtime and shift-work payments.

EPIC Training Ltd, Alban Row, 27–31 Verulam Road, St Albans, Herts AL3 4DG; 01727 869008;www.epicltd.com

RADIOGRAPHER

Radiography is a caring profession which calls for considerable technological expertise. There are two branches: diagnostic radiography and therapeutic radiography. Diagnostic radiographers are responsible for producing high-quality images on film and other recording materials which help doctors to diagnose disease and the extent of injuries. Therapeutic radiographers help to treat patients, many of whom have cancer, using X-rays, ionising radiation and sometimes drugs.

Qualifications and Training

All radiography qualifying courses are now at degree level. Courses are normally based in a university or higher education institution affiliated to a university, with half the time spent on clinical education in hospital departments associated with the university.

On graduation, entrants are eligible for State Registration by the Radiographers Board of the Council for Professions Supplementary to Medicine, which is an essential requirement for employment in the National Health Service. The requirements for entry to radiography courses are two A levels and three GCSEs at grade C or above, or equivalent. Entry is also possible through validated access courses, and applications from mature candidates are welcomed by many radiography education centres.

Personal Qualities and Skills

As well as having an interest in science, radiographers should be caring and compassionate but sufficiently level-headed not to get upset when dealing with

info

College of Radiographers, 207 Providence Square, Mill Street, London SE1 2EW; 020 7740 7200; fax: 020 7740 7204; www.sor.org

NHS Careers, PO Box 376, Bristol BS99 3EY; Careers helpline: 0845 6060 655; www.nhscareers.nhs.uk/index.html

A Factsheet 'What is a radiographer?' is available from NHS Careers

sick people. They need to be patient and calm when faced with patients who may be frightened or difficult. Good health and reasonable strength are needed for lifting people and heavy equipment. In addition, radiographers should be good humoured, able to work well in a team and assume responsibility.

Starting Salary

Starting salary varies from around £17,000 to £19,000 in the NHS rising to a top level of £35,000+.

RAILWAY WORK

The rail industry employs a vast number of people: drivers, revenue protection inspectors, customer service assistants, signal operators, engineers, fitters, clerical workers, technicians and managers. The latter are responsible for the day-to-day running of the railways or are in charge of departments such as planning, engineering, marketing and accounts.

Qualifications and Training

Train drivers do not require formal educational qualifications but are expected to have studied English, maths and a science. Training is on the job and a range of NVQs is available. Guards, signallers, station attendants and general rail workers are also trained on the job and work towards NVQs.

Technicians need four GCSEs, including maths, English and a science, and undertake apprentice training, working alongside experienced staff. NVQs at levels 2 and 3 are available in rail transport engineering: maintenance and rail transport engineering.

Management recruitment is normally at graduate level, although trainees with A levels may be sponsored on sandwich degrees. Training for graduates varies depending on the nature of their work and lasts up to two years.

Personal Qualities and Skills

All rail staff must have a strong interest in providing an efficient service and in promoting and caring for passengers' needs. In addition, drivers need perfect vision without glasses. Managers need qualities appropriate to their departments plus managerial and administrative skills.

Starting Salary

Different train operating companies pay different amounts; drivers earn around £13,500 while training, £24,000+ once qualified; operatives earn £9,500+, technicians £12,000+, clerical staff £10,000+ and graduate recruits £15,000+. Free or reduced-price travel is usually offered as an extra benefit.

GoSkills: Sector Skills Council for Passenger Transport, Concorde House, Trinity Park, Solihull, Birmingham B37 7UQ; 0121 635 5520; www.goskills.org

Careers in Rail; www.careersinrail.org

Centre for Rail Skills, 4 Lombard Street, London EC3V 9HD; 0845 345 2700; www.cfrs.org.uk

RECEPTIONIST

see Hospitality *and* Catering, *and* Business Administration

RECRUITMENT CONSULTANT

The aim of recruitment/employment consultants is to fit people to jobs. Agencies deal with all types of staff, from office and secretarial to highly complex and specialist technical roles. Much of the work involves selling to potential users and matching clients' demands. This includes interviewing prospective job candidates, keeping records of their details and matching them to employers' requirements.

Qualifications and Training

Many recruitment consultants have come into the industry after some experience of another job, for example, sales, personnel or office work. They are trained either in-house or on courses run by the Recruitment and Employment Confederation (REC). The REC offers two levels of qualification: the Foundation Award, suitable for those in their first year in the industry, and the Certificate in Recruitment Practice for those with more than one year's experience. Both qualifications can be studied by distance learning or at an evening class.

Personal Qualities and Skills

Recruitment consultants must be able to relate to people at different organisational levels, have good communication skills, work quickly and calmly under pressure and be organised and resilient.

Starting Salary

Varies greatly for trainees, but with experience consultants can earn a salary of £25,000+ with commission.

Recruitment and Employment Confederation, 36–38 Mortimer Street, London W1W 7RG; 020 7462 3260; fax: 020 7255 2878; www.rec.uk.com

REGISTRAR

The local registration service (LRS) is a network of register offices in England and Wales which registers births, stillbirths, marriages and deaths. These are staffed by a mixture of statutory officers and local government employees. The latter are known as 'deputies' to the statutory officers. England and Wales is divided into 366 registration districts, and each district has a Superintendent Registrar based at the register office. Some districts have outstations that are either visited or permanently staffed.

Qualifications and Training

No formal requirements other than a good general education are necessary. Training is on the job but vacancies are few.

Personal Qualities and Skills

Registrars must be able to get on with people, giving advice calmly and sympathetically and be even-tempered. They should be able to do their job well in situations of excitement, emotion and distress. Confidentiality must be maintained at all times. Good handwriting is important, and the ability to drive may be necessary in rural locations. Entrants must be prepared for weekend work.

Starting Salary

£12,000+.

info

Local authorities

Local Job Centre Plus and Careers/Connexions Centres

Local Government Careers; www.LGcareers.com

Office of Population Censuses and Surveys, St Catherine's House, 10 Kingsway, London WC2B 6JP; 020 7242 0262; www.statistics.gov.uk

REMOVALS

Removers play a key role in the chain of events leading up to departure from one home and arrival in another – which can be around the corner or on the other side of the world. It is the remover's job to see that all the customer's belongings are professionally packed and transported to their destination. The work may involve packing fragile objects quickly and efficiently, as well as travelling long distances. Some large companies have their own storage facilities, so employees may be involved in ensuring that furniture is stored safely.

Estimators are the technical salespeople in a removals company. They visit customers' homes and estimate the amount of packing space needed, the time it will take and the price.

Qualifications and Training

Employees can work towards NVQs for the removals and storage industry. Progression is also possible to supervisory level. An LGV (large goods vehicle) licence would be beneficial, but is not essential when starting out. Estimators should have a good standard of education with good passes preferably in English, maths, geography and modern languages, hold a full car driving licence and be able to express themselves clearly and persuasively. Training is on the job.

Personal Qualities and Skills

Removers should be fit and strong. They must be honest and have a sense of responsibility towards other people's possessions. Common sense and the ability to work in a team are important.

Starting Salary

Salaries vary from region to region in the UK depending upon the market and competition in the area. There is no set income and salaries are often paid hourly, especially with casual staff. Income varies with experience and skills: a new entrant can earn £10,000 per year; with experience it is possible to earn between £11,000 to £13,000 per year. A senior person earns over £17,000.

British Association of Removers Limited, 3 Churchill Court, 58 Station Road, North Harrow, Middlesex HA2 7SA; 020 8861 3331; fax: 020 8861 3332; www.removers.org.uk; e-mail: info@bar.co.uk

Local Job Centre Plus and Careers/Connexions Centres

RETAILING

The retailing industry covers a range of businesses: department stores, supermarkets, cash-and-carry and discount warehouses, mail order firms, local shops, and some manufacturing companies that sell direct to the public.

Display designer/visual merchandiser

Display designers are responsible for shop windows and displays inside stores. These may be to attract customers into a shop, promote a new product or reinforce a company image. Displays are often seasonal or themed. Some designers work to instructions from head office, others create their own designs. The work may include making props, arranging lighting and general care of the display areas. Some shops also employ visual merchandisers who arrange products according to an organisation's display policy.

Qualifications and Training

Some companies have their own training schemes but these are generally intended to supplement previous training. Many designers have completed a higher-level course in design. Specialised courses in visual merchandising management and retail design are available at degree, foundation degree and HND level at the London Institute. Other higher education courses in retail management can include a design option. Entry requirements for degrees are normally two or three A levels or equivalent; for foundation degrees and HNDs, one or two A levels or equivalent. Some art courses require applicants to have completed a foundation course in art and design. NVQs in visual merchandising at levels 2, 3 and 4 are available.

Personal Qualities and Skills

Artistic flair and a passion for and awareness of fashion are the most important attributes for this work. You should also have practical skills such as sewing,

Fashion Retail Careers

If you've always viewed the High Street simply as the host to your favourite shopping experiences – think again. Fashion retail is one of the fastest growing industries in the world today offering a wide range of lively, long-term careers to suit everyone.

Careers and Training

Opportunities start at 16, with the option of becoming a sales advisor in store after completing GCSE's. Whether full time or part time, experience in store gives an excellent grounding for a future career in retail.

Specific Retail Management Programmes are available to students who have studied to A-Level standard. These programmes provide structured development opportunities. This means trainees can train and learn whilst in full time employment.

The Arcadia Group Limited is one of the UK's largest fashion retail companies, offering opportunities in Retail and Head Office. The group includes eight celebrated high street brands – Burton, Dorothy Perkins, Evans, Outfit, Miss Selfridge, Topshop, Topman and Wallis.

Arcadia offer a Retail Management Trainee Programme tailored to individuals with 2 A-levels or equivalent. The responsibilities of a Retail Manager are varied and interesting. They include:

- Inspiring and coaching team members
- Championing brand initiatives
- Delivering excellent customer service
- Keeping up to date with up and coming fashion trends
- Being aware of competitors

Retail Management is suited to individuals who wish to learn and develop valuable management skills from day one: from managing and developing staff to driving the business forward. Exposure to all these areas means this role provides experiences and opportunities to build a long and successful future career.

Personal Qualities

For all careers within Fashion Retail, passion for the customer and the industry are necessary to be successful. Team working and communication skills are also essential. For more information on Arcadia's opportunities and on what qualities and qualifications are useful for each career, visit the Arcadia Group website **www.arcadiagroup.co.uk/recruitment**

What's it really like?

Beth Newland, Management Trainee, Dorothy Perkins Ipswich

"Before I began the Management Trainee Programme with Arcadia I had been working in an independent department store part time whilst studying for my A-Levels. I enjoyed the busy and lively retail environment, so I decided that Retail was the sector I wanted to build my career within. I knew I wanted to progress as quickly as I could, so I began to research companies that would give me the training I needed to achieve this. Arcadia's Management Trainee Programme – known as the MTP – provided the best and most diverse training and development. The programme was for individuals with 2 A-levels or equivalent and a keen interest in fashion retail. It had a good mix of 'on the job' training and structured activities and workshops to motivate trainees and encourage learning.

"After completing an online application form and attending an assessment centre, I was so happy to hear that I had been successful and had been offered a position in Dorothy Perkins Ipswich. Since joining I have made sure I have been involved in everything I possibly can. I manage the store on a regular basis and have had placements in other stores. I am responsible in my store for account openings and customer service and regularly hold training sessions for the store team. I also look after recruitment and induction of all new staff and organise the visual merchandising – dressing the windows and mannequins in the latest trends. The role is so varied!

"All Trainees also get to attend development workshops that train us on core management skills. As well as being fantastic learning opportunities they also give us all the chance to meet up and discuss everything you have been involved in.

"I learn something new every day. I cannot wait to manage my own store on completing the programme and put everything I have learnt into practice!"

and be physically fit. You need to work well as part of a team and have an overall understanding of the particular retail business you work for. In some jobs you will need to be able to produce drawings of your work, either on paper or with Computer Aided Design (CAD).

Starting Salary

Starting salaries for junior designers are around £10,000 to £12,000. With three or four years' experience, you could earn up to £20,000 a year. A display manager with a top fashion or department store could earn £50,000, but these opportunities are few and far between.

info

British Display Society, 146 Welling Way, Welling, Kent DA16 2RS; 020 8856 2030; www.messiterdesign.co.uk

Arts Advice; 0800 093 0444; www.artsadvice.com

Skillsmart Retail: The Sector Skills Council for Retail, 40 Duke Street, London W1A 1AB; 0800 093 5001; www.skillsmartretail.com

General staff

Work opportunities include shop assistants, warehousing staff, cashiers, visual merchandisers, managers – store or department – and buyers. Larger concerns will also have administrators, personnel officers, and transport and logistic departments. In some shops – in a profession such as pharmacy, or in a trade such as butchery – the owner or manager must have special training. Most people in the retail trade have to work on Saturdays, and increasingly at least one late night a week, but there is often a rota system to make the working week more flexible. Sunday trading is the norm for most shops, requiring stores to have a full complement of staff. In large stores, bank holiday working is often recompensed by time off plus extra payment.

The growth in online shopping has affected all sectors of the retail industry and led to a growth of retail-related call centre work and work for packers and dispatchers to fulfil those orders.

Qualifications and Training

Sales staff generally do not need academic qualifications and training is on the job. Entrants may work towards NVQs at levels 1 to 4. However, to be taken on as a junior trainee or trainee supervisor, three to four GCSEs or equivalent are required. Trainee managers and buyers need two A levels, and increasingly companies recruit graduates as trainee managers.

Personal Qualities and Skills

Employees in retailing should enjoy talking to and helping people and have a pleasant manner. The ability to communicate in a friendly and helpful way is essential. Those involved with handling money and checking stock should be numerate and methodical.

Starting Salary

Sales assistants start on between £9,500 and £12,000. Supervisors earn up to £17,500. Some stores offer staff discounts and a few pay a clothing and grooming allowance.

info

Skillsmart Retail: The Sector Skills Council for Retail, 40 Duke Street, London W1A 1AB; 020 7399 3450; www.skillsmart.com

Department Stores and local Job Centre Plus and Connexions/Careers Centres

ROAD TRANSPORT

(*see also* Logistics)

This industry includes road haulage, plus passenger transport and commercial companies that have their own transport and delivery facilities. Passenger transport covers bus and coach services. Commercial companies need to plan the flow of materials or parts for manufacturing and the subsequent delivery of their products to their customers. Similarly, retail organisations need transport to bring merchandise to their outlets. The work divides into loading, moving and unloading, involving a wide range of operative and administrative staff: drivers, warehouse staff, depot managers, mechanics, clerical staff, transport planners and many others. There is a variety of public-sector and private-sector employers.

Qualifications and Training

Jobs range from those needing few formal qualifications to those that require a degree. There are NVQs in road passenger and road freight transport for operative staff; and Edexcel (BTEC)/SQA National Certificates for those with four GCSEs or equivalent; the Institute of Logistics and Transport offers a range of professional qualifications from entry level upwards. In England and Wales the Foundation and Advanced Modern Apprenticeships in road haulage and distribution are available. In Scotland NVQ/SVQ training at level 2 through Skillseekers and at level 3 through Skillseekers Modern Apprenticeships is available. Degrees in transport management are available at a number of universities.

Personal Qualities and Skills

Drivers need to be physically strong, responsible, careful and able to communicate effectively. Transport managers need good numeracy and ICT skills, and to be able to think analytically and plan effectively.

Starting Salary

A newly qualified driver will earn around £10,000–12,000, while an experienced driver carrying dangerous goods can earn £25,000+. Graduate trainees start between £18,000 and £24,000.

Skills for Logistics, 14 Warren Yard, Warren Farm Office Village, Milton Keynes MK12 5NW; 01908 313360; www.skillsforlogistics.org; e-mail: info@skillsforlogistics.org

British International Freight Association, Institute of Freight Forwarders, Redfern House, Browells Lane, Feltham, Middlesex TW13 7EP; 020 8844 2266; fax: 020 8890 5546; www.bifa.org; e-mail: bifa@bifa.org

Institute of Logistics and Transport, 11–12 Buckingham Gate, London SW1E 6LB; www.iolt.org.uk

Institute of Transport Administration, IoTA House, 7B St Leonards Road, Horsham, West Sussex RH13 6EH; 01403 242412; fax: 01403 242413; www.iota.org.uk

GoSkills, Concorde House, Trinity Park, Solihull, Birmingham B37 7UQ; 0121 635 5520; fax: 0121 635 5521; www.transfed.org

info

ROOFER

see Construction

ROUNDSPERSON

The roundsperson we are all most familiar with is probably the person who delivers milk and other dairy products to people's doorsteps on a daily basis.

In fact, working as a roundsperson can involve delivering and selling goods and services of many kinds to private homes and business premises. Examples include doing a sandwich round to businesses, selling ice cream or fast food and running mobile shops, selling many different kinds of goods. Usually, you work for yourself or you operate a franchise for a franchising company.

Qualifications and Training

You do not need any formal qualifications to do this work, but some companies set their own entry tests, and you need good basic maths skills for calculating prices and making out bills. You need a full driving licence and many companies prefer applicants to be over 21 years old. If you are selling fast food, you will need a licence to trade from your local Environmental Health Department. You could do a number of relevant NVQs in customer service and sales. If you are employed by a retailer or a franchising company, it usually provides specific training about its own products and services.

Personal Qualities and Skills

For most of the time you are working on your own, but you have to enjoy and be good at dealing with customers. You must be well organised with good numeracy skills and usually some computer skills these days. You have to be highly motivated, well organised and not mind working some antisocial hours or being out in all weathers.

Starting Salary

When you start off it is hard to earn more than about £10,000, though with experience this can rise to £15,000 to £20,000 and there are only a few types of round (milk and sandwiches, for example) where you are likely to receive seasonal tips.

info

British Franchise Association, Thames View, Newtown Road, Henley-on-Thames, Oxfordshire RG9 1HG; 01491 578050; www.british-franchise.org.uk

Improve: The Food and Drink Manufacturing and Processing Sector Skills Council, Providence House, 2 Innovation Close, Heslington, York YO10 52F; 0845 644 0448; www.improveltd.co.uk

Dairy Training and Development Council, 19 Cornwall Terrace, London NW1 4QP; 020 7486 7244; www.dairytraining.org.uk

Local Job Centre Plus and Connexions/Careers Centres

ROYAL AIR FORCE

The Royal Air Force is responsible for the airborne defence of the UK and its allies. It consists of a small flying force, almost exclusively officers, supported by non-commissioned airmen and airwomen working in a variety of trades such as engineering, communication and air traffic control work as well as supporting jobs such as catering, medical and dental support workers, photographers, security guards and musicians. A few non-commissioned officer airmen and airwomen work as crew in specialities such as air signallers, air electronics operators or air loadmasters.

Ground opportunities for officers include air traffic and fighter control, engineering, physical education, intelligence, catering, administration, supply and education. There are also provost (police) officers, medical officers, dental officers, nursing officers, legal officers and chaplains.

Qualifications and Training

Non-Commissioned Personnel

For some jobs no academic qualifications are needed. For entry to scientific and technical trades, three to five GCSEs, often including science and maths, are required. Musicians need to have passed Grade 8 or have a higher qualification; dental/nursing staff need the appropriate professional qualifications. The minimum age for entry to most trades is 16; the upper age limit is normally 30, but there is some variation between trades.

Ground recruits attend an initial seven-week course covering physical fitness and weapons training which is followed by specialist training. Aircrew have a 12-week basic training course followed by specialist training. Many airmen and airwomen will work towards NVQs or other nationally recognised qualifications throughout their career.

Officers

Minimum academic entry requirements are two A levels and five GCSEs at A–C (including English and maths) or equivalent. The normal upper age limit is 26 (24 for pilots) but qualified specialists can apply up to the age of 39. Graduates are preferred for some specialisms and student sponsorships are available. Those wanting to train as pilots take aptitude tests to assess coordination and speed of reaction. Applicants must meet nationality and residence requirements and pass a medical examination. For some jobs good eyesight and colour vision is essential. Women may apply to all branches except the RAF Regiment.

Training for all new officers starts with an intensive 24-week course which covers operational and leadership skills. This is followed by training relevant to the chosen specialisation, which varies in length from a few weeks to up to three years for pilots.

Personal Qualities and Skills

Air Force personnel must enjoy teamwork and a disciplined regime and be willing to go into combat. They need physical fitness, dedication, commitment, initiative and a sense of responsibility.

Starting Salary

New entrants earn around £14,650 a year. Senior airmen/women earn up to £25,000 a year. Warrant officers, the highest non-commissioned ranks, can earn over £38,000 a year. Graduate officer cadets start on £20,173. Officer commissions are confirmed upon successful completion of initial officer training and, with increments for the possession of a degree, on commissioning the salary increases to approximately £25,000.

Local RAF Careers Offices; 0845 605 5555; www.rafcareers.com

Joint Services Command and Staff College, Faringdon Road, Watchfield, Swindon SN6 8TS; 01793 788000; www.da.mod.uk/JSCSC

Royal Aeronautical Society (RAES), 4 Hamilton Place, London W1J 7BQ; 020 7670 4300; www.raes.org.uk

ROYAL MARINES

The Royal Marines acts as the emergency strike force of the Royal Navy. Its personnel are trained for amphibious assaults and commando operations on land. It has a well-deserved reputation for toughness, and training is arduous. Marines are sent at short notice to deal with emergency situations, which include natural disasters as well as military operations. There are six specialist areas in the Royal Marines. These are Ships Detachment (serving on Royal Navy ships), Air Squadron, Special Boat Squadron, Jungle and Arctic Warfare and Embarked Force (working at sea and forming part of the amphibious Task Force). Most commandos serve as Riflemen but there are some specialist and support trades. The Royal Marines is an all-male service.

Qualifications and Training

Officers

Full career entry is between 17 and a half and 23, and at least two A levels or equivalent are required. Undergraduates may be recruited on a cadetship scheme and sponsored at university. Graduates can enter up to the age of 25. Initial training is 15 months followed by 9 months working in a specialist unit. Officers specialise in particular areas of work such as radio communications, amphibious operations or special reconnaissance work, but are trained in all the activities undertaken by the Marines.

Other Ranks

Entry to the Royal Marines is between 17 and a half and 28 and does not require formal qualifications but many recruits have GCSEs and some have A levels. All candidates must pass the Royal Navy selection test. The minimum height requirement is 1.65 m (5 ft 6 in) with appropriate height to weight ratio. Initial training lasts 30 weeks and is followed by a period of more advanced training with the opportunity to work towards the appropriate qualifications. Before returning to civilian life Marines can learn a new trade or supervisory and management skills at a Royal Navy vocational training centre.

Personal Qualities and Skills

The same basic qualities are needed as for the other services: discipline, dedication, fitness, initiative and an ability to work with others. Marines spend long periods away from home, often in difficult and dangerous locations with climates ranging from tropical to arctic. High standards of physical fitness and stamina are essential. Around 900 Marines are recruited each year and entry is competitive.

Starting Salary

New entrants earn £11,774 a year. Able ratings earn between £13,866 and £25,042 a year. Midshipmen/women and sub lieutenants earn between £14,727 and £21,301 a year. Lieutenants earn from £32,809 to £39,018 a year. Lieutenant commanders receive up to £49,497 a year, and commanders can earn up to £64,123 a year. There are extra payments for special duties or for being separated from your family. Your pay may be less if you are living in subsidised accommodation.

The Royal Navy; www.royal-navy.mod.uk

Joint Services Command and Staff College, Faringdon Road, Watchfield, Swindon SN6 8TS; 01793 788000; www.da.mod.uk/JSCSC

Leaflets and advice are available from all local armed forces careers offices.

ROYAL NAVY

(*see also* ROV Pilot Technician)

Navy personnel work in the nation's combat fleet and at its land bases. Like the other services, the Navy uses many trades and skills. Royal Navy ratings are non-commissioned servicemen and women working in one of six branches: warfare, engineering, supply, medical, Fleet Air Arm and deep navy (submarines). Officers command and are responsible for the welfare of the ranks. They may work in warfare, engineering, supply, aviation or training. Special Officers work as doctors, dentists, nursing officers or chaplains.

Qualifications and Training

Officers

There are two main entry routes – direct entry from school, university or civilian employment or by promotion from the ranks. Some scholarships are available for sixth formers and undergraduates. Minimum entry requirements are two A levels or equivalent.

An increasing number of officers are graduates. Applicants must be under 23 (26 for graduates). Experienced engineers must be under 32 on entry; age limits for Special Officers can be up to 44.

All officers spend two to five terms at the Britannia Royal Naval College at Dartmouth, which will include some time spent at sea. After this they go on to further training which varies in length according to specialism.

Ratings

The minimum age for entry to most jobs is 16. Medical and dental assistants and nurses need to be slightly older. The upper age limit for communications technicians and artificer apprentices is 27; for other trades 32. Academic requirements vary according to the trade but are between two and five GCSEs or equivalent. Medical and dental assistants and nurses may need professional qualifications. All applicants have to pass a test in reasoning, English, numeracy and mechanical comprehension and a medical. Jobs in submarines are not open to women.

Initial basic training is eight weeks followed by specialist training relevant to the trade chosen. Some of this time will be spent at sea.

Personal Qualities and Skills

A liking for the sea is important. Other requirements are the same as for the other services: discipline, dedication, fitness, initiative and an ability to work with others. Different trades demand specific skills – languages are useful for those working in communications, while a knowledge of science and technology is needed by those working with sophisticated equipment.

Starting Salary

On entry ratings earn £11,432. Able ratings earn from £13,461 to £24,313. Officers start on £14,494 on entry and salaries rise to between £18,323 and £24,313.

SALES REPRESENTATIVE

A sales representative may work for a manufacturer, wholesale distributor or service industry, persuading potential customers to buy the firm's products and also looking after the needs of existing customers. The representative is usually assigned a geographical area and travels around it on the firm's behalf. It is possible to be a representative for any number of products, from soap powder to pharmaceutical supplies to office equipment, machine tools and beauty products.

Qualifications and Training

Requirements for trainees vary, but most firms look for four GCSEs grades A–C or equivalent and in some companies recruitment is at graduate level. Sales reps may study for examinations set by such bodies as the Chartered Institute of Marketing or the Managing and Marketing Sales Association. Diplomas and certificates are also issued by various trade associations representing particular types of product. Technical sales representatives usually have a degree or equivalent in the relevant subject.

Personal Qualities and Skills

An outgoing, friendly personality, a manner that inspires confidence and the ability to speak forcefully and persuasively, plus persistence and stamina, are all important.

Starting Salary

Salaries start at between £11,000 and £20,000, rising to around £15,000 to £24,000 in two or three years. Medical and technical products sales tend to offer the higher salaries. Many sales jobs include commission for sales made, bonuses for successful work and free petrol or other benefits.

Chartered Institute of Marketing (CIM), Moor Hall, Cookham, Maidenhead, Berks SL6 9QH; 01628 427500; www.cim.co.uk

Institute of Sales & Marketing Management (ISSM), Harrier Court, Lower Woodside, Bedfordshire LU1 4DQ; 01582 840001; www.ismm.co.uk

SECURITY WORK

Security guards and security officers work for all kinds of organisations and businesses, where buildings, property and people need protection. They work to prevent theft and other criminal activities and to alert the police when the need arises. Typical tasks for security guards and officers include door supervision, checking people who enter a premises to confirm identity, patrolling buildings on foot or monitoring them from a control room, guarding cash and other valuables as it is delivered or removed or when it is in transit, and checking individuals and observing behaviour at airports or other public places. Many security staff begin as security guards and then progress to becoming security officers or supervisors with responsibility for coordinating security arrangements and training other security staff.

Qualifications and Training

No specific entry qualifications are required, but you must be at least 18 – many companies prefer you to be 21. You often need a driving licence and you may have to pass some written tests and have a medical. Many companies will carry out extensive checks on your past work record to ensure that you are trustworthy and honest.

Since March 2006 The Security Industry Association has introduced a new training scheme that incorporates a security guard qualification and a licence to work as a security guard. The training takes 30 hours and is usually completed over a few days. It is possible to do City & Guilds courses equivalent to GNVQ levels 2 and 3 in security guard work, and many companies provide a range of short courses in relevant skills such as dog handling, or use of electronic monitoring.

Personal Qualities and Skills

You need to be self-confident and mature – able to challenge people when necessary, but also polite and helpful. You should be able to write short reports and also have good basic IT skills. You need to be physically fit, and able to concentrate for long periods while remaining highly observant. You should be

info

British Security Industry Association Limited, Security House, Barbourne Road, Worcester WR1 1RS; 01905 21464; fax: 01905 613625; www.bsia.co.uk; e-mail: info@bsia.co.uk

Security Industry Training Organisation, Security House, Barbourne Road, Worcester WR1 1RS; 01905 20004; fax: 01905 724949; www.sito.co.uk; e-mail: info@sito.co.uk

National Security Inspectorate, Queensgate House, 14 Cookham Road, Maidenhead, Berks SL6 8AJ; 0870 205 0000, fax: 01628 773367, www.nsi.org.uk; e-mail: nsi@nsi.org.uk

Security Industry Authority (SIA), PO Box 9, Newcastle upon Tyne NE82 6YX; 0845 243 0100; www.the-sia.org.uk

able to work on your own, but also work as part of a team and know when to seek help, support or advice.

Starting Salary

New security guards are often paid the minimum wage, or something close to it; £5.05 an hour, or £10,000 to £12,000 depending on the hours you work. Senior security officers with experience and some supervisory responsibility earn between £15,000 and £22,000 a year.

SERVICE MECHANIC

(*see also* Engineering *and* Electrician)

Mechanics are needed to service and repair business machines such as photocopiers, as well as domestic machines such as washing machines and televisions. Service mechanics are employed by machine manufacturers. Although some work may be done in the company's workshop, more frequently the mechanic will visit offices or private homes. As office equipment and domestic appliances become increasingly dependent on computer technology the work is becoming more IT-related.

Qualifications and Training

These vary, but formal academic qualifications are not always necessary. Some employers require City and Guilds certificates in mechanical, electrical or electronic engineering. Modern Apprenticeships and related NVQs are available.

Personal Qualities and Skills

Service mechanics spend a great deal of their time on other people's premises, so a polite and friendly manner plus the ability to work quickly and neatly are useful. A driving licence is usually essential.

Starting Salary

For those with experience, £16,000+.

Local Job Centre Plus and Careers/Connexions Centres

SHEET METAL WORKER

see Manufacturing

SHIPBROKER

Shipbrokers act as go-betweens for ship owners, looking for cargo to fill their vessels, and charterers, seeking to ship their dry cargo and tanker requirements. Sale and purchase of vessels is also an important service offered to clients. Brokers are paid commission on the contracts arranged. The Baltic Exchange in London is the centre of the chartering market. It is a self-regulated market and the Exchange maintains a register of those seeking employment, which its member companies may consult. Vacancies are also advertised on the website. Additionally, shipbrokers/ship's agents in ports make arrangements when a ship calls for customs clearance – loading and discharging cargoes, meeting crew requirements and so on. Port agents who attend to cargo liners may also be involved in marketing and documenting cargo. In order to maintain contact with the international scene, shipbrokers tend to work long hours and to travel abroad frequently.

Qualifications and Training

There are no specific academic qualifications needed for ship broking beyond a good general educational background. However, members of a firm who wish to make a career in the shipping business usually study for the examination leading to membership of the Institute of Chartered Shipbrokers. Such study can be part-time or by correspondence course, and covers not only shipping practice but more general studies in law, economics and international trade. The Institute also offers a foundation diploma in shipping for those just starting in the business.

Personal Qualities and Skills

A good business sense, the ability to learn through practical experience, and willingness to work long and irregular hours and to travel are all necessary.

Starting Salary

Salaries start at between £15,000 and £20,000, rising to £22,000 to £23,000 after two or three years.

info

British International Freight Association (BIFA), Redfern House, Browells Lane, Feltham, Middlesex TW13 7EP; 020 8844 2266; www.bifa.org

The Chartered Institute of Logistics and Transport (CILT) UK, 11–12 Buckingham Gate, London SW1E 6LB; 01536 740104; www.ciltuk.org.uk

Skills for Logistics, 14 Warren Yard, Warren Farm Office Village, Milton Keynes MK12 5NW; 01908 313 360; www.skillsforlogistics.org/

SIGNWRITER

see Art and Design

SOCIAL WORK/SOCIAL CARE

Home carer

Home carers provide emotional and practical support for the elderly, people with physical disabilities, mental health problems and a range of other illnesses.

The role of the home carer includes housework, shopping, dressing, bathing, toileting and supervising medication. Carers are offered training and support by a home care organiser, who also provides team supervision. Most home carers work for local authorities or private agencies.

Home care organiser

Home care organisers undertake assessment of a person's needs and their financial circumstances. They decide whether or not the person is eligible for support and exactly what financial support he or she needs. They then arrange for home care provision. They work in teams alongside social workers and care managers, mainly in local authorities, the voluntary sector or private agencies.

info

British Association of Social Workers, 16 Kent Street, Birmingham B5 6RD; 0121 622 3911; www.basw.co.uk

General Social Care Council, Goldings House, 2 Hay's Lane, London SE1 2HB; 020 7397 5800; Registration helpline: 0845 070 0630; www.gscc.org.uk

Skills for Care (England), Albion Court, 5 Albion Place, Leeds LS1 6JP; 0113 245 1716; www.topss.org.uk

Scottish Social Services Council (SSSC), Compass House, Discovery Quay, 11 Riverside Drive, Dundee DD1 4NY; 01382 207101; www.sssc.uk.com

Care Council for Wales (CCW), 6th Floor West Wing, South Gate House, Wood Street, Cardiff CF10 1EW; 029 2022 6257; www.ccwales.org.uk

Northern Ireland Social Care Council (NISCC), 7th Floor Millennium House, Great Victoria Street, Belfast BT2 7AQ; 028 9041 7600; www.niscc.info

Social Work Admissions System (SWAS), Rose Hill, New Barn Lane, Cheltenham GL62 3LZ; 01242 223707; www.ucas.ac.uk

www.socialworkcareers.co.uk; 0845 60464

Qualifications and Training

For home carers, NVQs in care are available. For a home care organiser, some relevant experience and NVQs in care or management, a diploma in domiciliary care management, and a certificate/diploma in management studies are all qualifications that are increasingly required.

Personal Qualities and Skills

All individuals working in the area of social work need patience and a warm, sympathetic personality. They need to have excellent communication skills, be good listeners, trustworthy, and have compassion for others.

Starting Salary

For home carers, salaries vary locally but are around Minimum Wage levels. A home care organiser may earn £13,000 to £19,000 depending on qualifications and experience.

Probation officer

The aims of the National Probation Service for England and Wales (NPS) are: protecting the public; reducing re-offending; the proper punishment of offenders in the community; ensuring offenders are aware of the effects of crime on the victims of crime and the public; and the rehabilitation of offenders.

All probation work with offenders combines continuous assessment and management of risk with the provision of expert supervision programmes designed to reduce re-offending. Approximately 70 per cent of offenders supervised will be on community supervision orders and 30 per cent in prison. Probation staff are regularly seconded to work in youth offending teams, prisons and with a range of crime prevention agencies.

In Scotland, the functions of the probation officer are performed by social work departments in local authorities.

Qualifications and Training/Entry Requirements

Professional training in England and Wales is through the Diploma in Probation Studies which is managed by the 42 probation services working with nine regional consortia. This is an integrated programme of education and training that combines work- and university-based learning through a community justice NVQ level 4 award and an undergraduate degree. Trainee probation officers are appointed to probation areas following a rigorous recruitment and selection process and are paid a training salary. Programmes leading to the Diploma in Probation Studies are normally completed within 24 months. The minimum age for appointment as a probation officer is 22, so training cannot be undertaken by those under 20. Entry requirements for those under 21 are two passes at A level and three at GCSE, or three at A level and one at GCSE; candidates over 21 but under 25 years need five passes at GCSE, and candidates over 25 years may be accepted without formal qualifications, but have to demonstrate academic potential. Experience of related work, though not necessarily with offenders, is essential and can be gained through volunteering.

Entry in Scotland is through a course of professional training leading to a degree in social work.

Personal Qualities and Skills

Probation officers need to be able to develop imaginative, relevant strategies to help offenders lead law-abiding lives. They need to be good listeners and have an understanding of different ethnic and cultural backgrounds. They also need to be assertive, able to exercise and maintain authority and cope with aggression.

Starting Salary

Trainee probation officers can earn between £14,500 and £15,500. Main grade probation officers earn around £25,000 to £28,000 a year. Criminal justice social workers in Scotland earn between £17,000 and £28,000. The government is planning to restructure the Probation Service in the next three years and this may alter pay and conditions.

info

National Probation Service, Horseferry House, Dean Ryle Street, London SW1P 2AW; 020 7217 0659; www.probation.homeoffice.gov.uk

Probation Board for Northern Ireland, 80–90 North Street, Belfast BT1 1LD; 028 9026 2400; www.pbni.org.uk

Skills for Justice, 9 Riverside Court, Don Road, Sheffield S9 2TJ; 0114 261 1499; www.skillsforjustice.com

Scottish Social Services Council (SSSC), Compass House, 11 Riverside Drive, Dundee DD1 4NY; 01382 207101; www.sssc.uk.com

Wales Probation Training Consortium, 4–7 The Broadway, Pontypridd CF37 1BA; 01443 494333; www.probation.walestraining.gov.uk

Social workers and social carers

Social workers and social carers provide support for individuals, families and groups within the community. They work in a variety of settings and with many different client groups, eg, adults with mental health problems or learning disabilities, children, older people, young offenders, drug users – anyone who is disadvantaged in some way. Most social workers are employed by local authorities and work in teams based around particular client groups – children and young people, adults with disabilities, etc. Some work for voluntary organisations and other non-governmental groups.

Social care assistant

Social care assistants work in residential care homes and day centres, providing support to clients and professional staff who may be nurses, social workers or other care professionals. They may help with basic physical, but non-medical care, such as washing and dressing and assisting clients at meal times and with social activities.

Social work assistant

Social work assistants work with social workers and while they don't have responsibility for individual cases they will often meet clients and do a lot of the follow-up work, for example, contacting other agencies to arrange support for clients. They set up meetings, follow up enquiries and help keep track of cases.

Qualifications and Training

No specific academic qualifications are required for assistant's posts, but individual authorities or care providers may ask for some GCSEs and certainly will look for a background of dealing with people. There are opportunities to qualify to NVQ level 3 while working and some assistants do progress to management level.

Personal Qualities and Skills

Being warm, friendly and able to deal comfortably with people who face all kinds of difficulties is very important. Being practical, enthusiastic and encouraging is also important.

Starting Salary

For social care assistants the pay is often at or close to the Minimum Wage. Social work assistants earn from £9,000 to £13,000.

For further information see Social Worker.

Social worker – children and young people

More than half of all social workers work in some way with children. This may be in one of the specific areas outlined below or it may be as part of an area social work team working with local children and families. Child protection is an important part of the social worker's role.

Social worker – day care settings

Day care settings where social workers are employed include day care provision for adults and older people with a range of special needs, which might be emotional, behavioural or physical. It is often a qualified social worker who manages a day care centre.

Social worker – education settings

These social workers are sometimes referred to as 'education welfare officers'. It is their job to work with those school pupils who, for whatever reason, are failing to attend school properly. Education social workers work with the pupils and their families to try to get to the root of the problem and get the pupil back into school.

Social worker – healthcare settings

Social workers attached to hospitals work with patients who are about to be discharged from, or who have just been discharged from hospital, after a long stay. Their main client groups are older people or people who have had major accidents or serious long-term illnesses. The social worker helps clients to plan for their return home and to access whatever support services they need.

Social worker – mental health settings

Working with clients who have mental health problems, these social workers support their clients in the community, in hospitals or in sheltered accommodation. Social workers help assess risks, work out what support needs their clients have and help them to access such services as education, or a return to employment.

Social worker – residential settings

Social workers in residential settings work with clients who are resident in care homes. Their clients may be children, young adults with learning or physical disabilities, or frail elderly people who are unable to continue living in their own homes.

Qualifications and Training

The main routes to qualifying are either through a three-year social work degree, a two-year postgraduate diploma, or accelerated degree for graduates of other subjects. Preferred degree subjects include social sciences, social policy and psychology. Non-graduates with plenty of relevant experience can do a diploma course. All the courses are a combination of theoretical study and practical placements. Once qualified there are advanced courses in different areas of practice such as childcare, mental health work or social work teaching.

Personal Qualities and Skills

Social workers must be warm and caring, but be able to keep calm and not get upset by potentially distressing situations. They must be comfortable working with many different types of people. They should also be well organised, quick thinking and good at problem solving.

Starting Salary

Starting salaries range from £17,000 to £28,000 depending on qualifications and experience. Slightly lower salaries may be paid in the voluntary sector.

SPORTS AND RECREATION FACILITY MANAGEMENT

Sport and recreation facility managers are responsible for the efficient running of leisure centres, swimming pools, sports halls and associated facilities. Managers usually start their careers as recreation assistants and progress through supervisory and assistant manager positions via on-the-job training and professional development.

Qualifications and Training

The Institute of Sport and Recreation Management (ISRM) offers a comprehensive programme of training and qualifications designed to cover all aspects of sport and recreation facility management and operation ranging from recreation assistant, NVQ level 2 and supervisor, NVQ level 3, to management, NVQ levels 4 and 5.

HND courses and a range of degrees in recreation management and sports sciences are available.

Personal Qualities and Skills

A liking for people, a strong interest in sport, and organising skills are essential. Swimming and lifesaving ability are essential for swimming pool work.

Starting Salary

Recreation assistants at 18 years old, around £10,000; managers' salaries are variable depending upon level of responsibilities, type of facility, location, qualifications and experience, and can range from £13,000 to £25,000.

Institute of Sport and Recreation Management, Gifford House, 36–38 Sherrard Street, Melton Mowbray, Leicestershire LE13 1XJ; 01664 565531; www.isrm.co.uk; e-mail: info@isrm.co.uk

Fitness Industry Association (FIA), 4th Floor, 61 Southwark Street, London SE1 0HL; 020 7202 4700; www.fia.org.uk

Institute of Leisure and Amenities Management (ILAM), ILAM House, Lower Basildon, Reading, Berks RG8 9NE; 01491 874800; www.ilam.co.uk

Institute of Sport and Recreation Management (ISRM), Sir John Beckwith Centre for Sport, Loughborough University, Loughborough, Leics LE11 3TU; 01509 226 474; www.isrm.co.uk

Register of Exercise Professionals (REPs), 8–10 Crown Hill, Croydon, Surrey CR0 1RZ; 020 8686 6464; www.exerciseregister.org/

SkillsActive, Castlewood House, 77–91 New Oxford Street, London WC1A 1PX; 020 7632 2000; www.skillsactive.com

Institute of Leisure and Amenity Management, ILAM House, Lower Basildon, Reading, Berkshire RG8 9NE; 01491 874800; fax: 01491 874801; www.ilam.co.uk; e-mail: info@ilam.co.uk

SPORT

While relatively few earn a significant living from being a professional sportsperson, there are many other occupations within the sports sector.

Coach

Coaches help individuals and teams identify areas for improvement in physical fitness levels and for specific sports skills. They also plan and implement training programmes in a wide variety of sports provided by sports centres, clubs, schools, hotels and swimming baths.

Much coaching is done on a voluntary basis; however, there are opportunities for paid work, and many coaches work in a self-employed capacity. Some local authorities employ coaches to offer facilities for local schools at one or more centres in the authority. Such coaches are expected to be able to coach in most of the following sports: badminton, basketball, climbing (on indoor walls), ice skating, swimming, squash, tennis, trampolining and weight training. Increasingly, there is a need for coaches in the summer months to work in outdoor activity centres.

Qualifications and Training

Coaches must gain recognised coaching qualifications, which are awarded by the governing bodies of the various sports and acquired either at evening class or weekend school. Swimming coaches must also hold a national lifeguard award. All coaches need to have and develop their knowledge of related areas such as injury, sports science and nutrition.

Personal Qualities and Skills

Coaches need the ability to communicate, as well as perseverance, patience and tact. The ability to inspire children or adults of very different abilities is also needed.

Starting Salary

Salaries vary greatly. Local authority coaches receive £11+ an hour. In private health clubs and gyms the rate is often far higher.

info

Sports Coach UK, 114 Cardigan Road, Headingley, Leeds LS6 3BJ: 0113 274 4802; fax: 0113 275 5019; www.sportscoachuk.org; e-mail: coaching@sportscoachuk.org

Sport England, 3rd Floor, Victoria House, Bloomsbury Square, London WC1B 4SE; 020 7273 1500; 020 7383 5740; www.sportengland.org; e-mail: info@sportengland.org

Sport Scotland, Caledonia House, South Gyle, Edinburgh EH12 9DQ; 0131 317 7200; fax: 0131 317 7202; www.sportscotland.org.uk; e-mail: library@sportscotland.org.uk

Sports Council For Wales, Sophia Gardens, Cardiff CF11 9SW; 029 2030 0500; www.sports-council-wales.co.uk; e-mail: scw@scw.co.uk

SkillsActive, Castlewood House, 77–91 New Oxford Street, London WC1A 1PX; 020 7632 2000; www.skillsactive.com

Physiotherapist

see Physiotherapy

Teacher

see Teaching

Sportsperson

There are opportunities in sport for professional sportspeople and for careers in coaching. Not all sports allow players to be professionals, and there are others, such as snooker, where there is room for only a very few professionals. Sports attracting professionals in relatively large numbers are football, cricket, golf, horse racing, Rugby League and tennis.

Sportspeople's careers are generally short, but if, during their careers, they have made a name for themselves, there may be opportunities in journalism, broadcasting or consultancy.

Qualifications and Training

Professional sportspeople naturally need to be excellent at their sport. Those in team games generally begin by playing for their school, town or county side. In this context, a young player may be noticed by professional selectors. In the case of football, it is not necessary to join a local football league club; apprentices are taken on from all over the country. Because a club apprentice has no guarantee that he will ever play for the first side, some clubs allow apprentices time off to obtain academic qualifications.

Personal Qualities and Skills

As well as talent, professional sportspeople must possess dedication, perseverance, commitment and be highly competitive.

Starting Salary

Salaries for professionals are often low initially, but the rewards for top performers may be very high. The amount of money earned varies enormously depending upon the sport. Coaches' salaries vary according to whether the work is full- or part-time, what type of work they are doing and the number of hours.

info

SkillsActive, Castlewood House, 77–91 New Oxford Street, London WC1A 1PX; 020 7632 2000; www.skillsactive.com

Sport England, 3rd Floor, Victoria House, Bloomsbury Square, London WC1B 4SE; 0845 8508 508; www.sportengland.org

Sport Scotland, Caledonia House, South Gyle, Edinburgh EH12 9DQ; 0131 317 7200; www.sportscotland.org.uk

Sports Council for Northern Ireland, House of Sport, Upper Malone Rd, Belfast BT9 5LA; 028 9038 1222; www.sportni.net/

Sports Council for Wales, The National Sports Centre, Sophia Gardens, Cardiff CF1 9SW; 029 2030 0500; www.sports-council-wales.co.uk

STATISTICIAN

Every business and every government department uses the information gathered from statistics to plan its workload, market its products, analyse behaviour, etc. Statisticians are concerned with the collection, analysis and interpretation of numerical data. Statisticians design and plan surveys and use various software packages to help them in their analysis.

Qualifications and Training

Most entrants to this profession have a degree in statistics, mathematics or another degree or postgraduate qualification that has an in-depth level of statistical work as part of the course. Sometimes entrants with A levels or good GCSEs can work their way up from other administrative or routine data management jobs if they have an obvious flair for dealing with and interpreting numbers. The Royal Statistical Society also offers some distance learning and part-time courses for people already in work, but most candidates studying these already possess a degree.

Personal Qualities and Skills

You need to have a really good understanding of statistical and other numerical ideas, but it is also important that you can interpret them and explain your findings in a way that less mathematically minded colleagues will understand. You need good IT skills and good problem solving and analytical ability.

Starting Salary

Starting salaries range between £17,000 and £29,000. Commerce and industry pay higher salaries than local government, the Civil Service, education and the National Health Service. Salaries rise to £30,000 to £40,000 with experience.

info

Biomathematics and Statistics Scotland, The University of Edinburgh, James Clerk Maxwell Building, The King's Buildings, Edinburgh EH9 3JZ; 0131 650 4900; www.bioss.sari.ac.uk/index.html

Eurostat: The Statistical Office of the European Communities, Bâtiment Jean Monnet, Rue Alcide de Gasperi, L-2920 Luxembourg; europa.eu.int/comm/eurostat/

Government Statistical Service (GSS), 1 Drummond Gate, Pimlico, London SW1V 2QQ; 01633 819060; www.statistics.gov.uk

Office for National Statistics (ONS), Customer Contact Centre, Room 1.015, Office for National Statistics, Cardiff Road, Newport NP10 8XG; 0845 601 3034; www.statistics.gov.uk/

Royal Statistical Society (RSS), 12 Errol Street, London EC1Y 8LX; 020 7638 8998; www.rss.org.uk

SURVEYING

Surveying covers a wide variety of work within one profession, and a number of professional bodies offer qualifications in the different areas (see below). There are also technician qualifications. Surveying technicians work in all the same fields as surveyors but without being professionally qualified.

Aerial surveying

A specialisation of land surveying (see below), aerial surveying involves photogrammetry – the use of aerial photographs as a basis for calculations. Qualifications are offered by the Architecture and Surveying Institute (ASI) and the Institute of Civil Engineering Surveyors.

Archaeological surveying

This relatively new specialisation involves working on an archaeological dig, making plans, maps and cross-sections of the excavations. It requires the skill of a cartographer as well as that of a land surveyor. The Architects' and Surveyors' Institute has members in this discipline.

Building surveying

The structural surveying of properties and reporting on their condition and valuation is carried out by building surveyors/building engineers. They advise on necessary repairs and maintenance, and prepare plans and specifications for alterations and improvements. Local and central government employ a large proportion of qualified building surveyors, although many are in private practice. Qualifications in this area are available from the Association of Building Engineers (ABE), the ASI and the Royal Institution of Chartered Surveyors (RICS).

General practice

This includes auctioneering, estate agency, valuation and estate management. People working in this area are responsible for the selling or letting, surveying, valuation and management of both urban and rural property. Qualifications in general practice are offered by the ABE, the ASI and the RICS.

Hydrographic surveying

The hydrographer surveys and charts underwater areas, such as ports and harbours and offshore areas where drilling for oil takes place. Hydrographic surveying qualifications are offered by the ASI and the RICS.

Land surveying

The land surveyor measures and charts the earth's physical features so that maps can be drawn. The scale of the work can range from a one-house building site to a whole region of Africa, and there are opportunities in public services (the Ordnance Survey and the Ministry of Defence, for example), as well as in private practice or large commercial organisations. Qualifications are offered by the ASI and the RICS.

Minerals surveying

Minerals surveyors assist in the design, development and surveying of quarries and underground mines, ensuring safety for the workers as well as optimum profitability for the company extracting the minerals. They also value mineral workings for rating and taxation, and therefore need to be all-rounders with knowledge of geology, the management of mineral workings, taxation and planning legislation. This area of surveying is unique in having its qualifications and duties laid down by law. Minerals surveyors must hold the surveyor's certificate granted on behalf of the Secretary of State for Industry by the Mining Qualifications Board. They must be at least 21 and have at least four years' practical experience (including 2,000 hours underground) in order to sit the exam for this certificate. Further qualifications are provided by the RICS and the ASI.

Quantity surveying

In private practice, quantity surveyors work with an architect to draw up design specifications in line with the client's budget. When the finished design is agreed, the quantity surveyor draws up a bill of quantities, detailing the materials and labour that will be needed. Building contractors work on this bill of quantities in preparing their tender for the job; they will use their own quantity surveyors to estimate their costs. Quantity surveyors also monitor costs as the work progresses and is completed. If they train for this work while employed by construction contractors, they usually take the qualification of the RICS. Professional qualifications are also offered by the ASI.

Rural practice

This is often combined with land agency, and concerns the use and development of agricultural land. The qualifying bodies in this area are the ASI and the RICS.

Qualifications and Training

The RICS offers a range of qualifications in the different areas of surveying. Normally entrants need three A levels or equivalent for entry into an RICS-approved degree or diploma course. An alternative is undertaking an HND or

HNC in a related surveying discipline, which can give advanced entry to those courses. On successful completion of an RICS-approved degree or diploma, graduates enrol onto the Assessment of Professional Competence (APC), which is two years' practical training while in employment, concluding with an RICS professional assessment interview. Various degree backgrounds are valuable for surveying; one-year full-time and two-year part-time postgraduate conversion courses are available.

Technicians need a relevant HNC/HND or NVQ level 4 followed by the Assessment of Technical Competence. This is two years' RICS structured training while working, which concludes with the RICS technical assessment interview. Those who have gained technical membership of RICS can take a bridging course to become a Chartered Surveyor.

Personal Qualities and Skills

Logical and orderly thinking, ability in figure work and detailed drawings are called for in this precision work. Communication skills and business acumen are essential. Good oral and written English is an asset, and some areas may require specialised mathematical ability.

Starting Salary

The average starting salary for chartered surveyors is £14,000–18,000. After qualification, salaries increase to £20,000–25,000.

Chartered Institute of Building (Faculty of Architecture and Surveying), Englemere, Kings Ride, Ascot, Berkshire SL5 7TB; 01344 630700; fax: 01344 630777; www.ciob.org.uk; e-mail: reception@ciob.org.uk

Association of Building Engineers (ABE), Lutyens House, Billing Brook Road, Weston Favell, Northampton NN3 8NW; 0845 1261058; fax: 01604 784220; www.abe.org.uk; e-mail: building.engineers@abe.org.uk

Royal Institution of Chartered Surveyors (RICS), 12 Great George Street, Parliament Square, London SW1P 3AD; 0870 333 1600; www.rics.org; e-mail: contactrics@rics.org

Royal Institution of Chartered Surveyors in Scotland, 9 Manor Place, Edinburgh EH3 7DN; 0131 225 7078; fax: 0131 240 0830; www.rics-scotland.org.uk

RICS Contact Centre (for general enquiries), Surveyor Court, Westwood Way, Coventry CV4 8JE; 0870 333 1600; www.rics.org; e-mail: contactrics@rics.org

TAXATION

Those who work in the area of taxation deal with the payment of taxes, which is a source of revenue for public expenditure.

Tax adviser/technician

Tax advisers/technicians work for private firms or independently, offering assistance to other firms/individuals who need guidance through the complications of the tax laws. A tax adviser is able to advise clients on how to plan and present their taxable income so that they legally pay the least tax possible.

Tax technicians work for firms of accountants or solicitors, in clearing banks and for consultancy firms that offer a complete tax service to their clients. However, the largest area of work involves corporate tax in organisations that have their own tax department to prepare corporate tax and VAT returns on behalf of the company.

Qualifications and Training

Many tax advisers qualify first as accountants, but a growing number begin with A levels as tax trainees. The Chartered Institute of Taxation offers a qualifying exam for candidates already qualified as accountants or lawyers. The Association of Taxation Technicians is a starting point for all other tax trainees, and offers an exam. This may be sufficient in itself for those candidates who do

info

Chartered Institute of Taxation, 12 Upper Belgrave Street, London SW1X 8BB; 020 7235 9381; fax: 020 7235 2562; www.tax.org.uk; e-mail: post@tax.org.uk

Association of Taxation Technicians, 12 Upper Belgrave Street, London SW1X 8BB; 020 7235 2544; fax: 020 7235 4571; www.att.org.uk; e-mail: info@att.org.uk

For a downloadable guide see: www.insidecareers.co.uk/tax

not expect to give detailed planning advice in their careers, or provide a stepping stone to the Institute's exam.

Personal Qualities and Skills

Tax advisers/technicians must be prepared for continuous professional development, be able to keep up to date with numerous tax changes, have an analytical mind, be able to apply lateral thinking and have good communication skills.

Starting Salary

The starting salary is similar to others in finance at £15,000+; those with experience earn high salaries.

Tax inspectors

Tax inspectors work for HM Revenue & Customs, formed from the merger of the Inland Revenue and HM Customs & Excise Departments. It is the government department responsible under the direction of the Treasury for the efficient administration of income tax, tax credits, corporation tax, capital gains tax, petroleum revenue tax, inheritance tax, National Insurance contributions and stamp duties. Inspectors are responsible for the tax affairs of businesses and individuals, ensuring they pay the right amount at the right time, helping them to obtain their entitlements and meet their obligations. Inspectors detect and deter non-compliance and encourage voluntary compliance by carrying out enquiry work.

Qualifications and Training

To join the Inspector Development Programme you must have a 1st or 2nd class honours degree, or have membership of one of the professional bodies for accountants in the UK. You can join as a Revenue Executive if you do not have a degree and it is then possible to gain promotion to the Inspector Development Programme after you have had some work experience and if you can demonstrate the appropriate competences. There is a lot of variation in different geographical regions on how easy it is to move onto the Inspection Development Scheme.

Personal Qualities and Skills

You have to be very good at analysing information and you must possess an enquiring mind and be able to adopt an imaginative approach to situations. You need good numeracy skills, and familiarity wlth IT, especially record and data management systems, is an advantage. You need to be an excellent communicator, with good interviewing skills.

Starting Salary

Starting pay for recruits joining the Inspector Development Programme is between £22,430 and £28,200 in London and £20,040 to £25,320 elsewhere. After four years, at the end of the training programme, you can expect to move into a pay band ranging from £42,250 to £54,170 in London and £37,630 to £47,590 elsewhere.

Chartered Institute of Public Finance & Accountancy (CIPFA), 3 Robert Street, London WC2N 6RL; Tel: 020 7543 5600; www.cipfa.org.uk

www.hmrc.gov.uk

TEACHING

Most formal teaching is done in schools, while lecturing is carried out in universities and other further and higher education establishments.

Lecturer

Further Education

Lecturers in this field may teach anyone over the age of 16. The range of subjects taught in further education is diverse and growing rapidly. Most lecturers have a particular expertise but are increasingly expected to teach outside their specialist area. They may work on vocational and/or academic courses. In order to meet the demands of their clients, further education colleges offer courses on a full- or part-time basis. These include evening courses and short courses.

Higher Education

Lecturers in universities and other higher education institutions (HEIs) teach mainly undergraduates. As well as teaching, many carry out research, write articles and books, give outside lectures and broadcasts. Competition is fierce and it is unlikely that a new graduate will be able to enter higher education as a first job.

Qualifications and Training

Lecturers in HEIs must have first- or upper-second class degrees; many have postgraduate qualifications, and some have further degrees. In the new universities, lecturers may be drawn from industry or commerce.

Qualifications for lecturers in further education vary, depending on the subject taught. A degree, a professional qualification and a teaching qualification are all acceptable and desirable. There are one-year full-time and two-year part-time courses available for those intending to teach in further education.

Personal Qualities and Skills

All teachers/lecturers must have a high level of knowledge of, and enthusiasm for, their subject, combined with a desire to communicate this to others. They must have the ability to organise and deliver their material in a way that is understandable to their students.

Starting Salary

Lecturers on a full-time contract earn between £24,886 and £29,800, and senior lecturers earn between £28,850 and £36,546. Many lecturers are not on full-time contracts and they are paid on a pro rata basis.

info

Lifelong Learning UK (LLUK), 4th Floor, 32 Farringdon Street, London EC4A 4HJ; 0207 332 9535; www.lifelonglearninguk.org

The Higher Education Academy, Innovation Way, York Science Park, Heslington, York YO10 5BR; 01904 717500; www.heacademy.ac.uk

Association of University Teachers (AUT), Egmont House, 25–31 Tavistock Place, London WC1H 9UT; 020 7670 9700; www.aut.org.uk

Teacher

Teaching offers a wide variety of openings working with children and young people of all ages and backgrounds.

The work of a teacher varies according to the age group being taught. Nursery and Foundation Stage teachers take the under-fives, Key Stage 1 primary teachers take five- to seven-year-olds and Key Stage 2 teachers take 7–11-year-olds. Secondary education (Key Stages 3 and 4) starts at 11 and continues (in some cases) to 18 or 19. In addition, teachers are needed in sixth-form colleges and the numerous further and higher education establishments. Teachers at primary level (up to age 11) generally teach a variety of basic subjects, and specialist subject teachers are not introduced until secondary level, although specialist music or sports teachers may be brought in at an earlier age.

The majority of pupils attend state schools, although there are also openings in private education. There are also opportunities for teachers in special schools: for the handicapped (either boarding or day establishments), for disturbed children (in community homes or approved schools), for those with special educational needs and in children's hospitals, where long-term patients are expected to take lessons.

Qualifications and Training

Anyone wishing to teach in a state-maintained school in England and Wales must normally hold Qualified Teacher Status (QTS), obtained by completing an approved course of initial teacher training (ITT). The two main routes to achieving QTS are: the Bachelor of Education (BEd) degree (some institutions offer a BA or BSc degree with QTS) – usually four years; or a subject degree appropriate for the national curriculum subject to be taught, followed by a postgraduate certificate in education (PGCE) – three years plus one year.

Graduate and Registered Teacher Programmes (GRTP) enable schools to employ people who are not yet qualified to teach and undertake training leading to QTS while working. The GRTP involves one year of postgraduate training and requires a first degree to qualify. The RTP requires applicants to have successfully completed two years of higher education (or the part-time equivalent) and to complete a degree while training. The GRTP cannot be undertaken in Scotland, and the General Teaching Council for Scotland does not currently accept teachers who have trained via the GRTP in England or Wales.

All applications for all training routes, regardless of subject or teaching level, must have attained the standard equivalent to at least grade C in both GCSE English language and maths. GCSE science is also required from those born after 1 September 1979 wanting to teach primary or middle school pupils. Entry requirements for BEd courses are five subjects at GCSE grades A to C, two of which must be at A level or equivalent.

While there are significant similarities between teaching in Scotland and teaching in England and Wales, there are also many differences, from entry into the profession to pay and conditions and continuing professional development. There are six teacher education institutions in Scotland: University of Paisley at the Ayr campus, University of Edinburgh, University of Glasgow, University of Strathclyde, Northern College at the Aberdeen and Dundee campuses (Dundee offers primary courses only).

Courses are at undergraduate and postgraduate level. All teachers in local authority schools in Scotland must be registered with the General Teaching Council for Scotland (GTCS). The GTCS is responsible for making the decision whether a teaching qualification attained outside Scotland is acceptable. The process is called Exceptional Admission.

Personal Qualities and Skills

Teachers need good academic ability; they must also be able to communicate their knowledge clearly and in an interesting fashion. They must also be able to establish a good relationships with pupils, parents of pupils and colleagues, and be prepared to take on considerable responsibility. Patience and a sense of humour are great assets.

Starting Salary

Newly qualified teachers (NQTs) in England, Wales and Northern Ireland start on the main salary scale of £18,558 to £27,123. Where you start on that scale is determined by your qualifications and experience. Salaries in Scotland are now very similar to those for the rest of the UK. After you have gained some experience you can apply to go onto a higher scale, which pays between £29,000 and £33,000. The highest salaries are paid in London and some other inner city areas.

info

Department for Education and Skills (DfES); Sanctuary Buildings, Great Smith Street, London SW1P 3BT; 0870 000 2288; www.dfes.gov.uk

General Teaching Council for Scotland (GTC), Clerwood House, 96 Clermiston Road, Edinburgh EH12 6UT; 0131 314 6000; www.gtcs.org.uk/

General Teaching Council for England (GTC), Whittington House, 19–30 Alfred Place, London WC1E 7EA; 020 7023 3909; www.gtce.org.uk/homepage.asp

GTTR (Graduate Teacher Training Registry), Rose Hill, New Barn Lane, Cheltenham, Glos GL52 3LZ; 0870 112 2205; www.gttr.ac.uk

Scottish Executive Education Department, Victoria Quay, Edinburgh EH6 6QQ; 0131 556 8400; www.scotland.gov.uk/Topics/Education

Training and Development Agency for Schools (TDA), Portland House, Bressenden Place, London SW1E 5TT; 0870 4960 123; www.tda.gov.uk

Teaching assistant

Teaching assistants or classroom assistants provide help and support for qualified teachers in the classroom. They can work in any school, but there are more employed at primary school level helping younger children with reading, writing and mathematics. They often provide particular support to children with special needs or whose first language is not English. They also help prepare lesson materials.

If a job ad describes the post as 'Learning Support Assistant' rather than a classroom or teaching assistant, the work involves supporting an individual child who has particular special needs, such as a sensory impairment, or a physical or psychological disability.

Qualifications and Training

At present, this varies from LEA (local education authority) to LEA, though the government does plan to introduce a standard training model. Many LEAs do not ask for any formal qualifications, but some ask for GCSEs in English and mathematics.

Personal Qualities and Skills

Teaching assistants must be able to build good relationships with children and have a lot of common sense. They should be able to work well as part of a team, and being imaginative and creative is also useful.

Starting Salary

Teaching assistants are often paid on an hourly rate and this is sometimes close to the minimum wage, though it can be £6.50 to £8.00 an hour. A lot of the work is part time and available only during term time.

TELECOMMUNICATIONS

The telecommunications industry continues to change and develop rapidly. Although there have been job cuts in this sector, there are still a large range of career opportunities. Deregulation of the industry around the world has resulted in many mergers and alliances to take advantage of the greater need for communications in business, as well as home use of the internet, digital TV and WAP cell phones.

Technicians

The sector recruits large numbers of hardware technicians and software engineers but telecommunications companies also employ people in accountancy, sales and marketing, training, finance, human resources and production planning.

Technicians in the industry are involved in finding faults in telecommunications systems and ensuring that networks and equipment are working properly. This includes installing, setting up, testing and repairing equipment in businesses or people's homes, such as phones, cable, satellite or digital TV, fax machines or computers. Some technicians install and maintain the communications links for power and rail companies. There are also opportunities for such work in the armed services. Engineers and IT specialists combine technical expertise with strategic vision to enhance existing services, particularly in mobile and internet technologies.

Qualifications and Training

Technicians normally need at least four GCSEs grades A–C or equivalent in maths, English, science and technology. Many have other qualifications such as a National Certificate or diploma in electronics or telecommunications technology. Modern Apprenticeships are available, as are NVQs in testing and approval, fitting, maintenance and operation of telecommunications switching, transmission, radio (or mobile telephones), cabling and power systems.

Engineers and IT specialists are normally graduates with relevant degrees in computer science, telecommunications or electronics. Graduates from a range of degree backgrounds are recruited as trainees to commercial posts.

Personal Qualities and Skills

An interest in technological developments, good communication and interpersonal skills and the ability to work as part of a team.

Starting Salary

Technicians start around £11,000 to £15,000 and with experience can earn from £20,000 to £30,000. Graduate trainees' salaries are around £18,000+.

British Telecom, 81 Newgate Street, British Telecom Centre, London EC1A 7AJ; 0207 356 5000; www.bt.com

Vodafone: www.vodafone.co.uk

Orange: www.orange.co.uk

T-Mobile: www.t-mobile.co.uk

Sector Skills Council for IT, Telecoms and Contact Centres, 1 Castle Lane, London SW1E 6DR; 020 7963 8920; fax: 020 7592 9138; www.e-skillsnto.org.uk; e-mail: info@e-skillsnto.org.uk

info

THEATRE

Theatre comprises much more than the actors and directors who receive the publicity. Many other people are involved in a theatrical production. Lighting and sound effects are created and handled by electricians; scenery and props are built, arranged and moved by technicians; the practical aspects of the production are organised and run by the stage manager and assistants. The designer creates the sets; the wardrobe mistress makes the costumes and the director or producer is responsible for the production as a whole. Other staff include the publicity officer, house manager and box office staff.

Actors

see Performing Arts

Box office

The box office is in charge of ticket sales. The manager is responsible for promotion and marketing, for hiring his or her staff and for checking the takings. Experience of accounts or general management is useful. This office makes a good starting place for anyone interested in arts administration.

Designer

The designer is responsible for sets and costumes, working closely with the director, and produces drawings of sets and costumes. The scenery and costume departments will work from these drawings and also from scale models of the sets.

Director

The director is in charge of the actors, dancers, designers, singers and technicians, working within the managerial brief and, in consultation with producer and playwright, responsible for casting. The director's main work is in taking rehearsals and in turning the play into a theatrical production. The casting director auditions actors and arranges financial details with the actors and their agents.

Lighting designer

The theatre electrician may be in sole charge of the lighting or, in a large company with sophisticated equipment, be part of a team headed by an expert who will design a lighting plan. Appropriate electrician's qualifications are needed.

Press office/marketing

These departments deal with publicity for the theatre. Press officers provide editorial content and liaise with the press, arrange for photo sessions and interviews. Staff often have a background in journalism or advertising. The marketing department produces posters, advertisements and programmes. An arts graduate with secretarial training may find work here. Tact, self-confidence and a pleasant voice are useful qualities.

Producer

The producer chooses the play, rents the theatre, engages the director and actors and is responsible for paying the bills. The producer is responsible for raising the money for the production.

Production manager/technical director

They are responsible for budgets, contracting and scheduling. This is a project management role and is usually a promotion from stage manager posts.

Production staff

A large theatre may have a series of production workshops; smaller theatres may combine several jobs in one:

- Armoury: the armoury is responsible for making armour or weapons, for special effects like gunfire and shells and for decorative metalwork. The members of the team are experts, for example gunsmiths.
- Carpenters' workshop: technical drawing and carpentry skills come in useful for building sets. RADA offers a course for theatre carpentry.
- Metal workshop: here the heavy metalwork is designed and manufactured, for example for steel supports and complex trees. A welding qualification is useful.
- Paint workshop: this is where the sets are painted. Knowing how to create the right textures and effects is part of the scene painter's skill.

- Property-making shop: properties are often bought but in many productions, some props – for example, a throne or special upholstery – have to be specially made. An enthusiasm for research and an eye for detail are needed.
- Wardrobe and wigs: although costumes and wigs may be hired, many are made by the wardrobe department. A good knowledge of period fashion and skills in dressmaking and tailoring are needed. Casual help is also needed when there is much sewing for a new production. Special hats are usually produced by a freelance milliner. Accessory making is another specialist job, as is wig and beard making, for which a City and Guilds certificate is a useful qualification. The wardrobe department is also responsible for looking after costumes and repairing and cleaning them.

Stage manager

The stage manager is responsible for the smooth running of rehearsals and productions, ensuring that properties and costumes are ready when required, that actors know when they are needed, for supervising lighting, scene making and scene changes, and responsible for effects, music, curtain calls and prompting. A stage manager will often have assistants (assistant stage managers, ASMs and deputy stage managers, DSMs) and will also be helped by scene shifters. A stage manager may sometimes become a producer or director.

Theatrical agent

Agents try to find work for the actors on their books. Experience and good contacts are essential. Payment is usually 10 to 15 per cent of the client's fee.

Qualifications and Training

Designer

Most designers will have completed a full-time art and design course.

Director

A thorough grounding in the dramatic arts is essential. A degree in drama is useful. There are a few trainee director posts, mostly under the auspices of the Arts Council. A director will have had extensive experience of the theatre, probably as a stage manager or acting. Some directors come to the theatre from film or television, which also offer training.

Production

NVQs are available at levels 1, 2 and 3 for theatre technicians.

Personal Qualities and Skills

Designer

A theatre designer needs a thorough knowledge of period settings and costumes, and what looks effective on stage, as well as a sense of style and an ability to work within a budget and adapt to a variety of stage shapes.

Director

Directors need creativity, strong character, the ability to direct and weld together a team of people and a strong sense of the theatre. The casting director needs tact and the ability to cope with crises.

Producer

Tact, persuasiveness, sound business sense, flair for organisation and knowledge of what 'sells' in the theatre are all necessary.

Stage Manager

Managers need organising ability, tact, calmness in a crisis, a good memory, an eye for detail, a practical approach and an interest in the literary and technical aspects of theatrical production.

Starting Salary

Salaries are generally low in this sector. Some of the work is part time, seasonal, or on short contracts, but salaries pro rata start at around £8,000, with £12,000 to £20,000 for more specialised jobs or for people with a lot of experience.

info

The Conference of Drama Schools, CDS Ltd, PO Box 34252, London NW5 1XJ; 020 7692 0032; www.drama.ac.uk

Creative and Cultural Skills: The Sector Skills Council for the Creative and Cultural Industries, 1 Marshall Court, Marshall Street, Leeds LS11 9YP; 0113 244 6879; www.cciskills.org.uk/

EQ: Diversity and Opportunity in Creative Industries, Suite E237, Dean Clough, Halifax, West Yorkshire HX3 5AX; 01422 381618; www.thinkeq.org.uk/

Equity – The British Actors Union, Guild House, Upper St Martins Lane, London WC2H 9EG; 020 7379 6000; www.equity.org.uk

National Council for Drama Training, 1–7 Woburn Walk, Bloomsbury, London WC1H 0JJ; 020 7387 3650; www.ncdt.co.uk

Royal Academy of Dramatic Art, 62–64 Gower Street, London WC1E 6ED; 020 7636 7076; www.rada.ac.uk

Royal National Theatre, South Bank, London SE1 9PX; 020 7452 3400; www.nationaltheatre.org.uk

Society of British Theatre Designers, 17 Bermondsey Street, London SE1 1XT; 020 7403 3778; www.theatredesign.org.uk

THERAPY

There is a vast range of therapeutic disciplines and treatments and below is a selection of the most popular and common ones.

Art therapy

Art therapy is used as a treatment for psychological and emotional disorders. Drawing, painting, modelling and sculpture are among the creative activities employed. Art therapy is a State Registered profession. All training courses need to be approved by the Council for Professions Supplementary to Medicine (CPSM) and the British Association of Art Therapy. Details are on the Health Professions Council website.

Most art therapists work in hospitals, some in special schools and child guidance clinics, and some in prisons, detention centres and community homes. As posts are often part time, therapists usually work for more than one institution within an area.

Qualifications and Training

Entry to postgraduate courses requires a degree in art and design or related subject, one year's clinical experience and a minimum age of 23. Candidates without a degree but with relevant working backgrounds are also considered. The postgraduate qualification is usually a two-year full-time course or a three-year part-time course.

Personal Qualities and Skills

Art therapists should have the ability to apply art in a practical way, together with a great deal of patience and the maturity to work with people in emotional or psychological need. A background in art practice is also necessary.

Starting Salary

Salaries start between £19,000 and £22,000, and unless you move into a management role they do not rise much above £24,000. These figures are based on National Health Service pay scales; you may be able to earn more working for other organisations and projects.

British Association of Art Therapists (BAAT), 24–27 White Lion Street, London N1 9PD; 020 7686 4216; www.baat.org

Health Professions Council (HPC), Park House, 184 Kennington Park Road, London SE11 4BU; 020 7582 0866; www.hpc-uk.org

The Institute for Arts in Therapy and Education (IATE), 2–18 Britannia Row, London N1 8PA; 020 7704 2534; www.artspsychotherapy.org

Dance/movement therapy

This form of therapy uses movement and dance as a medium through which the individual can engage creatively in a process of growth and personal integration. Dance movement therapists work with individuals and groups in health, education and social service settings. Their clients include people who are emotionally disturbed or have learning difficulties, and those who want to use this therapy for personal growth.

Qualifications and Training

A postgraduate qualification in dance music therapy is required. The University of Roehampton and Goldsmiths College both offer this qualification.

Personal Qualities and Skills

A good understanding of dance and movement and communication skills is needed, as is an understanding of the clinical environment.

Starting Salary

Salaries in the National Health Service are between £19,000 and £24,000. Some other organisations and projects may pay either a little more or a little less than this.

info

Association of Dance and Movement Therapists (ADMT), 32 Meadfoot Lane, Torquay TQ1 2BW; www.admt.org.uk

Health Professions Council (HPC), Park House, 184 Kennington Park Road, London SE11 4BU; 020 7582 0866; www.hpc-uk.org

Music therapist

Music therapy is an interactive, primarily non-verbal intervention. It provides a process through which clients can express themselves, become aware of their feelings and interact more easily. The therapist uses live, improvised music to draw the client into an interactive musical relationship. Therapists work with people of all ages, in a wide variety of settings, including special schools, psychiatric hospitals, hospices and day centres. Music therapy is used in many clinical areas, including communication disorders, developmental delay, learning disabilities, mental health problems, physical difficulties, emotional problems, challenging behaviour and terminal illness.

Qualifications and Training

Music therapy is a State Registered profession and the Council for Professions Supplementary to Medicine recommends that postgraduate students should be at least 23 years old. The training is a postgraduate diploma course lasting between one and two years. Some courses offer a part-time option. Before training as a music therapist, students need first to have completed a three-year musical training leading to a diploma or degree. People from related disciplines, such as psychology or education, may also sometimes be accepted onto a training course if they have sufficient practical musical skills.

Personal Qualities and Skills

Music therapists need to be highly skilled musicians, and be able to use music creatively. Therapists also need to develop an understanding of their own reactions and responses. For this reason, student therapists are required to have their own personal therapy during training. Training courses generally prefer students to be over 25 when they begin training.

Starting Salary

Starting salaries are in the region of £17,500 to £18,000.

info

Association of Professional Music Therapists, APMT Administrator, 61 Church Hill Road, East Barnet, Herts, EN4 8SY; 020 8440 4153; www.apmt.org; e-mail: APMToffice@aol.com

British Society for Music Therapy, 61 Church Hill Road, East Barnet, Herts, EN4 8SY; 020 8441 6226; fax: 020 8441 4118; www.bsmt.org; e-mail: info@bsmt.org

Occupational therapist

Occupational therapists work with people who have physical, mental or social problems, either from birth or as the result of accident, illness or ageing. Their aim is to enable people to achieve as much as they can for themselves. They start with a thorough assessment of each client and his or her lifestyle, in order to establish what the person wants to achieve. Treatment can involve adapting living and working environments, teaching coping strategies and discovering the most beneficial therapeutic activities.

Although occupational therapists often work as part of a team, they have more autonomy than other healthcare workers in the way they apply their knowledge and expertise. They work in hospitals, social service departments, individuals' homes, residential and nursing homes, schools, universities, charities and prisons. They may also work in private practice.

Employment and promotional opportunities are excellent and all UK-educated occupational therapists receive a qualification that is recognised by the World Federation of Occupational Therapists, giving them opportunities to work abroad.

Qualifications and Training

Entry to the profession is normally on completion of a full- or part-time degree in occupational therapy. Most courses require three A levels or equivalent; mature students will be considered without these academic requirements. Accelerated two-year full-time courses are also available to graduates of other disciplines. Part-time in-service programmes are also available for those employed as occupational therapy support workers or technical instructors. Some part-time courses can be studied irrespective of employment status. Although courses vary, all include the principles and practice of occupational therapy, behavioural, biological and medical sciences, and periods of clinical practice in a variety of hospital and community settings.

Personal Qualities and Skills

In addition to academic ability, potential occupational therapists require sensitivity, tolerance, problem-solving skills and the ability to work as part of a team. Reliability, honesty and patience are also important, as well as enthusiasm, dedication and the desire to help and care for others.

Starting Salary

£19,000 on entry for a graduate, rising to over £36,500 for the highest grade of occupational therapy managers. Additional allowances include London and fringe zone weightings, as well as stand-by and on-call payments.

info

British Association of Occupational Therapists, 106–114 Borough High Street, Southwark, London SE1 1LB; 020 7357 6480; www.baot.org.uk

Health Professions Council (HPC), Park House, 184 Kennington Park Road, London SE11 4BU; 020 7582 0866; www.hpc-uk.org

Speech and language therapist

Speech and language therapists (SLTs) identify, assess and treat people who have communication and/or swallowing disorders. A large proportion of these will be children but SLTs also help adults who may have communication or swallowing problems caused by disease, accident or psychological trauma. Some SLTs specialise in a particular patient group, for example in the areas of severe learning difficulties, hearing impairment or neurological disorders, while others choose more general, broad-based practice. The NHS is the largest employer of SLTs, working in community clinics, hospitals, special schools and homes for the mentally or physically disabled. Some of the larger voluntary organisations also employ SLTs. Often the SLT works closely in a team which may include members of the medical, teaching, therapeutic, psychological and other caring professions.

Qualifications and Training

Speech and language therapy is a degree-entry profession. Courses leading to professional qualifications are offered at 15 universities and colleges of higher education throughout the UK. There are a number of two-year postgraduate diploma and Master's courses available to candidates with relevant degrees.

Entry qualifications for courses vary from one institution to another, but the minimum is five GCSEs and two A levels or equivalent. A good balance of language and science is expected. Other equivalent qualifications are considered on merit. All courses will consider applications from mature students (over 21), who are encouraged to apply in the normal way.

Students who successfully pass all academic and clinical components of an accredited course are eligible to obtain a certificate to practise and to enter the professional register of the Royal College of Speech and Language Therapists as full professional members.

Opportunities also exist to work as a speech therapist's assistant. An NVQ in care at level 3 is available.

Personal Qualities and Skills

It is essential that speech therapists themselves should have clear speech and be able to listen actively. In addition, they must have an interest in people as individuals, as well as an enquiring mind, initiative, patience, imagination and a willingness to take responsibility.

Starting Salary

£19,000–24,000.

Royal College of Speech and Language Therapists, 2 White Hart Yard, London SE1 1NX; 020 7378 1200; www.rcslt.org; e-mail: postmaster@rcslt.org

NHS Careers, PO Box 376, Bristol BS99 3EY; Careers helpline: 0845 6060 655; www.nhscareers.nhs.uk

Therapy assistant

Occupational, physiotherapy and speech and language therapy departments in hospitals and clinics employ assistants in each of these three professional areas. The work of assistants varies according to which profession they are working in, but there are many common features of their work. They may carry out introductory interviews with patients, though they cannot make formal assessments or plan treatment programmes. They help patients with programmes of exercises or other activities once these have been planned by a qualified therapist. They observe and monitor patients during exercises or other activities and they may be required to do some administrative work.

Qualifications and Training

These vary between different hospitals and healthcare trusts and within the three disciplines concerned. While there are no standardised formal entry qualifications, most applicants have at least five GCSEs including English, maths and a science. Many have A levels, and some applicants with degrees enter this work. Many people do it after A levels to gain experience of a healthcare profession before progressing to higher education and a career as a healthcare professional. A great deal of training is provided on the job, working with professionals, and there are also a variety of NVQs available at levels 2, 3 and 4.

Personal Qualities and Skills

You need to have excellent interpersonal skills, be kind, patient and understanding, but also able to be firm and positive. You must be practical so that you can handle technical equipment, and be physically fit, emotionally robust and keenly observant. An interest in medicine and science is essential.

Starting Salary

Since the major National Health Service salary review, Agenda for Change, in 2005, there is a lot of variation in individual pay according to your level of skills and experience and your range of responsibilities. A typical starting salary range for assistant is £14,000 to £18,000.

info

Skills for Health, 1st Floor, Goldsmiths House, Broad Plain, Bristol BS2 0JP; 0147 822 1155; www.skillsforhealth.org.uk

Health Professions Council (HPC), Park House, 184 Kennington Park Road, London SE11 4BU; 020 7582 0866; www.hpc-uk.org

British Association of Occupational Therapists, 106–114 Borough High Street, Southwark, London SE1 1LB; 020 7357 6480; www.baot.org.uk

Chartered Society of Physiotherapists, 14 Bedford Row, London WC1R 4ED; 0207 306 666; www.csp.org.uk

Royal College of Speech and Language Therapists (RCSLT), 2 White Hart Yard, London SE1 1NX; 020 7378 1200; www.rcslt.org.uk

Local hospital occupational therapy, physiotherapy and speech and language therapy departments

TOWN AND COUNTRY PLANNER

Planners are concerned with reconciling the needs of the population for buildings, shopping centres, schools and leisure centres with the necessity of preserving and enhancing the natural and built environment. They collect information about the present use of land, the position of roads and other features, as well as drawing up plans for new schemes. Planners in development control ensure that buildings or developments intended for a particular area are suitable and do not conflict with existing buildings or the surrounding environment. Planners work for local and central government, environmental agencies, and to an increasing extent in private practice. There are also varied opportunities for planning support staff.

Qualifications and Training

To enter a degree or diploma course in town planning, five GCSE passes and two A levels are desirable. Useful subjects include maths, English language, geography and history or a foreign language. Those with Royal Town Planning Institute (RTPI)-accredited degrees or diplomas in town planning have satisfied the academic requirement for election to corporate membership of the Institute. To achieve membership, these candidates also need to be able to demonstrate two years' experience in town and country planning. Planning courses are available at undergraduate and postgraduate levels, full- and part-time and on a distance-learning basis.

Planning support staff are normally expected to have good GCSE grades in English, maths and other appropriate subjects, but relevant experience might be a deciding factor for more mature candidates. There are colleges that offer courses for support staff on a part-time or block-release basis. Qualifications gained are the Edexcel (BTEC) certificate, higher certificate or higher diploma in planning or the SQA certificate or higher certificate in planning. An NVQ at level 3 in town planning support is also available for support staff.

Personal Qualities and Skills

Town planners and support staff need to have a knowledge of many subjects: economics, sociology, architecture and geography. Planners must be able to work in a team and cooperate with experts in other subjects. Planners need to take advice and opinions from many different people, and therefore need to be able to reconcile the conflicting views of various interest groups. They must be good communicators and have imagination, and an interest in, and understanding of, both people and the environment.

Starting Salary

Qualified planners about £12,000–19,000, support staff £9,000–15,000 upwards depending on qualifications and experience.

Royal Town Planning Institute, 41 Botolph Lane, London EC3R 8DL; 020 7929 9494; fax: 020 7929 9490; www.rtpi.org.uk; e-mail: careers@rtpi.org.uk.

A downloadable brochure about *Careers in Town Planning and Town Planning Support* is available from RTPI website.

TRADING STANDARDS OFFICER

Trading standards officers are employed by local authorities and responsible for enforcing a very wide range of legislation aimed at protecting consumers and traders. Laws relate to food and consumer product safety, credit, descriptions of goods and services, prices, animal health and welfare. While most operations are carried out through random inspections, officers are also required to investigate complaints and, where appropriate, take matters to court.

Qualifications and Training

The most common route to qualification is via one of the four approved degree courses in consumer protection run in the UK. Non-graduates can get into this work, but only if they have considerable relevant experience. Trading Standards Departments employ assistants who work with trading standards officers; these roles include consumer protection advisers and fair trading officers. Entry qualifications for these posts are more flexible, and from this work you can train as a trading standards officer through a combination of day release, block release and distance learning. All trading standards officers must take the Diploma in Trading Standards, though a degree in consumer protection gives you several exemptions from the diploma examinations. With an appropriate degree, training takes around 18 months, otherwise it takes three to four years.

Personal Qualities and Skills

You need to have a broad range of skills including very good communication skills, be able to interview effectively and be confident if appearing in court. You need good practical skills for using special weighing machines and other technical equipment, and you should be very well organised and able to work as part of a team, but also to use your initiative.

Starting Salary

Salaries for trainees range from £16,000 to £18,000, and from £20,000 to £26,000 once you have qualified.

info

Trading Standards Institute, First Floor, 1 Sylvan Court, Sylvan Way, Southfields Business Park, Basildon, Essex SS15 6TH; 0870 872 9000; 0870 872 9017 (careers information); fax: 0870 872 9025; www.tradingstandards.gov.uk; e-mail: institute@tsi.org.uk

Local government careers; www.LGcareers.com – for further careers information; www.LGjobs.com – for current job vacancy adverts in local councils all over the country

TRAFFIC WARDEN

Traffic wardens are civilians who work in conjunction with local police forces. They check parking meters and penalise drivers parking on double yellow lines or in other illegal places. They may also be required to do school crossing patrols or traffic control duty, as well as receiving vehicles towed into the police pound and looking out for out-of-date car licences.

Qualifications and Training

Each Police Authority sets its own entry requirements, but there is usually no need to have formal educational qualifications; instead you have to pass a written test, which includes maths and English. Training is on-the-job, sometimes being supervised by a police officer, and many areas send you on a short, introductory course.

Personal Qualities and Skills

You need to be calm, confident and possess a degree of common sense to do this work. You should be a good communicator, able to deal with aggression without becoming aggressive yourself.

Starting Salary

Salaries vary between geographical locations, with London salaries being the highest. The general range is between £15,000 and £18,000.

UK Police Service Portal;
www.police.uk

Police Recruitment;
www.policecouldyou.co.uk

Metropolitan Police;
www.met.careers.co.uk

TRAVEL AND TOURISM

Occupations in the travel and tourism sector cover being involved in arranging travel and accommodation for business and pleasure, and providing information on places of interest. It also includes work for airlines.

Airline staff

There are two sides to working for airlines: in front of the public such as with cabin crew and check-in staff, and behind-the-scenes staff such as reservations and cabin crew support.

Cabin crew support collate the information that is required to fly an aircraft. They plan the fuel required, organise crew rosters, book overnight hotels and much more.

A despatcher is employed to make sure the plane leaves on time, and checks that the passengers are alerted and that food and drink has been delivered to the plane. The despatcher also oversees the boarding of passengers.

Ground operations staff load and unload baggage, marshall aircraft into parking positions and oversee toilet and water services.

Cabin crew secure the safety of the passengers and are the most visible element of the airline team. During the flight they serve food and drink and sell duty-free goods.

Training and Qualifications

Most airlines have induction programmes specific to the type of work applied for. Airlines look for students who have taken relevant preliminary training such as the air cabin crew NVQ, languages, or a good marketing or business course. First aid courses are also useful to have on your CV.

Cabin crew need good health and must be over 5 ft 2 in. They also need to be able to swim (a legal requirement). Language qualifications are also essential for most airlines.

Personal Qualities and Skills

Good communication skills and being able to handle the public are essential. Staying calm in stressful situations is also necessary. Cabin crew support staff need to demonstrate reliability.

Starting Salary

Flight planning officer £15,784 plus shift allowances, cabin crew starting £12,000 rising to £25,000 plus subsidies.

info

Aviation Training Association, Dralda House, Crendon Street, High Wycombe HP13 6LS; www.aviation-training.org (this organisation has ceased operation but its website remains with a useful list of resources)

British Airports Authority; 0845 6060234; www.baa.co.uk

Careers and Jobs in Travel and Tourism (Kogan Page)

Tour managers

Tour managers are employed by major tour companies as official guides for parties of tourists travelling with them. The manager is responsible for the welfare of the tourists and must deal with any worries or complaints. In addition, managers are responsible for all the paperwork necessary when the party stays overnight in a hotel or crosses a border. Much of the work is seasonal and generally only senior staff are employed on a permanent basis.

Qualifications and Training

A good general education including GCSE passes in English, geography and maths is usually required by the travel trade. Qualifications in relevant languages and experience of living and working abroad are an obvious advantage; a manager on a particular tour will need an insight into local customs and fluency in the relevant languages. Most training takes place on the job and there are NVQs available.

Personal Qualities and Skills

Tour managers must have patience, tact and a pleasant personality. They need to be able to get on with a wide variety of people of all nationalities and from all walks of life, without becoming flustered or panic-stricken in a crisis.

Starting Salary

Around £150+ a week with full accommodation. There are also opportunities to earn more money by organising extra trips for the tourists.

info

Institute of Travel and Tourism, Studio 3, Mill Studio, Crane Mead, Ware, Herts SG12 9PY; 0870 770 7960; fax: 0870 770 7961; www.itt.co.uk; e-mail: enquiries@itt.co.uk

TTC Training, The Cornerstone, The Broadway, Woking, Surrey GU21 5AR; 01483 727321; fax: 01483 756698; www.ttctraining.co.uk; e-mail: info@ttctraining.co.uk

Major tour operators

Careers and Jobs in Travel and Tourism (Kogan Page)

Tourism officer

Tourism officers work for national or regional tourist boards and local authorities with the aim of attracting visitors to Britain or to a particular region. The work includes promoting attractions, working with press and public relations agencies, designers and photographers to advertise local features, researching local history to develop new attractions, and participating in exhibitions both nationally and overseas to promote the area. They work closely with businesses in attracting holidaymakers, tour operators, exhibitions and conferences to the area, and research future trends and needs. They are also responsible for overseeing the council's tourist information offices.

Qualifications and Training

Having a degree or HND in a business- or tourism-related subject can be an advantage, but personal qualities and proven business skills are just as important. NVQs in tourist information at levels 2–3 are available.

Previous tourist information centre experience, paid or voluntary, is invaluable. Marketing, travel agency or other retail experience is advantageous.

Personal Qualities and Skills

Good communication skills are essential, as are marketing and promotional experience and skills, including the ability to be creative, and write snappy copy to promote the area and various events. Excellent organisational skills and the ability to get on with a wide cross-section of people, from business leaders and councillors to residents and visitors, are important. A knowledge of languages, geography, history or archaeology can be an advantage for some posts.

Starting Salary

£12,000–14,000 for graduate entrants.

info

Local Government Careers; www.LGcareers.com – for further careers information; www.LGjobs.com – for current job vacancy adverts in local councils all over the country

National and local tourist boards

Institute of Travel and Tourism, Studio 3, Mill Studio, Crane Mead, Ware, Herts SG12 9PY; 0870 770 7960; fax: 0870 770 7961; www.itt.co.uk; e-mail: enquiries@itt.co.uk

TTC Training, The Cornerstone, The Broadway, Woking, Surrey GU21 5AR; 01483 727321; fax: 01483 756698; www.ttctraining.co.uk; e-mail: info@ttctraining.co.uk

Careers and Jobs in Travel and Tourism (Kogan Page)

Travel agent

Travel agents sell tickets for travel by air, land and sea on behalf of transport organisations. They make hotel bookings for individual travellers, business people or holidaymakers. Some travel companies deal only with business travel, and are also involved in arranging conferences and trade fairs. However, travel agents are best known for selling package holidays on behalf of tour operators. Many travel agents will also advise travellers on visas, foreign currency and necessary injections.

Qualifications and Training

Modern Apprenticeships and NVQ qualifications are available. No specific qualifications are asked for but GCSEs in maths, English and geography are an advantage. Computer literacy is becoming increasingly important.

info

Local Job Centre Plus and Careers/Connexions Centres

Institute of Travel and Tourism, Studio 3, Mill Studio, Crane Mead, Ware, Herts SG12 9PY; 0870 770 7960; fax: 0870 770 7961; www.itt.co.uk; e-mail: enquiries@itt.co.uk

TTC Training, The Cornerstone, The Broadway, Woking, Surrey GU21 5AR; 01483 727321; fax: 01483 756698; www.ttctraining.co.uk; e-mail: info@ttctraining.co.uk

Careers and Jobs in Travel and Tourism (Kogan Page)

Personal Qualities and Skills

Travel agents must enjoy dealing with the general public, and have a responsible attitude regarding the accuracy of information given, and good administrative and ICT skills.

Starting Salary

Varies according to job; assistants earn £8,000–13,000, managers £15,000+.

UNDERTAKER

see Funeral Director

UNDERWRITER

see Insurance

VALUER

see Land and Property

VETERINARY SCIENCE

(*see also* Animals)

Veterinary science is concerned with the care of animals, including both farm animals and domestic pets.

Veterinary nurse

Veterinary nurses (VNs) assist vets during operations and X-rays, sterilise instruments, look after animals recovering from surgery, and keep the animals and their cages clean. After qualification, the work of a veterinary nurse can include practice management, staff supervision, teaching and training other nurses or support staff. Some VNs choose to work outside veterinary practice in research establishments, colleges, zoos and breeding or boarding kennels.

Qualifications and Training

Entry requirements are five GCSEs at grade C or above, including English language and two passes in a physical or biological science and maths. Equivalent qualifications are accepted at the discretion of the Royal College of Veterinary Surgeons Review Officer. Alternatively, the British Veterinary Nursing Association's pre-veterinary nursing course, approved by the RCVS, enables the holder to enrol on to the veterinary nursing scheme without other GCSEs. A qualified nurse can go on to study for an advanced diploma in veterinary nursing (surgical and medical).

A BSc degree in veterinary nursing is available at a small number of universities and agricultural colleges. Entry requirements are at least two A levels or equivalent. A science subject is preferred.

Personal Qualities and Skills

You have to love animals and be calm, kind and patient when handling them. You have to be able to deal with sad or distressing situations and you must be able to communicate with people as well as their pets. You need to be practical, with an interest in science, and you can't be the least bit squeamish.

Starting Salary

Salaries start at close to £10,000 and once you are fully qualified and have some experience they rise to £16,000, though only a few veterinary practices would pay at this higher rate.

info

British Veterinary Nursing Association (BVNA), Suite 11, Shenval House, South Road, Harlow, Essex CM20 2BD; 01279 450567; fax: 01279 420866; www.bvna.org.uk; e-mail: bvna@bvnaoffice.plus.com

Royal College of Veterinary Surgeons, Belgravia House, 62–64 Horseferry Road, London SW1P 2AF; 020 7222 2001; www.rcvs.org.uk; e-mail: admin@rcvs.org.uk

Careers Working with Animals (Kogan Page)

Veterinary surgeon

Most vets work in private practice, usually starting out as a veterinary assistant and working their way up into a partnership or into their own business. Some specialise in small-animal treatment, including pets such as dogs, cats and birds, while others work with particular kinds of animals such as farm animals, racehorses or the more exotic zoo animals. Other vets go into research or industry. The Ministry of Agriculture, for instance, employs a substantial number to work on disease control, monitoring such epidemics as foot and mouth or swine vesicular disease. Others are employed by animal welfare organisations, such as the PDSA, in animal hospitals. Vets are also needed in the food-processing industries where their job is concerned with checking that conditions are humane and hygienic.

Qualifications and Training

A veterinary surgeon must hold a degree from one of the six veterinary schools in the UK. The six universities offering the course set their own entrance requirements but all demand an extremely high standard of A level passes or equivalent. Chemistry is essential, and other useful subjects are physics, maths, biology and zoology. The course lasts five years (six at Cambridge), and covers a formidable amount of academic and practical work, comparable to that needed to be a doctor.

Personal Qualities and Skills

Vets need to be sympathetic but detached. They must be excellent communicators, explaining and reassuring pet owners and farmers. Patience, calmness and, later on, a good business sense and problem-solving skills are also important.

Starting Salary

A newly qualified vet earns around £20,000 and with a few years' experience this rises to between £25,000 and £30,000. Many vets become partners in a business or run their own business, and can earn more than £45,000.

Royal College of Veterinary Surgeons, Belgravia House, 62–64 Horseferry Road, London SW1P 2AF; 020 7222 2001; www.rcvs.org.uk; e-mail: admin@rcvs.org.uk

WATCH AND CLOCK MAKER/REPAIRER

Watch and clock makers make timepieces by hand, sometimes to a design of their own.

Repairers receive watches and clocks from customers for servicing and repair. They must be able to examine a timepiece thoroughly for worn-out parts, clean and regulate a watch or clock, and repair or replace faulty parts. The work involves the use of precision tools and electronic equipment. Restoration is carried out on antique clocks and watches.

Qualifications and Training

The British Horological Institute (BHI) coordinates all watch and clock training organisations. A two-year HND in horology is available from the University of Central England. Applicants need three GCSEs, including maths and English, or to have completed the preliminary year of the BHI course. A one-year course in antique clock repair and restoration is offered by West Dean College in Chichester. St Loye's College in Exeter provides residential training in horology for students with disabilities.

The BHI also offers correspondence courses at preliminary, intermediate and final level which cover all aspects of horology from watch repairs, clocks, electric, electronic to heavy turret and master clocks. These courses lead up to internationally recognised qualifications.

Personal Qualities and Skills

Mathematical and drawing ability as well as dexterity are important. Applicants must have good eyesight, the physical skill and patience to do the intricate work required, and be able to work alone.

Starting Salary

Many horologists are self-employed and earnings vary enormously, starting from £8,000 to over £20,000 for those who have experience and a specialism.

info

British Horological Institute, Upton Hall, Upton, Newark, Nottinghamshire NG23 5TE; 01636 813795; fax: 01636 812258; www.bhi.co.uk; e-mail: info@bhi.co.uk

WELFARE ADVICE WORK

Advice worker

Advice workers assist their clients by providing information and confidential advice on a wide range of issues including debt, employment, housing, social security, education, immigration or legal issues. They either work in general advice centres such as Citizens Advice Bureaux, or in specialist services offering advice on one or more specific areas. Some advice workers are based in universities, colleges or various local authority departments.

Qualifications and Training

There are no specific entry requirements, though many applicants do have degrees, particularly in social science or psychology. Much of the training is on the job and there are some part-time diploma courses in advice work available at a few universities and colleges.

Personal Qualities and Skills

Getting on with people, being well organised and very good at researching answers to questions are all important in this work.

Starting Salary

Salaries tend to be fairly low for this work: £8,500 to £12,000 is typical. Where management and other responsibilities go with the work, up to £16,000 is more likely.

info

Federation of Independent Advice Centres (FIAC), 12th Floor, New London Bridge House, London Bridge Street, London SE1 9ST; 020 7407 4070; www.fiac.org.uk

Law Centres Federation, Duchess House, 18–19 Warren Street, London W1T 5RL; 020 7387 8570; www.information@lawcentres.org.uk

National Association of Citizens Advice Bureaux (NACAB), 115–123 Pentonville Road, London N1 9LZ; 020 7833 2181; www.nacab.org.uk

WINE TRADE

The wine trade has grown beyond the small merchant or importer, and most opportunities are now with large companies which import, retail and deal with the licensed trade, hotels and catering, off-licences, supermarkets and multiple stores. There are posts in marketing, advertising, packaging, promotion, market research, buying and quality control.

Qualifications and Training

Opportunities exist at GCSE, A and degree level for entry into the wine trade. On-the-job training is provided by the Wine and Spirit Education Trust (WSET), a registered educational charity set up by the drinks industry. They offer level 1 Foundation Certificate, Higher Certificate and Diploma courses. The University of Brighton offers a two-year full-time HND in wine studies.

Personal Qualities and Skills

These depend on the area entered, but a love and knowledge of wine are obviously important, plus relevant knowledge about the chief wine-growing areas, and their type of soil and climate. Tasters need a discriminating sense of taste and smell. Language skills can be an advantage.

Starting Salary

Trainee managers start on around £12,000 to £15,000 a year. Experienced wine merchants or managers earn £18,000 to £25,000. A highly successful and knowledgeable wine merchant can earn much more than this.

WRITER

For writers other than journalists, making a living purely from writing can be very difficult, so many writers, especially before they are established, have other careers as well. There are only a handful of people who become successful fiction writers or writers of really popular non-fiction such as biographies. There are some jobs for writers in residence with theatre companies and regional arts organisations, prisons or university departments, but many of these posts are temporary contracts.

Technical authors write user manuals and instruction books for anything from washing machines to computer software, and there are writers who specialise in writing textbooks and other teaching materials. Technical authors are often on permanent, or at least more secure contracts. Many writers of textbooks have other jobs in education.

Society of Authors, 84 Drayton Gardens, London SW10 9SB; 020 7373 6642; fax: 020 7373 5768; www.societyofauthors.net; e-mail: info@societyofauthors.net

Writers Guild, 15 Britannia Street, London WC1X 9JN, 020 7833 0777; fax: 020 7833 4777; www.writersguild.org.uk; e-mail: admin@writersguild.org.uk

Writers' and Artists' Yearbook (A&C Black); *The Writers' Handbook* (Macmillan)

Qualifications and Training

Generally writers are born, not made. However, it is possible to take courses in both creative and technical writing.

Personal Qualities and Skills

Writers must be self-disciplined, able to work on their own, highly motivated and persevering.

Starting Salary

Earnings vary enormously, but the majority of writers do not support themselves by their writing alone. Writers in residence can expect about £14,000–20,000. Technical authors earn £13,000–30,000.

YOUTH WORK

Personal adviser (Connexions)

Personal advisers are drawn from a variety of backgrounds, such as careers advice and guidance, youth work, health service, social services, youth justice and education. The Connexions service aims to provide a coherent system of support for young people in their transition to adulthood and working life. It came into operation in all areas of England in 2003 and is staffed by a network of personal advisers whose aim is to help 13- to 19-year-olds achieve their full potential by addressing barriers to learning. Some personal advisers may specialise in working with those who need additional support because of problems such as homelessness, mental illness or substance abuse.

The work of individual advisers will depend on their clients, and involve work with other agencies to broker access to specialist services. Most of an adviser's time will be spent in direct contact with young people, but some time will also be spent liaising with other organisations, working with parents and carers, and promoting links with the local community. There is also a certain amount of administrative work – producing accurate and up-to-date records to be shared with other professionals.

They are based in a variety of settings, including schools, colleges, youth and community centres and Connexions offices. At times, advisers may be called out to deal with crises in young people's lives. Most jobs will involve evening and weekend work. Some Connexions Partnerships will provide services during the evening and overnight, to respond to the needs of young people.

Qualifications and Training

To become a fully qualified personal adviser it is necessary to hold a relevant qualification at S/NVQ level 4, or equivalent, although some personal advisers will be working towards this level during training en route to qualified status. In addition, all personal advisers will be required to attend either the Diploma for Connexions Personal Advisers or the Understanding Connexions training programme.

The minimum age for entry to training is normally 21 and a driving licence is usually required. All candidates undergo police checks, so anyone with a conviction for a crime against children is barred from this type of work.

Personal Qualities and Skills

Advisers need strong communication and relationship-building skills to engage the trust and respect of young people. They need to be able to listen carefully and respond appropriately; a non-judgemental approach is essential. Personal advisers need to empathise with young people's concerns while maintaining professional and emotional detachment. A sense of humour, reliability, flexibility, good time management and team-working skills are also important.

Starting Salaries

Salaries vary between individual Connexions Partnerships. Trainees may start on £14,000 to £15,000; qualified staff with the Diploma for Personal Advisers between £19,000 to £21,000 (£23,000 to £25,500 in London).

Connexions website:
www.connexions.gov.uk

Local Connexions Partnership

Youth and community worker

Youth work promotes young people's personal and social development, provides support to help them achieve and progress into independence, and enables young people to have a voice in their communities and in society. This is accomplished through work with individuals, with and in groups, and with communities. In many instances youth workers work in partnership with professionals from other sectors, such as schools and colleges, careers, health organisations, the police and social services.

Youth and community workers work in a range of settings, including youth clubs, schools, colleges, community centres, as personal advisers within the Connexions Service and other specialist agencies offering information, advice and counselling. Some workers also work in mobile centres and with young people on the streets and in cafés. There are currently around 3,000 full-time youth workers employed in England and a far larger number of part-time and volunteer youth workers. The introduction of the Connexions Service in England, which offers advice, information and guidance to young people aged 13–19, has led to substantial numbers of new posts for people with youth work skills.

In Scotland, youth and community work is combined with adult education under the generic term 'community education'.

Qualifications and Training

For those seeking qualification as a full-time, nationally qualified youth worker, various routes, including full-time and part-time diploma and degree courses, postgraduate courses, and distance learning exist. Detailed information on courses can be obtained from the National Youth Agency, directly or via its website. Details of training and employment in Scotland and Wales can be obtained from Community Learning Scotland and the Wales Youth Agency, respectively.

NVQs in community work are available at levels 2/3 and 4. There is normally a minimum age requirement varying from 19 to 21 (18 for some degree courses), and applicants are usually expected to have substantial experience of work with young people or adults in community settings. This can be paid or unpaid. Mature entrants may be accepted without formal academic qualifications.

Personal Qualities and Skills

An interest in and understanding of the issues that affect people's lives, plus patience, stamina and a sense of humour are all qualities demanded of youth and community workers. They must also be able to plan, record and evaluate their work.

Starting Salary

Salaries of £16,000 to £23,000 are paid by local authorities, £12,000+ in the voluntary sector.

info

National Youth Agency, 17–23 Albion Street, Leicester LE1 6GD; 0116 285 3700; fax: 0116 285 3777; www.nya.org.uk; e-mail: nya@nya.org.uk

Community Learning Scotland, Rosebery House, 9 Haymarket Terrace, Edinburgh EH12 5EZ; 0131 313 2488; fax: 0131 313 6800; www.communitylearning.org; e-mail: info@cls.dircon.co.uk

Wales Youth Agency, Leslie Court, Lon-y-Llyn, Caerphilly CF83 1BQ; 029 2085 5700; fax: 02920 855701; www.wya.org.uk; e-mail: way@way.org.uk

YouthLink Scotland, Rosebery House, 9 Haymarket Terrace, Edinburgh EH12 5EZ; 0131 313 2488; fax: 0131 313 6800; www.youthlink.co.uk; e-mail: info@youthlink.co.uk

Z

ZOOLOGY

Zoo keeper

see Animals

Zoologist

Zoologists work in either research or teaching. Zoologists study anatomy, physiology, classification, distribution, behaviour and environment of all kinds of animals, from insects to elephants. When working in zoos, they usually coordinate conservation breeding programmes, collection planning and general conservation strategies. A very small number find jobs in industry, mainly in pharmaceutical and animal foodstuff companies. Research zoologists will probably work in one of the many government-backed centres on a variety of projects, including animal behaviour, pest control and the population ecology of birds.

Qualifications and Training

A degree in zoology, available at some universities, is needed for a career as a zoologist. Postgraduate training in specialisations such as entomology or nematology is also available.

Personal Qualities and Skills

Zoologists should have a scientific mind and an interest in research. They should also have keen powers of observation and be patient and confident.

Starting Salary

£15,000 upwards.

Institute of Biology, 20–22 Queensberry Place, London SW7 2DZ; 020 7581 8333; fax: 020 7823 9409; www.iob.org; e-mail: info@iob.org

Index

abbreviations viii
accountancy 1, 4, 8 *see also* taxation
  accountants 1, 4, 8
  accounting technician 8
actor *see* performing arts
actuary 9, 12
advertising 12–14 *see also* marketing; marketing researcher *and* public relations officer
  account executive 12
  account planner 12
  art editor/executive director 12
  artist 13 *see also* art and design
  copywriter and scriptwriter 13
  media executive 13
aerial erector 14
agriculture 15 *see also* farming
  agricultural contractor 15
  agricultural engineering *see* engineering
  agricultural surveying *see* surveying
ambulance service 16–18
  care assistants 16
  control and communication 16
  emergency medical dispatcher 17–18
  paramedics 16
  technicians 16
animals 18–27 *see also* veterinary science *and* zoology
  animal groomer 18–19
  animal technician 19–20
  dog trainer 20–21
  groom 21–22
  kennel work 22–23
  jockey 23, 24
  riding instructor 25
  RSPCA inspector 25–26
  stable lad 24
  zoo keeper 26–27
anthropologist 27–28
antique dealer 28
archaeology 29
  archaeological surveying *see* surveying
architecture 30–32 *see also* modelmaker
  architect 30–31
  architectural technologist 31–32
archivist 32–33
Army 34–35
art and design 35–40
  art therapist 40 *see also* therapy
  artist 35–36
  graphic designer 36
  illustrator 37
  industrial product designer 37–38
  interactive media design 38–39 *see also* information and communication technology
  interior designer 39 *see also* interior decorator
  signwriter 40
arts administration 40–41
astronomer 41–42
auctioneer 42 *see also* land and property
audiology technician 43

banking and finance 44–50
  banking 44–46
  building societies 46–47
  economist *see main entry*
  financial adviser 47–48
  investment work 48–49
  stockbroker 50
beauty 50–53
  make-up artist 52
  sales consultant 50–51
  therapist 51 *see also* hairdresser
biology 53–55
  biochemist 53–54
  biomedical scientist 54–55
  biotechnologist 55
book publishing *see* publishing: books
bookmaker 56
bookseller 56–57
brewing 57–58
broadcasting 58–63
  assistant floor manager and floor assistant 58
  audio assistant 58
  broadcast engineer 58
  camera operator 59
  costume designer 59
  costume dressmaker 59
  director 59
  dresser 59
  film editor/video editor 59
  floor manager 60
  journalist/reporter 60 *see also* journalism

producer 60
producer's assistant 60
production assistant 60
programme assistant 61
sound operator 61
studio manager 61
television make-up and hairdressing 61 *see also* beauty
vision mixer 61–62
business administration 63–68
company secretary 63–64
personal assistant 64–65
receptionist 65–66
secretary 66–67

call/contact centre 69–70
cardiac technologist 70–71
careers adviser 71–72
carpentry 72–73 *see also* construction
cabinet maker 72–73
carpet fitter 73–74
cartography 74–76
cartographer 74–75
Ordnance Survey work 75–76
catering *see* hospitality and catering
chemistry 76–77
analyst 76
chemist 76–77
child care 77–81
childminder 77–79
nursery nurse 79–80
pre-school workers 80–81
chiropodist (or podiatrist) 81–82
civil aviation 82–86
aeronautical engineer 82
air cabin crew 83, 84, 85
air traffic control 83, 84, 85
air traffic engineer 84, 85
aircraft maintenance engineer 83, 84, 85 *see also* engineering
pilot 84, 85
Civil Service 86–89
administrative staff 87
Diplomatic Service 87–88
professionally qualified staff 88
scientific staff 88–89
clothing industry 89–91 *see also* fashion
pattern cutter/grader 90
pattern cutter/spreader 91
coastguard 92
colour science and technology 93
complementary medicine 94–101
acupuncturist 94–95
aromatherapist 95
chiropractor 96–97
homeopath 97–98
massage therapist 98
naturopath 99
osteopath 100
reflexology 101
computing *see* information and communications technology
conservation 101–02 *see also* environment
environmental 102
heritage and arts 102
construction 103–04
building control surveyor 103–04
clerk of works 104
contract manager 104
construction trades 104–09
carpenter 104–05 *see also* carpentry
demolition work 105
demolition operative 105
scaffolder 105
steeplejack 105
interior and finishing trades 105–07
ceiling fixer 106
electrician 106 *see also main entry*
glazier 106
painter and decorator 106
plasterer 106
plumber 106
roofers 106–07
supervisory roles 107–08
construction project manager 108
site manager 108
site technician 107–08
trowel trades 107
bricklayer 107
stonemason 107
crafts 110–15
cabinet maker *see* carpentry
florist 110–11
jewellery trade 11–12
pottery 112–13
saddler 113–14
thatcher 114–15
Customs and Excise 115–16

dentistry 117–20
dentist 117–18
hygienist 118
nurse 119
orthodontist 120–21
technician 119–20
therapist 120
dietitian 121–22
disc jockey 122–23
diving 123–25
diver 123–24
ROV pilot technician 124–25
domestic service 125–26
butler 126
dresser 126–27

dressmaker *see* fashion
driving 127–33
  chauffeur 127–28
  courier 128
  driving examiner 129
  driving instructor 129–30
  lorry driver 130–31
  passenger transport 131–32
  taxi driver 132–33

economist 134–35 *see also* banking and finance
electrician 135–37
  auto 135
  highway 135
  installation 135
  instrumentation 135–36
  maintenance 136
  panel building 136
  repair and rewind 136
  service 136
  theatre 136–37
engineering 137–46 *see also* information and communication technology
  aeronautical 138, 145
  agricultural 138
  automobile 138
  biochemical 138
  biomedical 138
  building services 139
  chartered 143
  chemical 139
  civil 139
  control 139
  craft workers 144
  electrical and electronic 139–40
  energy 140
  fire 140
  gas 140
  incorporated 144
  instrument 140
  manufacturing systems 140
  marine 141
  mechanical 141
  mining 141
  municipal 141
  nuclear 141–42
  offshore 142 *see also* oil/gas rig work
  operations 142
  operators 144
  petroleum 142
  production 142
  recording 142
  structural 143
  technicians 144
  transport 143
  water 143
environment 146–49
  conservation 147–48
  energy conservation officer 146–47
environmental health 149–51
  environmental health officer 149–50
  health and safety adviser *see* health and safety
  pest controller 150–51
events organisation 151–54
  conference organiser 151–52
  events organiser 153
  exhibition organiser 153–54
  party/wedding organiser 152

farming 155–56 *see also* agriculture
  farm manager 155
  farm worker 155
fashion 156–61 *see also* clothing industry
  designer 157
  dressmaker 158
  leather production 158–59
  milliner 159–60
  model 160–61
film production 161, 163–67
  animation 161
  announcers 161
  archivists/librarians 161 *see also* archivist
  art and design 163 *see also main entry*
  camerawork 163
  costume/wardrobe 163
  direction 163
  engineering 163
  film, video and audio tape editing 163
  IT specialists 163
  journalists 164 *see also* journalism
  laboratory technician 164
  lighting 164
  make-up and hairdressing 164 *see also* beauty *and* hair
  management 164
  marketing and sales 164
  modelmaker *see main entry*
  producers 165
  production assistants 165
  production managers 165
  production operatives 165
  researchers 165
  runners/gofers 165
  setcraft/props 166
  sound 166
  special effects 166
  support staff 166
  transmission 166
  writers 166 *see also* writer

fire service 168–69
fish farmer 169–70
fisher 170–71
floristry *see* crafts
food science and technology 171–72
forensic scientist 172–73
forestry 173–74
foundry work 175
fundraising 176
funeral director 177
furniture and furnishing 178–79
  furniture manufacture 178–79
  upholstery 179

gardening 180–81 *see also* landscape architecture/architect *and* market gardening
  gardener 180–81
gas service engineer 181–82
geologist 182–83

hair 184–85
  hairdresser 184–85
  trichologist 185
health and safety 186–87
  adviser 186
  inspector 186
health service (non-medical) 187–88
  ancillary staff 187
  catering 187
  domestic services 187
  laundry 188
  management 188
  patient services 188
health visitor *see* nursing, health visiting and midwifery
healthcare assistant *see* nursing, health visiting and midwifery
home economics 189–90
  demonstrator 189
  home economist 189
  industry 189
  local authorities 189
  media, the 190
  teaching 190
horses *see* animals
horticulture 191–93
  advisory work 191
  amenity horticulture 191
  arboriculturist 191 *see also* forestry
  commercial horticulture 191
  market gardening 191–92
  research 192
  teaching 192
hospitality and catering 193–97
  chef/cook 193–94
  food service assistants 194
  hotel housekeeping 194
  hotel reception 194
  kitchen staff 195
  management 195–96
  publican 196–97
housing officer/manager 197–98
human resources 199–200
  adviser/manager 199
  training officer/manager 200

ICT *see* information and communication technology
illustration 202 *see also* art and design *and* medical illustration
indexer *see* publishing
information and communication technology 204, 207–11
  computer service technician 207
  data base administration 207
  hardware engineer 207
  IT operations 207
  IT research and development 208
  IT sales and marketing 208
  IT services 208
  multimedia programmer 208
  network engineer 208
  programmers 209
  software engineers 209
  systems analysts 209
  systems support staff 209
  trainers 209–10
  web designers 210 *see also* art and design
information science 202–04
  information scientist 202–03
  librarian/information manager 203–04
insurance 211–14
  agents and inspectors 212
  broker 212
  loss adjuster 212–13
  underwriter 213–14
interior decorator *see* construction trades
interior designer/inscape design 204

jewellery *see* crafts
journalism 216, 219–23
  broadcast journalist 221–22
  editor 216, 219
  journalist 219–21
  press photographer 222–23
  sub-editor 223

laboratory technician 224–25 *see also* biology
land and property 225–28
  estate agent 225–26
  gamekeeper 226–27
  land agent 227
  valuer 228

landscape architecture/architect 228–30 *see also* gardening
landscape designer 229
landscape manager 229
landscape scientist 229
law 230–44
advocate/barrister 231–32
barrister's clerk/advocate's clerk 232–33
court staff 233–35
court clerk 233–34
court reporter 234
justices' clerks' assistant 234
law costs draftsman 236–37
legal cashier/administrator 237
legal executive 238
legal services commission research assistant 235–36
notary public 238–39
solicitor 239–41
leisure and amenity management 241–42
linguistics, languages and translation 242–43
interpreter 242–43
translator 243
literary agent 245
local government 245–46
logistics 246–49 *see also* road transport
freight forwarding 247–48
logistics 248–49

magazine/newspaper publishing *see* publishing: magazines and newspapers
management consultant 250–51
management coach 250–51
manufacturing 251–56
factory worker 251–52
packaging technologist 252–53
sheet-metal worker/plater 253–54
toolmaker 254–55
welder 255–56
marine scientist 256–57
market researcher 261–62
marketing 257, 260
marketing executive 257, 260
meat industry 262–63
butcher 262–63
medical illustration 263–64
graphic designers 263
medical artists 263
medical photographers 263
medical videographers 263
medicine 264–67
general practitioner 264–65
hospital doctor 265
occupational physician 265
public health and community health medicine 266
research and teaching 266
merchant navy 267–69
communications 268
deck staff 268
engineering staff 268
hotel/entertainment services on cruise ships and ferries 268
metallurgist 270
meteorologist 270–71
microbiologist 271–72
midwifery *see* nursing, health visiting and midwifery
milk roundsperson *see* roundsperson
modelmaker 272
motor industry 273–76 *see also* engineering
garage work 273
motor body repairer 273–74, 276
motor vehicle valeter 275, 276
vehicle technician 274–75
music 276–79 *see also* performing arts
composer 276
musical instrument technologist 277
musician *see* performing arts
piano tuner 278–79
teacher 277–78
therapist 278

naval architect 280
neurophysiology technologist 281
nursing, health visiting and midwifery 282–86
health visitors 284–85
healthcare assistant 284
midwifery 285–86
nurses 282–83

oil/gas rig work 287–89
divers 287
drilling crew 287
engineers 288
geologist 288
geophysicist 288
optometry 289–92
dispensing optician 289–90
optometrist 290–91
orthoptist 291–92

painter and decorator *see* construction
patents 293–94
patent agent/patent attorney 293
patent examiner 293
patent officer 294
performing arts 295–300 *see also* music

actor 295
dancing 296–97
musician 297–98, 300
singer 298–300
pharmacy 300–02
community pharmacist 300
hospital pharmacist 300
industrial and research pharmacist 300–01
technician 302
photography 303–06
commercial photographer 303
institutional and specialist photography 303
manufacturing, retailing and service trades 305
photographic laboratories/imaging centres 305
photographic laboratory technician 305
photographic production 305
photojournalism and press photographer 303–05
physicist 306–07
physiotherapist 308
plumber *see* construction
police service 309–10
police constable support officer 309
police officer 309–10
political work 311–12
political party agent 311
political researcher 311
politician 311
public affairs consultant/lobbyist 311
Post Office 312–13
printing 313, 315–16
camera/scanner operator 313
finishing department 313
graphic design 315 *see also* art and design
office jobs 315
pre-press department 315
printing department 315
proofreader 315
prison officer 316–17
private investigator/detective 318
psychology 319–22
clinical psychology 319
counselling psychologists 319–20
educational psychologists 320
forensic psychology 320–21
health psychology 321
occupational psychologists 321–22
teaching and research 322
psychotherapist 322–23
public relations officer 323–24
publishing: books 324–28
designer 326 *see also* art and design
editorial 324–26
indexer 327–28
production controller 326
sales, marketing and publicity executives 327 *see also* marketing; public relations officer *and* sales representative
publishing: magazines and newspapers 328–30 *see also* journalism
advertisement sales representatives 329
design 328
production manager 328
purchasing officer/buyer 330–31

qualifications, Scottish xiii
quarrying 332

radiographer 333–34
railway work 334
receptionist *see* business administration *and* hospitality and catering
recruitment consultant 335
registrar 335–36
removals 336–37
retailing 337, 341–42
display designer/visual merchandiser 337, 341
general staff 341–42
road transport 342–43 *see also* logistics
roofer *see* construction
roundsperson 343–44
Royal Air Force 344–45
officer 345
Royal Marines 346–47
Royal Navy 347–48 *see also* diving (ROV pilot technician)

sales representative 349
security work 350–51
service mechanic 351 *see also* electrician *and* engineering
sheet metal worker *see* manufacturing
shipbroker 352
signwriter *see* art and design
social work and social care 353–58 *see also* social workers (with/in)
home care organiser 353–54
home carer 353
probation officer 354–55
social care assistant 355
social work assistant 356
social workers (with/in) 355, 356–58
children and young people 356

day care settings 356
education settings 357
health care settings 357
mental health settings 357
residential settings 357–58
and social carers 355
sport 359–61
coach 359–60
physiotherapist *see main entry*
sportsperson 360–61
teacher *see* teaching
sports and recreation facility management 358–59
statistician 362
surveying 363–65
aerial 363
archaeological 363
building 363
general practice 363
hydrographic 363
land 364
minerals 364
quantity 364
rural practice 364–65
taxation 366–68
adviser/technician 366–67
inspectors 367–68
teaching 368–71
lecturer 368–69
teacher 369–71
teaching/classroom assistant 371
telecommunications 372–73
technicians 372–73
theatre 373–76
actors *see* performing arts
box office 373
designer 373, 376
director 373–74, 376
lighting designer 374
press office/marketing 374
producer 374, 376
production manager/technical director 374
production staff 374–75
stage manager 375, 376
theatrical agent 375
therapy 377–82 *see also* dentistry *and* sport
art 377
assistants 381–82
dance/movement 378
music 378–79
occupational 379–80
speech and language 380–81
town and country planner 382–83
trading standards officer 383–84
traffic warden 384–84
travel and tourism 385, 388–91
airline staff 385, 388
tour managers 388–89
tourism officer 389–90
travel agent 390–91

undertaker *see* funeral director
underwriter *see* insurance
useful contacts/websites xvii

valuer *see* land and property
veterinary science 394–96 *see also* animals
veterinary nurse 394–95
veterinary surgeon 395–96

watch and clockmaker/repairer 397
welfare advice work 398
advice worker 398
wine trade 398–99
writer 399–400

youth work 401–03 *see also* careers adviser
personal adviser (Connexions) 401–02
youth and community worker 402–03

zoology 404
zoo keeper *see* animals
zoologist 404

Index of Advertisers

ACCA 5–7
The Actuarial Profession 10–11
Arcadia Group *inside front cover*, 338–40
BPIF (British Printing Industries Federation) 314
British Council xxi–xxiii
BUNAC v
The Chartered Institute of Purchasing and Supply xviii–xx
CIPD 201
City & Guilds ix
The Co-operative Bank *inside back cover*, xiv–xv
European Business School London xii
Explore Learning xxiv–xxv
i-to-i xxxii–xxxiii
London College of Communication 205–06
London Hotel School 392
The London School of Journalism 217–18
London School of Marketing 258–59
New York Film Academy 162
Pitman Training xxviii–xxix
PMA Training xxx–xxxi
Rok Group ii
Skillfast – UK xvi
The Society for Chiropodists and Podiatrists x–xi
University Centre, Doncaster xiii
University of Exeter, School of Business & Economics (MSc Accounting and Finance) 2–3
University of Exeter, School of Business & Economics (MSc Tourism, Development and Policy) 386–87
University of Leicester vi
University of Surrey xxvi–xxvii

Also available from Kogan Page

Interview and Career Guidance

Careers and Jobs in IT, David Yardley, 2004
Careers and Jobs in the Media, Simon Kent, 2005
Careers and Jobs in Nursing, Linda Nazarko, 2004
Careers and Jobs in the Police Service, Kim Clabby, 2004
Careers and Jobs in Travel and Tourism, Verité Reily Collins, 2004
Choosing Your Career, 2nd edition, Sally Longson, 2004
Great Answers to Tough Interview Questions, 6th edition, Martin Yate, 2005
How You Can Get That Job, 3rd edition, Rebecca Corfield, 2002
Preparing Your Own CV, 3rd edition, Rebecca Corfield, 2002
Readymade CVs, 3rd edition, Lynn Williams, 2004
Readymade Job Search Letters, 3rd edition, Lynn Williams, 2004
Right Career Moves Handbook, Sophie Allen, 2005
Successful Interview Skills, 4th edition, Rebecca Corfield, 2006
The Ultimate CV Book, Martin Yate, 2002
The Ultimate Interview Book, Lynn Williams, 2005
The Ultimate Job Search Book, Lynn Williams, 2006
The Ultimate Job Search Letters Book, Martin Yate, 2003

Titles in the Testing Series

The Advanced Numeracy Test Workbook, Mike Bryon, 2003
Aptitude, Personality and Motivation Tests, 2nd edition, Jim Barrett, 2004
The Aptitude Test Workbook, Jim Barrett, 2003
Graduate Psychometric Test Workbook, Mike Bryon, 2005
How to Master Personality Questionnaires, 2nd edition, Mark Parkinson, 2000
How to Master Psychometric Tests, 3rd edition, Mark Parkinson, 2004
How to Pass Advanced Aptitude Tests, Jim Barrett, 2002
How to Pass Advanced Numeracy Tests, Mike Bryon, 2002
How to Pass the Civil Service Qualifying Tests, 2nd edition, Mike Bryon, 2003
How to Pass the Firefighter Selection Process, Mike Bryon, 2004
How to Pass Graduate Psychometric Tests, 2nd edition, Mike Bryon, 2001
How to Pass the New Police Selection System, 2nd edition, Harry Tolley, Billy Hodge and Catherine Tolley, 2004
How to Pass Numeracy Tests, 3rd edition, Harry Tolley and Ken Thomas, 2006
How to Pass Numerical Reasoning Tests, revised edition, Heidi Smith, 2006
How to Pass Professional Level Psychometric Tests, 2nd edition, Sam Al-Jajjoka, 2004
How to Pass Selection Tests, 3rd edition, Mike Bryon and Sanjay Modha, 2005
How to Pass Technical Selection Tests, 2nd edition, Mike Bryon and Sanjay Modha, 2005
How to Pass Verbal Reasoning Tests, 3rd edition, Harry Tolley and Ken Thomas, 2006

How to Succeed at an Assessment Centre, 2nd edition, Harry Tolley and Robert Wood, 2005
IQ and Psychometric Tests, Philip Carter, 2004
IQ and Psychometric Test Workbook, Philip Carter, 2005
The Numeracy Test Workbook, Mike Bryon, 2006
Test Your Own Aptitude, 3rd edition, Jim Barrett and Geoff Williams, 2003
The Ultimate Psychometric Test Book, Mike Bryon, 2006

CD ROMS

Psychometric Tests, Volume 1, The Times Testing Series, Editor Mike Bryon 2002
Test Your Aptitude, Volume 1, The Times Testing Series, Editor Mike Bryon, 2002
Test Your IQ, Volume 1, The Times Testing Series, Editor Mike Bryon, 2002

For these titles and more, visit the Kogan Page website at
www.kogan-page.co.uk

The above titles are available from all good bookshops. For further information, please contact the publisher at the address below:

Kogan Page Limited
120 Pentonville Road
London N1 9JN
United Kingdom
Tel: 020 7278 0433
Fax: 020 7837 6348
www.kogan-page.co.uk